Arthur Haigh

The Attic theatre

A description of the stage and theatre of the Athenians, and of the dramatic performances at Athens

Arthur Haigh
The Attic theatre
A description of the stage and theatre of the Athenians, and of the dramatic performances at Athens

ISBN/EAN: 9783337303556

Printed in Europe, USA, Canada, Australia, Japan

Cover: Foto ©ninafisch / pixelio.de

More available books at **www.hansebooks.com**

The Attic Theatre

*A DESCRIPTION OF THE STAGE AND THEATRE
OF THE ATHENIANS, AND OF THE DRAMATIC
PERFORMANCES AT ATHENS*

BY

A. E. HAIGH, M.A.

LATE FELLOW OF HERTFORD, AND CLASSICAL LECTURER AT CORPUS
CHRISTI AND WADHAM COLLEGES, OXFORD

WITH FACSIMILES AND ILLUSTRATIONS

Oxford
AT THE CLARENDON PRESS
1889

PREFACE.

My purpose in this book has been to collect and piece together all the available information concerning the outward features and surroundings of the old Athenian dramatic performances; in other words, to write a history of the Attic drama from the theatrical, as opposed to the literary, point of view. The subject is one which has been practically revolutionised during the last half century, partly through the labours of various scholars in interpreting the notices of the old grammarians, but more especially owing to the rich discoveries of inscriptions relating to theatrical affairs, and the information supplied by excavations in the old Greek theatres. But in spite of the copious accession of fresh materials, it is now more than fifty years since any work has appeared in English, in which this particular department of Greek dramatic history has been treated in a comprehensive manner. The neglect is all the more remarkable, as the subject is undeniably of great interest and importance, and this for two distinct reasons. In the first place it is difficult to understand and appreciate the peculiar qualities of the existing Greek plays, without acquiring some knowledge of the circumstances under which they were produced, and the limitations within which the ancient dramatic poets had to work. In the second place, as the Attic drama was essentially a public institution, and formed one of the most conspicuous elements in the national life, the various details connected with its management are incidentally most instructive, because of the curious light which they throw upon the habits, feelings, and tastes of the old Athenians. It is owing to these several considerations that the present work has been undertaken.

Unfortunately, with the exception of a list of names and definitions in Pollux, and a few observations upon the theatre in Vitruvius, none of the ancient treatises, which dealt with the various portions of the subject, have been preserved. The materials have in consequence to be collected from the most multifarious sources—from casual remarks in ancient authors, from incidental references in the Greek dramas, from obscure and often contradictory notices in the scholiasts and grammarians, from old inscriptions, and the ruins of Greek theatres, from vases, statuettes, wall-paintings, and other works of art. In the treatment of questions, which depend upon evidence of this intricate and complex character, it is inevitable that great diversity of opinion should arise, and that numberless opportunities should be afforded for ingenious conjectures and fanciful combinations. As a matter of fact the whole history of the Attic drama has been to a certain extent obscured by the mass of controversy and hypothesis to which it has given rise. My purpose throughout the following pages has been to keep close to the original sources of information, to restrict myself unreservedly to such facts as seem to be fairly well established by the evidence, and to clear the subject of all those fine-drawn theories and conjectures, which have no definite foundation to depend upon. For every statement concerning the Attic drama I have been careful to quote the ultimate authority, and the plan which I have adopted, in the citation of evidence, has been as follows. Where a passage is appealed to in support of some mere matter of fact, about which there could be no particular difference of opinion, I have been content to simply give the reference. But in cases where the inference is more dubious, I have quoted the original authorities in full, so as to enable the reader to judge for himself as to the validity of the views adopted in the text. It would have been impossible, within the limits of a single volume, to discuss in detail all the points concerning which controversies have been raised. The more important questions I have treated at considerable length; but as regards matters of minute detail and trivial interest, I have merely given my own opinion in the text, and appended a complete statement of the evidence in the notes.

The various books, articles, monographs, and dissertations, which have been written on the subject of the Attic theatre and dramatic performances, are sufficient in themselves to constitute a considerable literature. It will be sufficient in the present place to enumerate those to which I have been principally indebted. Of writings in which the subject is treated as a whole the most important is Albert Müller's *Lehrbuch der Griechischen Bühnenalterthümer* (Freiburg, 1886)—a work which is conspicuous for the industry, learning, and sound judgment displayed in its compilation, and for the lucid manner in which an immense amount of information is compressed into a comparatively limited space. The exhaustive account which it contains of the bibliography of the subject is especially valuable. Another book which I have found of the greatest help is Schneider's *Das Attische Theaterwesen* (Weimar, 1835). It consists mainly of a citation in full of all the ancient passages which refer to performances in the theatre; and although Schneider's own views and inferences are now mostly antiquated, and his collection of 'Quelle' requires to be supplemented, the work will always be most interesting and serviceable to students of the Attic drama. The description of the Greek dramatic performances in the third volume of Bergk's *Griechische Literaturgeschichte* (Berlin, 1884) has been exceedingly useful and suggestive; and considerable assistance has been derived from the similar account in vol. ii. pt. 2 of Bernhardy's *Grundriss der Griechischen Litteratur* (Halle, 1880).

As far as the separate portions of the subject are concerned, I have been greatly indebted, for information regarding the Dionysiac festivals, to Böckh's dissertation, *Vom Unterschiede der Lenäen, Anthesterien, und ländlichen Dionysien* (*Abhandl. der Akad. der Wissensch. zu Berlin*, 1816–1817), and to A. Mommsen's *Heortologie* (Leipzig, 1864). The account of the regulations relating to the dramatic contests is based largely upon the evidence supplied by the recently discovered inscriptions, which have been collected and carefully edited by Köhler in the second volume of the *Corpus Inscriptionum Atticarum*. These inscriptions have, among other things, made it perfectly plain that the dramatic competitions had nothing to do with the tribes, but were merely contests between individuals. On the subject of the Proagon I have followed mainly Rohde's valuable article in *Rhein. Museum* xxxviii, and on the subject of the selection of the judges I have been greatly assisted by Sauppe's paper, *Ueber die Wahl der Richter*, etc. (*Sächs. Gesellschaft der Wissensch. zu Leipzig, phil.-hist. Classe*, 1855), and by Petersen's *Preisrichter der grossen Dionysien* (Progr. Dorpat. 1878). For various points connected with the production of a play I have consulted the dissertation by Lipsius, *Ueber die dramatische Choregie* (*Sächs. Gesell. der Wissensch., phil.-hist. Classe*, 1885), with advantage. To turn next to the question of the construction and arrangement of the Greek theatre. My principal authority, as far as regards the theatre of Dionysus at Athens, has been Kawerau's article *Theatergebäude*, in vol. iii. of Baumeister's *Denkmäler des klassischen Alterthums* (Munich and Leipzig, 1888). This article contains the results of Dr. Dörpfeld's recent investigations, together with a new plan of the theatre, and has in some respects superseded all the previous accounts. I may also mention Vischer's *Die Entdeckungen im Dionysostheater* (*Neues Schweizerisches Museum*, 1863), Julius' article, *Das Theater des Dionysos* (*Zeitschrift für bild. Kunst*, 1878), and J. R. Wheeler's *Theatre of Dionysus* (*Papers of the American School of Classical Studies at Athens*, vol. i). The description of the theatre at Epidaurus has been derived from the papers by Kabbadias in Πρακτικὰ τῆς ἐν 'Αθήναις ἀρχαιολογικῆς ἑταιρίας, 1881 and 1883. On the subject of the Greek theatre in general I would mention the exhaustive account by Wieseler in vol. 83 of Ersch and Gruber's *Allgemeine Encyklopädie* (Leipzig, 1866), from which I have obtained many interesting particulars. The plans and illustrations in Wieseler's *Theatergebäude und Denkmäler des Bühnenwesens bei Griechen und Römern* (Göttingen, 1851) have also been of the greatest service; and I have obtained some help from Strack, *Das altgriechische Theatergebäude* (Potsdam, 1843). Proceeding next to the question of the scenery I have to acknowledge my obligations to Niejahr's *Quaestiones Aristophaneae Scaenicae* (Greifswald, 1877), and Sommerbrodt's *De Aeschyli re scenica* (in *Scenica*, Berlin, 1876). On the subject of the acting and the actors in the Greek drama much information is to be derived from Grysar, *De Graecorum tragoedia*, etc. (Cöln, 1830); K. F. Hermann, *De distributione personarum inter histriones in tragoediis graecis* (Marburg, 1840); Beer, *Ueber die Zahl der Schauspieler bei Aristophanes* (Leipzig, 1844); and from Sommerbrodt's two articles *De Histrionibus* and *De Arte Histrionum*, in his *Scenica*. Concerning the costume of the Greek actors I have learned much from Dierk's two dissertations, *De tragicorum histrionum habitu scaenico apud Graecos* (Göttingen, 1883), *Ueber das Costüm der griechischen Schauspieler in der alten Komödie* (*Archaeol. Zeitung* xliii); and from Wieseler's *Das Satyrspiel* (Göttingen, 1848). I should also mention the valuable illustrations of theatrical masks and costumes to be found in Wieseler's *Theatergebäude und Denkmäler*, etc.; and those given by Maass in *Monumenti Inediti*, xi. 30–32, and by Robert in *Archaeol. Zeitung* for 1878, and in *Monum. Inedit.* xi. 13. In discussing the question of the relative proportion of speech, song, and recitative in the Greek drama I have frequently consulted Christ's *Metrik der Griechen und Römer* (Leipzig, 1879). Among works dealing with the chorus I would mention K. O. Müller's *Dissertations on the Eumenides* (Engl. transl., London, 1853), G. Hermann's *De choro Eumenidum* (Opusc. ii. p. 129 foll.), Schultze's *De chori Graecorum tragici habitu externo* (Berlin, 1857), Sommerbrodt's *De chori tragici principibus*, in *Scenica*, p. 5 foll., and lastly Arnoldt's *Die Chorpartieen bei Aristophanes* (Leipzig, 1873).

In conclusion I wish to express my obligations to Professor Gardner for his assistance in various questions connected with archæology, and to Mr. Evelyn Abbott for many valuable suggestions and criticisms. I have to thank the Council of the Hellenic Society for their permission to reproduce the two photographs of the theatre at Athens, and the illustration of a chorus of birds. I desire at the same time to acknowledge the great courtesy with which Dr. Dörpfeld, of the German Archæological Institute, has supplied me with the latest information concerning his excavations in the theatre of Dionysus, and his views on Greek theatres in general.

OXFORD, *June*, 1889.

CONTENTS.

	PAGE
CHAP. I. DRAMATIC CONTESTS AT ATHENS	1
§ 1. General Characteristics of the Attic drama	1
§ 2. First institution of dramatic competitions	6
§ 3. The City Dionysia	10
§ 4. Tragedy at the City Dionysia in the fifth century	15
§ 5. Trilogies and Tetralogies	21
§ 6. Tragedy at the City Dionysia in later times	27
§ 7. Comedy at the City Dionysia	30
§ 8. Order of Contests at the City Dionysia	33
§ 9. The Lenaea	36
§ 10. The Rural Dionysia and Anthesteria	42
§ 11. The Judges	44
§ 12. The Prizes	52
§ 13. Contests between actors	55
§ 14. Records of dramatic contests	59
CHAP. II. THE PRODUCTION OF A PLAY	65
§ 1. The Poets	65
§ 2. Appointment of the Choregi	71
§ 3. Selection of the Actors	75
§ 4. The training of the Chorus	79
§ 5. Expenses of the Choregia	82
§ 6. The Performances in the Theatre	86
§ 7. Reproduction of Old Plays	92
CHAP. III. THE THEATRE	101
§ 1. General character of a Greek theatre	101
§ 2. The old wooden theatres at Athens	103
§ 3. History of the Theatre of Dionysus	107

xii   CONTENTS.

		PAGE
§ 4. Site of the Theatre of Dionysus	.	110
§ 5. The Auditorium	.	113
§ 6. The Orchestra	.	125
§ 7. The Stage-buildings	.	136
§ 8. The Stage	.	141
§ 9. Relative position of Actors and Chorus	.	150
§ 10. Various details	.	158

CHAP. IV. THE SCENERY 164

 § 1. General character of the Scenery . . . 164
 § 2. Mechanical arrangements for the Scenery . . 170
 § 3. The entrances to the Stage 173
 § 4. Changes of Scene 178
 § 5. Stage Properties, etc. . . . 183
 § 6. The Ekkyklêma . . . 185
 § 7. The Mêchanê . . . 189
 § 8. Other Mechanical Contrivances . 192

CHAP. V. THE ACTORS 197

 § 1. Rise of the Actor's Profession . . . 197
 § 2. The distribution of the Parts among the Actors 207
 § 3. Extra Performers 212
 § 4. Costume of the Tragic Actors . . 216
 § 5. Costume of Satyric Actors . . 231
 § 6. Costume of Comic Actors . . 233
 § 7. Speech, Song, and Recitative . . 241
 § 8. Importance of the Voice in Greek Acting . 245
 § 9. Style of Greek Acting 249
 § 10. The Actors' Guild . . 251
 § 11. Social position of Actors . . 254
 § 12. Celebrated Athenian Actors . 255

CHAP. VI. THE CHORUS . . . 259

 § 1. History of the Chorus . 259
 § 2. Size of the Chorus . . 262
 § 3. Costume of the Chorus . . 263
 § 4. Arrangement of the Chorus . 268
 § 5. The Delivery of the choral part 276
 § 6. The Dancing . . . 283
 § 7. The Music . . 291

	PAGE
CHAP. VII. THE AUDIENCE	295
§ 1. Composition of the Audience	295
§ 2. Price of Admission	302
§ 3. The Distribution of the Seats	304
§ 4. Various arrangements in connection with the Audience	311
§ 5. Character of Attic Audiences	313
APPENDIX A	319
APPENDIX B	321
GREEK INDEX	329
GENERAL INDEX	333

LIST OF ILLUSTRATIONS.

View of the theatre of Dionysus from the east		*Frontispiece.*
View of the theatre of Dionysus from the south		to face p. 101
Ground-plan of the theatre of Dionysus		page 112
Part of the auditorium in the theatre of Dionysus		,, 118
Coin with view of the theatre of Dionysus		,, 121
Ground-plan of the theatre at Epidaurus		,, 130
Gates in the theatre at Epidaurus		,, 134
Part of the hyposkenion in the theatre at Epidaurus		,, 147
Scene from a comedy, showing the steps up to the stage		,, 148
A tragic actor		,, 218
Tragic masks		,, 222
Scene from a tragedy, showing the size of the cothurni		,, 224
Two tragic scenes		,, 230
Actors in a satyric drama		,, 232
Scene from a comedy of the Phlyakes		,, 234
Comic masks		,, 238
A comic scene		,, 240
Members of a satyric chorus		,, 265
A chorus of Birds		,, 267
Diagram illustrating the entrance of the chorus		,, 270
Throne of the priest of Dionysus		,, 308

THE ATTIC THEATRE.

CHAPTER I.

DRAMATIC CONTESTS AT ATHENS.

§ 1. *General Characteristics of the Attic drama.*

THE ancient Athenian drama was in many respects unlike any kind of dramatic performance that we are accustomed to in modern times. The difference extended not only to the character of the plays themselves, and the manner in which they were presented upon the stage, but also to the circumstances under which the production took place. In order to form an accurate conception of the external features of the old Greek drama it will be necessary to dismiss from the mind many of the associations with which the modern stage is connected. In the first place, the luxury of having theatrical entertainments at every season of the year was a thing never heard of among the ancient Athenians. The dramatic performances at Athens, instead of being spread over the whole year, were confined within very limited periods. They were restricted to the two great festivals of Dionysus, the Lenaea and the City Dionysia. It is true that at these festivals the number of plays exhibited was large enough to satisfy the most enthusiastic playgoer. Several days in succession were devoted entirely to the drama, and on each day tragedies and comedies followed one another without intermission from morning till evening. But with the exception of the two festivals of Dionysus there was no other occasion on which plays were acted in the Athenian theatre. There were dramatic exhibitions in the various townships of Attica during the Rural Dionysia; but in Athens itself the drama was restricted to the two periods already mentioned. In fact, as far as regards the time and duration of the performances, the ancient drama had much in common with the modern musical festival, in which at certain fixed seasons several days in succession are devoted entirely to music.

Another vital point of difference lay in the fact that the ancient drama was managed wholly by the state. To provide for the amusement of the people was considered to be one of the regular duties of the government. In England theatres are simply private enterprises. In some foreign countries certain theatres receive subventions from the state, and are subject to a code of rules; but for practical purposes their connexion with the state is only a slight one. But in Athens the superintendence of the annual dramatic performances was just as much a part of the public administration of affairs as was the repair of the dockyards, the equipment of fleets, or the despatch of armies. Poets and actors were both selected by the state. The cost of the performance was a tax upon the richer classes. Every wealthy citizen had in his turn to defray the expenses of a tragedy or a comedy, just as he had to pay for one of the ships of the fleet, or perform any other of the state burdens. The theatre was a public institution for the benefit of the whole people. Every Athenian citizen of whatever degree was entitled to be present at the annual dramatic performances; and if he was too poor to pay the entrance fee, he received the price of admission from the state.

The audience consisted practically of the whole body of the people. In a modern theatre, owing to its limited dimensions, the spectators are few in number, and have no representative character about them. But the theatre of Dionysus at Athens was capable of containing nearly thirty thousand people. Every

Athenian attended the performances at the Dionysia as a matter of course. The audience therefore to which the Athenian dramatic poet addressed himself was in reality a gathering of the whole body of his fellow-countrymen. In those days books were not plentiful, and their use was confined to a limited class. The ordinary Athenian depended for his literary pleasures upon the various public performances and recitations of poetical compositions. The drama was therefore much more to him than to a modern playgoer. At the present day, when continual supplies of fresh literature are accessible to every one, it is hard to realise the excitement and expectancy with which an Athenian looked forward to the annual exhibition of dramas at the Dionysia. It was here that his taste for novelty in literature was gratified. It was here that he found an equivalent for the books, magazines, and newspapers of modern civilization. Hence he was able to sit day after day, from morning to evening, listening to tragedy and comedy, without any feeling of satiety. The enthusiasm with which the drama was generally regarded, and the direct manner in which the author was brought into contact with the whole body of his countrymen, contributed to make the vocation of the dramatic writer one of the very greatest importance. The leading tragic poets especially are known to have exercised a most profound influence upon the national mind and character. They were spoken of as the teachers of the people. Their writings were invested with a sort of Homeric sanctity, and appealed to as authorities upon questions of science and morality. Maxims and quotations from their plays were upon every one's lips. Many passages in Plato and Aristophanes prove the enormous influence for good and evil which was exercised by the Greek tragic poets, and there is probably no other instance in history of a drama which was so thoroughly popular, and formed such an essential part of the national life [1].

Another prominent characteristic of the Attic stage, which distinguishes it from that of modern times, was the fact that almost every dramatic performance took the form of a contest.

[1] See especially Plat. Rep. 598 D, E; Aristoph. Ran. 1008 ff., 1054 ff.

In the best period of the Greek drama the production of a play by itself, as a mere exhibition, was a thing unknown. In later times celebrated plays by the great dramatists were sometimes exhibited alone. But in the period covered by the names of Aeschylus, Sophocles, Euripides, and Aristophanes, the only mode of exhibiting plays was by competing in the dramatic contests at the festivals of Dionysus. Prizes were offered by the state. A limited number of poets, after careful selection by the state, were allowed to take part in the competition. The result was decided by a jury publicly appointed. It is curious to notice how strongly implanted in the Greek nature was this passion for anything in the shape of a contest. It is seen in the case of most branches of poetry and music. Dithyrambs were generally produced in competitions at festivals between rival poets and choruses. Recitations of the old epic poems took the form of contests between rhapsodists. Public performances on flute and harp were mostly of the same character. There can be no doubt that the stimulus of rivalry and competition had a considerable effect upon the genius of the poets. It is remarkable in how many instances the Athenian dramatic writers retained the full vigour of their intellect even in extreme old age. For example, the tragedies composed in their latest years by the three great tragic poets show not the slightest symptoms of decaying power. The Agamemnon of Aeschylus, one of the most splendid products of the Greek drama, was brought out shortly before the poet's death. The Oedipus Coloneus of Sophocles and the Bacchae of Euripides were both written very late in life. The reason of this extraordinary vitality was no doubt partly due to the excitement caused by the public competitions in the theatre, which acted as a stimulus to the mind, and prevented that decay of power which usually accompanies old age.

But the most conspicuous difference between the ancient and modern drama lay in the essentially religious character of the former. The Athenian drama was not only an amusement for the people: it was also part of a great religious celebration. Throughout its history it never ceased to be closely connected with the religion of the state. It was developed originally out of the songs and hymns in honour of Dionysus, the god of wine. In later times its range was widened, and its tone secularised: but it continued to be performed solely at the festivals of Dionysus. Together with the other contests and ceremonials it was regarded as a celebration in honour of the god. The spectator who sat watching a tragedy or a comedy was not merely providing for his own amusement, but was also joining in an act of worship. Many facts tend to show the sacred character of the festivals of Dionysus, and the performances which accompanied them. The festivals themselves were not mere human institutions, but were established in obedience to the direct commands of the oracle. On these occasions the whole city gave itself up to pleasure, and to the worship of the genial wine-god. For the time being there was an end of business and litigation. Peace and harmony were supposed to prevail universally, and nothing was allowed to disturb the general enjoyment. Distraints for debt were forbidden by law during the continuance of the festival. Prisoners were temporarily released from gaol, to enable them to join in the worship of the god. Assaults and outrages, if committed during the Dionysia, were regarded as offences against religion, and were punished with the utmost severity. The ordinary course of law was not considered sufficient, and they were dealt with under an exceptional process at a special meeting of the Assembly. As a proof of the indignation which was aroused by such violations of the harmony of the festival it is recorded that on one occasion a certain Ctesicles was put to death for merely striking a personal enemy during the procession. To preserve the sanctity of the festival from contamination, no person suffering from civil disability was allowed to take part in a chorus at the Dionysia, or even to superintend the training of it. The performances in the theatre, being the most conspicuous part of the proceedings at the festival, were equally sacred in character. The god Dionysus was supposed to be present in person to witness and enjoy them. This belief was symbolised by a curious old custom. On the evening before the dramatic contests began, the Ephebi used to take the statue of the god out of its shrine, and carry it in procession by torchlight to the theatre, and place it in the orchestra in full view of the stage. There it remained until the end of the festival, in token of the presence of the god. The religious character of the dramatic performances is still further shown by the fact that most of the front seats in the theatre were given up to the priests of the different deities. In the centre of the front row, and in the best seat of all, sat the priest of Dionysus, presiding over the celebrations in honour of the god. The theatre itself was regarded as a temple of Dionysus, and possessed all the sanctity attaching to such a place. Any form of insult committed there during the Dionysia was doubly criminal. Merely to eject a man from a seat he had taken wrongfully was a piece of sacrilege punishable with death. The people who took part in the different contests, the poets, choregi, actors, and singers, were regarded as ministers of the god Dionysus. Their persons and dresses were sacred. To strike a choregus in the theatre, as Meidias struck Demosthenes, was an offence against religion and the gods. In order to understand the outward character and surroundings of the old Greek drama it is most essential to realise the fact that the whole proceedings were part of a religious celebration, and were intended to be an act of homage to the god, as well as an amusement for the people [1].

§ 2. *First institution of dramatic competitions.*

The date of the first institution of dramatic contests in Athens may be determined approximately, though the exact year cannot be fixed. During the earlier stages of the development of tragedy and comedy there was nothing in the

---

[1] Most of the details concerning the religious character of the proceedings at the Dionysia are derived from Demosth. Meid. §§ 8-10, 16, 51-53, 55, 58-60, 178-180. As to the release of prisoners see Demosth. Androt. § 68, and schol. ad loc. For the practice of placing the statue of Dionysus in the theatre see Corp. Inscr. Att. ii. 470, 471. Most of the front seats were given up to priests: see Corp. Inscr. Att. iii. 240-384; Hesych. v. νεμήσεις θέας.

shape of a contest. The first rude innovations upon the old hymns to Dionysus were mere tentative experiments by individuals, exhibited upon their own responsibility. Thespis has the credit of having introduced tragedy into Athens. At first he was without a rival or competitor, and gave exhibitions of the new form of art merely as a private enterprise. One of these performances is said to have been witnessed by Solon. As Solon died not later than 558 B.C., it follows that Thespis must have begun to exhibit before that date[1]. The progress of tragedy in popular favour was so rapid, that it was speedily accepted as a regular form of entertainment, and public contests were established even during the lifetime of Thespis. Aristophanes says distinctly that Thespis 'competed' with his tragedies. The Parian Marble puts the date of the first contest in which Thespis took part, and for which the prize was a goat, between the years 542 and 520 B.C. Suidas gives 535 as the date of the first appearance of Thespis. He is doubtless referring, not to his early exhibitions of the new form of art, but to his first appearance in a regular public contest. If these dates are to be relied upon, it follows that Thespis began his innovations during the first half of the sixth century, and that public competitions in tragedy were established early in the second half[2]. Everything connected with the life and art of Thespis is wrapped in great obscurity, and it is therefore uncertain how far the above traditions can be accepted as true. But at any rate there is no doubt that long before the end of the sixth century contests in tragedy were flourishing in full vigour. The names of three tragic poets, who lived in the generation after Thespis, are recorded. These were Choerilus, Phrynichus, and Pratinas. Choerilus is said to have first 'engaged in contests' in the year 523. Phrynichus won the prize for tragedy in 511. In 499 Aeschylus made his first public appear-

---

[1] Plut. Solon p. 95 B ἀρχομένων δὲ τῶν περὶ Θέσπιν ἤδη τὴν τραγῳδίαν κινεῖν, καὶ διὰ τὴν καινότητα τοὺς πολλοὺς ἄγοντος τοῦ πράγματος, οὔπω δὲ εἰς ἅμιλλαν ἐναγώνιον ἐξηγμένου, φύσει φιλήκοος ὢν καὶ φιλομαθὴς ὁ Σόλων ... ἐθεάσατο τὸν Θέσπιν αὐτὸν ὑποκρινόμενον κ.τ.λ.

[2] Aristoph. Vesp. 1479; Marmor Par. ep. 43 ἀφ' οὗ Θέσπις ὁ ποιητὴς [ἐφάνη], πρῶτος ὃς ἐδίδαξε [δρ]ᾶ[μα ἐν ἄ]στ[ει, καὶ ἐ]τέθη ὁ [τ]ράγος [ἆθλον], ἔτη κ.τ.λ.; Suidas v. Θέσπις.

ance. His competitors on this occasion were Choerilus and Pratinas. By this time it is probable that the arrangements for the tragic contests had been reduced to a regular system. During the greater part of the fifth century the ordinary rule was for three poets to take part in the competition, and for each poet to exhibit three tragedies and one satyric drama, making four plays in all. It is probable that this rule had already been established when Aeschylus made his first appearance in public. An arrangement of this kind would of course be the growth of time, and during the earlier tragic contests there was no doubt much irregularity in regard to the number of poets competing, and the number of plays exhibited. For instance, Pratinas is said to have brought out fifty plays, thirty-two of which were satyric dramas. He cannot therefore have been accustomed to exhibit three tragedies along with each satyric drama. On the other hand the number of plays ascribed to Choerilus was one hundred and sixty. It follows that during the greater part of his career he must have been accustomed to exhibit as many as four plays annually, else he could not have found occasions for producing so large a number. Hence it is probable that by the time of Aeschylus the system of tragic contests had already been reduced to that shape which afterwards prevailed, and that each poet was expected to produce four plays[1].

Comedy, as we learn from Aristotle, was much later than tragedy in being recognised by the state. For a long time it was kept up by voluntary enterprise, and not much importance was attached to it. The first Athenian comic poets of note were Chionides and Magnes. Chionides began to exhibit in 487 B.C. It is hardly likely that the date of his first appearance would have been preserved with such accuracy, if comedy had still been merely a private undertaking, without any connexion with the state. There seems therefore to be good ground for assuming that the institution of public contests in comedy was not later than 487 B.C.[2] At any rate it cannot have been later

---

[1] Suidas vv. Χοιρίλος, Φρύνιχος, Πρατίνας.
[2] Aristot. Poet. cc. 3, 5; Suidas v. Χιωνίδης.

than 459 B.C. This is proved by an inscription which records the names of the victors at the City Dionysia, and among them gives the name of the victor in comedy. The exact year to which the inscription refers is unknown, but at any rate it was anterior to 458 B.C. It follows that 459 is the very latest date to which the institution of public contests in comedy can be assigned [1].

Speaking roughly then the recognition of tragedy by the state, and the institution of annual competitions, date from the latter half of the sixth century. The similar recognition of comedy dates from the first half of the fifth century. These contests took place at the festivals of Dionysus. The Greek drama was essentially an offshoot of the worship of Dionysus, and throughout its history, as far as Athens was concerned, it continued to retain its close connexion with that worship. In other parts of Greece, when the drama had been fully established as a form of art, dramatic exhibitions were occasionally introduced into festivals with which originally they had no connexion. Thus they were introduced in later times into the Pythian games. But the Athenians were more conservative, and confined the drama to the festivals of Dionysus [2]. In Athens there were three of these festivals, the Anthesteria, the Great or City Dionysia, and the Lenaea. There were also the Rural Dionysia, celebrated in the various demes of Attica. Of the Athenian festivals the Anthesteria was the oldest [3]. But it had little, if any, connexion with the drama. The important festivals in the history of Greek drama were the City Dionysia and the Lenaea. They were themselves of late origin, and

---

[1] The inscription in Corp. Inscr. Att. ii. 971 a records the fact that at the City Dionysia Magnes won the prize for comedy, Aeschylus for tragedy. There is another inscription (given in the 'Εφημ. 'Αρχαιολ. 1886, pt. 4) which records that in 458 B.C. Euphronius won the prize for comedy, Aeschylus for tragedy. As this was the last appearance of Aeschylus as a tragic poet, it follows that the first inscription cannot refer to a later year than 459 B.C.

[2] Schol. Aristoph. Nub. 311; Plut. Symp. p. 674 D.

[3] Thucyd. ii. 15 calls the Anthesteria the ἀρχαιότερα Διονύσια, as opposed to the City Dionysia. That the Lenaea was a later institution than the Anthesteria seems to follow from the statement in Suidas v. τὰ ἐκ τῶν ἁμαξῶν σκώμματα· 'Αθήνησι γὰρ ἐν τῇ τῶν Χοῶν ἑορτῇ οἱ κωμάζοντες ἐπὶ τῶν ἁμαξῶν τοὺς ἀπαντῶντας ἔσκωπτόν τε καὶ ἐλοιδόρουν· τὸ δ' αὐτὸ καὶ τοῖς Ληναίοις ὕστερον ἐποίουν.

therefore offered a more suitable occasion for the introduction of a new form of art. The date of their institution and development is wrapt in obscurity. Various theories have been started as to their early history, but in the absence of definite facts it seems hardly worth while to hazard conjectures on such a subject. All that is required in an account of the Greek drama is to describe as fully as possible the character of these festivals during the fifth and succeeding centuries, and thus enable the reader to picture to himself the circumstances and surroundings which accompanied an Athenian theatrical performance.

§ 3. *The City Dionysia.*

By far the most splendid of the festivals of Dionysus was the Great or City Dionysia [1]. It was called the City Dionysia in opposition to the Lenaea. The significance of the names is not perfectly clear. The Lenaea was so called because it was held in the Lenaeum, or sacred enclosure of Dionysus on the south side of the Acropolis. The contests at this festival were called 'contests at the Lenaeum.' On the other hand, contests at the Great Dionysia were called 'contests in the city.' But as the Lenaeum was from the earliest times a part of the city, it is difficult to see the reason of the distinction [2]. And besides this, the contests at the Great Dionysia were, during all the period with which we are acquainted, held in the very same place as those at the Lenaea. The most plausible explanation is as follows. The Lenaea was a small festival; and the whole of the celebrations connected with it took place in or near the Lenaeum. At the Great Dionysia the festivities were on a larger

---

[1] Διονύσια τὰ μεγάλα Corp. Inscr. Att. ii. 312, 331, Διονύσια τὰ ἐν ἄστει Corp. Inscr. Att. ii. 341, 402, 404, Διονύσια τὰ ἀστικά Thucyd. v. 20. To produce plays at the City Dionysia was ἐν ἄστει διδάσκειν Schol. Aristoph. Ran. 67, or εἰς ἄστυ καθιέναι Arg. ii. Aristoph. Aves. The play or plays so produced were διδασκαλία ἀστική

Plut. X orat. 839 D. A victory at the City Dionysia was νίκη ἀστική Diog. Laert. viii. 90.

[2] Aristoph. Acharn. 504 οὑπὶ Ληναίῳ τ' ἀγών. That the Lenaeum was from early times inside the city is plain from Thucyd. ii. 15.

scale; and in addition to the contests in the sacred enclosure of Dionysus there were also other ceremonies in various parts of the city, more especially the chorus in the market-place before the statues of the twelve gods. It is probable therefore that the festival was called the City Dionysia to denote the wider area over which the various celebrations were spread. The date of the City Dionysia can be fixed with a fair amount of certainty. It took place in Elaphebolion, a month which answers to the last half of March and the first half of April. It must have terminated on the 15th, and begun on the 10th or 11th[1]. It could hardly have lasted less than five days. The long series of performances and celebrations which had to be gone through could not have been packed into a smaller space of time. Whether it extended to six days is a point that cannot be determined.

Before proceeding to describe the dramatic part of the performances at the City Dionysia it may be as well first of all to collect together such information as is attainable concerning the general character of the festival. It was held at a time of year when the spring was just commencing, and the sea had again become navigable. Occasionally stormy weather interfered with the proceedings. In the time of Demetrius the procession through the city was prevented by a heavy fall of snow. But the winter was generally at an end[2]. The city was full of visitors from all parts of Greece. During the period of Athenian supremacy it was at this season of the year that the allies came to Athens to pay the annual tribute. Ambassadors frequently chose this time for the transaction of public business. There were also the crowds of visitors who were attracted

---

[1] This is proved by certain passages in Aeschines and Demosthenes. After the City Dionysia came the Pandia; next day was the ἐκκλησία ἐν Διονύσου; then followed the 18th of Elaphebolion, the day of the first assembly mentioned by Aeschines and Demosthenes. Hence the City Dionysia must have terminated on the 15th. See Aeschin. Ctesiph. § 68, Fals. Leg. § 61; Demosth. Meid.

§ 8. The feast of Asclepius and the Proagon were on the 8th, Aeschin. Ctesiph. § 67. But the Proagon took place 'a few days' before the City Dionysia, Schol. Aeschin. Ctesiph. § 67. The City Dionysia cannot therefore have begun before the 10th.

[2] Theophrast. Char. 3; Plut. Demetr. p. 894 B.

to Athens merely from a desire to see the splendours of the festival. The consequence was that the streets were thronged with strangers, and the city presented an animated appearance in marked contrast to the quietness of the winter festival of the Lenaea[1]. The Athenians were glad of the opportunity of displaying the magnificence of their city before such a vast concourse of foreign Greeks. The procession through the streets, the sacrifices to the gods, the dithyrambs, the tragedies, and the comedies were all calculated to impress strangers with the wealth and public spirit and literary taste of the Athenians. In addition to the ordinary proceedings of the festival one or two ceremonies of a striking character were introduced for the express purpose of emphasising the power of Athens in the eyes of the visitors. At the commencement of the performances in the theatre the tribute collected from the allies was solemnly deposited in the orchestra in the presence of the assembled multitude. On the same occasion the herald made an announcement concerning the crowns which had been bestowed by foreign states upon Athens or upon Athenian citizens, and the crowns themselves were brought forward and laid in the orchestra beside the tribute[2]. By scenes of this kind the festival was made an occasion for glorifying Athens in the presence of foreign Greeks. In the fourth century, after the fall of the Athenian Empire, the political splendour of the City Dionysia came to an end. But the magnificence of the spectacle and the vastness of the gathering do not seem to have been in any way diminished. Visitors were attracted from all parts of Greece, not by political business, but by the celebrity of the dramatic exhibitions. Demosthenes speaks of the 'multitudes of strangers' who were present, and Aeschines describes the audience at the City Dionysia as consisting of 'the whole Greek nation[3].' Though Athens was shorn of her political power, the crowds which continued to attend the festival testified to her unimpaired supremacy in art and literature.

---

[1] Aristoph. Achar. 505, 506; Thucyd. v. 23.
[2] Isocrat. Orat. viii. § 82; Aeschin. Ctesiph. §§ 32–48.
[3] Dem. Meid. § 74; Aeschin. Ctesiph. § 43.

THE CITY DIONYSIA.

One of the most brilliant spectacles at the City Dionysia was the great procession in honour of Dionysus, which was probably held upon the first day of the festival. Athenians of every class, men, women, and even girls, made a point of being present to witness or take part in it. Vast crowds filled the streets; and the casual encounters which took place on these occasions often served as a foundation to the plots of the New Comedy[1]. The members of the procession wore brilliantly-coloured garments and ornaments of gold. Many of them had their faces covered with masks. Some were in chariots; others walked on foot. Among the people who took part in the procession were the choregi to the different choruses. For instance, when Demosthenes was choregus, he had a golden crown and mantle made specially for use at the procession. Alcibiades on a similar occasion was dressed in purple, and excited much admiration by his beauty[2]. It is not improbable that the performers in the various lyric and dramatic competitions also joined in the procession. Part of the show consisted of the trains of victims which were afterwards to be sacrificed to Dionysus. An old inscription records how the Ephebi offered a bull to Dionysus at the City Dionysia, after first taking it round in the procession. Many victims were publicly provided by the state, and many others were doubtless offered by individuals, or by different classes of the population. All these would be conducted round in the procession. Conspicuous among the train of people were the canephori, or virgins bearing upon their heads the baskets containing the sacrificial implements. The procession, in the course of its march, halted in the market-place, and a chorus danced and sung in front of the statues of the twelve gods[3]. Further details concerning the order of the proceedings are nowhere recorded, but it is easy to imagine that the brilliant colours of the procession itself, the vast crowds of spectators, and the splendid

---

[1] Demosth. Meid. § 10; Menand. Frag. Incert. 32.

[2] Dem. Meid. § 22; Plut. Cupid. Divit. 527 E; Athen. 543 C.

[3] Ἐφημερὶς Ἀρχαιολογική, 1860, No. 4098, 1862, No. 180; Corp. Inscr. Gr. i. 157; Xen. Hipparch. iii. 2.

public buildings of Athens in the background, combined to form an effective spectacle.

The entertainments provided in the theatre during the City Dionysia were of two kinds. In the first place there were the dramatic competitions, at which tragedies, comedies, and satyric dramas were exhibited. In the second place there were the choral competitions, which consisted of performances of dithyrambs to the accompaniment of the flute. It is most important not to confuse together the details of these two classes of contest. Even in the most recent works upon the Greek drama many mistakes have been caused by filling out the description of the dramatic performances with facts and circumstances which had really nothing to do with them, but applied solely to the choral competitions. At the City Dionysia there were two of these choral competitions, one between choruses of boys, and the other between choruses of men [1]. The choruses were called cyclic choruses, because of the circular form in which they stood. Each of them was composed of fifty members. There were five choruses of boys and five choruses of men, and each chorus was supplied by one of the ten tribes of Attica. In this way all ten tribes took part in one or other of the two competitions [2]. The important point to remember in regard to

---

[1] Demosth. Meid. § 10 καὶ τοῖς ἐν ἄστει Διονυσίοις ἡ πομπὴ καὶ οἱ παῖδες [καὶ οἱ ἄνδρες] καὶ ὁ κῶμος καὶ οἱ κωμῳδοὶ καὶ οἱ τραγῳδοί. The words καὶ οἱ ἄνδρες have obviously fallen out. There is abundant evidence to prove that there were choruses of men, as well as of boys, at the City Dionysia. Corp. Inscr. Gr. 213 contains a list of all members of the tribe Pandionis who had been victorious παισὶν ἢ ἀνδράσιν at the City Dionysia. On the lists of victors at the City Dionysia (Corp. Inscr. Att. ii. 971 a-e) the contests enumerated are always the same, viz. choruses of boys, choruses of men, comedy, tragedy. Cp. Lysias Orat. xxi. § 2 ἀνδράσι χορηγῶν εἰς Διονύσια.

[2] There is a full account of the choruses of boys and men in Schol. Aeschin. Timarch. § 11 ἐξ ἔθους Ἀθηναῖοι [κατέστησαν] κατὰ φυλὴν πεντήκοντα παίδων χορὸν ἢ ἀνδρῶν, ὥστε γενέσθαι δέκα χορούς, ἐπειδὴ ⟨δὲ⟩ καὶ δέκα φυλαί. διαγωνίζονται δὲ ἀλλήλοις διθυράμβῳ, φυλάττοντος (MS. φυλάττοντες) τοῦ χορηγοῦντος ἑκάστῳ χορῶν τὰ ἐπιτήδεια. ὁ δ' οὖν νικήσας χορὸς τρίποδα λαμβάνει, ὃν ἀνατίθησι τῷ Διονύσῳ. λέγονται δὲ οἱ διθύραμβοι χοροὶ κύκλιοι, καὶ χορὸς κύκλιος. A chorus of men is called rather loosely αὐληταὶ ἄνδρες by Demosthenes (Meid. § 156), not because it consisted of flute-players, but because it sang dithyrambs to the accompaniment of the flute. This is made clear by other passages in the speech, e.g. §§ 15, 17. See Wieseler das Satyrspiel pp. 46–48. Misled by the phrase the author of the first argument to the Meidias erroneously asserts that there were αὐλητῶν χοροί at the City Dionysia.

these dithyrambic choruses is that the contest in which they were engaged was essentially a tribal one. In the dramatic competitions the rivalry was confined to the individual poets and choregi. The choruses were selected indiscriminately from the whole population. But each dithyrambic chorus represented one of the ten tribes. Its choregus was a member of that tribe. The singers were exclusively chosen from the same tribe[1]. The victory of the chorus was a victory for the tribe to which it belonged. The prize of victory, the tripod, though presented to the choregus, and erected in some public place at his expense, was regarded as appertaining equally to the tribe[2]. In the records of victories with dithyrambic choruses, preserved on inscriptions and elsewhere, the name of the tribe to which the chorus belonged is always given in a prominent position. On the other hand the records of dramatic victories give merely the names of the choregus, the poet, and the principal actor. There is no mention of any tribe[3]. It follows that the tribes had nothing to do with the dramatic contests. In order to avoid error it is most important to keep this fact clearly in view, that in the dithyrambic contests the competitors were really the ten tribes of Attica, while the drama was a matter with which only individual citizens were concerned.

§ 4. *Tragedy at the City Dionysia in the fifth century.*

We come now to the dramatic performances at the City Dionysia. These were of two kinds, tragic and comic. The

[1] Demosth. Meid. § 13; Antiphon orat. vi. §§ 12, 13.

[2] Lysias orat. xxi. § 2; Demosth. Meid. § 5 τῆς φυλῆς ἀδίκως ἀφαιρεθείσης τὸν τρίποδα. The choregus to a dithyrambic chorus was said χορηγεῖν τῇ φυλῇ, since he represented his tribe in the contest, while the dramatic choregus represented no one but himself; cp. Plut. X orat. 835 B ἐχορήγησε κυκλίῳ χορῷ τῇ αὑτοῦ φυλῇ ἀγωνιζομένῃ διθυράμβῳ: Isaeus orat. v. § 36 οὗτος γὰρ τῇ μὲν φυλῇ εἰς Διονύσια χορηγήσας τέταρτος ἐγένετο, τραγῳδοῖς δὲ καὶ πυρριχισταῖς ὕστατος. In this passage to be choregus to one's tribe is contrasted with being choregus to a tragic chorus. Bentley's emendation (Phalaris p. 360 τῇ μὲν φυλῇ εἰς Διονύσια χορηγήσας τέταρτος ἐγένετο τραγῳδοῖς, καὶ πυρριχισταῖς ὕστατος) is quite unnecessary, and contains the fatal error of making Dicaeogenes *fourth* in the tragic contest, though the number of competitors in tragedy never exceeded three.

[3] Corp. Inscr. Gr. vol. i. pp. 342–348; Corp. Inscr. Att. ii. 971. Cp. the record of victors at the City Dionysia quoted on p. 59.

first point to be considered is the number of the competing poets, and the number of the plays produced, at each celebration of the festival. The most difficult part of the enquiry is that which concerns tragedy during the fifth century. In the fourth century various changes and innovations were introduced, which call for separate consideration. The fifth century stands by itself, and the question as to the number of tragedies produced during that period at each celebration of the City Dionysia is one of considerable intricacy. But it deserves to be considered in detail, as it is of much more interest than a mere question of numbers, and practically involves the whole subject of trilogies and tetralogies. The practice of writing plays in trilogies and tetralogies produced the most profound effect upon the art of Aeschylus. Any enquiry therefore into the origin and character of this practice will throw light upon one of the most interesting parts in the history of the Greek drama. It will be best in the first place to enumerate all the records which bear upon the subject. Fortunately a sufficient number have been preserved to enable us to determine with moderate certainty the regulations as to the number of tragic poets and tragedies at the City Dionysia during the fifth century.

The earliest record is for the year 499 B.C., when Aeschylus made his first public appearance, and his competitors were Choerilus and Pratinas. Nothing is known as to the plays produced on this occasion [1]. The next record refers to the year 472. In this year Aeschylus produced the Phineus, Persae, Glaucus, and Prometheus, and was successful in winning the first prize. The Prometheus here mentioned was of course not the Prometheus Vinctus, but a satyric play in which the same myth was treated humorously, and of which two or three fragments are preserved [2]. For the year 467 there is a very complete record of the tragic competition. Aeschylus was again first, and his plays were the Laius, Oedipus, Septem versus Thebas, and satyric play Sphinx. Aristias was second with the Perseus, Tantalus, and satyric play Palaestae written by his father Pratinas. Polyphradmon

---

[1] Suidas v. Πρατίνας.   [2] Arg. to Aesch. Persae.

was third with the Lycurgean tetralogy[1]. According to this notice Aristias only exhibited three plays, while his competitors each exhibited four. But there can be little doubt that the name of one of his plays has dropped out accidentally, and that he produced four like the rest. This is proved by a comparison with the records of other tragic contests, of which a large number exist, referring to very different periods. In these records varieties are found both in the number of poets competing, and in the number of plays exhibited by each poet. But in one respect complete uniformity prevails. With the exception of the case before us there is no instance of poets competing in the same festival with a different number of plays. There can hardly then be any doubt that in the present instance the three poets each exhibited four plays. The next record is for the year 458. This was the year in which Aeschylus made his last appearance as a dramatic poet. He produced the Orestean tetralogy, consisting of the Agamemnon, Choephori, Eumenides, and satyric drama Proteus. The names of the other poets are not mentioned[2]. In addition to the above notices it is also known that on one occasion Aeschylus competed with the four plays composing his Lycurgean tetralogy. The tetralogy dealt with the fate of Lycurgus, king of the Edoni, and consisted of the Edoni, Bassarides, Neanisci, and satyric play Lycurgus. On another occasion he exhibited a trilogy dealing with the legend of Prometheus. This trilogy, of which the Prometheus Vinctus was the central play, no doubt concluded with a satyric drama; but there is no record of it among ancient writers[3]. After the death of Aeschylus there is a gap in our information till the year 438, when Sophocles and Euripides were competitors. Sophocles was first; Euripides second with the Cressae, Alcmaeon in Psophis, Telephus, and Alcestis. In 431 they were again competitors, but this time the first place was taken by Euphorion. Sophocles was second; Euripides third with the Medea,

---

[1] Arg. to Aesch. Theb.
[2] Arg. to Aesch. Agam.
[3] Schol. Aristoph. Thesm. 142; Arg. to Aesch. Prom.; Schol. Aesch. Prom. 94.

Philoctetes, Dictys, and satyric play Theristae. In 428 the Hippolytus of Euripides was produced; but for this year only the names of the poets have been preserved. Euripides was first, Iophon second, Ion third[1]. The year 415 was memorable for the defeat of Euripides by an obscure poet called Xenocles. On this occasion Xenocles was first with the Oedipus, Lycaon, Bacchae, and satyric play Athamas. Euripides was second with the Alexander, Palamedes, Troades, and satyric play Sisyphus. The only other record which bears upon the present subject is to the effect that after the death of Euripides, and therefore after 406 B.C., his Iphigeneia in Aulis, Alcmaeon, and Bacchae were produced by his son at the City Dionysia[2].

In the above notices and records the name of <u>the festival</u> at which the contest took place, and the plays were produced, is usually not mentioned. An exception is made in one case. It is expressly stated that it was at the City Dionysia that the three posthumous tragedies of Euripides were exhibited. Otherwise nothing is said about the festival. But there is not the slightest doubt that all the above notices refer to the City Dionysia. In one instance there is positive proof of the fact. An inscription recently discovered in the Acropolis shows that it was at the City Dionysia that the Orestean tetralogy was produced[3]. Various considerations make it practically certain that the other notices refer to the same festival. At the Lenaea the performances of tragedy were always comparatively unimportant. It is doubtful whether they existed at all during the earlier half of the fifth century. In the fourth century they

---

[1] Args. to Eurip. Alcest., Med., Hippol.

[2] Aelian Var. Hist. ii. 8; Schol. Aristoph. Ran. 67.

[3] This inscription was discovered in the Acropolis in 1886, and published in the 'Εφημερὶς 'Αρχαιολογική for 1886, pt. 4. It runs as follows: 'Επὶ Φιλοκλέους Οἰνηῒς παίδων, | Δημόδοκος ἐχορήγει· | 'Ἱπποθωντὶς ἀνδρῶν, | Εὐκτήμων 'Ελευσίνιος ἐχορήγει· | κωμῳδῶν Εὐρυκλείδης ἐχορήγει, | Εὐφρόνιος ἐδίδασκε· | τραγῳδῶν Ξενοκλῆς 'Αφιδναῖος ἐχορήγει, | Αἰσχύλος ἐδίδασκεν. The combination of four kinds of contests, with boys' choruses, choruses of men, comedies, and tragedies, proves that the festival was the City Dionysia. That the plays exhibited on this occasion by Aeschylus were the Orestean tetralogy is proved by the Arg. to the Agamemnon: ἐδιδάχθη τὸ δρᾶμα ἐπὶ ἄρχοντος Φιλοκλέους ὀλυμπιάδι ὀγδοηκοστῇ ἔτει δευτέρῳ. πρῶτος Αἰσχύλος 'Αγαμέμνονι, Χοηφόροις, Εὐμενίσι, Πρωτεῖ σατυρικῷ, ἐχορήγει Ξενοκλῆς 'Αφιδνεύς.

came to be confined to mere reproductions of old tragedies. It is impossible to suppose that the three great masters of tragedy,—Aeschylus, Sophocles, and Euripides,—during the height of their reputation, produced their plays at this relatively insignificant festival. The omission of all mention of the festival in the notices about their tragedies is in itself a conclusive proof that there could be no doubt upon the subject, and that it was a matter of general knowledge that they were brought out at the City Dionysia. The case was very different in comedy. Comedy flourished with equal vigour at both festivals. Hence in the records about the plays of Aristophanes care is generally taken to notify the festival at which they were produced. In the case of tragedy it was felt that any such specification was unnecessary.

From the notices and records enumerated above two conclusions may be drawn concerning the tragic contests at the City Dionysia during the fifth century. The number of poets who took part in the competition was limited to three, and each poet was expected to exhibit four plays, consisting of three tragedies and a satyric drama. As regards the number of poets, it might perhaps be suggested that the records give, not the names of all the competitors, but merely those of the three most successful ones. But the evidence of the comic didascaliae proves that this was not the case. It is known for a fact that after the beginning of the fourth century the number of competitors in comedy was five. But the comic didascaliae of the period invariably give the names of all five competitors, together with the plays they produced[1]. When therefore only three poets are mentioned, it follows that the number of competitors was limited to three. The practice of recording the names of all the competing poets need cause no surprise. As a matter of fact it was a considerable distinction for a poet to be allowed to exhibit at all at one of the annual festivals. In addition to the

---

[1] Arg. to Aristoph. Plutus ἐδιδάχθη ἐπὶ ἄρχοντος Ἀντιπάτρου, ἀνταγωνιζομένου αὐτῷ Νικοχάρους μὲν Λάκωσιν, Ἀριστο- μένους δὲ Ἀδμήτῳ, Νικοφῶντος δὲ Ἀδώνιδι, Ἀλκαίου δὲ Πασιφάῃ. Corp. Inscr. Att. ii. 972, 975.

testimony of the didascaliae there is the following direct evidence concerning the number of the tragic poets. It is expressly stated that in 499 the competitors in the tragic contest were the three poets Aeschylus, Choerilus, and Pratinas. Then again it is recorded of Sophocles that he 'won twenty victories, was often second, never third.' This form of statement seems clearly to imply that the number of competitors in tragedy never exceeded three[1]. Even on general grounds it is evident that the number could hardly have been greater. If there had been four or five poets, it would have implied the production of sixteen or twenty tragedies. But it is difficult to see how such a large number of tragedies could have been compressed within the limited period of the festival, along with the comedies and dithyrambs, and various other festivities and entertainments.

The fact then that each poet exhibited three tragedies and a satyric play is clearly demonstrated by the records, and also confirmed by a statement in Diogenes Laërtius[2]. The practice of terminating the tragic pieces with the boisterous licence of the satyric drama suggested to Ion of Chios, the tragic poet of the fifth century, his well-known remark that virtue, like a tragic poet's group of plays, should always contain a satyric element[3]. It is noticeable that on one occasion Euripides substituted the Alcestis, a short tragedy with a tinge of comedy about it, for the usual satyric drama. This may have been not infrequently the case, especially during the latter half of the fifth century. The

---

[1] Suidas v. Πρατίνας; vita Sophoclis (p. 3 Dindf.).

[2] Diog. Laërt. iii. 56 Θράσυλλος δέ φησι καὶ κατὰ τὴν τραγικὴν τετραλογίαν ἐκδοῦναι αὐτὸν τοὺς διαλόγους· οἷον ἐκεῖνοι τέτρασι δράμασιν ἠγωνίζοντο, Διονυσίοις, Ληναίοις, Παναθηναίοις, Χύτροις, ὧν τὸ τέταρτον ἦν σατυρικόν· τὰ δὲ τέτταρα δράματα ἐκαλεῖτο τετραλογία, εἰσὶ τοίνυν, φησίν, οἱ πάντες αὐτῷ γνήσιοι διάλογοι, κ.τ.λ. Thrasyllus was a philosopher who flourished in the time of the emperor Tiberius. The passage οἷον ἐκεῖνοι ... τετραλογία is apparently an explanatory interpolation by Diogenes himself. The statement that the four plays of a tetralogy were performed at four different festivals is manifestly absurd in itself, and abundantly disproved by the inscriptions. Moreover, it is expressly recorded that the Iphigeneia in Aulis, Alcmaeon, and Bacchae of Euripides were brought out together at the City Dionysia (Schol. Aristoph. Ran. 67).

[3] See note on next page.

statement in the last notice, that the Iphigeneia, Alcmaeon, and Bacchae of Euripides were brought out by his son at the City Dionysia, does not necessarily imply that they were brought out by themselves, without any satyric play to make up the number four. It is possible indeed that at this late period the satyric play had begun to be occasionally dispensed with. But on the other hand it is very likely that the satyric play in this case was supplied by the younger Euripides. That no mention of it is made in the above statement is easily intelligible, since the writer does not profess to give a record of the tragic contest for the year, but is merely concerned with the biography of the elder Euripides.

§ 5. *Trilogies and Tetralogies.*

The four plays exhibited by each poet might either be independent works of art, totally unconnected in subject, or they might deal with the same legend, and be fused together into a single artistic whole. When the four plays were connected by community of subject, they were called tetralogies. Similarly the three tragedies, regarded apart from the satyric drama, were called trilogies when connected together in this manner[1]. The practice of exhibiting trilogies and tetralogies is insepar-

---

[1] The general word for a play or group of plays produced by one poet at the same festival was διδασκαλία. Thus Ion remarked (Plut. Peric. p. 154 E) that virtue, like a τραγικὴ διδασκαλία, should contain a satyric element. The τραγικὴ διδασκαλία in Ion's time usually consisted of three tragedies and a satyric drama. Cp. also Anthol. Pal. vii. 37 ἡ δ' ἐνὶ χερσὶν Κούριμος, ἐκ ποίης ἥδε διδασκαλίης: Plut. X orat. 839 D διδασκαλίας ἀστικὰς καθῆκεν ἐξ ... καὶ ἑτέρας δύο Ληναϊκάς. The word τετραλογία was not applied to all groups of four plays, but only to those groups in which the separate plays were connected together by unity of subject. This is proved by the words of Suidas in his account of Sophocles: καὶ αὐτὸς ἦρξε τοῦ δρᾶμα πρὸς δρᾶμα ἀγωνίζεσθαι, ἀλλὰ μὴ τετραλογίαν. These words can only mean that Sophocles exhibited the same number of plays as his rivals, but that his plays did not form a tetralogy, that is to say, were not connected together by unity of subject. Another proof is afforded by the use of the word τετραλογία in Greek writers. There are four places in which it is applied to particular groups of plays. It is applied to the Oresteia of Aeschylus (Schol. Aristoph. Ran. 1155), the Pandionis of Philocles (Schol. Aristoph. Av. 282), the Lycurgeia of Aeschylus (Schol. Aristoph. Thesm. 135), and the Lycurgeia of Polyphradmon (Arg. to Aesch. Theb.). All these were groups of plays upon a single subject.

ably connected with the name of Aeschylus. Unfortunately there is no information as to the origin and development of the custom. It is not known whether he invented it, or inherited it from his predecessors. But we know that before the time of Aeschylus tragedy as a form of art had made but little progress. It was he that inspired it with dignity and splendour. It is far from likely that the 'rough and unfinished productions of his predecessors should have been cast in the elaborate mould of the tetralogy. And the largeness of design involved in tracing the same tragic story through three successive dramas is a conception peculiarly akin to the grandeur of Aeschylus' genius. Hence it is exceedingly probable, though not certain, that the system was his invention. He did not employ it on all occasions. In one of the records quoted above the four plays which he is said to have exhibited together are apparently quite unconnected in subject. These are the Phineus, Persae, Glaucus, and Prometheus, produced in 472. As a matter of fact the only tetralogies of Aeschylus for which there is direct evidence are the four already mentioned, dealing with the legends of Oedipus, Lycurgus, Prometheus, and Orestes. How many more he wrote is a matter of uncertainty. If the system of tetralogies was invented by him, it could hardly have been developed in its full completeness all at once. It is probable that he began his career by exhibiting groups of isolated plays. Even in later times the record just referred to proves that he did not invariably employ the form of the tetralogy.

Fortunately for our knowledge of the Greek drama, a specimen of the Aeschylean trilogy has been preserved in the Oresteia. This was the latest work of its author, and in it the trilogic form of composition is brought to the highest perfection. A great crime is committed, and its consequences are traced through successive plays, until finally the guilt is expiated, and the ministers of vengeance satisfied. The whole forms a magnificent work of art; and the separate plays, though complete in themselves, gain additional significance and impressiveness from their position in the trilogy. The general effect can be appreciated even by a modern reader, but must have been still more striking to an ancient audience, before whom the three plays were performed in succession in the course of the same morning. But it would be a mistake to suppose that all the trilogies of Aeschylus were equally perfect in construction. Probably in some cases they treated of one subject without possessing much real artistic unity. The three plays, while depicting successive stages in some great national legend, may have been strung together after the fashion of a chronicle or history, rather than welded into one compact whole. This seems to have been to some extent the case with the Oedipodeia. The third play of this trilogy, the Seven against Thebes, certainly did not bring the legend to a conclusion in the same artistic and satisfying manner in which the Oresteia is concluded by the Eumenides. The final scene of the Seven against Thebes is like the prelude to a new play. In this scene Antigone proclaims her resolve to bury the corpse of her brother in spite of Creon's prohibition, and the herald warns her of the risk she will incur by setting the authorities at defiance[1]. Here then is an instance of a trilogy which breaks off in the middle of a legend, at a point where there is no artistic necessity for it to do so. The concluding play of the three, instead of bringing matters to a final settlement, ends with a suggestion of future difficulties and crimes. A trilogy of this kind resembles the poems of the Epic Cycle, in which legends were linked together in chronological order, and the point at which the story began and ended was determined by purely accidental considerations. Other trilogies of Aeschylus may

[1] The didascalia to the Septem v. Thebas was first brought to light by Franz in 1848 (Didasc. zu Aesch. Sept., Berl. 1848). Previously to the discovery of this didascalia there was hardly any point upon which the critics were more unanimous than that the Septem must have been the middle play of a trilogy. The concluding scene, in which Antigone proclaims her resolve to bury the corpse of her brother, was supposed to obviously pave the way to the final play of the three, in which the same subject was treated as in the Antigone of Sophocles. The publication of the didascalia revealed the fact that the Septem was after all the concluding play of the group, and that the trilogy consisted of the Laius, the Oedipus, and the Septem. Nothing could have more clearly demonstrated the futility of endeavouring, by mere conjecture, to arrange the lost plays of Aeschylus in tetralogies.

have approximated to the same type. At any rate it is most unlikely that they were all as perfect and harmonious in construction as the Oresteia. Attempts have been made, especially by Hermann and Welcker, to take the titles of the lost plays of Aeschylus, and group them together into tetralogies. But it is clear that conjectural arrangements of this kind must be received with the very greatest caution, and this for two reasons. In the first place it is uncertain how many of the tetralogies of Aeschylus conformed to the perfect model of the Oresteia. In the second place it is probable that a large number of his plays were not composed in tetralogies at all.

The relation of the satyric play to the three tragedies which preceded it is a question of some importance in connexion with the composition of tetralogies. The usual theory seems to have been that the satyric play should deal with the same subject as the trilogy, but from a humorous point of view; and that some of the personages out of the trilogy should appear in it. The king or hero whose sufferings had already been depicted was now to be exhibited in a different aspect, amid the wild surroundings of a satyr's existence. It was necessary to give a certain tinge of poetry and romance to the composition, and not jar the feelings with a sense of incongruity, by introducing the tragic personage into scenes of ordinary comedy. This is well expressed in the lines of Horace :—

> Verum ita risores, ita commendare dicaces
> Conveniet Satyros, ita vertere seria ludo,
> Ne quicumque deus, quicumque adhibebitur heros,
> Regali conspectus in auro nuper et ostro,
> Migret in obscuras humili sermone tabernas,
> Aut dum vitet humum nubes et inania captet[1].

The satyric plays of Aeschylus seem, when they formed part of a tetralogy, to have been of this type. The Oedipodeia concluded with the Sphinx, the Lycurgeia with the Lycurgus. In both these plays some of the personages out of the preceding trilogy must have appeared. The Oresteia is called a tetralogy,

---

[1] Hor. Ars Poet. 225 foll.

and therefore the Proteus, the satyric play with which it concluded, was probably connected with the other three plays in subject. But in the absence of information it is impossible to say what that connexion was, and what personages took the leading part in the play. Curiously enough the satyric play Prometheus did not conclude the Promethean trilogy, as we should have expected, but was performed along with the Persae, and two other independent plays. The practice of terminating a trilogy with a satyric play upon the same subject may seem questionable to modern taste, and can hardly be defended on artistic grounds. Like many other customs of the Greek drama, it was an accident due to the circumstances in which tragedy originated. Tragedy was developed out of the odes to Dionysus sung by choruses of satyrs; and as it departed more and more from its original character, a regard for antiquity required that the satyric element should be retained in some form or another. Hence the practice of concluding every tragic performance with a satyric play of the old-fashioned type.

Sophocles is said to have been the first to abandon the system of writing plays in tetralogies[1]. Each of his dramas formed an independent work of art. It appears to be implied that before his time the practice of writing tetralogies had been very generally adopted; and it is only natural to suppose that the commanding genius of Aeschylus would cause his example to be widely followed. But the fashion set by Sophocles was adopted by the younger poets. In 467, the very next year after the first tragic victory of Sophocles, when Aeschylus produced his Theban tetralogy, and Polyphradmon his Lycurgeia, the third poet Aristias appears to have exhibited a group of independent plays[2]. After the death of Aeschylus the practice of composing tetralogies rapidly went into disuse. The records show that Euripides abandoned the system. In fact, during the latter half of the fifth century only three tetralogies are mentioned. A Pandionis was written by Philocles, the nephew of Aeschylus, who naturally continued

---

[1] Suidas v. Σοφοκλῆς.   [2] Arg. to Aeschyl. Theb.

the traditions of the Aeschylean system. An Oedipodeia, apparently a tetralogy, was composed by Meletus, the prosecutor of Socrates. Plato is said to have written a tetralogy in his youth, but to have abandoned poetry for philosophy before it was exhibited. In the course of the succeeding century the practice of writing tetralogies came to be so little regarded that Aristotle never even mentions it in his Poetics [1].

Some difficulty has been made as to the derivation of the words trilogy and tetralogy. As far as their etymology goes they ought to denote groups of speeches rather than groups of plays. In their dramatic sense the words do not occur frequently, and were of comparatively late origin. The word tetralogy, as applied to the drama, is not found before the time of Aristotle; the word trilogy not before that of Aristophanes the grammarian [2]. It is quite possible that the dramatic meaning of a tetralogy may have been a secondary one, and that the word was used at first in reference to oratory. It was the custom of the Greek orators to write groups of four speeches, two for the prosecution and two for the defence, about fictitious cases, to serve as models for their pupils. Three groups of this kind, composed by Antiphon, have come down to us, and are called tetralogies. It is very likely that this was the original meaning of the word, and that it was only in the course of the fourth century that it came to be applied by analogy to the drama. It would be convenient to have a generic term to denote groups of four plays composed about a single subject in the Aeschylean fashion. When the word tetralogy had once acquired this sense, it would be an easy step to form by analogy the

---

[1] Schol. Aristoph. Av. 282; Schol. Plat. Apol. p. 330, ed. Bekk.; Aelian Var. Hist. ii. 30.

[2] Schol. Aristoph. Ran. 1155 τετραλογίαν φέρουσι τὴν 'Ορέστειαν αἱ Διδασκαλίαι. The Didascaliae is the work of Aristotle. Diog. Laërt. iii. 61 ἔνιοι δέ, ὧν ἐστι καὶ 'Αριστοφάνης ὁ γραμματικός, εἰς τριλογίας ἕλκουσι τοὺς διαλόγους.

The other passages in which the word τετραλογία occurs in a dramatic sense are Diog. Laërt. iii. 56, ix. 45; Schol. Plat. Apol. p. 330; Schol. Aristoph. Ran. 1155, Av. 282, Thesm. 142; Arg. to Aeschyl. Theb. The word τριλογία only occurs in three places, viz. Schol. Aristoph. Ran. 1155; Diog. Laërt. iii. 61; Suidas v. Νικόμαχος.

word trilogy, to denote the three tragedies apart from the satyric play. Satyric plays were treated with comparative neglect in later times, and were easily separable from the tragedies which preceded them. Possibly also in many cases the three tragedies may have been connected in subject with one another, but independent of the satyric play. Hence the convenience of a term to denote the three tragedies by themselves. It is said that the grammarians Aristarchus and Apollonius preferred to disregard the satyric plays altogether, and to speak only of trilogies. But although the generic terms trilogy and tetralogy were of relatively late origin, it was customary at a much earlier period to give a common name to groups of plays composed on the tetralogic system. The poet Aristophanes cites the group of plays about Lycurgus under the title of the Lycurgeia; and in the same way he cites the group of plays about Orestes as the Oresteia[1]. These and similar titles no doubt dated from the time of Aeschylus himself.

§ 6. *Tragedy at the City Dionysia in later times.*

It has been worth while to discuss in some detail the question as to the number of tragedies produced each year at the City Dionysia during the fifth century, because of the interest of the subject. The fourth century is a period of decay as far as tragedy is concerned. For the first half of the century there is a complete blank in our information as to the system of tragic competitions at the City Dionysia. On coming to the latter half of the century it is found that considerable changes had been made. An inscription discovered in recent years gives a copious record of the tragic contests at the City Dionysia for the years 341 and 340[2]. From this record it appears that the satyric drama had now been completely separated from tragedy. The proceedings commenced with the performance of a single satyric play. Then followed a

---

[1] Aristoph. Thesm. 135, Ran. 1124.   [2] Corp. Inscr. Att. ii. 973.

representation of an old tragedy by one of the great tragic poets. In 341 the old tragedy was the 'Iphigeneia' of Euripides; in 340 it was the Orestes of Euripides. Then at length after the satyric play and the old tragedy had been performed, came the competition with new and original tragedies. The number of competing poets was still three, as it had been from the earliest times. But the number of tragedies varied from year to year. In 341 each poet exhibited three tragedies; in 340 each poet exhibited two. Here the information ends. It appears then that by the latter half of the fourth century the satyric drama had receded still further into the background. In the fifth century each poet had exhibited one satyric play at the end of his three tragedies. But now a single satyric play at the commencement of the proceedings was considered sufficient. The poet who was to have the honour of performing this play would be selected beforehand by the archon. There is no evidence to show when the new system came into existence; but it must have been in the course of the first half of the fourth century. Another point to be noticed is the gradual decrease in the number of new tragedies produced each year. In 341 it was nine; in 340 it was only six. It is impossible to say with certainty what was the practice during the first half of the fourth century. When the change in regard to the satyric drama was first made, the tragic poets may have continued to produce four plays apiece, substituting a tragedy for the old satyric play, just as Euripides had done in 438, when he exhibited the Alcestis. Or on the other hand the change may have consisted in simply discontinuing the satyric play, and leaving the tragic poets to compete with three tragedies only. There is very little evidence which bears upon the subject, but such as it is, it rather points to the conclusion that at first the number four was retained. Theodectes, the rhetorician and tragic poet, flourished in the middle of the fourth century. He wrote 'fifty tragedies,' and engaged in thirteen contests. These numbers seem to imply that in most of the contests in which he was engaged he exhibited four tragedies[1]. Again, Aphareus, the tragic poet, wrote thirty-five confessedly genuine tragedies, and engaged in eight contests ranging in date from 368 to 341. Here too the inference seems to be that he must have exhibited four tragedies on most of these occasions[2]. The only way to escape such an inference would be to suppose that both Aphareus and Theodectes wrote a considerable number of plays which were never intended for the stage. Such a practice was not unknown at this time. The tragic poet Chaeremon, the contemporary of Aphareus and Theodectes, wrote tragedies which were simply intended to be read[3]. But as yet the practice was unusual, and nothing of the kind is related of Theodectes and Aphareus. Hence the probability is that during the earlier part of the fourth century each poet at the City Dionysia exhibited four tragedies. But owing to the scantiness of the evidence it is impossible to come to any certain conclusion on the subject.

It has been seen that in 340 the total number of new tragedies produced at the City Dionysia was only six. The decrease in numbers points to the gradual decay of tragedy at Athens. With the close of the fourth century the productive period of Attic tragedy came to an end. The centre of literary activity was transferred from Athens to Alexandria, and to this city the more creative poetical minds were attracted. During the third century we meet with the names of many celebrated tragic poets at Alexandria. On the other hand, after the fourth century hardly a single Athenian tragic poet is mentioned. Competitions in tragedy continued to be held in Athens at the City Dionysia even down to Roman times. But in most cases the tragedies exhibited must have been old ones. It is true that in public decrees recording the proclamation of crowns at the City Dionysia the phrase 'at the performance of new tragedies' continues to occur as late as Roman times. But there can have been no significance in the phrase. It was merely an

---

[1] Suidas v. Θεοδέκτης; Steph. Byzant. v. Φάσηλις.
[2] Plut. X orat. 839 D.   [3] Aristot. Rhet. iii. 11.

instance of the retention of an old formula when its meaning was obsolete[1].

§ 7. *Comedy at the City Dionysia.*

The history of the tragic contests at the City Dionysia having now been traced down to the latest times, the contests in comedy have next to be considered. This is a subject of much less difficulty. It has already been pointed out that it was in the course of the earlier half of the fifth century that comedy was first recognised by the state. The performances of comedy, which had previously been mere voluntary undertakings, were now superintended by the archon, and regular public contests were instituted. It is impossible to determine the exact date of their institution. Nor is there any certain evidence to show whether it was at the Lenaea or the City Dionysia that comedy was first officially recognised. As far as the City Dionysia is concerned the only fact that can be established with certainty is that contests in comedy were fully elaborated at any rate as early as the year 459 B.C. This is proved by the inscriptions already referred to on a previous page[2]. Whether they had existed for many years previously is a question which there is no evidence to determine.

The number of poets who were allowed to take part in the comic contests at the City Dionysia differed at different periods. During the fifth century it was limited to three, as in tragedy. The Clouds, the Peace, and the Birds of Aristophanes were all brought out at the City Dionysia during the latter part of the fifth century; and on each of these occasions Aristo-

---

[1] Dio Chrysost. xiii, p. 246 (Dindf.). καίτοι τραγῳδοὺς ἑκάστοτε ὁρᾶτε τοῖς Διονυσίοις. Corp. Inscr. Att. ii. 334, 341, 402, 444-446, 465-471, 479, 481. These inscriptions range in date from about 270 B.C. to 50 B.C. There are slight differences in the formula, e.g. Διονυσίων τῶν μεγάλων τραγῳδῶν τῷ ἀγῶνι τῷ καινῷ, Διονυσίων τῶν ἐν ἄστει καινοῖς τραγῳδοῖς, Διονυσίων τῶν ἐν ἄστει τραγῳδῶν τῷ καινῷ ἀγῶνι, Διονυσίων τῶν ἐν ἄστει τῷ καινῷ ἀγῶνι, Διονυσίων τῶν μεγάλων τῷ καινῷ ἀγῶνι.

[2] Corp. Inscr. Att. ii. 971 compared with the inscription in Ἐφημ. Ἀρχαιολ. 1886, pt. 4. See above p. 9.

phanes was opposed by two competitors[1]. At the Lenaea during the fifth century the number of the competing poets was also three. In the beginning of the fourth century the number was raised to five at both festivals, and appears to have continued unchanged throughout the subsequent history of the Attic drama[2]. The reason of the increase was probably due to the disappearance of the chorus from comedy. A comedy without a chorus would be less expensive, and would take less time to perform. A larger number of comedies was therefore provided, and the number of poets had consequently to be increased.

It does not appear however that comedy was ever exhibited at Athens on the same large scale as tragedy. It has already been shown that during the most flourishing period of Attic tragedy each poet was accustomed to produce no less than four plays at the annual festival. But in comedy it was the invariable practice to compete with single plays only. In all the notices of comic contests which remain there is no instance of a poet competing with more than one play. The total number of comedies produced each year at the City Dionysia would be three during the fifth century, and five during the succeeding centuries. These figures appear small compared with the number of tragedies produced each year at the same festival. But although each poet competed with a single play, it was not impossible for a man to exhibit two comedies at the same contest. However in order to do so he had to appear really as two poets, and to compete as it were against himself. The total number of comedies remained the same, but the poet was allowed to appear twice over, and to run a double chance of success. Instances of such an occurrence are occasionally found. In 422 Philonides took the place of two poets, and exhibited both the Prelude and the Wasps. He was first with the

---

[1] Args. to Aristoph. Nubes, Pax, Aves.
[2] Arg. to Aristoph. Plutus; Corp. Inscr. Att. ii. 972, 975. It is not always known to which of the two festivals these various notices refer. But in every case the number of the poets appears as five. It is therefore practically certain that the number was raised to five at *both* festivals after the fifth century.

Prelude, and second with the Wasps, and his antagonist Leucon was third with the Ambassadors[1]. Both the Prelude and the Wasps were really plays of Aristophanes, but were brought out in the name of the poet Philonides. Again in 353 Diodorus made a double appearance, and was second with the Corpse, and third with the Madman[2]. Such instances of a poet taking the place of two competitors, and thus running a double chance of obtaining the first position, cannot have been of common occurrence. They were probably due, when they did occur, either to an exceptional dearth of new comedies, or to very marked inferiority on the part of the other poets who had applied for permission to compete.

It has already been pointed out that comedy was much later than tragedy in being officially recognised by the state. It also lasted much longer. One of the most brilliant periods of Attic comedy falls at a time when tragedy had practically come to an end. A sure symptom of decay, both in tragedy and comedy, was the tendency to fall back upon the past, and reproduce old plays, instead of striking out new developments. As regards tragedy this practice had already become prevalent by the middle of the fourth century. But in comedy the creative impulse was still at that time predominant. A fresh direction was being given to the art by the development of the New Comedy, or comedy of manners. There was not as yet any tendency to have recourse to the past. In the record of the exhibitions of comedy for the year 353 there is no trace of any reproduction of old plays. When the practice first commenced it is impossible to say. Probably it was not until the more productive period of the New Comedy had come to an end, and the creative instinct had begun to flag. There is a complete break in our information from the middle of the fourth century to the beginning of the second. When we come to the second century, the practice of reproducing old comedies is found to have become a regular occurrence. This appears from the series of inscriptions

---

[1] Arg. to Aristoph. Vespae. [2] Corp. Inscr. Att. ii. 972.

recording the comic exhibitions at the City Dionysia during the earlier half of the second century. It is seen that the five new comedies were regularly preceded by an old one, just as in tragedy, a hundred and fifty years before, the proceedings had commenced with the performance of an old play. Among the old comedies reproduced in this manner appear Menander's Ghost and Misogynist, Philemon's Phocians, Posidippus' Outcast, and Philippides' Lover of the Athenians. It is noticeable that all these plays belong to the New Comedy, and that there are no traces of any tendency to fall back upon the Middle or the Old Comedy. The records just referred to prove that the New Comedy retained its vitality and productiveness much longer than had been previously suspected, and that original comedies were frequently exhibited at the City Dionysia as late as the second century. On every occasion when there was a contest the full complement of five new plays was produced. How long this lasted it is impossible to determine. Even in these records of the second century there are symptoms of approaching decay in the productiveness of the comic drama. Almost every other year, and sometimes for two or three years in succession, occur the ominous words, 'This year there was no exhibition of comedies.' Probably by the end of the second century the performances of new and original comedies had become a very exceptional occurrence.

§ 8. *Order of Contests at the City Dionysia.*

The regulations concerning the dramatic contests at the City Dionysia have now been described in detail. Before passing on to the Lenaea it will be well to take a general survey of the various competitions at the City Dionysia. There were two dithyrambic contests, one between five choruses of boys, and the other between five choruses of men. There was a tragic contest in which three poets took part. During the fifth and earlier part of the fourth century each of these poets exhibited four plays. Later on the number of original plays began to be diminished, and the competition was preceded by an old tragedy. There was also a contest in comedy in which originally three poets took part; but in the course of the fourth century the number of poets was raised to five. Each poet exhibited a single comedy.

As to the order in which the various performances took place, and the method in which they were grouped together, there is very little evidence. One thing may be regarded as certain, and that is that the three groups of tragedies were performed on three successive days. It is difficult to see what other arrangement would have been possible, as two groups, consisting of eight tragedies, would have been too much for a single day[1]. As to the relative arrangement of dithyrambs, comedies, and tragedies not much can be laid down for certain. In all the records which refer to the City Dionysia the various competitions are always enumerated in the same order. First come the choruses of boys, then the choruses of men, then comedy, then tragedy. Also in the law of Evegorus the same order is observed in recounting the different performances at the City Dionysia[2]. It has been argued that this was the order in which the contests took place; that the dithyrambs came first, then the comedies, and the tragedies last of all. But there seems to be very little justification for such an inference. It is quite as likely that the order followed in these lists was based upon the relative importance of the different contests. In fact, the only piece of evidence in regard to the subject which has any appearance of certainty about it seems to show that at any rate during the fifth century the comedies followed the tragedies at the City Dionysia. This evidence is contained in a passage

---

[1] Aristotle in the Poetics (c. 24), speaking of the proper size of an epic poem, says that it should be shorter than the old epics, and about equal in length to the tragedies performed on a single day (πρὸς δὲ τὸ πλῆθος τραγῳδιῶν τῶν εἰς μίαν ἀκρόασιν τιθεμένων παρήκοιεν). It has already been shown that it is not quite clear what the practice was at the time to which Aristotle refers. But to suppose a performance of four tragedies on one day would harmonise very well with the statement of Aristotle. Four tragedies would contain about 6000 lines, and the Iliad contains about 15,000 lines, the Odyssey about 12,000.

[2] Corp. Inscr. Att. ii. 971; 'Εφημ. 'Αρχαιολ. 1886, pt. 4; Demosth. Meid. § 10.

in the Birds of Aristophanes. The Birds was performed at the City Dionysia. In that play the chorus, in the course of a short ode, remark how delightful it would be to have wings. They say that if one of the spectators was tired with the tragic choruses, he might fly away home, and have his dinner, and then fly back again to the comic choruses[1]. It follows that at that time the comedies were performed after the tragedies. In the fifth century there were three comedies performed at the City Dionysia, and three groups of tragedies. Most likely therefore each group of tragedies was performed in the mornings of three successive days, and was followed in the afternoon by a comedy. In the fourth century, when the number of comedies was raised to five, a new arrangement would be necessary. Possibly the comedies were then transferred to a single day by themselves. But on these and other points of the same kind there is really no available evidence. One thing is certain, that the whole series of performances, consisting of ten dithyrambs, three to five comedies, and twelve tragedies, cannot have taken up less than four days in the performance[2]. Even if they could have been compressed into three days, it would have exceeded the limits of human en-

[1] Aristoph. Av. 785–789 οὐδέν ἐστ' ἄμεινον οὐδ' ἥδιον ἢ φῦσαι πτερά. | αὐτίχ' ὑμῶν τῶν θεατῶν εἴ τις ἦν ὑπόπτερος, | εἶτα πεινῶν τοῖς χοροῖσι τῶν τραγῳδῶν ἤχθετο, | ἐκπτόμενος ἂν οὗτος ἠρίστησεν ἐλθὼν οἴκαδε, | κᾆτ' ἂν ἐμπλησθεὶς ἐφ' ἡμᾶς αὖθις αὖ κατέπτατο. Müller (Griech. Bühnen. p. 322) and others take ἐφ' ἡμᾶς to mean generally 'to us in the theatre'; and deny that it refers to the comic chorus in particular. But in that case there would be no point in the sentence. There is obviously a contrast between ὑμεῖς, the spectators, and ἡμεῖς, the comic chorus. The same contrast is strongly emphasised throughout the previous group of trochaics, vv. 753–768. Lipsius (Berichte der K. S. Gesellschaft der Wissenschaften zu Leipzig, philol.-histor. Classe, 1885, p. 417) adopts the old conjecture τρυγῳδῶν for τραγῳδῶν, and supposes that the contrast is between ἡμεῖς, the chorus of Birds, and οἱ τρυγῳδοί, the *other* comic choruses. Hence he infers that at the City Dionysia all the comedies were performed on a single day by themselves. But τρυγῳδοί is a perfectly gratuitous emendation, and makes the whole passage both feeble and obscure.

[2] Polus is said to have acted eight tragedies in four days when he was seventy years old (Plut. An seni &c. 785 C). If it was at the City Dionysia, he might have done so, supposing that the old tragedy was performed on the first day, and the new tragedies on the three following days. But as there is nothing to show whether the feat of Polus was performed at Athens or elsewhere, it is impossible to base any conclusions upon the statement.

durance to have sat out performances of such enormous length. The festival as a whole, with the procession and other minor amusements, lasted probably either five or six days, as was previously pointed out.

§ 9. *The Lenaea.*

We now come to the other great Athenian festival of Dionysus at which dramatic performances took place. The name of this festival was the Lenaea. It derived its name from the Lenaeum, an enclosure on the south-east of the Acropolis, sacred to Dionysus, the god of the wine-press. It was also called 'the contest at the Lenaeum,' or 'the festival of Dionysus at the Lenaeum.' A victor at this festival was said to have 'won a prize at the Lenaeum[1].' On the other hand, the Great Dionysia was called 'the festival of Dionysus in the City.' It has already been remarked that the Lenaeum was itself within the city, and that the contests at the Lenaea and the City Dionysia were held in the very same place. The distinction of names was probably due to the fact that while the Lenaea was a small festival, and took place entirely within the sacred enclosure, the City Dionysia was altogether on a grander scale, and many of the ceremonies which accompanied it were celebrated in different parts of the city. The Lenaea was held in the month of Gamelion, corresponding to the last half of January and the first half of February. It was still winter, and the sea was dangerous for voyagers. Hence there were few strangers or visitors in Athens. The Lenaea was in fact a domestic sort of festival, confined to the Athenians themselves. The proceedings were quiet and insignificant, in comparison with the splendour of the City Dionysia, when Athens was crowded with visitors from all parts of Greece. In the Acharnians, which was exhibited at the Lenaea, Aristophanes remarks that he can abuse Athens as much as he likes, without incurring the imputation of lowering

---

[1] Heysch. v. ἐπὶ Ληναίῳ ἀγών; Aristoph. Acharn. 504; Corp. Inscr. Att. ii. 714 Διονύσια τὰ ἐπὶ Ληναίῳ; Schol. Aeschin. Fals. Leg. § 15 νικᾶν ἐπὶ Ληναίῳ; Diog. Laërt. viii. 90 νίκη Ληναϊκή; Plut. X orat. 839 D διδασκαλία Ληναϊκή.

her in the eyes of foreigners[1]. The proceedings at the Lenaea consisted of a procession, and of exhibitions of tragedy and comedy. The procession was not like that at the City Dionysia, but was more in imitation of the proceedings at the Anthesteria, and was accompanied by the rough jesting and ribald abuse which were characteristic of the worship of Dionysus and Demeter. There were no dithyrambic contests during the period with which we are concerned. The festival as a whole was much shorter than the City Dionysia[2].

Tragedy at the Lenaea seems to have been at all times subordinate to comedy. The law of Evegorus, in enumerating the proceedings at the City Dionysia and the Dionysiac festival in the Peiraeeus, places tragedy last in each case, as being the most important. But in the list of the proceedings at the Lenaea it places comedy last, obviously because comedy was the principal feature of the festival. It is uncertain when tragic competitions at the Lenaea were first instituted. An argument has been founded on the didascaliae prefixed to the plays of Aeschylus, Sophocles, and Euripides. In these didascaliae there is no mention of the festival at which the plays were produced. Hence it has been argued that during that period there can only have been one festival at which tragic competitions took place. If there had been two festivals, then, it is said, the didascaliae would have recorded the name of the particular festival at which the tragedies they refer to were exhibited. As they do not do so, it would follow that during the lifetime of the three great tragic poets the only tragic contests in existence were those at the City Dionysia, and that tragedy at the Lenaea was unknown before the very end of the fifth century. But the argument is unsound. The omission

---

[1] Bekk. Anecd. p. 235, 6; Plat. Symp. 223 C; Theophrast. Char. 3; Aristoph. Acharn. 501 foll.

[2] Demosth. Meid. § 10 καὶ ἡ ἐπὶ Ληναίῳ πομπὴ καὶ οἱ τραγῳδοὶ καὶ οἱ κωμῳδοί. Suidas v. τὰ ἐκ τῶν ἁμαξῶν σκώμματα. That there were no dithyrambs at the Lenaea during the period we are dealing with is proved by the above quotation from the Meidias, and also by Corp. Inscr. Gr. no. 213, which contains a list of the festivals at which dithyrambic choruses competed, viz. the City Dionysia, Thargelia, Prometheia, and Hephaesteia. The inscription in Ἐφημ. Ἀρχαιολ. 1862, i. 219, recording a victory at the Lenaea with a dithyramb, must refer to late times.

of the name of the festival in the didascaliae does not prove so much as is supposed. It is known for a fact that there were tragic contests at the Lenaea as early as the year 416, for in that year Agathon won a tragic victory at the Lenaea. But there are two notices about plays of Sophocles subsequent to this date, in which there is no mention of the festival. It is stated that the Philoctetes was produced in 409, and the Oedipus Coloneus in 401; but in neither case is the name of the festival mentioned[1]. It cannot therefore be contended that the omission of the festival in the tragic didascaliae proves that during that time there was only one festival at which tragedies were exhibited. All it proves is that the City Dionysia was of much more importance than the Lenaea, and that every one was supposed to know that this was the festival at which the great tragic poets were competitors.

As to the date of the institution of tragic contests at the Lenaea, there is positive evidence to prove that they were of regular occurrence before the year 416. An inscription which was previously given in a very mutilated condition in Böckh's collection has been recently published in a more complete form[2]. It is a record of tragic competitions in the years 419 and 418. In both these years the number of competing poets was two, and each of them exhibited three tragedies. There is no mention of a satyric play. It seems certain that the record must refer to the Lenaea, since it has been shown that at the City Dionysia the number of competitors was regularly three, and that each of them exhibited four plays. If then the Lenaea is the festival referred to, it would appear that tragic contests at the Lenaea were a regular institution as early as 419 B.C. For how many years they had existed previously is uncertain. There is a dubious notice about Euripides which may perhaps bear upon the subject[3]. It is

---

[1] Athen. p. 217 A; Args. to Soph. Phil. and Oed. Col.

[2] Corp. Inscr. Att. ii. 972. The record for the year 418 runs as follows:—ἐπὶ Ἀρχίου ... | Τυροῖ, Τ ... , ... , | ὑπεκρίνετο Λυσικράτης. | Καλλίστρατος ... . . , |
'Αμφιλόχῳ, 'Ιξίονι, | ὑπεκρίνετο Καλλιπίδης· | ὑποκριτὴς Καλλιπίδης ἐνίκα.

[3] Vita Eurip. (p. 4 Dindf.) ἤρξατο δὲ διδάσκειν ἐπὶ Καλλίου ἄρχοντος κατὰ ὀλυμπιάδα πα' ἔτει α', πρῶτον δὲ ἐδίδαξε τὰς Πελιάδας, ὅτε καὶ τρίτος ἐγένετο.

said that Euripides began to exhibit tragedies in the year 455, and that 'the first play he brought out was the Daughters of Pelias, on which occasion he was third.' If the statement is to be depended upon, and is not a mere looseness of expression on the part of the grammarian, it implies that Euripides competed on this occasion with a single play. If so it must have been at the Lenaea, and it would follow that there were tragic contests at the Lenaea as early as 455, but on a small scale, three poets competing with a single tragedy apiece. At any rate, during the last quarter of the fifth century tragedy had become a regular part of the proceedings at the Lenaea. Until the middle of the fourth century new tragedies continued to be performed at this festival. In 367 Dionysius, the tyrant of Syracuse, won the prize for tragedy at the Lenaea. Aphareus, whose dramatic career extended from 368 to 341, exhibited at the Lenaea on two occasions. Theodectes, the pupil and friend of Aristotle, was victorious on one occasion at the Lenaea[1]. As to the details of the contest, and the number of poets and plays, there is not enough evidence to form any conclusion. In 419 and 418 there were two poets, each exhibiting three tragedies. If the inference from the notice about Euripides is reliable, it would follow that at first each poet only exhibited a single play. Very likely the arrangements were changed from time to time[2]. By the middle of the fourth century the career of Attic tragedy began to draw to a close. There were signs of decay in productive power. New tragedies were not so plentiful as in previous times; and henceforward they were given only at the City Dionysia. Tragedy at the Lenaea came

---

[1] Diod. Sic. xv. 74; Plut. X orat. 839 D. Theodectes is known to have won eight tragic victories (Steph. Byzant. v. Φάσηλις). From Corp. Inscr. Att. ii. 977 frag. *b* it appears that he won seven victories at the City Dionysia. It follows that one of his victories must have been at the Lenaea.

[2] No inference can be drawn from the expression in Plat. Symp. 173 A (ὅτε τῇ πρώτῃ τραγῳδίᾳ ἐνίκησεν 'Αγάθων), and in Diod. Sic. xv. 74 (Διονυσίου τοίνυν δεδιδαχότος 'Αθήνησι Ληναίοις τραγῳδίαν), to the effect that Agathon and Dionysius exhibited single tragedies. Probably τῇ πρώτῃ τραγῳδίᾳ νικᾶν is a loose expression for 'winning one's first tragic victory'; and διδάσκειν τραγῳδίαν means generally 'to exhibit in the tragic contests.' It seems certain that in Agathon's time it was customary for each poet to exhibit three tragedies at the Lenaea; and the number was probably not less in the time of Dionysius.

to be confined to the reproduction of old plays. It is about the middle of the fourth century that the phrase 'at the City Dionysia, at the performance of the new tragedies' begins to appear, in public documents and elsewhere, implying that at the Lenaea only old tragedies were exhibited[1]. For how long a period afterwards tragedy in this shape continued to form a part of the Lenaea is a point which cannot be determined.

Comedy, as we have seen, was the principal feature of the Lenaea. Public contests in comedy were instituted by the state in the course of the earlier half of the fifth century. From the very first they no doubt formed part of the proceedings at the Lenaea. But there is no actual evidence on the subject till the time of Aristophanes. Four of his plays—the Acharnians, Knights, Wasps, and Frogs—are known to have been brought out at the Lenaea. From the arguments prefixed to these plays it appears that during the fifth century it was the custom at the Lenaea, as well as at the City Dionysia, for three comic poets to take part in the competition, each exhibiting a single play. In the fourth century, as was previously shown, the number of poets was raised to five, and this continued to be the number in subsequent times. Comedy continued to flourish at the Lenaea, as well as at the City Dionysia, until the third century. Eudoxus, a poet of the New Comedy, is said to have obtained three victories at the City Dionysia, and five at the Lenaea[2]. It is therefore clear that during the third century the comic competitions were kept up with full vigour at both festivals. Indeed, considering the vast number of plays which were written by the poets of the Middle and New Comedy, and the fact that only five plays could be produced at one festival, it would require not less than two festivals in the year to give an opportunity for the production of the plays that were written.

---

[1] Plut. de exil. 603B πλὴν μίαν ἡμέραν, ἐν ᾗ Ξενοκράτης καθ' ἕκαστον ἔτος εἰς ἄστυ κατῄει Διονυσίων καινοῖς τραγῳδοῖς. Aeschin. Ctesiph. § 34 τραγῳδῶν ἀγωνιζομένων καινῶν. Dem. de Cor. § 84 καὶ ἀναγορεῦσαι τὸν στέφανον ἐν τῷ θεάτρῳ Διονυσίοις, τραγῳδοῖς καινοῖς. Corp. Inscr. Att. ii. 331, 341, 402, &c.

It has been suggested that the 'new tragedies' at the City Dionysia were opposed, not to old tragedies at the Lenaea, but to the one old tragedy which was performed each year at the City Dionysia. But the old interpretation is much the most probable.

[2] Diog. Laërt. viii. 90.

After the third century there is no further evidence as to the performances of comedy at the Lenaea.

Before leaving this part of the subject a few observations may be made concerning the <u>comparative importance of the dramatic performances at the two festivals</u>. The City Dionysia was of course a much grander and more splendid gathering than the Lenaea. Its superiority is shown by the fact that at the City Dionysia aliens were not allowed to take part in the choruses, and metics were forbidden to serve as choregi[1]. At the Lenaea there were no such prohibitions. It must have been a much greater honour for a poet to produce his plays at the City Dionysia, before the crowds of visitors and natives, than at the comparatively quiet Lenaea. This was especially the case in regard to tragedy. The great tragic poets, after their reputation was established, would confine themselves to the City Dionysia; and it is probable that the tragedies at the Lenaea were mostly the work of inferior poets, or of young and untried ones. Such slight evidence as we possess is in favour of this opinion. Agathon won his first victory at the Lenaea. The poet Callistratus, who exhibited at the Lenaea in 418, is absolutely unknown, except for the inscription which records his name[2]. Probably also foreign poets were in most cases confined to the Lenaea. Thus it was at the Lenaea that Dionysius, the tyrant of Syracuse, won his victory[3]. The case was not quite the same in respect to comedy. It appears that Aristophanes produced his plays indifferently at the Lenaea as well as the City Dionysia[4]. It must be remembered that comedy was the great feature of the Lenaea, while tragedy was an appendage. Also the Old Comedy, with its local and personal allusions, would be best appreciated by a purely Athenian audience. It is not therefore remarkable that the leading poets of the Old Comedy should have been as anxious to exhibit at the Lenaea as at the greater festival. There is also the fact that comic poets only exhibited one play at a time. Even if they competed at both

---

[1] Schol. Aristoph. Plut. 954.
[2] Athen. p. 217 A; Corp. Inscr. Att. ii. 972.
[3] Diod. Sic. xv. 74.
[4] Args. to Aristoph.'s Comedies.

festivals in the same year, it would only involve the composition of two comedies, as opposed to the three or four tragedies of the tragic poet. Consequently a comic poet of a productive intellect would be bound to exhibit at both the festivals. But when the New Comedy, with its plots of general interest, had taken the place of the Old Comedy of personal allusion and satire, it can hardly be doubted that it was a much greater honour to exhibit at the City Dionysia than at the Lenaea. There would no longer be any advantage in the small and purely Athenian audience.

§ 10. *The Rural Dionysia and Anthesteria.*

After the drama had been thoroughly established at Athens, the different Attic demes proceeded to institute dramatic performances at their own Rural Dionysia. These festivals were held in the month of Poseidon, corresponding to the modern December. The Dionysiac festival at the Peiraeeus was celebrated on a large scale, and was a gathering of some importance. There was a procession, followed by competitions in comedy and tragedy. On one occasion Euripides brought out a new tragedy at the Peiraeeus, and we are told that Socrates came to see it. There were performances of tragedy and comedy at Collytus; and it was here that Aeschines acted the part of Oenomaus in the play of Sophocles, whence he is styled by Demosthenes 'the rustic Oenomaus.' Exhibitions of tragedy were of regular occurrence at Salamis and Eleusis, and it was customary on these occasions to make public proclamation of the crowns which had been bestowed upon deserving citizens. At Aixone there were performances of comedies, but no mention is made of tragedies. At Phlya there were dramatic performances, probably of both kinds. The remains of a theatre have been discovered at Thoricus. From these few indications it is plain that the drama was cultivated with great energy throughout the country districts of Attica[1]. Prob-

---

[1] Demosth. Meid. § 10 ὅταν ἡ πομπὴ   καὶ οἱ τραγῳδοί. Aelian Var. Hist. ii.
ᾖ τῷ Διονύσῳ ἐν Πειραιεῖ καὶ οἱ κωμῳδοὶ   13; Aeschin. Timarch. § 157 ἐν τοῖς

ably it was only on very rare occasions, and at the more important demes, that new and original plays were brought out. The performances would generally be confined to the reproduction of plays which had been successful in the competitions at Athens. The proceedings took the form of contests between troupes of actors, who exhibited plays of established reputation. Prizes were offered by the different demes, and companies seem to have been formed in Athens for the purpose of travelling about the country, and taking part in these provincial competitions. Aeschines was at one time tritagonist in a company of this kind, having been hired for a provincial tour by Simylus and Socrates, 'the Ranters,' as they were called[1]. The number and frequency of these rustic performances exhibit in very clear light the vigorous life and widespread popularity of the old drama. Even the country districts of Attica, in the course of their annual festivals, must have become familiar with the masterpieces of Attic tragedy.

In Athens itself the only festivals at which dramatic performances took place were the Lenaea and the City Dionysia. At the Anthesteria, the oldest of the Athenian festivals of Dionysus, there were competitions between comic actors, but no regular performances of dramas. Our knowledge of these competitions is derived from a rather obscure statement about Lycurgus the Orator. It is said that he re-introduced an old custom, which had latterly fallen into disuse. This custom appears to have been as follows. At the Chytri, the last day of the Anthesteria, a contest between comic protagonists was held in the theatre, and the protagonist who was victorious was allowed the undisputed right of acting at the forthcoming City Dionysia[2]. The Chytri took place about a month before the

κατ' ἀγροὺς Διονυσίοις κωμῳδῶν ὄντων ἐν Κολλυτῷ. Dem. de Cor. § 180; Corp. Inscr. Att. ii. 469, 470, 585, 594; Ἐφημ. Ἀρχαιολ. 1884, p. 71; Isaeus orat. viii. § 15; Wieseler Denkmäler &c. p. 7.

[1] Dem. de Cor. § 262.

[2] This appears to be the meaning of the passage in Plut. X orat. 841 F εἰσήνεγκε δὲ καὶ νόμους, τὸν περὶ τῶν κωμῳδῶν ἀγῶνα τοῖς Χύτροις ἐπιτελεῖν ἐφάμιλλον ἐν τῷ θεάτρῳ, καὶ τὸν νικήσαντα εἰς ἄστυ καταλέγεσθαι, πρότερον οὐκ ἐξόν, ἀναλαμβάνων τὸν ἀγῶνα ἐκλελοιπότα. The contest is plainly the same as the ἀγῶνες Χύτρινοι quoted from Philochorus by the Scholiast on Aristoph. Ran. 220.

City Dionysia. Of course the privilege of acting as protagonist at the City Dionysia was a very considerable one. There were only five comedies performed, and consequently only five protagonists would be required. There would naturally be a keen competition among the comic actors of the time to get themselves selected among the five. The victor in this contest at the Chytri was selected as a matter of course. There is nothing to show what the nature of the contest was; but most likely it consisted in the recitation of selected portions of a comedy. This competition between comic actors at the Anthesteria is the only trace to be found, as far as Athens is concerned, of anything connected with the drama taking place at any festival other than the Lenaea and City Dionysia.

§ 11. *The Judges.*

The institution of the dramatic contests at the different Attic festivals has now been described in detail. As regards the management of the competition many points still remain to be considered, viz. the selection of the judges, the mode of giving the verdict, the prizes for poets and actors, and the public records of the results. First as to the judges. The number of the judges in the comic contests was five[1]. The number in the tragic contests was probably the same, but there is no direct evidence upon the subject. The selection of the judges was a most elaborate affair, and consisted of a combination of two principles, that of election by vote, and that of appointment by lot. A large preliminary list of judges was first elected by vote. At the beginning of the contest a second list of ten judges was chosen by lot from the first one. At the end of the contest a third list of five judges was selected by lot from the second list, and these five judges decided the result of the competition. The object of all these elaborate arrangements and precautions was to make the names of the actual judges a matter of uncertainty as long as possible, and to prevent them from being tampered with by the partisans

---

[1] Schol. Aristoph. Aves 445; Suidas v. ἐν πέντε κριτῶν γόνασι.

of the different competitors. The details of the whole process were as follows[1]. Several days before the actual commencement of the festival the Council, assisted by the choregi, drew up the preliminary list of judges. A certain number of names were selected from each of the ten tribes of Attica. The different choregi, as was natural, endeavoured to get their own partisans upon the list. The names of the persons chosen were then inscribed upon tablets, and the tablets were placed in ten urns, each urn containing the names belonging to a single tribe. The urns were then carefully locked up and sealed in the presence of the prytanes and choregi, handed over to the custody of the treasurers, and deposited in the Acropolis. The preliminary list of judges was kept a secret from every one

[1] There is no consecutive account in any ancient writer of the mode of selecting the judges and of voting. Our knowledge of the subject has to be pieced together from the three following passages: (1) Plut. Cim. p. 483 E ἔθεντο δ' εἰς μνήμην αὐτοῦ καὶ τὴν τῶν τραγῳδῶν κρίσιν ὀνομαστὴν γενομένην. πρώτην γὰρ διδασκαλίαν τοῦ Σοφοκλέους ἔτι νέου καθέντος, Ἀψεφίων ὁ ἄρχων, φιλονεικίας οὔσης καὶ παρατάξεως τῶν θεατῶν, κριτὰς μὲν οὐκ ἐκλήρωσε τοῦ ἀγῶνος, ὡς δὲ Κίμων μετὰ τῶν συστρατήγων προελθὼν εἰς τὸ θέατρον ἐποιήσατο τῷ θεῷ τὰς νενομισμένας σπονδάς, οὐκ ἀφῆκεν αὐτοὺς ἀπελθεῖν, ἀλλ' ὁρκώσας ἠνάγκασε καθίσαι καὶ κρῖναι δέκα ὄντας, ἀπὸ φυλῆς μιᾶς ἕκαστον. (2) Isocrat. xvii. § 33 Πυθόδωρον γὰρ τὸν σκηνίτην καλούμενον, ὃς ὑπὲρ Πασίωνος ἅπαντα καὶ λέγει καὶ πράττει, τίς οὐκ οἶδεν ὑμῶν πέρυσιν ἀνοίξαντα τὰς ὑδρίας καὶ τοὺς κριτὰς ἐξελόντα τοὺς ὑπὸ τῆς βουλῆς εἰσβληθέντας; καίτοι ὅστις μικρῶν ἕνεκα καὶ περὶ τοῦ σώματος κινδυνεύων ταύτας ὑπανοίγειν ἐτόλμησεν, αἳ σεσημασμέναι μὲν ἦσαν ὑπὸ τῶν πρυτάνεων, κατεσφραγισμέναι δ' ὑπὸ τῶν χορηγῶν, ἐφυλάττοντο δ' ὑπὸ τῶν ταμιῶν, ἔκειντο δ' ἐν ἀκροπόλει, τί δεῖ θαυμάζειν εἰ κ.τ.λ. (3) Lysias iv. § 3 ἐβουλόμην δ' ἄν, μὴ ἀπολαχεῖν αὐτὸν κριτὴν Διονυσίοις, ἵν' ὑμῖν φανερὸς ἐγένετο ἐμοὶ διηλλαγμένος, κρίνας τὴν ἐμὴν φυλὴν νικᾶν, νῦν δὲ ἔγραψε μὲν ταῦτα εἰς τὸ γραμματεῖον, ἀπέλαχε δέ. καὶ ὅτι ἀληθῆ ταῦτα λέγω Φιλῖνος καὶ Διοκλῆς ἴσασιν· ἀλλ' οὐκ ἔστ' αὐτοῖς μαρτυρῆσαι μὴ διομοσαμένοις περὶ τῆς αἰτίας ἧς ἐγὼ φεύγω, ἐπεὶ σαφῶς ἔγνωστ' ἂν ὅτι ἡμεῖς ἦμεν αὐτὸν οἱ κριτὴν ἐμβαλόντες, καὶ ἡμῶν εἵνεκα ἐκαθέζετο. The first of these passages refers to a dramatic contest, the third to a dithyrambic one. It is uncertain to which the second refers. But there is no reason to suppose that the mode of selecting the judges was different in the dramatic and the dithyrambic contests. That a second list of judges was appointed by lot from the larger list *before* the commencement of each contest, and that this second list consisted of ten persons, one from each of the ten tribes, seems to be proved by the words of Plutarch, κριτὰς μὲν οὐκ ἐκλήρωσε τοῦ ἀγῶνος ... ἀπὸ φυλῆς μιᾶς ἕκαστον. That there was another selection of judges by lot *after* the contest, and that the number of judges who actually decided the result was smaller than the number of those who sat through the performance and voted, is proved by two expressions in the above passages: (1) ἔγραψε μὲν ταῦτα εἰς τὸ γραμματεῖον, ἀπέλαχε δέ, i. e. he voted in my favour, but his vote was not drawn; (2) ἡμῶν εἵνεκα ἐκαθέζετο. Καθίζειν and καθέζεσθαι were the regular words used of a judge at a contest. It is clear therefore that the person

except the Council and the choregi. The penalty for tampering with the urns was death. The reason for all the secrecy was obviously to prevent undue influence being brought to bear upon the persons nominated. It is not known from what class the nominees were selected, or whether any property qualification was necessary. It is plain that the judges in the dramatic and dithyrambic contests had a very delicate office to perform. If their verdict was to be of value, it was necessary that they should be men of culture and discernment. It is most likely therefore that there was some limitation upon the number of persons qualified to act in this capacity.

Until the time of the festival the preliminary list of citizens remained sealed up in urns in the Acropolis. On the first day of the competitions the ten urns were produced in the theatre, and placed in some prominent position. The persons whose names were contained in the urns were all present in the theatre. Probably they received a special summons from the archon shortly before the festival. At the commencement of the contest the archon proceeded to draw a single name from all the urns in succession. The ten persons, whose names were drawn, constituted the second list of judges, and each of them represented one of the ten tribes of Attica. After being selected by lot in the manner described, they were called forward by the archon, and took a solemn oath that they would give an impartial verdict[1]. They were then conducted to seats specially appointed for them, and the contest began. At the end of the performances each of them gave his vote, writing upon a tablet the names of the competitors in order of merit[2]. These tablets,

here referred to sat through the performance as a judge, but that after the performance was over his vote was not drawn by lot. It may be remarked that any doubt as to the truth of the story in Plutarch does not destroy its value as an example of the mode of judging in the Athenian theatre.

[1] Dem. Meid. § 17 ὀμνύουσι παρεστηκὼς τοῖς κριταῖς. Aristoph. Eccles. 1160 μὴ 'πιορκεῖν, ἀλλὰ κρίνειν τοὺς χοροὺς

ὀρθῶς ἀεί. The judges addressed by Aristophanes here and elsewhere were of course the second body of judges, from whom the third body of five was chosen at the end of the contest.

[2] Special seats were assigned to the judges at Alexandria, and no doubt the Attic custom was followed there : cp. Vitruv. vii. praef. § 5 cum secretae sedes iudicibus essent distributae. For the practice of recording the votes on a

ten in number, were then placed in an urn, and the archon proceeded to draw forth five of them at random. The majority of these five votes decided the competition, and the persons whose votes were drawn from the urn constituted the ultimate body of five judges. It thus appears that up to the very last the judges who recorded their votes were not sure whether the votes would eventually have effect, or turn out to be so much waste paper. This uncertainty was of course a great obstacle to intimidation and bribery. After the competition was over, and the verdict announced, the names of the five judges, whose votes had decided the day, were not kept secret. It was known how each of them had voted. But the other votes, which had been recorded but not drawn from the urn, were destroyed without being made public[1]. It was of course considered a much greater honour to win a victory by the unanimous vote of all five judges, than by a mere majority of one[2]. But it is very doubtful whether any public record was kept of the number of votes by which a victory was gained.

Whether the decision of the judges was generally given with discernment, and how far it corresponded with the ultimate verdict of posterity, is a question of some interest. Both Aeschylus and Sophocles were usually successful, and this speaks highly for the taste of the judges. Aeschylus won thirteen victories; and as he produced four plays on each occasion, it follows that no less than fifty-two of his plays obtained the first prize. Whether the total number of his plays was seventy or ninety, the proportion of victories was very large[3]. Sophocles was equally fortunate. He won eighteen victories at the City Dionysia. The number of his plays, as given by different authorities, varies from a hundred-

---

tablet cp. Aelian Var. Hist. ii. 13 καὶ προσέταττον τοῖς κριταῖς ἄνωθεν 'Αριστοφάνην ἀλλὰ μὴ ἄλλον γράφειν. Lysias iv. 3 ἔγραψε μὲν ταῦτα ἐς τὸ γραμματεῖον.

[1] This follows from Lysias iv. § 3 ἐβουλόμην δ' ἄν μὴ ἀπολαχεῖν αὐτὸν κριτὴν Διονυσίοις, ἵν' ὑμῖν φανερὸς ἐγένετο ἐμοὶ διηλλαγμένος, κρίνας τὴν ἐμὴν φυλὴν νικᾶν· νῦν δὲ ἔγραψε μὲν ταῦτα εἰς τὸ γραμματεῖον, ἀπέλαχε δέ.

[2] Aristoph. Aves 445-447 ΧΟ. ὄμνυμ' ἐπὶ τούτοις, πᾶσι νικᾶν τοῖς κριταῖς | καὶ τοῖς θεαταῖς πᾶσιν. ΠΕ. ἔσται ταυταγί. | ΧΟ. εἰ δὲ παραβαίην, ἑνὶ κριτῇ νικᾶν μόνον.

[3] Vita Aeschyli; Suidas v. Αἰσχύλος.

and-four to a hundred-and-thirty. Thus on the lowest estimate considerably more than half his plays gained the first position [1]. Euripides was not so successful. He only won five victories, though he wrote between ninety and a hundred plays. The cause of his failure was partly due to the fact that he often had the misfortune to contend against Sophocles. He was beaten by Sophocles in 439 and 432, and probably on many other occasions of which no record has been preserved. But at other times he was defeated by very inferior poets. In 415 he was beaten by Xenocles, and on another occasion by the obscure poet Nicomachus [2]. But the most surprising verdict of which there is any record is the defeat of the Oedipus Tyrannus of Sophocles by Philocles the nephew of Aeschylus [3]. Of course the other three plays, along with which the Oedipus Tyrannus was produced, may not have been of equal merit. Still it must always seem an extraordinary fact, and a proof of the uncertainty of Athenian judges, that a play which is generally allowed to be one of the greatest dramas of antiquity should have been defeated by a third-rate poet such as Philocles.

Verdicts of this indefensible character might be due to various causes. The judges might be corrupt or might be intimidated. The spirit of emulation ran very high at these contests, and men were often not very particular as to the means by which they obtained the victory. There is an instance in one of the speeches of Lysias. The defendant is showing that the prosecutor had been on very friendly terms with him a short time before. The proof he brings forward is that when he was choregus at the City Dionysia, he got the prosecutor appointed on the preliminary list of judges for the express purpose of voting for his own chorus. The prosecutor was pledged to vote for the chorus of the defendant, whether it was good or

---

[1] The victories of Sophocles are given as 18 by Diod. Sic. (xiii. 103), as 20 in the Vita Soph., and as 24 by Suidas v. Σοφοκλῆς. That he won 18 victories at the City Dionysia is proved by Corp. Inscr. Att. ii. 977, frag. a. It is possible that he won other victories at the Lenaea, though it is not probable that he exhibited at that festival during the later part of his career. The number of his plays is given as 123 by Suidas, and as 104 or 130 in the Life.

[2] Vita Eurip., Args. to Alcestis and Medea; Aelian Var. Hist. ii. 8; Suidas v. Νικόμαχος.

[3] Arg. to Soph. Oed. Tyr.

bad. He appears to have actually done so; but unfortunately, at the final drawing, his name was not selected, and his vote was therefore of no value[1]. Another example of the use of corruption is afforded by the case of Meidias, who is said to have won the victory with his chorus of men at the City Dionysia by bribing or intimidating the judges[2]. Similarly at a contest of boys' choruses, Alcibiades, in spite of his outrageous conduct on the occasion, won the first prize, because some of the judges were afraid to vote against him, and others had been bought over to his side[3]. The verdict of each individual judge was made public. Hence it is easy to see that judges might often be afraid to incur the hostility of rich and unscrupulous citizens by voting against them. The above instances all refer to dithyrambic contests. No doubt in these cases, as the whole tribe was concerned with the result, party feeling ran exceptionally high. In the dramatic competitions only individuals were engaged, and there was less general excitement about the result. Yet even here corrupt influences were sometimes employed. Menander, the greatest comic poet of his time, was often defeated by Philemon owing to jobbery and intrigue similar to that described above[4].

One not unfrequent cause then of unfair verdicts must have been corruption and intimidation. There is also another point to be kept in view, in estimating the value of the decisions of the ancient judges. The plays of Sophocles and Euripides were no doubt immeasurably superior, as literary works, to the plays of Philocles, Xenocles, and Nicomachus, by which they were defeated. And yet in these and similar instances the verdicts of the judges may perhaps have had some justification. One is apt to forget the importance of the manner in which the play was presented upon the stage. Even in modern times an inferior play, if well mounted and acted, is more impressive than a good play badly performed. This must have been still more the

---

[1] Lysias iv. § 3.
[2] Dem. Meid. §§ 5, 17, 65.
[3] Andocid. Alcibiad. § 20 ἀλλὰ τῶν κριτῶν οἱ μὲν φοβούμενοι οἱ δὲ χαριζόμενοι νικᾶν ἔκριναν αὐτόν.
[4] Aul. Gell. N. A. 17. 4.

case in the ancient drama, where the singing and dancing of the chorus formed such an important element in the success of the performance. It can easily be seen that, however well a play was written, if it was ill-mounted, and if the chorus was badly trained, this would greatly diminish the chances of success. Now the ancient poet was dependent upon his choregus for the mounting of the piece and for the selection of the chorus. If the choregus was rich and generous, the play was put upon the stage in the very best manner, with all the advantages of fine dresses and a well-trained chorus. An ambitious choregus spared no pains to do his part of the work thoroughly. But if the choregus was a miserly man, he tried to do the thing as cheaply as possible. He hired inferior singers, and cut down the prices of the dresses and other accessories. Hence the success of a play depended nearly as much upon the choregus as upon the poet. Several examples illustrate this fact. Demosthenes, shortly before his death, is said to have dreamt that he was acting in a tragedy in a contest with Archias; but although he was highly successful, and produced a great impression upon the audience, he was defeated in the contest because of the wretched manner in which the play was mounted upon the stage. Then there is the case of Nicias. He was a man of great wealth, but not of commanding talents. Accordingly he tried to win popularity by the magnificence with which he performed his duties as choregus. The result was that although he took part in many competitions, he was always victorious. Antisthenes is another instance of a rich choregus who, although he knew nothing about music and poetry, was always successful in his contests, because he spared no expense in the preparations[1]. There is an example of a different kind of choregus in one of the speeches of Isaeus. A certain Dicaeogenes regarded his office of choregus merely as a burden, and tried to perform it in the most economical manner. The result was that he was always unsuccessful. He engaged in a dithy-

---

[1] Plut. Demosth. 859 D εὐημερῶν δὲ καὶ κατέχων τὸ θέατρον ἐνδείᾳ παρα- σκευῆς καὶ χορηγίας κρατεῖσθαι, id. Nicias, 524 D; Xen. Memor. iii. 4. 3.

rambic and tragic contest, and in a contest of pyrrhic dancers. On the first occasion he was last but one, on the other two occasions he was last[1]. Obviously the tragic poet who had the misfortune to be associated with Dicaeogenes would have a very small chance of success. The above examples show very clearly that the money of the choregus was almost as important towards securing victory as the genius of the poet.

It is necessary therefore, in criticising the verdicts of the Athenian judges, to remember that we know nothing of the circumstances of the different performances, and of the extent to which the choregus may have been responsible for success or failure. Possibly if all the facts were known in regard to the occasions when Sophocles and Euripides were defeated, it would be found that there was some justification. The best critics would attend mainly to the merits of the piece in itself, apart from the splendour of the accompaniments. But the mass of the spectators would be dazzled by gorgeous dresses and effective singing and dancing. And the mass of the spectators had a great deal to do with the verdict. If they were strongly in favour of a particular poet, it was difficult for the judges to act in opposition to their wishes. The judges were liable to prosecution and imprisonment, if their verdict was supposed to be unjust; and the case would of course be tried before a jury chosen from the very audience they had thwarted[2]. It was hardly therefore to be expected that they would venture to give a verdict in opposition to the loudly pronounced opinion of the multitude. That the multitude on occasions made their wishes known most emphatically, and brought great pressure to bear upon the judges, is shown by Aelian's account of the first performance of the Clouds. The story is a fable, but is interesting as an illustration of the occasional behaviour of an Athenian audience. It is said that the people were so delighted with the Clouds, that they applauded the poet more than they had ever done before, and insisted on the judges placing the name of Aristophanes first upon the list[3]. Such unanimous expressions

[1] Isaeus v. § 36. [3] Aelian Var. Hist. ii. 13.
[2] Aeschin. Ctesiph. § 232.

of opinion on the part of the spectators could hardly be resisted by judges who had the fear of prosecution before their eyes. Plato laments on several occasions the despotism exercised by the audience in the theatre. In former times, he says, the verdict was not decided by 'hisses and unmusical shouts, as at the present day, nor by applause and clapping of hands,' but the rabble were compelled by the attendants to keep quiet. In another place he says that the judge should be the instructor, not the pupil, of the audience, and should refuse to be intimidated by their shouts into giving a false verdict. But at the present day, he adds, the decision rests with the multitude, and is practically decided by public vote, and the result is the degeneracy of the poets and spectators alike[1]. These passages of Plato prove how much the judges were under the dominion of the audience; and a general audience would be especially likely to be carried away by the splendour of the choregic part of the exhibition, by the music, dancing, and scenery. But on the whole, in spite of occasional cases of corruption, and in spite of the despotism of the multitude, one would be inclined to say, arguing from results, that the judges performed their duties well. The best proof of their fairness lies in the continued success of Aeschylus and Sophocles.

§ 12. *The Prizes.*

When the contest was ended, and the decision of the judges had been announced, the names of the victorious poet and of his choregus were publicly proclaimed by the herald, and they were crowned with garlands of ivy in the presence of the spectators. The crowning probably took place upon the stage, and was performed by the archon[2]. There is no mention of any special prize for the choregus, in addition to the honour of the crown and the public proclamation of his victory. It is usually stated that the successful choregus received a tripod from the

---

[1] Plato, Legg. 700C–701 A, 659 A–C. Ληναίοις; Aristid. vol. ii. p. 2 (Dindf.)
[2] Alciphron ii. 3; Plut. An seni &c. τοῦτον στεφανοῦν καὶ πρῶτον ἀναγορεύειν.
p. 785 B; Athen. p. 217 A στεφανοῦται

state, which he erected upon a monument in some public place, with an inscription recording his victory. But this was only the case in the dithyrambic contests. There is no mention or record of a tripod being bestowed upon the choregus of a dramatic chorus. All the notices of tripods as the prize of victory refer to dithyrambic contests[1]. The memorials of victory erected by the choregi to the dramatic choruses appear to have taken the form of tablets, differing in style and costliness according to the wealth and taste of the individuals. For instance, Themistocles after his victory with a tragic chorus erected a 'tablet' in honour of the event, as also did Thrasippus after his victory in the comic contests. It is a trait in the character of the mean man in Theophrastus, that when he has been successful with a tragic chorus, he erects merely a wooden scroll in commemoration of his victory[2]. It appears then that the only prize or symbol of victory which was bestowed upon the choregus to a dramatic chorus was the crown of ivy.

As to the rewards for the poets, the tradition was that in the earliest times the prize for tragedy was a goat, the prize for comedy a basket of figs and a jar of wine[3]. After the dramatic contests had been regularly organised, each of the competing poets received a payment of money from the state, differing no doubt in amount, according to the place he gained in the competition[4]. Nothing is known as to the value of these prizes, but it must have been something considerable, as the

---

[1] Dem. Meid. § 5; Lysias xxi. § 2; Schol. Aeschin. Timarch. § 11; Isaeus vii. § 40; 2nd Arg. to Dem. Meid. p. 510. The monuments of Lysicrates and Thrasyllus, which were surmounted with tripods (Stuart and Revett, Antiquities of Athens, vol. i. chap. iv. pt. 3, vol. ii. p. 31), were in honour of victories with dithyrambic choruses; cp. Corp. Inscr. Gr. 221, 224.

[2] Plut. Themist. 114 C πίνακα τῆς νίκης ἀνέθηκε. Aristot. Pol. viii. 6 ἐκ τοῦ πίνακος ὃν ἀνέθηκε Θράσιππος. Theophrast. Char. 22 ταινία ξυλίνη. Cp. Lysias xxi. § 4 κωμῳδοῖς χορηγῶν Κηφισοδώρῳ ἐνίκων, καὶ ἀνήλωσα σὺν τῇ τῆς σκευῆς ἀναθέσει ἐκκαίδεκα μνᾶς. In this last case some article of theatrical costume seems to have been dedicated as a memorial of the victory. It is known that masks were occasionally dedicated in this way by successful actors.

[3] Marmor Par. epp. 39, 43.

[4] Schol. Aristoph. Ran. 367 τὸν μισθὸν τῶν κωμῳδῶν ἐμείωσαν; Eccles. 102 τὸν μισθὸν τῶν ποιητῶν συνέτεμε; Hesych. v. μισθός· τὸ ἔπαθλον τῶν κωμικῶν ... ἔμμισθοι δὲ πέντε ἦσαν. As the competitors in comedy were five, this last passage proves that *all* the competing poets received a reward of money.

demands upon the time and energy of the ancient dramatist were very great. He had not merely to write his plays, but also to superintend their production. Hence the profession of the dramatic poet was distinctly an arduous one, and the rewards would be correspondingly large. The exact amount is unknown, but some idea of the scale on which the sums were graduated, according to the place of each poet in the competition, may be gathered from the analogy of the dithyrambic contests instituted by Lycurgus in the Peiraeeus. In these contests not less than three choruses were to take part, and the prizes were to be ten minae for the first chorus, eight for the second, and six for the third[1]. The payment of the dramatic poets was probably arranged in a somewhat similar proportion. Towards the end of the fifth century the prizes were reduced in amount by certain commissioners of the Treasury, named Archinus and Agyrrhius. Accordingly in the Frogs of Aristophanes these two statesmen are placed in the list of bad men who are not allowed to join the chorus of the initiated[2]. The fact that all of the competing poets received a reward of money need cause no surprise. They were the poets chosen, after selection, to provide the entertainment at the annual festivals. They were not selected until their plays had been carefully examined by the archon, and found to be of the requisite merit. To be allowed to exhibit at all was a considerable distinction. There was nothing dishonourable for an ordinary poet in being placed last in the competition. Of course, for one of the great dramatic writers such a position was regarded as a disgrace. When Aristophanes was third, it is spoken of as a distinct rebuff. But to obtain the second place was always creditable. It is mentioned as a proof of the greatness of Sophocles that he 'obtained twenty victories and was often second.' When he was defeated for the first place by Philocles, the disgrace consisted, not in his being second, but in his being beaten by such an inferior poet[3]. At the same time

---

[1] Plut. X orat. 842 A.
[2] Aristoph. Ran. 367, and Schol. ad loc.
[3] Arg. Aristoph. Nub.; Vit. Soph. Aristid. vol. ii. p. 344 (Dindf.)

to be second was never regarded as a 'victory.' The title of victor was reserved for the first poet. This is proved by the passage about Sophocles just quoted, and also by the fact that in the list of victors in the contests at the City Dionysia only the names of the first poets in the tragic and comic contests are enumerated. It is clearly owing to an error that the second poet is sometimes spoken of as a victor[1].

§ 13. *Contests between actors.*

In addition to the rewards just mentioned, prizes for acting were instituted in later times. At first the principal competitors in the dramatic contests were the choregus and the poet. Upon their efforts the success of a play mainly depended. It was to them that the rewards of victory were assigned, and it was their names which were recorded in the public monuments. But as time went on the profession of the actor gradually increased in importance. Eventually the success of a play came to depend principally upon the actors. The competition was extended to them. A prize was offered for the most successful actor as well as for the most successful poet. The names of the actors began to be recorded in the public monuments. The exact date of these innovations is unknown; but the inscriptions prove that the competition between the tragic actors had become a regular institution by the year 420 B.C. There is no record of a competition between comic actors before the year 354 B.C.[2] It is therefore probable that the actors' contest was established in tragedy much sooner than in comedy. At any rate the importance of the tragic actor began to be recognised at an earlier period than that of the comic actor, as is proved by the lists of the victors at the City Dionysia.

---

[1] Arg. Aristoph. Vesp. ἐνίκα πρῶτος Φιλωνίδης. Arg. Nub. ὅτε Κρατῖνος μὲν ἐνίκα Πυτίνῃ, Ἀμειψίας δὲ Κόννῳ. Arg. Pax ἐνίκησε δὲ τῷ δράματι ὁ ποιητής ... δεύτερος Ἀριστοφάνης Εἰρήνῃ.

[2] Corp. Inscr. Att. ii. 972. The conclusion of the 2nd Arg. to the Pax (τὸ δὲ δρᾶμα ὑπεκρίνατο Ἀπολλόδωρος, ἡνίκα ἑρμῆν λοιοκρότης) is emended by Rose into ἐνίκα Ἕρμων ὁ ὑποκριτής. If this were correct, it would prove the existence of contests between comic actors as early as 421 B.C. But the emendation is exceedingly doubtful. Dindorf suggests Ἀπολλόδωρος, ἡνίκα ἔτ' ἦν ὑποκριτής.

In the earlier lists belonging to the first half of the fifth century no actors' names are recorded. The only names given are those of the choregus and the poet. But after the middle of the fifth century, in every record of a tragic contest, the name of the actor begins to be appended, as well as the name of the poet. On the other hand, there is no mention of a comic actor even as late as the middle of the fourth century. It follows that at this period the comic actors were thought much less worthy of record than the tragic actors; and it is probable that the contest in acting was only adopted in comedy after it had already existed for some time in tragedy. After the middle of the fourth century competitions in acting became a regular accompaniment of all dramatic performances whether tragic or comic[1].

These contests were limited to the principal actors or protagonists in each play. The subordinate actors, the deuteragonist and tritagonist, had nothing to do with them. The principal actor in a Greek play was a much more important personage than even the 'star' in a modern company. The actors in a Greek play were limited to three in number, and each of them had to play several parts in succession, by means of changes in dress and mask. Hence the protagonist had to perform not only the principal part, but also several of the subordinate ones. Besides this the composition of a Greek tragedy was designed almost solely with the view of bringing out into strong relief the character of the principal personage. The incidents were intended to draw forth his different emotions: the subordinate characters were so many foils to him. The success of a Greek play depended almost wholly upon the protagonist. In the ordinary language of the times he was said to 'act the play,' as if the other performers were of no importance. To take an example from existing inscriptions, it is recorded that in 341 'Astydamas was victorious with the Parthenopaeus, acted by Thessalus, and the Lycaon, acted by Neoptolemus.' This is the regular form of the old records both in tragedy and comedy. Demosthenes uses similar lan-

[1] Corp. Inscr. Att. ii. 971–973, 975.

guage. Referring to the Phoenix of Euripides, he says that 'Theodorus and Aristodemus never acted this play.' The form of the language is proof of the overwhelming importance of the protagonist[1]. These considerations will remove any surprise which might have been felt at the fact of the contest in acting being confined solely to the principal actor in each play.

As to the nature of the contest, the only other point to be noticed is that the success of the actor was quite independent of the success of the play in which he was performing. Thus in one of the comic contests of the second century the prize for acting was won by Onesimus. But the play in which he acted, the Shipwrecked Mariner, only won the second place. The successful comedy, the Ephesians, was acted by Sophilus. Similarly in the tragic contests of the year 418 the prize for acting was won by Callippides; but the poet Callistratus, whose three tragedies he performed, was only second. The tragedies of the successful poet were acted by Lysicrates. It will be seen that in this contest each of the tragic poets had one protagonist all to himself, and his three plays were performed by the same actor. This was the usual practice in the tragic contests during the fifth century. But in the fourth century a new arrangement was made. All the protagonists acted in turn for all the poets. If a tragic poet exhibited three plays, each play was performed by a different protagonist, and the same protagonists appeared in the plays of his rivals. Under this system the competition between the actors was necessarily quite independent of that between the poets. But even in the earlier period of tragedy, when one actor and one poet were closely associated together, we have seen that the success of the poet did not imply the success of the actor. The two competitions were quite separate. The same was always the case in comedy[2].

The actors' contests which we have hitherto been describing took place at the performance of new tragedies and comedies, and existed side by side with contests between poets and choregi. But there were other occasions in which actors met

---
[1] Corp. Inscr. Att. ii. 973; Dem. Fals. Leg. § 246.
[2] Corp. Inscr. Att. ii. 975 *b*, 972, 973.

in competition. The reproduction of old plays generally took the form of contests between actors. These contests were of two kinds. In the first kind each actor performed a different play. At the same time the victory was decided, not by the merits of the play, but by the skill of the actor. There are several references to competitions of this sort. For instance, before the battle of Arginusae, Thrasyllus is said to have dreamt that he was engaged in a contest in the theatre at Athens, and that he and his fellow-generals were acting the Phoenissae of Euripides, while their opponents were acting the Supplices[1]. The most frequent occasion for reproductions of old plays in this manner must have been afforded by the Rural Dionysia in the different townships of Attica. At most of these festivals there were dramatic performances, which were generally confined to the exhibition of old tragedies and comedies. The town offered a prize for acting, and the leading Athenian actors came down with their companies and took part in the competition, each performing a different play. As far as tragedy is concerned, similar contests must have existed at the Lenaea in later times, after the tragic performances at this festival had come to be confined to the reproduction of old plays. But in the case of comedy there are no traces of such contests at the great Athenian festivals. The fertility of Attic comedy was so great that there was no deficiency in the production of new and original comedies within the period we have to deal with.

The first then of the two kinds of competitions with old plays was of the character just described. Each actor performed a different play. The second kind differed from the first in this respect, that each actor performed the same play. For instance, Licymnius, the tragic actor, is said to have defeated Critias and Hippasus in the Propompi of Aeschylus. Andronicus, another tragic actor, was successful in the Epigoni on one occasion; and it is implied that his oppo-

[1] Diod. Sic. xiii. 97. Of course the story is an anachronism, as competitions with old tragedies did not exist at Athens in the time of the Peloponnesian War. But it illustrates the practice of later centuries.

nents acted the same play[1]. In contests of this description it is not probable that the whole play was acted by each of the competitors, but only special portions of it. The contest would be useful for purposes of selection. It has been shown that in later times all performances of new tragedies and new comedies were preceded by the reproduction of a single play by one of the old poets. The actor who was to have the privilege of performing the play would have to be selected by the state. It is very probable that the selection was determined by a competition of the kind we are describing, in which a portion of an old play was performed by each of the candidates. The contests between comic actors at the Chytri have already been referred to. Most likely they were of the same description.

§ 14. *Records of dramatic contests.*

It is difficult in modern times to fully realise the keenness of the interest with which the various dramatic contests were regarded by the old Athenians, and the value which was attached to victories obtained in them. The greatest statesman was proud to be successful with a chorus in tragedy or comedy. It was a proof both of his taste and of his munificence. The tragic poet held as high a place in the popular estimation as the orator or the general. Victorious competitors were not content with the mere temporary glory they obtained. Every care was taken to perpetuate the memory of their success in a permanent form. Elaborate records were also erected by the state. A description of the various kinds of memorials, of which fragments have been preserved, will be a convincing proof of the enthusiasm with which the drama was regarded in ancient times.

It may be assumed that from the earliest period records of the results of the different contests were preserved by the

---

[1] Alciphron iii. 48 κακὸς κακῶς ἀπόλοιτο καὶ ἄφωνος εἴη Λικύμνιος ὁ τῆς τραγῳδίας ὑποκριτής. ὡς γὰρ ἐνίκα τοὺς ἀντιτέχνους Κριτίαν τὸν Κλεωναῖον καὶ Ἵππασον τὸν Ἀμβρακιώτην τοὺς Αἰσχύλου Προπομποὺς κ.τ.λ. Athen. p. 584 D Ἀνδρονίκου δὲ τοῦ τραγῳδοῦ ἀπ' ἀγῶνός τινος, ἐν ᾧ τοὺς Ἐπιγόνους εὐημερήκει, πίνειν μέλλοντος παρ' αὐτῇ κ.τ.λ.

state in the public archives. In addition to this, the choregi in the dramatic competitions were accustomed to erect monuments of some sort or another in commemoration of their victory. The inscriptions upon these monuments were of the briefest character, and consisted merely of the names of the poet and choregus, and of the archon for the year. Probably in later times the name of the actor was appended. The following notice is from the monument erected by Themistocles in honour of his victory with a tragic chorus in the year 476 B.C.[1]:—

> Choregus, Themistocles of Phrearria:
> Poet, Phrynichus:
> Archon, Adeimantus.

In addition to these choregic records, elaborate monuments of various kinds were erected by the state in or near to the theatre of Dionysus. Considerable fragments of these monuments have been discovered by recent excavations. They may be divided into three classes. The first class consisted of records of all the contests at some one particular festival. Such records were of the most general description, and consisted merely of a list of victors' names. Fragments have been discovered of the records of the contests at the City Dionysia during the fifth and fourth centuries[2]. The style is the same throughout. The boys' choruses are mentioned first, then the choruses of men, then comedy, and tragedy last of all. In the dithyrambic contests the names of the victorious tribe and choregus are given; in the dramatic contests the names of the victorious choregus and poet. The only difference between the earlier and later portions of the record is that towards the end of the fifth century the name of the tragic actor begins to be appended. The following specimen, which refers to the year 458, is of especial interest, since it was in this year that Aeschylus brought out his Orestean tetralogy:—

> Archonship of Philocles:
> Boys' chorus, tribe Oeneïs:
> Choregus, Demodocus:
> Chorus of men, tribe Hippothontis:
> Choregus, Euctemon of Eleusis:

[1] Plut. Themist. 114 C.
[2] Corp. Inscr. Att. ii. 971; 'Εφημ. 'Αρχαιολ. 1886, pt. 4.

Comedy:
Choregus, Eurycleides:
Poet, Euphronius:
Tragedy:
Choregus, Xenocles of Aphidna:
Poet, Aeschylus.

The second class of public monuments was devoted to the record of one particular kind of contest at a particular festival. It went into much greater detail than the class already mentioned. Fragments of several monuments of this class have been preserved. There is part of a record of the tragic contests at the Lenaea towards the end of the fifth century, and of the tragic contests at the City Dionysia in the fourth century. There are fragments of a record of comic contests in the fourth century, and very considerable remains of a record of comic contests in the second century[1]. In these lists the names of all the competing poets are given, together with the titles of the plays they produced, and the names of the actors who performed them. At the end comes the name of the actor who won the prize for acting. If there was any reproduction of an old tragedy or comedy, the name of the play is given, together with the name of the actor. The following specimen is a record of the tragic contests at the City Dionysia in the year 340 B.C.:—

Archonship of Nicomachus: Satyric Play,
The Lycurgus of Timocles:
Old Tragedy, actor Neoptolemus;
Play, the Orestes of Euripides:
Poets: Astydamas first
With the Parthenopaeus, actor Thessalus,
The Lycaon, actor Neoptolemus:
Timocles second with the Phrixus,
Actor Thessalus,
The Oedipus, actor Neoptolemus:
Evaretus third
. . . . . actor Thessalus,
. . . . . actor Neoptolemus:
Prize for acting, Thessalus.

The records of the comic contests are numerous, but in no case do they extend over a whole year. The general style of them will be best exemplified by giving the first part of one year's list, and the last part of another:—

[1] Corp. Inscr. Att. ii. 972, 973, 975.

> Archonship of Xenocles: Old Comedy,
>> Actor Monimus: Play, Menander's Ghost:
>> Poets: Paranomus first with . . . ,
>> Actor, Damon:
>> Criton second with the Aetolian,
>> Actor, Monimus:
>> Biottus third with the Poet,
>> Actor Damon:
>>> &c., &c.

The following is the termination of another list:—

> Sogenes fourth with the Devoted Slave,
> Actor Hecataens:
> Philemon the Younger fifth with the Girl of Miletus:
> Actor, Crates:
> Prize for acting, Onesimus.

The third class of monument was of a different kind altogether. It consisted of lists of tragic and comic actors, and tragic and comic poets, with numerals after each of them, denoting the number of victories they had won in the course of their career. There were separate lists for the City Dionysia and the Lenaea. There were consequently eight lists in all, four for each festival. Numerous fragments have been discovered, but unfortunately the most interesting parts are not always the best preserved[1]. Still they throw light upon several small points in connexion with the drama. One fragment confirms the account of Diodorus, that the number of Sophocles' victories was eighteen. At any rate that is proved to have been the number of his victories at the City Dionysia. Cratinus is represented as having won three victories at the City Dionysia and six at the Lenaea. This tallies exactly with the account of Suidas, who gives the total number of his victories as nine[2]. The following specimen is a list of comic poets, with the number of their victories at the City Dionysia:—

Xenophilus I.	Hermippus IIII.
Telecleides V.	Phrynichus II.
Aristomenes II.	Myrtilus I.
Cratinus III.	Eupolis III.
Pherecrates II.	

None of the public monuments, of which fragments have been

---

[1] Corp. Inscr. Att. ii. 977.   [2] Diod. Sic. xiii. 103; Suidas v. Κραтῖνος.

recovered, appear to have been erected before the third century
B.C. But there can be no doubt that similar monuments had
existed at a much earlier period. These records, together with the
choregic inscriptions and the documents in the public archives,
must have been the source from which Aristotle derived the
information contained in his two books about the contests at the
Dionysia. Of these two books the first was called 'Dionysiac
Victories,' and though it is never quoted by ancient writers, it
probably contained the same sort of information as the first and
third classes of public monuments. The other book was called
the 'Didascaliae,' and is very frequently referred to and quoted
from[1]. It contained lists of the poets who competed at each
festival, together with the names of the plays they produced.
It was therefore similar to the second class of monuments.
The origin of the title of the book is as follows. 'Didascalia,'
in its dramatic sense, meant originally the teaching and training
of a chorus. It then came to denote the play or group of plays
produced by a poet at a single festival[2]. Lastly, it was used to
denote a record of the circumstances of the production of a
play or group of plays. It is in this sense that Aristotle used
it as the title of his book. The work would not be a mere compilation from existing records and monuments. It must have
required some care and research. For instance, when a poet
had his plays brought out vicariously, we cannot doubt that the
name of the nominal author was entered in the public records,
and not that of the real poet. Aristophanes usually brought
out his plays in this manner. Then again a poet's plays were
sometimes brought out after his death in the name of his son.
In these and similar cases it would be the duty of the compiler
of a work like Aristotle's to correct the mistakes of the public
records, and to substitute where necessary the name of the real
poet of the play. Corrections of this kind were no doubt made
by Aristotle and his successors. The Didascaliae of Aristotle
is the ultimate source of our information as to the production

---

[1] Diog. Laërt. v. 1. 26. A complete list of the quotations from Aristotle's Διδασκαλίαι is given in Bekker's Aristotle, vol. v. p. 1572.

[2] See above, p. 21 note; chap. ii. p. 80.

and the success of the plays of the great Athenian dramatists. Callimachus, the grammarian of Alexandria, wrote a book of a similar kind, based upon Aristotle's work. It was from Callimachus that Aristophanes, the grammarian, derived the information which he incorporated in his Arguments to the Greek plays. The existing Arguments are mainly fragments of the work of Aristophanes. The facts about the production of the plays are thus ultimately derived from Aristotle[1]. The authenticity of the information contained in these Arguments has been strikingly proved by a recent discovery. The list of victors at the City Dionysia for the year 458, which was dug up at Athens a year or two ago, tallies in every particular with the facts recorded in the Argument to the Agamemnon of Aeschylus[2].

---

[1] Suidas v. Καλλίμαχος; Schol. Aristoph. Nub. 552; Etym. Mag. v. πίναξ; Trendelenburg, Grammat. Graec. de Arte Trag. Judic. p. 3 foll.

[2] Ἐφημ. Ἀρχαιολ. 1886, pt. 4. See above, p. 18.

CHAPTER II.

THE PRODUCTION OF A PLAY.

§ 1. *The Poets.*

It has already been pointed out that the dramatic performances at Athens were managed entirely by the state. No such thing was known as for an individual citizen to give an exhibition of plays as a private speculation. The drama was one of the principal ornaments of the great festivals of Dionysus, and the regulation of the drama was as much the duty of the government as the management of a public sacrifice or other religious ceremonial. Of the two festivals to which dramatic performances were confined, the Lenaea was superintended by the archon basileus, while the archon eponymus was responsible for the City Dionysia[1]. These two archons had therefore to undertake the general arrangement of the dramatic exhibitions at their respective festivals. They had not much to do with the details of preparation. Their functions mainly consisted in selecting the proper persons, and setting them to work, and seeing that they performed their duties satisfactorily. At Athens this was a matter of some complexity. Several persons had to co-operate in the production of a play. The expenses of the chorus were defrayed by the choregus, who fulfilled this duty as one of the public burdens to which the richer citizens were liable. The play was written, and the chorus trained, by the poet. The principal actor, at any rate in later times, was chosen by the state, and assigned to the poet by lot. It was the duty of the archon to bring together

[1] Pollux viii. 89, 90.

these three persons, the choregus, the poet, and the actor, and to see that they did not neglect the work of preparation. It is the object of the present chapter to explain in detail the system on which these preliminary arrangements were conducted, as well as the other circumstances which attended the production of a play at Athens.

When a poet wished to bring out a play, he sent in his application to the archon. If he was a young poet, he would probably be content to exhibit at the Lenaea, and would apply to the archon basileus. The City Dionysia was reserved for the more distinguished poets. The plays offered for exhibition were carefully examined by the archon, who proceeded to select, from among the various applicants, the number of poets required by the particular festival[1]. If it was tragedy at the City Dionysia that he was superintending, three poets would be chosen. If it was comedy, the number of poets would be three, or in later times five. When a poet applied for permission to exhibit, he was said to 'ask for a chorus,' because the first step taken by the archon was to assign him a choregus, who defrayed the expenses of his chorus. Similarly, when the archon acceded to a poet's application, he was said to 'grant him a chorus[2].' The number of applicants must often have been very large, especially for the City Dionysia; and to decide between their rival claims would be a task of great delicacy. It appears that the whole responsibility was thrown upon the archon. It was he who selected the poets, and assigned the choruses[3]. It was inevitable that functions of this kind should sometimes have been performed with partiality and unfairness. An author who had interest with the archon for the year would have a better chance of obtaining a chorus than a mere stranger. Mention

---

[1] Suidas v. χορὸν δίδωμι· ἐν ἴσῳ τῷ εὐδοκιμεῖν καὶ νικᾶν· παρὰ γάρ τοῖς Ἀθηναίοις χοροῦ ἐτύγχανον κωμῳδίας καὶ τραγῳδίας ποιηταὶ οὐ πάντες ἀλλὰ οἱ εὐδοκιμοῦντες καὶ δοκιμασθέντες ἄξιοι. To be allowed to compete was an honour, but was not regarded as a victory, as Suidas asserts. The title of victor was reserved for the poet who obtained the first place in the competition. See chap. I, p. 55.

[2] Athen. p. 638 F; Suidas l. c.

[3] Aristot. Poet. c. 5; Cratinus, Βουκόλοι, frag. I. (Meineke Frag. Com. Gr. ii. p. 27).

is made of an archon who refused a chorus to the great comic poet Cratinus. Another archon is said to have given a chorus to one Cleomachus in preference to Sophocles[1]. The only check upon such favouritism was public opinion. In a place like Athens, where the magistrates were entirely at the mercy of the people, and were subjected to severe scrutiny at the end of their year of office, it would be impossible for an archon to disregard public opinion in a very flagrant manner. It is therefore probable that in most cases the best poets were chosen.

It is often stated erroneously that there was a law regulating the age at which poets were permitted to compete. One of the scholiasts on the Clouds says that no poet was allowed to exhibit until he had reached the age of thirty. Another scholiast puts the age at forty or thirty. These are the only authorities for the existence of any such law[2]. Their statements upon the point appear to be mere conjectures, invented to explain the fact that Aristophanes did not at first produce his plays in his own person. Possibly they were misled by a confused recollection of the law that no man could be choregus to a chorus of boys until he had reached the age of forty. In regard to poets, there cannot have been any law of the kind they mention. Take the case of Aristophanes. His first play was the Banqueters, which he brought out in another man's name in 427, while he was still 'almost a boy.' Three years later he brought out the Knights in his own name. If he was almost a boy in 427, he cannot have been anything like thirty when he exhibited the Knights[3]. The other great poets began to exhibit at a very early age. Aeschylus was only twenty-five at the time of his first dramatic contest. Sophocles won his first tragic victory at the age of twenty-eight. Euripides began to contend when he was twenty-six[4]. All that appears to have been required was that the poet should have reached the age of twenty, passed his docimasia, and been enrolled in the list of

---

[1] Cratinus l. c.
[2] Schol. Aristoph. Nub. 510, 530.
[3] Schol. Aristoph. Ran. 504; Arg. to Aristoph. Equites.
[4] Suidas v. Αἰσχύλος; Marmor Par. ep. 56; Vita I Eurip.

citizens. Before this it is not likely that he would be allowed to take part in the contests. Eupolis is said to have been only seventeen when he began to produce comedies. But if this was really the case, probably his earlier plays were brought out by friends, and not in his own name[1].

It seems to have been not an uncommon practice for a poet to have his plays produced by a friend, instead of coming forward in his own person. Various reasons might induce him to do so. In the first place a young poet might feel diffident of his powers, and might wish to conceal his identity until he had tested them by experience. This seems to have been the reason why the first three plays of Aristophanes, the Banqueters, the Babylonians, and the Acharnians, were produced by Callistratus[2]. Aristophanes did not come forward in his own name till the year 424, when he brought out his Knights. In the parabasis of this play he explains at some length the reasons which induced him to keep in the background at first. His reasons were partly the difficulty of writing comedies, partly the fickleness of the Athenians, partly a feeling that one ought to proceed warily in the business, and advance by slow degrees, just as the steersman of a ship begins by serving as a common oarsman. He says nothing about any law which would have prevented him producing his early plays in his own name, but ascribes his conduct entirely to youthful modesty. Referring to the same subject in the Clouds he expresses similar ideas in a metaphorical way, by saying that at the time when the Banqueters came out his Muse was still a virgin, and too young to have a child of her own[3]. One reason then for this vicarious production of plays was merely the diffidence of youth, and a desire to make the first experiments anonymously. A second and quite a different motive was that which actuated old poets, when they allowed their sons to bring out their plays, and have the credit of the authorship, in

---

[1] Suidas v. Εὔπολις.
[2] Schol. Aristoph. Nub. 531; Anon. de Comoed. (Dindorf, Prolegom. de Comoed. p. 24); Suidas v. Σαμίων ὁ δῆμος; Arg. Aristoph. Acharn.
[3] Aristoph. Equit. 512-544, Nub. 528-531.

order to give them a successful start in their dramatic career. Aristophanes for this reason entrusted to his son Araros the production of his two latest comedies. Iophon also was suspected of exhibiting in his own name the tragedies of his father Sophocles[1]. A third case was that in which wealthy citizens, who had a wish for poetical distinction, bought plays from needy authors, and exhibited them as their own. Plato, the poet of the Old Comedy, is said to have been compelled by poverty to sell his comedies in this manner[2]. A fourth reason was probably the desire to avoid the labour and the trouble of bringing out a play. The earlier dramatic poets were stage-managers as well as authors, and the superintendence of the production of a play was part of the business of their profession. But in later times when play-writing had a tendency to become more entirely a literary pursuit, authors appear to have entrusted their plays to friends who had more experience in theatrical affairs. It is true that a professional trainer might be procured, who thoroughly understood the business of producing a play. But still a certain amount of trouble and responsibility must have devolved upon the person in whose name the play was brought out, and to whom the archon granted the chorus. It was most likely some reason of this kind which induced the tragic poet Aphareus never to bring out his plays in his own name[3]. He was quite as much a rhetorician as a dramatist, and probably knew nothing at all about the details of stage-management. Though he exhibited tragedies on eight occasions, they were always entrusted for production to a friend. A similar reason may have induced Aristophanes, during the middle of his career, to entrust so many of his plays to Callistratus and Philonides. For instance, the Birds and the Lysistrata were exhibited by Callistratus, the Wasps, the Proagon, the Frogs, and the Amphiaraus by Philonides[4]. In addition to the examples already mentioned there are other instances of vicarious pro-

---

[1] Arg. to Aristoph. Plutus; Schol. Aristoph. Ran. 73.
[2] Suidas v. Ἀρκάδας μιμούμενοι.
[3] Plut. X orat. 839 D.
[4] Args. to Aristoph. Av., Lysist., Vesp., Ran.

duction, where it is very difficult to discover what the motives really were. Philip, one of the sons of Aristophanes, is said to have 'frequently competed with plays of Eubulus.' The Autolycus of Eupolis was brought out by an obscure poet called Demostratus[1]. In these cases there may have been special circumstances which are unknown to us. But as far as our information goes, the only plausible reasons for having plays brought out vicariously appear to be the four already mentioned, the timidity of youth, the stress of poverty, kindness towards a relative, or the desire to escape responsibility. Other reasons have been suggested. For instance it has been conjectured that on certain occasions a poet's friend might have a better chance than the poet himself of obtaining a chorus from the archon. But there does not seem to be much plausibility in the suggestion. No one would be more likely to obtain a chorus from the archon than a poet of well-established reputation. The reasons already given are the only ones which stand the test of examination.

As to the relationship between the poet and the friend who produced his plays for him a few points require to be noticed. It was the nominal poet who made the application to the archon, received the chorus, and undertook the whole responsibility[2]. At the same time it appears that the name of the real poet was often perfectly well known. Of course if secrecy was an object, this would not be so. When a father gave his plays to his son, he kept his own name concealed. The real authorship was only revealed in later times. Iophon was merely suspected of having competed with the plays of his father Sophocles, and was not known for certain to have done so. But in other instances the real poet was known from the very first. Aristophanes in the Knights says that many people had been asking him why he gave his plays to Callistratus, and did not ask for a chorus in his own name. Again in the Wasps, which was brought out by Philonides, the chorus refer to the author of

[1] Vit. Aristoph. (Dindf. Prolegom. de Comoed. p. 39); Athen. p. 216 D. θαυμάζειν ὑμῶν φησιν πολλοὺς αὐτῷ προσιόντας, | καὶ βασανίζειν, ὡς οὐχὶ πάλαι
[2] Aristoph. Equit. 512, 513 & δὲ χορὸν αἰτοίη καθ' ἑαυτὸν κ.τ.λ.

the play in terms which are only applicable to Aristophanes[1]. It follows that from the very first the real authorship of the plays of Aristophanes was more or less an open secret. Hence it is most likely that when the author of the Babylonians was prosecuted by Cleon, it was the real author Aristophanes, and not the nominal author Callistratus, who was attacked. At the same time the nominal author was the one officially recognised by the state. There can be no doubt that it was his name which was entered as victor in the public archives, and that he received the prize and the other rewards of victory, such as the public proclamation and the crown. The existing didascaliae in cases of vicarious production give the name of the real author, with a note to the effect that the play was actually brought out by such and such a person. This can hardly have been the form adopted originally in the public records, but must be due to the corrections of Aristotle and his successors.

§ 2. *Appointment of the Choregi.*

To return to the preliminary arrangements in connexion with the dramatic exhibitions. For every play or group of plays a choregus was required to provide and pay for the chorus. The appointment of the choregi was a matter for which the archon was responsible[2]. For the dithyrambic contests each tribe was bound to provide one choregus. These contests, as was pointed out in the last chapter, were essentially a tribal affair. There were five choruses of boys and five choruses of men; and each of the ten tribes took part in the contest, and provided one choregus and one chorus. But it is a mistake to apply the same system to the tragic and comic choruses, and to suppose, as is usually done, that each tribe had to supply a choregus for tragedy and comedy as well. The dramatic contests had nothing to do with the tribes, but were contests between individuals. Consequently the choregi were chosen without distinction from the whole body of the citizens, and were not specially appointed by the tribes.

---

[1] Aristoph. Equites l. c., Vespae 1016–1022.   [2] Demosth. Meid. § 13.

Whenever a man is said to have been choregus for his tribe, it is a chorus of boys or men that is referred to, and not a dramatic chorus[1]. If each of the ten tribes had supplied a choregus for the dramatic choruses, there would have been more of them than was necessary, since the number of tragic and comic choruses at any one festival was never more than eight, and in early times was only six or five. As far then as tragedy and comedy are concerned, the choregi were chosen, without any distinction of tribe, from the general body of citizens. The dramatic choregia was a burden, which, like the other public burdens, had to be undertaken in turn by the members of the wealthier classes. The order was fixed by law. But a man of more than usual ambition or generosity might volunteer for the office of choregus out of his proper turn. The defendant in one of the speeches of Lysias points out that he had been choregus to no less than eight choruses in a space of nine years, in addition to such expenses as the war-tax and the trierarchy. He adds that if he had only undertaken such burdens as he was compelled to perform by law, he would not have spent a quarter of the money[2].

A man was liable to be selected as choregus as soon as he had reached the age of twenty, and been enrolled as a full citizen. The defendant in the speech of Lysias just referred to passed his docimasia in the archonship of Theopompus, and in that very same year he acted as choregus to a tragic chorus, and to a chorus of men[3]. There was a law that no one should be choregus to a boys' chorus till he had reached the age of forty. But this law had nothing to do with the choruses of men, or the choruses in tragedy or comedy[4]. There was occasionally some difficulty in finding a sufficient number of rich men to fill the office. In the time of Demosthenes the tribe Pandionis was for three years unable to supply a choregus for the dithyrambic contests. At a much earlier period, towards the end of

---

[1] Demosth. Meid. § 13; Plut. X orat. 835 B; Isaeus orat. v. § 36, where to be choregus to one's tribe is contrasted with being choregus to a tragic chorus. Corp. Inscr. Gr. 224, &c.

[2] Lysias orat. xxi. §§ 1–5.
[3] Lysias l. c.
[4] Aeschin. Timarch. §§ 11, 12; Harpocrat. v. ὅτι νόμος.

the Peloponnesian War, when there had been long and heavy drains upon the resources of the state, it was found necessary to lighten the burden of the choregia. Accordingly in 406 a law was passed enacting that each dramatic chorus at the City Dionysia should be provided by two choregi instead of one. Thus the cost to individuals was diminished by half[1]. The same law was probably passed in reference to the choruses at the Lenaea. It was only a temporary expedient, due to the distress caused by the Peloponnesian War. At any rate there are several instances in later times of single individuals acting as choregi to tragic choruses. For example, a certain Aristophanes was tragic choregus twice, Meidias once[2]. Towards the end of the fourth century, or the beginning of the third, the choregia was abolished altogether. A new system was introduced in its stead. The providing and the training of all the choruses was undertaken by the state, and an officer called the Agonothetes was elected annually to carry out the arrangements. His duties would mainly consist in providing the dithyrambic choruses. By the beginning of the third century the chorus had practically disappeared from comedy. Tragedy at Athens was in most cases confined to the reproduction of old plays, and it is very doubtful whether in these reproductions the chorus was retained in its integrity. Such dramatic choruses as were still required in this late period were provided by the Agonothetes, acting as the representative of the people[3].

When the archon had selected the poets whose plays were to be performed at the approaching festival, and the list had been made up of the choregi who were to supply the choruses, the next thing to be done was to arrange the choregi and poets together in pairs. Each choregus had one poet assigned to him, for whose chorus he was responsible. There is no definite information as to the manner in which this arrangement

---

[1] Demosth. Meid. § 13; Schol. Aristoph. Ran. 406.
[2] Lysias orat. xix. §§ 29, 42; Dem. Meid. § 156.

[3] Corp. Inscr. Gr. 225, 226; Corp. Inscr. Att. ii. 302, 307, 314, 331; Köhler's article in Mittheil. des deut. arch. Inst. iii. p. 231 ff.

was carried out in the case of tragic and comic choruses. But in the case of the dithyrambic choruses there are full accounts of the manner in which similar arrangements were made; and it will not be difficult, from the analogy of these proceedings, to form a fairly clear conception of the proceedings in regard to tragedy and comedy. Every dithyrambic chorus required a flute-player. These flute-players were first selected by the state, and then distributed among the different choregi. Some time before the festival a meeting of the ecclesia was held, at which the distribution took place under the superintendence of the archon. The proceedings were quite public, and any Athenian citizen who wished could be present. The system was as follows. There were of course ten choregi and ten flute-players. The choregi first drew lots for order of choice, and then each chose his own flute-player. The choregus who had obtained the privilege of choosing first selected the flute-player whom he considered to be the best of the ten. So they went on till all the flute-players were chosen. The scene was a lively one. The success of the choregus, and in consequence the success of his tribe, depended to a certain extent upon his luck in getting a good or bad flute-player. Hence the whole process was followed with the greatest interest by the crowds of spectators present. As each lot was drawn, the result was greeted with expressions of triumph or disappointment by the partisans of the different choregi[1]. The above information is derived from the account given by Demosthenes, in the speech against Meidias, of the preliminary arrangements for the dithyrambic contests. Nothing is there said about the choice or assignation of the poets. Probably in this contest only old dithyrambs were reproduced, and there were no poets to be assigned. That such was often the case is proved by inscriptions[2]. But

---

[1] Demosth. Meid. §§ 13, 14; and Arg. to Meidias, p. 510.

[2] Mittheil. des deut. arch. Inst. x. p. 231 Νικίας Νικοδήμου Ξυπεταίων ἀνέθηκε νικήσας χορηγῶν Κεκροπίδι παίδων· Πανταλέων Σικυώνιος ηὔλει· ᾆσμα 'Ελπήνωρ Τιμοθέου· Νέαιχμος ἦρχεν. In this case the dithyramb performed was the Elpenor of the celebrated poet Timotheus. When old dithyrambs were performed, and no poet was necessary, a professional trainer was hired to look after the chorus. Such was the διδάσκαλος mentioned by Demosthenes (Meid. § 17).

when the contest was with original dithyrambs, and poets were required, they seem to have been allotted to the choregi in much the same manner as the flute-players. The defendant in one of the speeches of Antiphon says that, when he was choregus to a chorus of boys at the Thargelia, the poet Pantacles was assigned to him by lot[1]. The system then in the case of the dithyrambic choruses was that at a meeting of the ecclesia, held under the superintendence of the archon, the choregi drew lots for the flute-players, and (where necessary) for the poets. Probably much the same system was adopted in tragedy and comedy. Some time before the festival the choregi would meet, and after the order of choice had been determined by lot, each choregus would choose his poet. Quite as much depended upon this allotment, in the case of tragedy and comedy, as in the case of the dithyrambic contests. A choregus who obtained an inferior poet would be heavily handicapped in the competition; and a poet who was joined to a mean and unambitious choregus would be equally unfortunate. If a matter of such importance had been left to be decided by individual will, it would have given endless opportunities for unfairness and favouritism. The best precaution against such an evil was to arrange the matter by lot.

§ 3. *Selection of the Actors.*

Poets and choregi having been associated together in pairs, there still remained the selection and appointment of the actors. The manner in which they were appointed differed very considerably at different periods. To take the case of tragic actors first. Before the time of Aeschylus, when tragedy was more

---

[1] Antiphon orat. vi. § 11 ἐπειδὴ χορηγὸς κατεστάθην εἰς Θαργήλια καὶ ἔλαχον Παντακλέα διδάσκαλον κ.τ.λ. Pantacles was a poet, and not a mere trainer of choruses, like the διδάσκαλος hired by Demosthenes. This is proved by a passage in Etym. Mag. v. διδάσκαλος· ἰδίως διδασκάλους λέγουσιν οἱ Ἀττικοὶ τοὺς ποιητὰς τῶν διθυράμβων ἢ τῶν κωμῳδιῶν ἢ τῶν τραγῳδιῶν. Ἀντίφων ἐν τῷ περὶ τοῦ χορευτοῦ· ἔλαχόν, φησι, Παντακλέα διδάσκαλον· ὅτι γὰρ ὁ Παντακλῆς ποιητής, δεδήλωκεν Ἀριστοτέλης ἐν ταῖς Διδασκαλίαις. When there was a poet, a professional trainer was not usually required. The poet undertook the training of the chorus.

a lyrical than a dramatic performance, consisting of long choral odes interspersed with recitatives, actors did not exist as a separate class. Only one actor was required in each play, and his part was taken by the poet[1]. But when Aeschylus increased the number of actors to two, and converted tragedy from a lyrical into a dramatic form of art, the poets ceased to perform in their own plays, and the actor's profession came into existence. For the next fifty years or so it does not appear that the state took any part in the selection of the actors. It left the matter in the hands of the poets. Particular actors are found to have been permanently connected with particular poets. Aeschylus is said to have first employed Cleander as his actor, and to have afterwards associated a second actor with him in the person of Mynniscus. Tlepolemus acted continuously for Sophocles. It is stated, on the authority of Ister, that Sophocles was accustomed to write his plays with a view to the capacities of his actors[2]. This story, whether true or not, shows that he chose his actors himself, at any rate during the earlier part of his career. But long before the end of the fifth century the system was altogether changed. As the actors grew in importance their selection was no longer left to the choice of individual poets, but was undertaken by the state. The actors chosen by the state were distributed among the poets by lot. Towards the end of the fifth century we no longer hear of particular poets and actors being permanently connected together. The statement of Thomas Magister, that Cephisophon was the actor of Euripides, appears to be a mere conjecture, as Cephisophon is nowhere else described in that way. Under the new arrangement the mode of distribution was as follows. Three protagonists were first of all selected by the archon. There is no information as to the way in which they were selected. They may have been chosen by means of a small competition, similar to that between comic actors at the Chytri. The subordinate actors were not chosen by the state, but each protagonist was allowed to provide his

---

[1] Aristot. Rhet. iii. 1.
[2] Vit. Aeschyl.; Schol. Aristoph. Clouds 1267; Vit. Soph. and Eurip.

own deuteragonist and tritagonist. When the three leading actors had been chosen they were assigned to the three competing tragic poets by lot. Probably the system was the same as in the assignation of the flute-players to the dithyrambic choruses. The poets would first draw lots for order of choice, and then each poet would choose his actor. The actor performed all the tragedies of the poet to whom he was allotted. Thus in 418 the three tragedies of Callistratus were acted by Callippides; the three tragedies of his rival were acted by Lysicrates. The actor who won the prize for acting was permitted to compete as a matter of course at the next festival without having to submit to the process of selection by the archon. Such was the system adopted during the latter half of the fifth century[1]. How long it lasted cannot be determined; but when we come to the middle of the fourth century, a further alteration is found to have been introduced. By this time the importance of the actors had increased to a still greater extent. In fact, Aristotle says that in his day the success of a play depended much more upon the actor than the poet[2]. It was probably felt that under the old arrangement the poet who obtained by lot the greatest actor had an unfair advantage over his rivals. A new system was therefore introduced, by which the talents of the actors were divided with perfect equality among the poets. Each tragedy was performed

[1] Suidas v. νεμήσεις ὑποκριτῶν· οἱ ποιηταὶ ἐλάμβανον τρεῖς ὑποκριτὰς κλήρῳ νεμηθέντας, ὑποκρινομένους τὰ δράματα· ὧν ὁ νικήσας εἰς τοὐπιὸν ἄκριτος παραλαμβάνεται. The interpretation of this passage had long been a mystery; but the discovery of the existence of an actors' contest, side by side with that between the poets, has made the matter comparatively clear. Obviously ὁ νικήσας denotes, not the victorious poet, nor yet the actor who acted for him, but the actor who won the prize for acting. Τοὐπιὸν apparently means 'the next festival.' The victorious actor was allowed to act at the next festival as a matter of course. The 'three actors' are the three protagonists required at each tragic contest, and not the three actors required by each poet. This is proved by the words ὧν ὁ νικήσας, which imply that the three actors mentioned all took part in the actors' contest. But the actors' contest was limited to the protagonists; the subordinate actors had nothing to do with it. See chapter I, p. 56. Moreover, it is known that in the time of Demosthenes the subordinate actors were hired by the protagonists; and this was probably the case at a much earlier period. Cp. Demosth. Fals. Leg. § 10 ἔχων Ἰσχανδρον τὸν Νεοπτολέμου δευτεραγωνιστήν. Ibid. § 246; de Cor. § 262.

[2] Aristot. Rhet. iii. 1.

by a separate actor. All the actors appeared in turn in the service of each of the poets. Thus in 341 Astydamas exhibited three tragedies. His Achilles was acted by Thessalus, his Athamas by Neoptolemus, his Antigone by Athenodorus. The three tragedies of each of his competitors were performed by the same three actors[1]. By this arrangement no poet had any advantage over his rivals, but as far as the excellence of the actors was concerned all were on exactly the same level. The system just described appears to have been retained without alteration during the remaining period of Attic tragedy.

The mode of distributing the actors in comedy was much the same as that in tragedy. During the earlier part of the fifth century the poets were left to choose their own actors. Thus the comic poet Crates is said to have begun his career as actor to Cratinus. But in later times no instances are to be found of comic actors being permanently connected with particular poets. The story that Philonides and Callistratus were actors of Aristophanes is a mere fiction of one of the old commentators, based upon a misunderstanding[2]. It is evident, therefore, that the state began to undertake the selection and appointment of the comic actors about the same time that a corresponding change was made in regard to tragedy. No doubt the mode of distribution was identical. The actors were first appointed by the state, and the poets then drew lots for them. As the comic poets competed with single plays, only one method of distribution was possible, and there was no need of the further alteration which was afterwards made in tragedy. The number of poets in the comic contests was originally three, and in later times five. A corresponding number of actors would be required. Sometimes however a smaller number was selected, and one actor appeared in two comedies. In 353 Aristomachus was the actor assigned both to Simylus and Diodorus. In later times Damon is found occasionally acting in two comedies at

---

[1] Corp. Inscr. Att. ii. 973.
[2] Schol. Aristoph. Equit. 534; Vita Aristoph. (Dindf. Prolegom. de Comoed. p. 36). The commentator, misunderstanding the expression that certain plays of Aristophanes were brought out by Philonides and Callistratus (ἐδιδάχθη διὰ Φιλωνίδου κ.τ.λ.), concluded that these persons were actors.

the same competition[1]. It is not likely that such a course was adopted except on occasions when it was impossible to obtain five comic actors of fairly equal merit.

§ 4. *The training of the Chorus.*

The archon had now for the present finished his part of the business. He had seen that the proper number of poets, actors, and choregi had been chosen. He had seen that each choregus was provided with his own poet and actor. It was now the duty of choregus and poet to attend to the subsequent preparations. The choregus was responsible for the selection and payment of the chorus. He had also to provide a room for them to rehearse in[2]. Very little is known concerning the relations between the choregus and his chorus. Such few details as have been recorded refer rather to the dithyrambic, than to the dramatic, choruses. The dithyrambic contests were contests between the tribes, and each dithyrambic chorus was selected exclusively from the tribe which it represented in the competition. Each tribe had a specially appointed agent, who was employed by the choregus to collect his chorus for him[3]. But the drama had nothing to do with the tribes, and there was no limitation upon the selection of the dramatic choruses. Aristotle happens in one place to remark that a tragic and a comic chorus often consisted of much the same individual members[4]. It is quite clear, therefore, that the dramatic choruses were chosen from the general body of citizens, and not from particular tribes, and that a man might serve in two of these choruses at the same time. There was probably a class of professional singers who made their livelihood by serving in the dramatic choruses. A rich choregus would have a great advantage over his rivals by offering higher pay, and so securing better singers. The stories about the boarding and

---

[1] Corp. Inscr. Att. ii. 972, 975 *c* and *d*. Pollux iv. 106, ix. 42).
[2] Xen. Hiero ix. 4, Resp. Athen. i. 13. The training room was called διδασκαλεῖον (Antiphon orat. vi. § 11), or χορηγεῖον (Bekk. Anecd. p. 72, 17;
[3] Antiphon orat. vi. §§ 11–13; Pollux iv. 106. The agent was called χορολέκτης.
[4] Aristot. Pol. iii. 3.

lodging of the choreutae also refer mainly to the dithyrambic choruses. The choregus in Antiphon's speech lodged his chorus in his own house, and gave special directions that every delicacy which was ordered by the trainer should be provided for them. But this was a chorus of boys. The professionals who served in the dramatic choruses are not likely to have been lodged in the house of the choregus, especially as they were often in the service of two choregi at the same time. However, it seems that the diet of the choruses was well attended to, so that the members should appear in the best possible condition on the day of the contests. Plutarch mentions eels, lettuce, garlic, and cheese as delicacies provided for the choruses. The appetite of the Attic choreutae passed into a proverb[1].

During the earlier period of the Athenian drama the principal part in the training and instruction of the chorus was undertaken by the poet himself. In fact, the regular name at Athens for a dramatic or dithyrambic poet was didaskalos, or 'the teacher,' owing to the part he took in teaching his play or poem to the chorus. In the same way, when a poet brought out a tragedy or a comedy, the technical expression was that he 'taught' such and such a play. The play, or group of plays, exhibited by a single poet was called a 'teaching[2].' In addition to the evidence supplied by these expressions, there is also no lack of direct testimony as to the important part taken by the older poets in the production of their plays. In fact, they were quite as much stage-managers as poets. The older dramatic writers, such as Thespis, Pratinas, Cratinus, and Phrynichus, were called 'dancers,' not only because of the prominent part which the chorus and the dancing filled in their plays, but also because they gave instruction in choric dancing. Aeschylus is said to have

---

[1] Antiphon l.c.; Plutarch Glor. Athen. 349 A; Suidas v. φαρυγγίνδην· ὡς ἀριστίνδην σκώπτοντες γὰρ τὴν γαστριμαργίαν τῶν χορευτῶν Ἀττικοὶ οὕτω λέγουσι.

[2] Suidas v. διδάσκαλος; Aristoph. Ran. 1026 εἶτα διδάξας Πέρσας κ.τ.λ.

Anthol. Pal. vii. 37 (of a mask of Antigone or Electra) ἐκ ποίης ἥδε διδασκαλίης; Plut. Pericles 154 E ἀλλ' Ἴωνα μὲν ὥσπερ τραγικὴν διδασκαλίαν ἀξιοῦντα τὴν ἀρετὴν ἔχειν τι πάντως καὶ σατυρικὸν μέρος ἐῶμεν.

superintended personally the whole of the training of his choruses, and to have invented many new dances and movements for them. His innovations in regard to the scenery and the dresses of the actors entirely transformed the outward appearance of the drama[1]. This intimate connexion between the poet and the stage, between the literary and the theatrical part of dramatic production, continued to exist during the great period of Athenian drama. Sophocles appeared personally in some of his plays. In the Thamyris he played the harp. In the Nausicaa he won great applause by the skill with which he played ball in the scene where Nausicaa is sporting with her maidens[2]. Euripides also seems to have superintended the training of his choruses in person, as there is a story in Plutarch which represents him as singing over one of his odes to the choreutae[3].

Originally then the principal part of the training was done by the poet himself. He was assisted in his task by a subordinate, who looked after the routine part of the work, and was called a hypodidaskalos, or 'assistant teacher.' This was the proper term to denote the professional trainer, as opposed to the didaskalos, or poet[4]. But towards the end of the fifth and the beginning of the fourth century the practice in these matters underwent a change. Poetry and stage-management began to be sharply discriminated from one another. A class of literary dramatic writers arose, such as Theodectes and Aphareus, who were quite as much rhetoricians as poets. They knew nothing about the details of training a chorus, or preparing a play for representation. Under these circumstances the greater part of the management was undertaken by the professional trainer. The term didaskalos, which had originally been confined to the poet, was now applied to these hired trainers[5]. A class of men came into existence who made it their business to look after the instruction of choruses. One of these, named Sannio, is men-

---

[1] Athen. pp. 21 C, 22 A; Vit. Aeschyli; Philostrat. Vit. Apol. vi. 11 (vol. i. p. 220, ed. Kayser).
[2] Eustath. Odyss. p. 1553.
[3] Plut. De Andiendo, 46 B.

[4] Photius v. ὑποδιδάσκαλος; Plat. Ion p. 536 A.
[5] Thus the trainer hired by Demosthenes for his chorus is called διδάσκαλος, Dem. Meid. § 17.

tioned by Demosthenes, and was celebrated for his skill in training tragic choruses. These professional trainers were hired and paid by the choregus. A rich choregus had a great advantage in being able to secure the most skilful trainer. Socrates mentions the case of a certain choregus called Antisthenes, who knew little or nothing about music and choruses himself, but was always successful in his competitions, because he took care to provide himself with the very best trainers procurable[1]. It is obvious that in these later times, when the poets ceased to attend to the details of stage-management, the importance of the professional trainers must have very much increased. The hiring of a good trainer would be one of the first conditions of success.

§ 5. *Expenses of the Choregia.*

It will now be possible to form some conception of the expenses which the choregus had to meet. The principal item was the hire of the chorus during the whole period of training. This part of the expenditure was borne entirely by the choregus without any assistance from the state[2]. Then again, he had to provide an instructor for his chorus. As the competition between rich choregi was of the keenest character, the services of a really good instructor must have been expensive. In the third place, a flute-player was required. In the dithyrambic choruses the flute-players were selected by the

---

[1] Dem. Meid. §§ 58, 59; Xen. Mem. iii. 4. 3.

[2] Xen. Resp. Athen. i. 13 χορηγοῦσι μὲν οἱ πλούσιοι, χορηγεῖται δὲ ὁ δῆμος ... ἀξιοῖ οὖν ἀργύριον λαμβάνειν ὁ δῆμος καὶ ᾄδων καὶ τρέχων καὶ ὀρχούμενος ... ἵνα αὐτός τε ἔχῃ καὶ οἱ πλούσιοι πενέστεροι γίγνωνται. First Arg. to Demosth. Meidias, p. 509 χορηγὸς ... ὁ τὰ ἀναλώματα παρέχων τὰ περὶ τὸν χορόν. Plut. Glor. Athen. 349 B. The statement of the Scholiast on Dionysius Thrax (Bekk. Anecd. p. 746), that every comic and tragic poet was supplied with a chorus 'supported by the state,' appears to be merely a loose way of saying that the dramatic choruses were provided by choregi appointed by the state. The author of the 2nd Arg. to the Meidias says that the choregus 'received sums of money for the support of the chorus.' But his authority is of the weakest description. He is utterly mistaken as to the Dionysiac festivals, imagining that the Great Dionysia was a triennial affair, as opposed to the Small or annual celebration. Hence his testimony is of no value in the face of other authorities.

state, and assigned by lot to the choregi. There is no evidence to show whether the flute-player of a dramatic chorus was chosen by the choregus or by the state; but in any case the choregus would have to pay his salary. Fourthly, the various mute characters that appeared upon the stage, such as the attendants upon kings and queens, were supplied by the choregus. This is proved by the story in Plutarch of a tragedian at Athens who was going to act the part of a queen, and who refused to perform unless the choregus would provide him with a train of female attendants dressed in expensive fashion [1]. The number and splendour of the mute characters would add greatly to the magnificence of the spectacle, and form a considerable item in the expenses of a wealthy choregus. It is also probable that in early times, when the actors were chosen by the poets, their salary was paid by the choregus. But later the selection and payment of the actors were undertaken entirely by the state [2]. The principal part then of the expenditure of the choregus consisted in paying the salaries of the various persons just mentioned. In addition to this, he had to provide the dresses of the chorus, which were often very magnificent. For example, the comic poet Antiphanes mentions the case of a choregus who ruined himself by dressing his chorus in gold. Demosthenes supplied his chorus of men with golden crowns [3]. Sometimes the love of splendour degenerated into mere vulgar ostentation. Unnecessary magnificence in the appointments of a comic chorus is mentioned by Aristotle as a proof of vulgarity. On the other hand, economical choregi saved expense by hiring second-hand dresses from the dealers in theatrical costumes [4]. Another item in the expenses of the choregia was the supply of dresses for the various mute characters and subordinate personages. With the dresses of the actors themselves the choregus had probably nothing to do. As for the

[1] Plut. Phocion. p. 750 C.
[2] The actors were assigned by the state to the poets, and not to the choregi: hence it is quite clear that in later times the choregi did not pay for them. See Suidas v. νεμήσεις ὑποκριτῶν.
[3] Antiphanes apud Athen. p. 103 E; Dem. Meid. § 16.
[4] Aristot. Eth. Nic. iv. 6; Pollux vii. 78 τοὺς δὲ τὰς ἐσθῆτας ἀπομισθοῦντας τοῖς χορηγοῖς οἱ μὲν νέοι ἱματιομίσθας ἐκάλουν, οἱ δὲ παλαιοὶ ἱματιομισθωτάς.

ordinary kinds of scenery, they were part of the permanent fixtures of the theatre, and would be provided by the lessee. But when anything very special in the way of scenery was required by the necessities of a particular play, it is most probable that the expenses in such cases were borne by the choregus. As far, then, as can be gathered from ancient notices, the expenses of the choregia consisted in the hire of the chorus, the instructor, the flute-player, and the mute characters; in providing dresses for the chorus and the mute characters; and in supplying such exceptional scenery as the theatre did not possess.

A choregus who was anxious for victory, and who was ready to spend money over the production of the play, would easily be put to very considerable expense. The defendant in one of the speeches of Lysias gives some interesting details about the expenses of the different kinds of choruses. He is enumerating the various public burdens which he undertook since he was enrolled as a citizen, and the amount of money which he spent upon each of them. A tragic chorus cost him thirty minae. He spent sixteen minae upon a comic chorus, and fifteen upon a chorus of boys. It follows that a comic chorus was only about half as expensive as a tragic one, and cost about the same as a chorus of boys. On the other hand, a chorus of men at the City Dionysia cost fifty minae. These figures bear out the statement of Demosthenes, that a chorus of men was much more expensive than a tragic chorus. The chorus of men consisted of fifty members; and the payment of so large a number, together with the dresses and crowns which the choregi used to provide them with, would easily account for the expense. A tragic chorus consisted of only fifteen members, and yet it cost about twice as much as a comic chorus, which consisted of twenty-four. But we must remember that the tragic chorus had to perform in several plays, the comic chorus in only one. Also it does not appear to have been customary to spend very much money upon a comedy. In another speech of Lysias, a certain Aristophanes is said to have expended fifty minae over two tragic choruses,

THE EXPENSES OF THE CHOREGIA.

He was therefore rather more economical than the person mentioned above, who spent thirty minae over one[1]. It would be very interesting to be able to form some conception of the amount which these sums would represent at the present day. But of course it is exceedingly hard to find a standard by which to measure the comparative value of money in two such different civilizations as that of ancient Athens and that of modern England. It appears that in the time of Aristophanes the daily wages for common and unskilled labour were three obols[2]. If we take as a modern equivalent the case of the agricultural labourer who gets ten shillings a week, or one shilling and eight-pence per day, it follows that three obols in ancient Attica were equivalent to about one shilling and eight-pence at the present time. If this calculation is anywhere near the mark, then a choregus who spent thirty minae on a tragic chorus would be spending a sum equivalent to about £500 of our money. The sixteen minae paid for a comic chorus would represent about £266. Comparisons of this kind are very conjectural; but they enable one to form some idea of the immense sums of money which must have been spent at Athens in the course of a single year upon dramatic and choral performances. There were eight dramatic and ten dithyrambic choruses at the City Dionysia. There were seven or eight dramatic choruses at the Lenaea. Besides this there were dithyrambic choruses at the Thargelia, Prometheia, and Hephaesteia; and dithyrambic and pyrrhic choruses at the Panathenaea. The expenses of all these choruses were drawn from a single small state, about the size of an English county, in which wealth was by no means abundant. It is easy to see that there was not much exaggeration in the complaint of Demosthenes, that the Athenians spent more upon their festivals than they ever spent upon a naval expedition[3].

If the choregi neglected their duties, and were careless about the efficiency of their choruses, it was the duty of the archon to

---

[1] Lysias orat. xxi. §§ 1–5, xix. §§ 29, 42; Dem. Meid. § 156.
[2] Aristoph. Eccles. 307; Böckh, Public Economy of Athens, i. p. 157 (Engl. transl.).
[3] Demosth. Philipp. i. § 35.

bring pressure to bear upon them[1]. But such interference was not often necessary. On the contrary the rivalry between the choregi was so keen, and their desire for victory so great, that it often led them into expenses which they could not afford. Demosthenes says that men frequently spent all their property upon these competitions[2]. The choregus in Antiphanes has already been referred to, who reduced himself to beggary by his extravagance in providing golden dresses for his chorus. Besides the mere spirit of emulation there was another inducement to lavish vast sums upon these choregic displays. For a wealthy politician it was an easy means of gaining popularity, and increasing his influence in the state. Nicias is said to have owed a great deal of his power to the splendour of his choruses, upon which he spent more money than any of his contemporaries or predecessors[3]. With the double motives of ambition and emulation at work, it was natural that considerable jealousy should be excited between the rival choregi, the 'anti-choregi,' as they were called. Sometimes this hostility ended in blows. When Taureas and Alcibiades were competitors with choruses of boys, a dispute having arisen as to the parentage of one of the boys in Alcibiades' chorus, the matter ended in a personal conflict in the orchestra. Demosthenes, in his speech against Meidias, cites many examples of the bitterness and animosity with which choregi regarded one another. He adds that there would have been some excuse for the assault of Meidias upon himself if it had been caused by the jealousy of a rival choregus[4].

§ 6. *The Performances in the Theatre.*

When the preparations were all completed, a few days before the actual festival there was a preliminary ceremony

---

[1] Xen. Hiero ix. 4 καὶ γὰρ ὅταν χοροὺς ἡμῖν βουλώμεθα ἀγωνίζεσθαι, ἆθλα μὲν ὁ ἄρχων προτίθησιν, ἀθροίζειν δὲ αὐτοὺς προστέτακται χορηγοῖς καὶ ἄλλοις διδάσκειν, καὶ ἀνάγκην προστιθέναι τοῖς ἐνδεῶς τι ποιοῦσιν.
[2] Dem. Meid. § 61.
[3] Plutarch Nicias p. 524 D.
[4] Dem. Meid. §§ 58–66; Andocid. Alcibiad. § 20.

called the Proagon. It took place in the Odeum, a sort of smaller theatre to the south of the Acropolis, not far from the theatre of Dionysus. The Proagon was a kind of show or spectacle, and served as an introduction to the actual performances at the festival. Each of the tragic poets who were about to compete in the approaching contest appeared upon the stage in the presence of the people, accompanied by his choregus, his actors, and the members of the chorus. All of them wore crowns upon their heads; but the actors were without their masks and their stage dresses. As they paraded upon the stage some announcement was made to the people, of which the exact nature is not known. But it is very likely that this occasion was taken for making known to the people the names of the poet and his actors, together with the titles of the tragedies shortly to be performed, and other information of a similar character. At the same time the people would have an opportunity of becoming acquainted with poets and actors who were making their first appearance. The splendour of the dresses of choruses and choregi, upon which great sums of money were spent, would make a spectacle of some magnificence, and appeal to the popular taste. At the Proagon which followed shortly after the death of Euripides it is said that Sophocles appeared upon the stage in a dark-coloured dress, and introduced his actors and chorus without the usual crowns. It is nowhere definitely stated that the comic and dithyrambic poets and choruses took part in the Proagon. But the whole of our information about the ceremony is derived from one or two brief and casual notices, in which very few details are given. It is hardly probable that only tragedy should have been represented. The magnificence of the spectacle would be very much increased by the large and gorgeously-dressed choruses of boys and men[1].

On the evening before the festival the statue of the god Dionysus was taken out of his temple by the Ephebi, and

---

[1] Our knowledge of the Proagon is derived from the following passages:— Schol. Aeschin. Ctesiph. § 67 ἐγίγνοντο πρὸ τῶν μεγάλων Διονυσίων ἡμέραις ὀλίγαις ἔμπροσθεν ἐν τῷ ᾠδείῳ καλουμένῳ τῶν τραγῳδῶν ἀγὼν καὶ ἐπίδειξις ὧν

conveyed by torchlight to the theatre. It was there placed in the orchestra, in full view of the stage, so that the god might enjoy the approaching exhibitions as well as his worshippers[1]. This curious ceremony, of which the existence has only lately been discovered from inscriptions, gives additional appropriateness to the selection of Dionysus in the Frogs as the representative of dramatic criticism at Athens. He was the one spectator who had been present at every dramatic performance from first to last. The ceremony is often referred to by later writers in the course of their denunciations of the gladiatorial shows with which the theatre at Athens had come to be polluted. The blood of human beings, they say, is shed in the very orchestra which the god Dionysus occasionally visits; and he is implored not to come near the scene of such defilement[2].

During the period of the actual contests the audience met in

μέλλουσι δραμάτων ἀγωνίζεσθαι ἐν τῷ θεάτρῳ δι' ὃ ἐτύμως προάγων καλεῖται. εἰσίασι δὲ δίχα προσώπων οἱ ὑποκριταὶ γυμνοί. Vita Euripid. λέγουσι δὲ καὶ Σοφοκλέα, ἀκούσαντα ὅτι ἐτελεύτησε, αὐτὸν μὲν ἱματίῳ φαιῷ ἤτοι πορφυρῷ προελθεῖν, τὸν δὲ χορὸν καὶ τοὺς ὑποκριτὰς ἀστεφανώτους εἰσαγαγεῖν ἐν τῷ προάγωνι, καὶ δακρῦσαι τὸν δῆμον. Aeschin. Ctesiph. §§ 66, 67 ὁ γὰρ μισαλέξανδρος νυνὶ φάσκων εἶναι ... γράφει ψήφισμα ... ἐκκλησίαν ποιεῖν τοὺς πρυτάνεις τῇ ὀγδόῃ ἱσταμένου τοῦ ἐλαφηβολιῶνος μηνός, ὅτ' ἦν τῷ Ἀσκληπιῷ ἡ θυσία καὶ ὁ προάγων. Schol. Aristoph. Wasps 1104 οἱ δ' ἐν ᾠδείῳ ἐστὶ τόπος θεατροειδής, ἐν ᾧ εἰώθασι τὰ ποιήματα ἀπαγγέλλειν πρὶν τῆς εἰς τὸ θέατρον ἀπαγγελίας. That the Proagon was a contest is out of the question. The contest was to follow some days later. Nor can it have been a dress rehearsal, as part of one day would not have sufficed for the rehearsal of twelve tragedies and five comedies. Προάγων denotes 'the ceremony before the contest,' just as πρόγαμος means 'the ceremony before the marriage.' The word ἀπαγγέλλειν, in the note of the Scholiast on the Wasps, must denote some announcement about the plays, and not an actual performance of them. That there was a Proagon before the Lenaea as well as the City Dionysia seems natural in itself, and is implied by the use of the plural in such inscriptions as Corp. Inscr. Att. ii. 307 ἐπετέλεσε δὲ καὶ τοὺς προάγωνας τοὺς ἐν τοῖς ἱεροῖς κ.τ.λ. The passage in Plato's Symposium 194 A (ἐπιλήσμων μέντ' ἂν εἴην, ὦ Ἀγάθων, ... εἰ ἰδὼν τὴν σὴν ἀνδρείαν καὶ μεγαλοφροσύνην ἀναβαίνοντος ἐπὶ τὸν ὀκρίβαντα μετὰ τῶν ὑποκριτῶν καὶ βλέψαντος ἐναντία τοσούτῳ θεάτρῳ, μέλλοντος ἐπιδείξεσθαι σαυτοῦ λόγους, καὶ οὐδ' ὑπωστιοῦν ἐκπλαγέντος κ.τ.λ.) probably refers to the Proagon.

[1] Corp. Inscr. Att. iv. 470, 471.
[2] Philostrat. vit. Apoll. iv. 22 (vol. i., p. 142, ed. Kayser); Dio Chrysostom. xxxi. § 121 (631 R). The discovery of the practice of placing the statue of Dionysus in the orchestra explains the passage in Aristoph. Equit. 535, 536 (ὃν χρῆν διὰ τὰς προτέρας νίκας πίνειν ἐν τῷ πρυτανείῳ, | καὶ μὴ ληρεῖν, ἀλλὰ θεᾶσθαι λιπαρὸν παρὰ τῷ Διονύσῳ) which previously caused some difficulty.

the theatre every morning soon after daybreak. Considering the number of plays which had to be produced, it was necessary that the proceedings should begin at an early hour[1]. The vast gathering of spectators, like all public meetings at Athens, was first of all purified by the offer of a small sacrifice. Then libations were poured in front of the statue of the god Dionysus[2]. If the festival was the City Dionysia, before the tragedies began the opportunity was taken to proclaim the names of citizens upon whom crowns had been bestowed, together with the services for which they had been granted. The proclamation before such a vast multitude of citizens was naturally considered a very great honour. During the period of Athenian supremacy another striking ceremony preceded the tragedies at the City Dionysia. The tribute collected from the dependent states was divided into talents, and solemnly deposited in the orchestra. Then the orphans whose fathers had been killed in battle, and who had been educated by the state, and had now reached the age of manhood, were brought forward upon the stage equipped in complete armour. The herald made a proclamation, recounting what the state had done for them, and they were then publicly discharged from state control to take their place as ordinary citizens[3]. After these preliminaries had been gone through the dramatic performances commenced. The order in which the different plays were to be performed was determined by lot. Each poet, as his turn came, was summoned by name by the public herald and ordered to produce his play. The phrase employed seems to have been 'lead in your chorus.' But it is not likely that the poet appeared in person at the head of his chorus. And in fact most plays began with speeches from the stage, and the chorus only came in later on. The phrase was an old formula, applicable to the times when tragedy and comedy were mainly lyrical, and the poet was the chief actor and led in

---

[1] Aeschin. Ctesiph. § 76 ἅμα τῇ ἡμέρᾳ ἡγεῖτο τοῖς πρίσβεσιν εἰς τὸ θέατρον. Demosth. Meid. § 74.
[2] Suidas v. καθάρσιον; Pollux viii. 104; Plut. Cimon p. 483 E; Philostrat. vit. Apoll. iv. 22.
[3] Aeschin. Ctesiph. §§ 48, 153, 154, 230, 231; Isocrates περὶ εἰρήνης § 82.

his chorus in person. It was retained after its literal significance had become obsolete[1]. The summons to each poet was accompanied in later times by the blowing of a trumpet. The object was to ensure that the performers should be ready at the proper time. On one occasion an actor called Hermon had left the building, expecting that his comedy would come on late. But as it was called for sooner than he expected, there was a hitch in the proceedings owing to his absence. The blowing of the trumpet was therefore instituted to mark the commencement of each new performance, and let people in the neighbourhood of the theatre know at what rate the contest was progressing[2]. The order in which the poets competed was determined by lot, as stated above. It was considered an advantage to be drawn last, as the latest performance left the most vivid impression upon the minds of the judges. This would be especially the case in such competitions as lasted over three days. The Ecclesiazusae of Aristophanes was drawn first for performance. The poet therefore, in the course of this play, implores the judges not to let the ballot damage his chances, but to judge the choruses on their merits, unlike the courtesans, who forget all except their latest lovers[3].

At the end of each competition the judges wrote their verdicts upon tablets. Five of these tablets were drawn by lot, and decided the result. The names of the victorious poet and choregus were then proclaimed by the herald, and they were crowned with a chaplet of ivy in the presence of the spectators. At the conclusion of the festival the successful poet celebrated his victory by a solemn sacrifice, followed by a grand banquet, at which most of his friends were present. The members of the chorus were also there, and probably the choregus and the actors. The scene of Plato's Symposium is

---

[1] Aristid. περὶ ῥητορικῆς vol. ii. p. 2 (Dindf.). Aristoph. Acharn. 11 ὁ δ' ἀνεῖπεν, εἴσαγ', ὦ Θέογνι, τὸν χορόν. The passage from Philochorus (Athen. p. 464 E καὶ τοῖς χοροῖς εἰσιοῦσιν ἐνέχεον πίνειν καὶ διηγωνισμένοις ὅτ' ἐξεπορεύοντο ἐνέχεον πάλιν) affords no warrant for assuming, with Müller (Griech. Bühnen. p. 373), that before the commencement of each play the poet and his chorus entered the orchestra and offered a libation to Dionysus.

[2] Pollux iv. 88.

[3] Aristoph. Eccles. 1154 ff.

laid in Agathon's house the day after the banquet in honour of his first tragic victory. Socrates had avoided the banquet itself, because of the crush of people, but came next day to a more private gathering. A victory, especially at the City Dionysia, was regarded as a splendid distinction. On one occasion Ion of Chios, after winning the first prize in both the tragic and the dithyrambic contests at the same festival, showed the extent of his joy by making a present of a jar of Chian wine to every Athenian citizen[1].

The next day but one after the conclusion of the City Dionysia a special assembly of the people was convened in the theatre of Dionysus to discuss matters connected with the festival. No doubt a similar assembly was held after the Lenaea, though the fact is nowhere actually stated. At this assembly the conduct of the archon, who had had the management of the festival which was just over, was taken into consideration. Any neglect of his duties, or any unfairness in the choice of poets and actors, would be punished. At the same time crowns and other distinctions were voted in honour of officials who had performed their duties in connexion with the festival satisfactorily. It has been pointed out that the judges in the dramatic and dithyrambic contests were liable to prosecution and punishment if they were suspected of dishonesty in their verdicts. Probably such charges were brought forward and decided at this assembly in the theatre. Then came the hearing of complaints as to any violation of the sanctity of the festival. It was illegal during the days of the festival to make distraints upon debtors. All assaults and offences against the person, however trifling in themselves, were regarded as sacrilege if they were committed during the festival. Complaints of this kind were brought forward at the assembly in the theatre, and a special procedure called the Probolê was adopted in regard to them. The aggrieved person stated his charges before the assembled people: the defendant made his reply: the people then proceeded to vote. If they acquitted the

---

[1] Plat. Symp. 173 A, 174 A; Athen. p. 3 F; Schol. Aristoph. Pax 835.

defendant there was an end of the matter. But if they voted against him the prosecutor then carried the case before the ordinary law-courts, where of course the previous verdict of the people weighed very much in his favour[1].

§ 7. *Reproduction of Old Plays.*

The process of bringing out a play at Athens has now been traced from first to last, from the selection of the poet by the archon to the meeting of the people in the theatre at the conclusion of the festival. Hitherto only the production of new and original plays has been discussed. The reproduction of old plays is a matter of some interest in connexion with the history of the drama. At Athens, during the great period of the Attic drama, plays were exhibited once, and once only. A repetition of the same play was a most exceptional occurrence. The theatre was large enough to contain the whole body of the citizens: every man had a chance of seeing a play when it was first brought out; and there was not therefore any need for it to be repeated in order to give a fresh audience a chance of witnessing it. The Athenians were fond of novelty. Aristophanes, in the Clouds, takes credit to himself for his originality, and for his cleverness in never introducing the same plot twice over[2]. This love of novelty prevented the repetition or reproduction of old plays at Athens, as long as there was an unfailing supply of new ones. And during the flourishing period of the drama there was never any lack of productive talent. The number of poets, both in tragedy and comedy, was more than sufficient to supply the demand for new dramas. Hence, after a play had been once performed, unless it was of very exceptional merit, it was never seen again, as far as the Athenian stage was concerned. It is stated on the authority of Dicaearchus that the Frogs of Aristophanes 'was so much admired on account of its parabasis that it was actually repeated[3].'

---

[1] Demosth. Meid. §§ 8–10; Corp. Inscr. Att. ii. 114, 307, 420.

[2] Aristoph. Nub. 545–548.

[3] Arg. Aristoph. Ran, οὕτω δὲ ἐθαυμάσθη τὸ δρᾶμα διὰ τὴν ἐν αὐτῷ παράβασιν ὥστε καὶ ἀνεδιδάχθη, ὥς φησι Δικαίαρχος.

The language here used implies that such a repetition was a very unusual occurrence. It is true that when the Capture of Miletus, the historical play of Phrynichus, caused such a commotion in the theatre, the Athenians are said to have passed a law that 'for the future no one should exhibit this drama [1].' But the law must have referred to its reproduction at the Rural Dionysia. It has already been pointed out that it was customary to bring out in the rural demes plays which had been successful in Athens; and by the time of Phrynichus it is probable that many of the more important demes, especially those in the immediate neighbourhood of Athens, had their dramatic contests. The decree about the Capture of Miletus must have referred to these rural festivals. The statement of Dicaearchus makes it perfectly plain that in Athens itself, during the fifth century, a play was never repeated, unless it was of unusual merit, and the people specially demanded its reproduction.

Even successful plays then were only exhibited once. But if a play was unsuccessful, the poet was allowed to revise and rewrite it, and to compete with it again in its improved shape [2]. The revision of unsuccessful plays seems to have been a common practice with the Athenian dramatic writers. It is mentioned as rather a peculiarity in the comic poet Anaxandrides, that when one of his comedies was unsuccessful, he used to destroy it at once, without taking the trouble to revise it, and try his fortunes with it a second time [3]. Many plays were revised and re-exhibited in this manner, and in consequence many plays existed in ancient times in a double form. The Thyestes, the Phineus, the Tyro, and the Lemnian Women of Sophocles were all exhibited a second time in an improved shape. The Hippolytus of Euripides which we at present possess is a revised edition pruned of its original defects. The Autolycus and Phrixus of Euripides also existed in a double form. The Clouds of Aristophanes in its original shape was very unsuccessful, and was altered in many important particulars

---

[1] Herod. vi. 21.
[2] A revised edition of a play was called διασκευή, Athen. p. 110 C.
[3] Athen. p. 374 A.

before it reached the form in which we now possess it. Among the other plays of Aristophanes, the Peace, the Plutus, and the Thesmophoriazusae were brought out a second time in a revised form. Instances of the revision of plays are not uncommon among the writers of the Middle and New Comedy. Sometimes the original title was retained in the revised version, as for instance in the Heiress of Menander. Sometimes a new title was adopted. Thus the Braggart Captain of Diphilus appeared subsequently as the Eunuch[1].

It seems then that during the fifth century the dramatic competitions at Athens were limited to new plays, or to plays which had been so far altered and revised as to be equivalent to new ones. The one exception to the rule was in the case of Aeschylus. In the Life of Aeschylus it is said that the Athenians felt such an admiration for him, that they passed a decree after his death that any one who offered to exhibit his plays should receive a chorus from the archon. This does not mean that his plays were to be performed as a mere isolated exhibition, apart from the regular contests. Such a reproduction of old plays appears to have been unknown at Athens during the fifth century. The meaning is that any person might be allowed to compete at the ordinary tragic contests with plays of Aeschylus instead of new plays of his own. If any one offered to do so, the archon was bound to give him a chorus. He would then take his place as one of the three competing poets; but while his rivals exhibited new and original tragedies, he would confine himself to reproducing tragedies of Aeschylus. Probably the men who undertook these revivals were in most cases celebrated actors. In this way the plays of Aeschylus were often brought into competition with the plays of later writers, and appear to have been generally successful. Philostratus refers

---

[1] Arg. to Aristoph. Nub., Pax; Arg. Eurip. Hippolytus. For the facts about the other plays see Nauck's Frag. Trag. Graec. pp. 146, 170, 217, 226, 350, 492; and Meineke's Frag. Com. Graec. ii. 1074, 1130, iv. 116, 377. Additional instances of revision of plays are to be found in the Autolycus of Eupolis, the Synoris of Diphilus, and the Phryx of Alexis. The Demetrius of Alexis appeared subsequently as the Philetaerus, the Ἄγροικοι of Antiphanes as the Butalion. See Meineke's Frag. Com. Graec. ii. 440, iii. 36, 403, 500, iv. 412.

to the custom[1]. He says that the Athenians invited Aeschylus after his death to the festivals of Dionysus, and that his plays were acted over again, and were victorious a second time. This passage makes it quite clear that the tragedies of Aeschylus were exhibited in the ordinary contests, and not as a separate performance by themselves. There is a reference in the beginning of the Acharnians to a competition of this kind. Dicaeopolis had come to the theatre to see the tragic contests. He was expecting that the performance would commence with plays of Aeschylus; but to his disgust the frigid Theognis was the first to be called upon. Here then is a picture of a contest in which the tragic poet Theognis was opposed by a competitor who exhibited, not plays of his own, but plays of Aeschylus[2]. It is to the practice of reproducing his plays after his death that Aeschylus alludes in the Frogs, when he remarks that his poetry has not died with him, like that of Euripides. Quintilian refers to the same custom, though his language is not quite accurate. He says that the tragedies of Aeschylus were sublime, but rough and unfinished; and therefore the Athenians permitted subsequent poets to polish and revise them, and exhibit them at the competitions in their amended form; and in this way many of his plays won the prize. This story of the revision of the plays of Aeschylus by subsequent poets is not confirmed by anything in the Greek authorities, nor is it probable in itself. In the fourth century a law was passed providing for the preservation of the exact original text of the plays of Aeschylus, Sophocles, and Euripides. It is hardly likely that the Athenians of the fifth century should have been less conservative about the text of Aeschylus than the Athenians of the fourth, to whose taste Aeschylus had begun to seem antiquated. It is most probable therefore that the story of the subsequent correction of the plays is a mistake of Quintilian's[3].

From this reproduction of old plays of Aeschylus must be carefully distinguished those instances where plays, which

[1] Philostrat. vit. Apoll. vi. 11 (vol. i. p. 220, ed. Kayser).
[2] Aristoph. Acharn. 9–12.
[3] Aristoph. Ran. 868, 869; Quintil. Inst. x. 1. 66; Plut. X orat. 841 F.

Aeschylus had left unpublished at his death, were produced for the first time by his son Euphorion. It is said that Euphorion won four victories with his father's unpublished tragedies. In a similar manner the Oedipus Coloneus of Sophocles was produced for the first time by his grandson four years after the poet's death. And after the death of Euripides, his Iphigeneia in Aulis, Alcmaeon, and Bacchae were brought out by his son at the City Dionysia. On such occasions as these, when a poet's unpublished plays were exhibited by a relative after his death, although no doubt the real authorship of the plays was perfectly well known at the time, the relative appeared as the nominal author. He asked for a chorus from the archon in his own name. The plays he produced were new ones. There is therefore no similarity between instances of this kind, and those occasions when a man asked for a chorus, not in his own name, but in order to produce old plays of Aeschylus[1].

At Athens then during the fifth century the reproduction of old plays was confined to tragedies of Aeschylus, and remarkably successful dramas such as the Frogs of Aristophanes. Otherwise when a play had been once exhibited on the Athenian stage, it was relegated to the Rural Dionysia. It was not till the fourth century that the reproduction of old plays developed into a regular custom. The practice was at first confined to tragedy. This branch of the drama had passed beyond the period of healthy growth, and already showed symptoms of decay. The three great tragic poets of the fifth century had in their several lines exhausted the capabilities of Attic tragedy. Their successors were mostly feeble imitators of Euripides. Under such circumstances the tendency to fall back upon the old tragedies naturally became more and more frequent. The reproductions were of two kinds, as was pointed out in the last chapter. Sometimes an old tragedy was exhibited by itself, as a prelude to the new tragedies. This was the case at the City Dionysia in the latter

---

[1] Suidas v. Εὐφορίων; Arg. Soph. Oed. Col.; Schol. Aristoph. Ran. 67.

part of the fourth century. Sometimes a number of old tragedies were performed in competition by different actors. In such cases the prize was given to the best actor, and not to the best tragedy. The tragic contests at the Lenaea in later times were probably of this kind. Very few details are known as to the management of these reproductions. Probably the leading actors applied to the archon, and if selected by him they received a chorus, and undertook the general superintendence of the revival. The middle of the fourth century was the great age of Athenian acting. The principal actors of the period filled a more important place in the history of tragedy than did the tragic poets themselves. The different interpretations of the old tragedies by the celebrated actors excited more interest than the feeble productions of the contemporary dramatists. Apparently the actors were sometimes inclined to tamper with the old plays, and to introduce what they considered improvements, just as the plays of Shakespeare were adapted for the stage by Garrick in the last century. A law was passed by the orator Lycurgus to put a stop to this practice. It was enacted that a public copy should be made of the works of Aeschylus, Sophocles, and Euripides, and deposited in the state archives; and that the actors, in their performances, should not be allowed to deviate from the text of the copy[1]. It is very probable that this authorised version eventually found its way to Alexandria. Ptolemy the Third was a great collector of manuscripts. He borrowed from the Athenians an old copy of the works of Aeschylus, Sophocles, and Euripides, promising to return it after he had made a transcript, and depositing fifteen talents as security. The transcript was made in the best possible style. Ptolemy then proceeded to keep the original manuscript for himself, and sent back merely the transcript to Athens. The

[1] Plut. X orat. 841 F εἰσήνεγκε δὲ καὶ νόμους ... τὸν δέ, ὡς χαλκᾶς εἰκόνας ἀναθεῖναι τῶν ποιητῶν, Αἰσχύλου, Σοφοκλέους, Εὐριπίδου, καὶ τὰς τραγῳδίας αὐτῶν ἐν κοινῷ γραψαμένους φυλάττειν, καὶ τὸν τῆς πόλεως γραμματέα παραναγιγνώσκειν τοῖς ὑποκρινομένοις· οὐκ ἐξεῖναι γὰρ αὐτὰς ὑποκρίνεσθαι. The general meaning of the passage is clear, though the text is corrupt. Various emendations have been proposed, e. g. παρ' αὐτὰς ὑποκρίνεσθαι, Wyttenbach; αὐτὰς ἄλλως ὑποκρίνεσθαι, Grysar; γὰρ ἄλλως ὑποκρίνεσθαι, Dübner.

Athenians had to console themselves with the fifteen talents which were forfeited. This old copy of the tragic writers was most probably that made in accordance with the law of Lycurgus[1].

Athenian comedy, as was pointed out in the last chapter, continued to grow and develop long after tragedy had come to an end. Reproductions of old comedies at Athens do not seem to have become prevalent till towards the end of the third century. As far as our information goes such reproductions were confined to the exhibition of a single old comedy as a prelude to the new ones. In all the instances recorded the plays are taken from the New Comedy. The Old Comedy, with its special and personal allusions, would have been unsuited for popular representation in a later age[2].

To return once more to tragedy. The fourth century was especially the age of great actors, just as the fifth century had been the age of great poets. The leading actors of the fourth century were chiefly celebrated for their impersonations of characters out of the great tragedies of the past. From the frequent references to the subject it is possible to collect some interesting details as to the popular taste in regard to these revivals. The three great masters of tragedy, Aeschylus, Sophocles, and Euripides, occupied a position by themselves in popular estimation, and quite overshadowed all other poets. This is proved by the law of Lycurgus providing for the strict preservation of the text of their works, and prohibiting the interpolations of the actors. But though the existence of the law shows that the tragedies of Aeschylus were occasionally reproduced, and were therefore liable to corruption, it does not appear that in this later age Aeschylus was very popular upon the stage. The only allusion to a particular revival of his plays is that which occurs in one of the letters of Alciphron, where the tragic actor Licymnius is said to have been victorious in the Propompi of Aeschylus[3]. On the other hand the reproductions of plays of Sophocles and Euripides are very

---

[1] Galen Comm. ii. on Hippocrat. Epidem. iii. (p. 607 Kühn).
[2] See chap. I, p. 32.
[3] Alciphron Epist. iii. 48.

frequently referred to. And it is a significant fact that when the actor Satyrus was consoling Demosthenes for the ill-success of his first speech before the assembly, and wished to point out to him the defectiveness of his elocution, he asked him to repeat 'a speech out of Sophocles or Euripides,' implying that these were the two poets whom everyone knew[1]. In the Poetics of Aristotle the laws of the drama are based upon the plays of Sophocles and Euripides, while Aeschylus is comparatively disregarded. The simplicity of his plots, and the elevation and occasional obscurity of his language were distasteful to an age which looked for ingenuity in the management of the incidents, and rhetorical facility in the style. These qualities were found to perfection in Euripides: hence his great popularity. There can be no doubt that Euripides was the favourite poet of the fourth century. A striking proof of the fact is supplied by the records of the tragic performances at the City Dionysia for the years 341–339 B.C. In each of these years the old tragedy selected for exhibition was one by Euripides. In 341 it was the Iphigeneia, in 340 it was the Orestes. The title of the play produced in 339 is lost, but the author was Euripides[2]. Other plays of his which were favourites upon the stage at this time were the Cresphontes, the Oenomaus, and the Hecuba, in all of which Aeschines is said to have played the part of tritagonist. The Oenomaus and the Hecuba are also mentioned as plays in which the great actor Theodorus was especially effective. In the dream of Thrasyllus before the battle of Arginusae the plays which were being acted were the Phoenissae and the Supplices of Euripides[3]. Though the story of the dream is apocryphal, these two tragedies were doubtless popular ones during the fourth century. As to the plays of Sophocles, it is said that Polus, the contemporary of Demosthenes, and the greatest actor of his time, was celebrated for his performance of the leading parts in the Oedipus Tyrannus, the Oedipus Coloneus, and the Electra. The Antigone of Sophocles was often acted

---

[1] Plut. Demosth. p. 849 A.
[2] Corp. Inscr. Att. ii. 973.
[3] Demosth. de Cor. §§ 180, 267;

Aelian Var. Hist. xiv. 40; Plut. Fort. Alexand. 333 F; Diod. Sic. xiii. 97.

by Theodorus and by Aristodemus. A certain Timotheus used to make a great impression in the part of Ajax. Lastly, the Epigoni of Sophocles is mentioned in connexion with Andronicus, another contemporary of Demosthenes[1]. It is interesting to observe that of the plays which the popular taste of the fourth century had begun to select for revival by far the greater number are among those which are still extant.

[1] Aul. Gell. vii. 5; Stob. Flor. 97, 28 (ii. p. 211 Meineke); Demosth. Fals. Leg. § 246; Schol. Soph. Ajax 865; Athen. p. 584 D.

Collotype. Oxford University Press.

THEATRE OF DIONYSUS, FROM THE SOUTH.
Copied by permission of the Council of the Hellenic Society from a photograph
published for the Hellenic Society by the Autotype Company.

CHAPTER III.

THE THEATRE.

§ 1. *General character of a Greek theatre.*

THE regulations concerning the dramatic competitions at Athens have now been described in detail, together with the circumstances attending the production of a play. The next point to be considered is the construction and general arrangement of the theatre. It would be beyond the scope of the present work to attempt to give any account of all the Greek theatres of which remains are in existence. In the following pages our attention will be confined mainly to the theatre of Dionysus at Athens, which will serve as a specimen of the Greek type of theatre in general. The theatre at Athens, whether regarded from the historical or the architectural point of view, is one of the most interesting buildings in the world. It was the prototype of all other ancient theatres, both Greek and Roman. It was the theatre in which the plays of the great Athenian dramatists, from Aeschylus to Menander, were produced. In connexion with a building of such importance the smallest details are not without interest. The object of the chapter will be, in the first place, to give an account of the existing remains and present condition of this theatre; and, in the second place, to endeavour to determine what must have been its original form and appearance during the great days of the Attic drama, before the primitive design had been obscured by later alterations. At the same time it will be necessary to make occasional references to other Greek theatres, both for the purpose of illustration and comparison, and also in order to fill up the gaps in our information caused by the ruinous condition of the Athenian theatre. Of the other theatres, the most interesting is that of Epidaurus. It is by far the best preserved of all theatres of purely Greek origin. It has lately been excavated in a thorough and systematic manner, and the result of the excavations has been to throw an altogether new light upon various questions connected with the Greek stage.

The construction and general arrangement of a Greek theatre differed widely from any form of theatre to be found at the present day. In this respect, as in most others, a comparison between the ancient and modern drama reveals as many points of contrast as of similarity. The Greek theatre was of course exposed to the open air, and had no roof or covering of any kind. It was generally built upon the slope of a hill in or near the city. It was of enormous magnitude, compared with a modern theatre, being intended to contain at one and the same time the whole theatre-going population of the city. The largest part of it consisted of the auditorium, or tiers of stone seats for the spectators. These seats rose one above the other like a flight of steps, and were arranged in the form of a semi-circle with the two ends prolonged. The flat space at the bottom of the auditorium, corresponding to the stalls and pit in a modern theatre, was called the orchestra, or 'dancing-place,' and was used by the chorus only, the spectators being entirely excluded from it. At the further end of the orchestra, facing the tiers of seats, rose the stage and the stage-buildings. The stage was a long and narrow platform, much higher than a modern stage, and only a few feet in depth. It was reserved for the actors, as opposed to the chorus. Thus it is obvious that the general spectacle presented by the interior of a Greek theatre during the representation of a drama must have been quite unlike anything we are accustomed to in modern times. The open-air building, the performance in broad daylight, the vast crowds of spectators, the chorus grouped together in the centre, the actors standing on the lofty stage behind them—all these characteristics of a Greek theatrical exhibition must have combined to produce a scene to which there is no exact parallel at the present day. This fact should be kept clearly in view, in discussing all questions connected with the Greek stage. Many errors have been caused, and many unnecessary difficulties have been raised, owing to the failure to realise the essential difference between the external features of the ancient and the modern drama.

§ 2. *The old wooden theatres at Athens.*

The type of theatre described above was of course only developed very gradually by the Athenians. It came into existence side by side with the growth of their drama. At first there was no permanent theatre. Attic tragedy and comedy grew out of the dithyrambs and phallic songs which were performed by choruses in honour of Dionysus. For such exhibitions all that was required was an orchestra, or circular dancing-place. The chorus performed in the middle, the spectators ranged themselves all round the ring. The first innovation was the introduction of the table upon which the leader of the chorus took his stand, while he carried on a dialogue with the rest of the choreutae in the intervals between the choral odes[1]. As the dialogue between the leader and the chorus was the germ out of which the drama was subsequently developed, in the same way the table on which the leader took his stand was the prototype of the stage in the later Greek theatre. The next step was the introduction of a single actor by Thespis. The actor had to play many parts in succession, and it was necessary that he should have some room or covered place to change his dress and mask in. A tent or booth was erected for the purpose at the back of the small platform on which he performed. Out of this tent or booth were gradually developed the stage-buildings of the Greek theatre. The recollection of their origin was preserved in their name. Even in the latest times, when the stage-buildings of a Greek theatre had come to

---

[1] Poll. iv. 123 ἐλεὸς δ᾽ ἦν τράπεζα ἀρχαία, ἐφ᾽ ἣν πρὸ Θέσπιδος εἶς τις ἀναβὰς τοῖς χορευταῖς ἀπεκρίνατο.

be elaborate structures of stone, they were still called by the name 'skênê,' which means properly a booth or tent. The platform and dressing-room for the actor, having now become a regular accompaniment of a dramatic performance, occupied one end of the original orchestra. The spectators, who had formerly been ranged all round the circle in which the chorus was performing, had to confine themselves to two-thirds of that circle. The remaining portion was taken up by the stage. At this early period the seats provided for the spectators were only temporary erections. They were called 'ikria,' and consisted of wooden benches rising in tiers one above the other, and resting on wooden supports [1]. The stage and the dressing-rooms were also mere temporary constructions of wood. But in these rude erections, hastily put up each year for the annual performances, were already to be found all the essential parts of the later Greek theatres. Nothing more was required than to change the material from wood to stone, and to introduce greater elaboration into the design. In course of time the booth and platform of the Thespian period were developed into imposing stage-buildings; the wooden benches became permanent amphitheatres of stone.

In this sketch of the early history of the Greek theatre one point deserves especial notice. The <u>most important part</u> of the whole building, and that which formed the starting-point in the process of development, <u>was the orchestra</u>, or place for the chorus. The auditorium and the stage-buildings were only later additions. In all theatres of purely Greek origin the orchestra continued to maintain its prominent position. All the other parts were subordinated to it. The general conception of a Greek theatre was that of a building with a circular dancing-place in the centre, and with tiers of seats arranged round two-thirds of the ring, while the remaining side was occupied by the stage. The result of this arrangement was that all the spec-

---

[1] Hesych. v. παρ' αἰγείρου θέα· ... τὰ ἴκρια, ἅ ἐστιν ὀρθὰ ξύλα, ἔχοντα σανίδας προσδεδεμένας, οἷον βαθμούς, ἐφ' αἷς ἐκαθέζοντο πρὸ τοῦ κατασκευασθῆναι τὸ θέατρον. Cp. also Bekk. Anecd. p. 354; Hesych. and Suidas v. ἴκρια; Eustath. Od. p. 1472.

tators had an equally good view of the orchestra, and the chorus performing in it; while many of them had only a very poor view of the stage. In theatres built under Roman influence this was not so much the case. The arrangements were considerably modified. The orchestra and auditorium were restricted in size to a semicircle[1]. The consequence was that the stage became a much more prominent object, and all the spectators had a fairly good view of it. But in purely Greek theatres, which were built as much for choral performances as for dramatic ones, the orchestra was always the principal object of attention. The primary purpose of the whole design was to give every member of the audience a clear and direct view of the orchestra. The view on to the stage was a matter of secondary importance.

It was not till the fifth century that the Athenians felt the need of a permanent stone theatre. Before that time they were content with the wooden erections just described. As to the place in which the early dramatic performances were held, two distinct traditions have been preserved. According to one set of notices they were held in the market-place; according to the other set they were held in the Lenaeum, the sacred enclosure of Dionysus to the south-east of the Acropolis[2]. It seems unnecessary to choose between these two statements. It is most probable that both of them are true, and that dramatic performances were held in each of the places mentioned. The Lenaeum would of course be the most appropriate scene for such performances, being sacred to Dionysus, in whose worship the drama originated. It was in fact in the Lenaeum that the stone theatre was subsequently built. But the market-place was also in any Greek city a natural place for exhibitions of various kinds. Plato, referring to his ideal city, lays down the law that tragic poets shall not be allowed to 'erect their stages in the

---

[1] All theatres, in which the orchestra consists of an exact semicircle, are either Roman, or built under Roman influence. See Vitruv. v. 6, 7.

[2] They were held in the market-place according to Phot. v. ἴκρια, Eustath. Od. p. 1472; in the Lenaeum according to Hesych. v. ἐπὶ Ληναίῳ ἀγών, Phot. v. Λήναιον, Bekk. Anecd. p. 278.

market-place[1].' There seems therefore to be no reason to doubt that in early times at Athens dramatic representations were given in the market-place as well as in the Lenaeum. The exact site of the primitive performances in the Lenaeum has probably been discovered by Dr. Dörpfeld. In the course of his recent excavations in the theatre of Dionysus he has come across the remains of an old orchestra some yards to the south-east of the orchestra of the existing theatre[2]. This old orchestra was doubtless the scene of the exhibitions of Thespis and his immediate successors. It appears also that in early times there was a regular orchestra in the market-place. In the course of the fifth century this orchestra disappeared, but the portion of the market-place in which it had originally stood continued to be called The Orchestra at a much later period. In Plato's time books were sold there. Socrates, in his Apology, remarks that any one could buy the works of Anaxagoras in The Orchestra for a drachma[3]. It was here no doubt that in early times, while the orchestra was still in existence, dramatic representations were occasionally given. There was an old proverb in use at Athens, which the commentators explained by a reference to the primitive drama. A bad seat at any spectacle was called 'the view from the poplar.' It was said that at the old dramatic exhibitions the wooden benches for the spectators reached as far as a certain poplar, and that the people who could not get seats on the benches used to scramble up the poplar[4]. Whether the poplar was supposed to be in the Lenaeum or the market-place is uncertain. The whole story

[1] Plat. Legg. 817 C.
[2] Dr. Dörpfeld, in a letter of Nov. 7th, 1888, writes to me as follows: 'Von der alten Orchestra ist ein Stück, aus polygonalen Kalk-Steinen erbaut, erhalten. Der Mittelpunkt dieser alten Kreisrunden Orchestra liegt von dem Mittelpunkt der Lykurgischen Orchestra einige Meter weiter nach Südost.'
[3] Phot. v. ὀρχήστρα, πρῶτον ἐκλήθη ἐν τῇ ἀγορᾷ. Timaeus Lex. Plat. v. ὀρχήστρα· τόπος ἐπιφανὴς εἰς πανήγυριν, ἔνθα Ἁρμοδίου καὶ Ἀριστογείτονος εἰ-κόνες. The statues of Harmodius and Aristogeiton were in the market-place: cp. Rangabé, ii. 565 εἰκόνα στῆσαι ... ἐν ἀγορᾷ πλὴν παρ' Ἁρμόδιον καὶ Ἀριστογείτονα. See Wachsmuth die Stadt Athen, p. 170. The passage in Plato's Apology (p. 26 D) doubtless refers to the orchestra in the market-place, and not to that in the theatre.
[4] Eustath. Od. p. 1472; Suidas v. ἀπ' αἰγείρου θέα; Hesych. vv. αἰγείρου θέα, παρ' αἰγείρου θέα, θέα παρ' αἰγείρῳ.

has a rather suspicious appearance, and was very likely mere guesswork, invented to account for a current proverbial expression.

§ 3. *History of the Theatre of Dionysus.*

The determination of the Athenians to build a stone theatre was due to an accident at one of their dramatic performances. In the year 499 the competitors in the tragic contest were Pratinas, Choerilus, and Aeschylus. While Pratinas was exhibiting, the wooden benches for the spectators collapsed. In order to avoid such dangers in the future it was resolved to build a permanent theatre[1]. Some doubt has been thrown upon the credibility of this tradition because of the fact that Aristophanes speaks of 'benches' (ikria) in connexion with the theatre[2]. Hence it has been argued that in the time of Aristophanes the seats in the theatre must have been of wood, and that consequently the construction of a stone theatre cannot have been anterior to the fourth century. But the use of the word 'ikria' by Aristophanes was merely the survival of an old term, after it had become no longer literally correct. Such survivals are common enough in all languages, and might be illustrated by numerous examples. It would be just as plausible to argue that during the fifth century the seats in the Pnyx were of wood, because Aristophanes, in the Acharnians, speaks of the presidents jostling one another for the 'front bench[3].' But there is another passage in Aristophanes which proves that they were of stone. In the well-known scene in the Knights, where Demos is represented as sitting in the Pnyx, the sausage-seller comes forward and presents him with a cushion to alleviate the discomfort of 'sitting on the hard rock[4].' This example shows

---

[1] Suidas v. Πρατίνας.
[2] Aristoph. Thesm. 395, 6 ὥστ' ε'θὺς εἰσιόντες ἀπὸ τῶν ἰκρίων | ὑποβλέπουσ' ἡμᾶς. The word ἴκρια is also used of the seats in the theatre by Cratinus, Frag. Incert. 51 ἰκρίων ψόφησις, and by Dio Chrysost. Or. 33, p. 3 Dindf. ἐπεὶ δὲ Σωκράτης ἄνευ σκηνῆς καὶ ἰκρίων ἐποίει τὸ τοῦ θεοῦ πρόσταγμα.

[3] Aristoph. Acharn. 24, 25 εἶτα δ' ὠστιοῦνται πῶς δοκεῖς | ἐλθόντες ἀλλήλοισι περὶ πρώτου ξύλου.
[4] Aristoph. Equit. 754 ὅταν δ' ἐπὶ ταυτησὶ καθῆται τῆς πέτρας, 783 ἐπὶ ταῖσι πέτραις οὐ φροντίζει σκληρῶς σε καθήμενον οὕτως, and Schol. ad loc.

the danger of arguing from a single phrase in Aristophanes. There can be no doubt that when Aristophanes employs the word 'ikria' in reference to the theatre of his time, it is merely an instance of the survival in common language of a term which had originated in connexion with the wooden theatres of the sixth century. We may therefore conclude that the stone theatre was commenced after the accident in 499[1]. It was not finally completed till the latter part of the fourth century, but doubtless at a much earlier period enough was done to make it sufficient for all practical purposes. There is very little information concerning the progress of the building. It is known that in the year 330 B.C. works were being carried on in connexion with it. A decree of the people has been preserved, belonging to that year, in which a vote of thanks is passed to a certain Eudemus of Plataea, for lending a thousand yoke of oxen for 'the construction of the Panathenaic race-course and the theatre[2].' The final completion was due to Lycurgus. As Lycurgus died about 325 B.C., it follows that the work must have been brought to a termination sometime between the years 330 and 325. Considerable doubt exists as to the condition of the theatre before the time of Lycurgus, and as to the exact character of the works

δείκνυσι γὰρ αὐτῷ προσκεφάλαιον ... ἵνα μὴ ἐπὶ ψιλοῖς τοῖς βάθροις ἐπικαθέζηται.

[1] Wilamowitz-Möllendorf, in Hermes for 1886, p. 597 ff., argues in favour of the view that there was no stone theatre at Athens in the fifth century. His reasons are as follows:
—(1) The use of the word ἴκρια by Aristophanes and Cratinus. (2) The passage in Bekk. Anecd. p. 354 αἰγείρου θέα· Ἀθήνῃσιν αἴγε ὅς ἦν, ἧς πλησίον τὰ ἴκρια ἐπήγνυντο εἰς τὴν θέαν πρὸ τοῦ θεάτρου γενέσθαι· οὕτω Κρατῖνος. He says this proves that the stone theatre was not commenced in the time of Cratinus. But all it proves is that Cratinus used the proverbial expression αἰγείρου θέα. (3) The story in Suid. v. Αἰσχύλος that the collapse of the wooden benches was the cause of Aeschylus'

banishment to Sicily. This is said to contradict the tradition that the collapse took place in 499 B.C. But the connexion of Aeschylus' retirement to Sicily with the fall of the benches is obviously a foolish conjecture of some commentator. Aeschylus, as poet, would be in no way responsible for the safety of the benches. Other equally impossible conjectures were invented to account for the same circumstance. Aeschylus' first retirement to Sicily took place before 476, the date of the foundation of Aetna. Yet according to one story it was due to disgust at his defeat by Sophocles in 468; according to another it was due to the terror caused by his chorus of Eumenides in 458.

[2] Corp. Inscr. Att. ii. 176.

which he carried on there. It is uncertain whether they consisted mainly in new erections, or in restorations of the old building. Unfortunately the various notices upon the subject are too vague and general in their language to admit of any definite inference[1]. All that is certain is that the theatre was finally completed by about 325 B.C.

After the fourth century there is no further record concerning the history of the building for many centuries. In late Roman times, probably in the third century A.D., a new stage in the Roman fashion was erected by a certain Phaedrus, who commemorated the fact by an inscription upon one of the steps, to the effect that 'Phaedrus, son of Zoïlus, ruler of life-giving Attica, erected this beautiful stage.' At this point all traces of the history of the theatre are lost. During the Middle Ages it disappeared so completely from view, that its very site was forgotten. For a long time modern travellers knew nothing upon the subject. The true site was first pointed out by Chandler. In 1862 excavations were commenced by the German architect Strack, and continued for three years. The theatre was again exposed to view, and large portions of it were found to have been preserved. Some further discoveries were made in 1877. Lastly, in 1886, new excavations have been carried on under the direction of Dr. Dörpfeld, acting for the German Archaeological Institute. The result of these latest investigations has been to throw considerable additional light upon the original arrangement of the orchestra and stage-buildings[2].

---

[1] Plut. X orat. 841 C καὶ τὸ ἐν Διονύσου θέατρον ἐπιστατῶν ἐτελεύτησε; ibid. Psephism. iii. πρὸς δὲ τούτοις ἡμίεργα παραλαβὼν τούς τε νεωσοίκους καὶ τὴν σκευοθήκην καὶ τὸ θέατρον τὸ Διονυσιακὸν ἐξειργάσατο καὶ ἐπετέλεσε. Paus. i. 29. 16 οἰκοδομήματα δὲ ἐπετέλεσε μὲν τὸ θέατρον ἑτέρων ὑπαρξαμένων. Hyperid. apud Apsines, Rhet. Gr. i. p. 387 (Spengel) ταχθεὶς δὲ ἐπὶ τῇ διοικήσει τῶν χρημάτων εὗρε πόρους, ᾠκοδόμησε δὲ τὸ θέατρον, τὸ ᾠδεῖον, τὰ νεώρια, τριήρεις ἐποιήσατο, λιμένας. The statement of Hyperides, that the theatre was 'built' by Lycurgus, is obviously a rhetorical exaggeration. All the other authorities, including the Psephism, say that it was merely 'completed.'

[2] Wheeler's Theatre of Dionysus, in Papers of the American School at Athens, vol. i.; Baumeister's Denkmäler des Klassischen Alterthums, vol. iii., v. Theatergebäude.

§ 4. *Site of the Theatre of Dionysus.*

Such is the history of the theatre, as far as it can be collected from ancient notices and records. In proceeding to describe its form and construction it will be convenient to take the different portions in succession. A Greek theatre is naturally divided into three parts, the auditorium, the orchestra, and the stage-buildings. In the following description the auditorium will be considered first, the orchestra next. The stage-buildings, as forming the most difficult part of the whole subject, will be reserved for the last. The object of the chapter, as already stated, is partly to describe the present condition of the theatre, partly to determine its original shape and appearance. As far as the latter object is concerned there are three principal sources of information. The most important evidence is of course that afforded by the existing ruins. Where these are defective, or where the original construction has been obliterated by later alterations, the gaps in our knowledge can occasionally be supplied by the evidence from the ruins of other theatres, more especially the theatre of Epidaurus. A third great source of information consists in the notices scattered up and down the works of the ancient grammarians and commentators. These notices, though often confused and contradictory, and though sometimes hardly applicable to the theatre at Athens in the fifth and fourth centuries, are nevertheless of the greatest value in illustrating and supplementing the evidence supplied by the actual ruins.

The site chosen for the new theatre was on the south-eastern slopes of the Acropolis. There was here an enclosure called the Lenaeum, sacred to Dionysus, the god of the 'lenos,' or wine-press. The spot was also called the Marshes. Within this enclosure were two temples of Dionysus, of which the foundations have recently been discovered. The oldest of these was the nearest to the Acropolis, and is that marked D in the accompanying plan. It contained the statue of Dionysus Eleuthereus. It was probably this statue which was taken into the theatre every year during the dramatic performances, and deposited in the orchestra. The more recent temple stood a few yards to the south of the old one, and is indicated by the letter E in the plan. It contained a statue of Dionysus by a certain Alcamenes, made of ivory and gold. Nearly in front of the more ancient temple of Dionysus stood the old orchestra in which Thespis and his successors had performed. The site chosen for the new theatre was a few yards to the north-west of the old orchestra[1]. The reasons for the choice are obvious. In the first place it was natural that the theatre, being regarded as a sort of temple of Dionysus, and being designed for celebrations in his honour, should be erected in his sacred enclosure. In the second place the slopes of the Acropolis afforded an excellent foundation for the tiers of seats, and the necessity of erecting costly substructures was avoided. In one respect the position of the theatre differed from that usually adopted in later times. The auditorium faced almost directly towards the south. This arrangement was generally avoided by the Greeks, and Vitruvius expressly warns architects against the danger of adopting it, because of the terrible heat caused by the midday sun glaring into the concavity of the theatre[2]. But at Athens there were special reasons on the other side. If the theatre was to be built in the Lenaeum at all, the only natural position for the auditorium was along the slopes of the Acropolis, and facing towards the south. We must also remember that at Athens the competitions for which the theatre was principally designed were held in the late winter or the early spring, when the cold was more to be dreaded than the heat. For performances at this period of the year the theatre was admirably adapted. It not only received the full warmth of the sun, but was also protected from the north wind by the rocks of the Acropolis behind it. At Athens therefore there were special reasons for preferring the southern aspect. The

---

[1] Hesych. v. ἐπὶ Ληναίῳ ἀγών; Thucyd. ii. 15; Pausan. i. 20. 3; Baumeister's Denkmäler des Klassischen Alterthums, vol. iii. p. 1736.
[2] Vitruv. v. 3. 2.

112 THE THEATRE. [Ch.

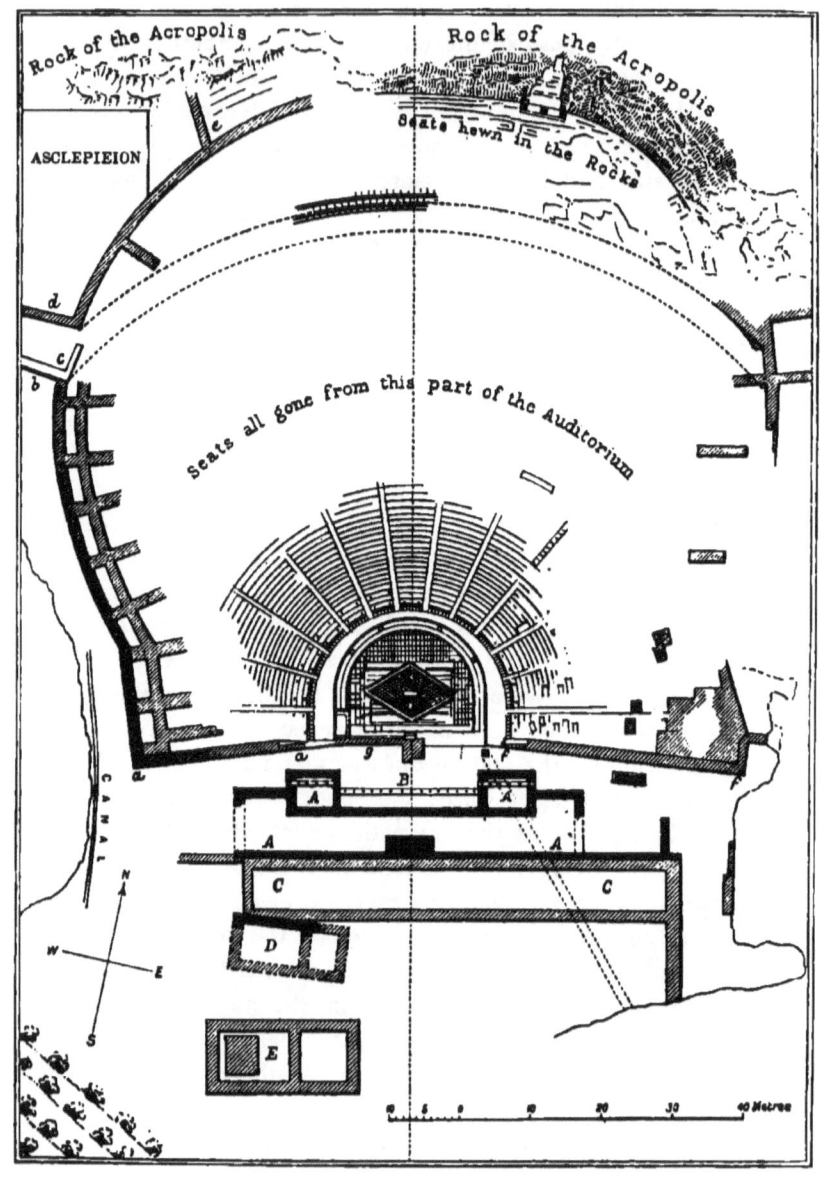

official name of the building was The Theatre of Dionysus. It was also sometimes called The Lenaic Theatre[1].

§ 5. *The Auditorium.*

Following the arrangement previously mentioned we come first of all to the auditorium. A plan of the existing remains of the theatre is here inserted[2]. Together with the two views of the theatre, which are given in the frontispiece and at the commencement of the present chapter, it will enable the reader to understand the following details without much difficulty. The auditorium, or the portion of the theatre containing the seats for the spectators, was called the 'cavea' in Latin; but there was no technical term for it in Greek. In almost all Greek theatres it was built upon the side of a hill, so that the natural slope of the ground might serve as a foundation for the tiers of seats. At Athens the rising ground at the foot of the Acropolis was utilised for this purpose. It was only at the extremities of the two wings, on the east and the west, that artificial substructures were necessary, in order to bring the back seats up to the proper height. In the other parts of the building the rising ground served as a foundation, after being altered to the requisite shape. The walls by which the auditorium was bounded on the outside have been preserved to a certain extent, and suffice to mark clearly the original shape of the building. On the western side of the theatre, from *a* to *b*, there are two boundary walls, an inner and an outer one. The inner wall is built of conglomerate, and

[1] Corp. Inscr. Att. ii. 240 τὸ θέατρον τὸ Διονυσιακόν. Cp. Phot. and Hesych. (v. ἴκρια) τὸ ἐν Διονύσου θέατρον; Poll. iv. 121 τὸ Ληναϊκὸν (θέατρον).

[2] The plan is taken from Baumeister's Denkmäler, v. Theatergebäude, and, as Dr. Dörpfeld informs me, contains substantially the results of his recent excavations. Dr. Dörpfeld's own more elaborate plan has unfortunately not yet been published. My authorities for the description of the existing remains of the theatre have been Vischer's article in the Neues Schweizerisches Museum, 1863, Bd. 3; Wheeler's Theatre of Dionysus, in Papers of the American School at Athens, vol. i.: Das Theater des Dionysus, by Julius and Ziller, in Zeitschrift für bildende Kunst, vol. xiii.; Murray's Handbook to Greece, vol. i. p. 228 ff.; Baumeister's Denkmäler des Klassischen Alterthums, vol. iii. v. Theatergebäude.

formed the real supporting wall of the auditorium in this part. The outer wall is built of Peiraic limestone, and merely served as a cover and protection to the inner one. The two walls are connected at intervals by lateral arms, which are also continued some distance beyond the inner wall. On the eastern side of the building almost all traces of the boundary walls have disappeared, but probably the general construction was very much the same as that on the western side just described. At the point b a wall of Peiraic limestone, marked c in the plan, and closely connected with the wall a-b, runs off westwards. The small piece of wall stretching northwards from c is of mediaeval construction. A little to the north of wall c another wall d, made of conglomerate, also runs off westwards in a nearly parallel direction. Between these two walls the boundary wall of the theatre is discontinued. It is obvious therefore that at this point there was an entrance into the auditorium. Very possibly there was a similar entrance on the opposite side; but the remains there are not sufficiently well preserved to determine the question. From the point d the boundary wall proceeds in a curve towards the north-east. There is no inner wall in this part, as in the lower half of the western side. The single wall which here forms the boundary of the theatre is built of conglomerate faced with Peiraic limestone, and is continued in the same line with the outer wall from a to b. At the point e some extra seats are built upon the rocky slopes of the Acropolis, outside the boundary wall of the theatre, and supported by a special wall marked e. Further eastwards the rock of the Acropolis abutted upon the theatre, and has been hollowed out into a regular curve. This is without doubt the portion of the theatre referred to by the ancients as Katatomê, or 'The Cutting[1].' In the rock is a natural grotto enlarged by artificial means, and 34 ft. long by 20 ft. broad. Here

---

[1] Harp. v. κατατομή· Ὑπερείδης ἐν τῷ κατὰ Δημοσθένους· καὶ καθήμενος κάτω ὑπὸ τῇ κατατομῇ. Φιλόχορος δὲ ἐν ἕκτῃ οὕτως· Αἰσχραῖος Ἀναγυράσιος ἀνέθηκε τὸν ὑπὲρ θεάτρου τρίποδα καταγυρώσας, νενικηκὼς τῷ πρότερον ἔτει χορηγῶν παισί, καὶ ἐπέγραψεν ἐπὶ τὴν κατατομὴν τῆς πέτρας. Bekk. Anecd. p. 270. 21 κατατομὴ ἡ ὀρχήστρα ἡ νῦν σίγμα, ἢ μέρος τι τοῦ θεάτρου κατετμήθη, ἐπεὶ ἐν ὄρει κατεσκεύασται κ.τ.λ.

Thrasyllus erected an elaborate monument to commemorate his victory with a chorus of men in 319 B.C. In the front of the grotto stood three columns supporting an entablature, and surmounted by a statue of Dionysus. On the architrave was an inscription recording the victory of Thrasyllus. Inside the grotto were statues of Apollo and Artemis, destroying the children of Niobe. In modern times the grotto has been converted into a chapel of Our Lady. The columns and entablature were in excellent preservation when Stuart visited Athens, but they were shattered by a mine during the Greek revolution. Above the grotto are two columns, which were erected to commemorate victories with dithyrambic choruses. On the capitals can still be seen the holes made to receive the legs of the tripods[1]. After the Katatomê there are very few remains of the boundary of the theatre upon the eastern side. But enough is left to show the general outline, as may be seen from the plan. The two wings of the auditorium are terminated on the south by the walls marked *a–a* and *f–f*. The walls are of unequal length, the eastern wall being about 111 ft., the western only 88 ft. The eastern wing was therefore considerably wider than the western. The two walls are of conglomerate faced with Peiraic limestone. They are not in the same straight line, but if continued inwards would meet in an obtuse angle in the orchestra. A comparison of the various Greek theatres shows that two different plans were adopted in regard to the position of these walls. Sometimes, as in the theatre at Athens, they were so arranged as to form an angle if prolonged. This is the case with most of the theatres of Asia Minor, and the same plan has been adopted in the theatres at Epidaurus, Mantineia, and the Peiraeeus. Some-

---

[1] Paus. i. 21. 5. Stuart and Revett's Antiquities of Athens, ii. 8. The inscription on the monument was as follows (Corp. Inscr. Gr. 224), Θρασύλλος Θρασύλλου Δεκελεεὺς ἀνέθηκεν χορηγῶν νικήσας ἀνδράσιν Ἱπποθωντίδι φυλῇ, Εὔϊος Χαλκιδεὺς ηὔλει, Νέαιχμος ἦρχεν, Καρκίδαμος Σώτιος ἐδίδασκεν. In the view of the theatre given at the commencement of the chapter the katatomê, together with the grotto and the two choregic columns, are clearly visible. Above the grotto is seen the old wall of Cimon, covered over with a modern casing.

times, on the other hand, the walls were arranged in one and the same straight line, so as to be exactly parallel with the stage. The theatres of Sicily are mostly of this pattern, as is also the theatre at Megalopolis[1].

The above description, together with the plan, will give a fair idea of the general outline of the auditorium. It will readily be seen that the Athenian theatre had <u>none of that symmetry and harmonious beauty</u> of design which is conspicuous in so many of the later Greek theatres. Its shape was far from regular. A glance at the plan of the theatre of Epidaurus, which was built by the younger Polycleitus in the middle of the fourth century, will show at once the great inferiority of the Athenian theatre in point of grace and symmetry of outline[2]. In most Greek theatres the auditorium was of the same width from one end to the other, and was shaped in a symmetrical curve. In the theatre at Athens the two wings of the auditorium are narrowed so considerably towards the south, as to be less than half the depth of the central part. The outside boundary does not run in a regular curve, but is very much flattened where it encounters the rock of the Acropolis, and terminates in a straight line at each of the southern corners. But the strangest point of all is that the eastern wing, at its termination, is several yards wider than the western wing—an arrangement utterly destructive of symmetry of design. A similar disregard for mere appearance is shown by the erection of extra seats on the slopes of the Acropolis outside the north-western boundary wall. The theatre at Athens was built for use rather than for show. It was not, like the theatre at Epidaurus, designed on one symmetrical plan. Its shape was determined by the conformation of the ground and by the situation of the adjoining rocks. Hence the irregularity of its outline. Although therefore it is the most interesting of Greek theatres on account of its historical associations, in point of mere beauty it cannot take the highest rank.

We now come to the interior of the auditorium. The boundary

[1] Müller's Griech. Bühnenalterthümer, p. 29.
[2] See the plan of the theatre of Epidaurus on p. 130.

between the auditorium and the orchestra is denoted by the dark line in the plan. It will be observed that in the theatre of Dionysus the inside boundary of the auditorium consists of a semicircle with the two ends prolonged in parallel straight lines. This was not the plan usually adopted in Greek theatres. In most of the later theatres the two ends of the semicircle were prolonged in the same curve as before, so that the inside boundary of the auditorium formed about two-thirds of a regular circle. The effect of this arrangement was that the spectators sitting at the extremities of the two wings faced towards the centre of the orchestra, and away from the stage. This need not surprise us when we remember that in purely Greek theatres the orchestra was always the most important part of the whole building. But the arrangement adopted at Athens, of prolonging the two ends of the semicircle in a straight line, had the advantage of giving the spectators on the wings a much better view of the stage. The same plan was also adopted in the theatre of the Peiraeeus, and in the theatres at Acrae in Sicily, and Termessus in Asia Minor. At Epidaurus a third plan was pursued, differing from both the above. The two ends of the semicircle were prolonged, not in a straight line, nor yet in the same curve as before, but in the shape of an ellipse, so that while they converged to a certain extent, they did not converge so much as in the ordinary Greek theatres[1]. This arrangement is perhaps the most beautiful of the three. But as far as the view of the stage is concerned the design adopted in the theatre of Dionysus has decidedly the advantage.

The interior of the auditorium consisted of a series of stone seats rising tier above tier in a gentle slope from the boundary of the orchestra to the outside extremities of the building. Immediately under the cliff of the Acropolis the seats were carved out of the living rock. With this exception they were made of Peiraic limestone. In some of the upper portions of the theatre they were fixed upon conglomerate foundations. But in most parts they were placed directly upon the bare earth, and

---

[1] Müller's Bühnenalterthümer, p. 29.

were therefore easily capable of being removed. For this reason the greater number of them have disappeared, having been taken away during the Middle Ages for building purposes. All that remain are from twenty to thirty rows in the bottom of the auditorium, and portions of a few rows at the top. From these however it is possible to obtain a clear conception of the style and arrangement of the auditorium. In order to make the following description clearer, an illustration is here inserted,

consisting of a restoration of the extremity of the eastern wing[1]. In this illustration *a* is the orchestra, *b* the eastern entrance into the orchestra, *c* the southern boundary wall of the east wing of the auditorium.

To proceed with the description of the seats. The lowest step of the auditorium rose a few inches above the level of the orchestra, and then sloped gently upwards towards the first row of seats. It was built of large slabs of stone. It was wider at the sides than in the centre, the width at the sides being nine feet ten inches, the width at the centre only six feet seven inches. The line of seats therefore did not coincide exactly with the boundary line of the auditorium and orchestra,

[1] The illustration is copied, with a few alterations, from the Zeitschrift für bildende Kunst, xiii. p. 197.

but receded slightly on the two wings. The first row of seats consisted of marble thrones with backs to them. In the front of each throne was an inscription recording the title of the priest or official for whom the seat was reserved. The thrones were 25 inches wide, and 23½ inches deep. In the centre was the throne of the priest of Dionysus, slightly larger than the others, and elaborately and beautifully carved. Behind the line of thrones was a passage 33 inches wide. Then came a small step, 7 inches high, and 17½ inches deep, for the people on the seat above to rest their feet upon. Then began the first of the ordinary tiers of seats, which were continued in exactly the same style from this point up to the top of the building. Their shape and dimensions were as follows. Each seat was 12½ inches high, and was hollowed out slightly in front, so that the person sitting on it could put his heels back as far as he liked. The depth of the seat was 33 inches, and its surface was divided into three distinct portions. The first part was for sitting upon, and was 12½ inches deep. The second part was several inches lower, and was intended to receive the feet of the persons upon the seat above. It was 16½ inches across. The third part was merely a narrow edge, of the same level as the first part, and 4 inches in depth. Thus the whole surface came to 33 inches. All the seats throughout the building, with the exception of the row of thrones, were of exactly the same construction. Along the front of each tier of seats were vertical lines engraved in the stone at intervals of about 13 inches. The lines were doubtless intended to help in discriminating each person's seat from his neighbour's.

For the purpose of giving access to the different parts of the auditorium a series of passages ran in divergent lines, like the spokes of a wheel, from the orchestra up to the outside boundary. The passages were fourteen in number, and the two upon the extreme south at each side adjoined immediately upon the boundary walls. In a theatre like that at Athens, where an immense number of people had to be accommodated with seats in tolerable proximity to the orchestra and stage, the greatest economy had to be observed in the use of space. These vertical passages were therefore made only 27½ inches wide, so that not more than one person could ascend at a time. The arrangement of the steps along the passages was altogether exceptional. In every Greek theatre, except that at Athens, each tier of seats had two steps corresponding to it in the vertical passages. But at Athens there was only one step for each tier of seats; and as the seats were 12½ inches high, while the steps were only 8½ inches, it was necessary to make up the difference by building the steps with a sloping surface. The surface was furrowed over, to render the ascent more easy. The fourteen passages divided the auditorium into thirteen blocks. Such blocks were called 'cunei' or 'wedges' in Latin, because of their shape. In Greek they were called 'kerkides,' from their resemblance to the 'kerkis,' or tapering rod used in weaving[1]. The front row in each 'kerkis' contained five marble thrones, with the exception of the two 'kerkides' on the extreme south of each wing, which contained six thrones each; so that the total number of marble thrones was sixty-seven. In addition to the vertical passages all Greek theatres of any size were also intersected by one or two longitudinal passages, called 'praecinctiones' in Latin. These passages divided the auditorium into sections, called 'belts' or 'girdles' in Greek technical terminology[2]. In the theatre of Dionysus no traces of such passages can be discovered, owing to the total destruction of the upper part of the auditorium. But we have seen that there was an entrance into the building on the western side at the point marked *c* in the plan. There was in all probability a corresponding entrance on the opposite side, and a longitudinal passage ran from entrance to entrance, following the direction of the tiers of seats in the manner indicated by the dotted lines in the plan. This supposition is confirmed by a coin in the British Museum, which contains on one side a rude representation of the Theatre at Athens. In spite of the roughness and inaccuracy of the design, there are clear traces of a longitudinal passage intersecting the upper portion of the auditorium. A copy

---

[1] Pollux, iv. 123.
[2] διαζώματα, Corp. Inscr. Gr. 4283; ζῶναι, Malal. p. 222.

of the coin is here inserted[1]. The position of the 'praecinctio' in the Athenian theatre has not a very symmetrical appearance. But symmetry of design was not the characteristic of the theatre of Dionysus. In most Greek theatres the auditorium was of the same width from end to end, and was divided by the longitudinal passages into equal and symmetrical portions. The plan of the theatre of Epidaurus will serve as a specimen[2]. But in the theatre at Athens it was impossible to arrange the longitudinal passage in this manner, owing to the narrowness of the wings of the auditorium. As to the vertical passages, in the

Athenian theatre they appear to have run in a straight line from the bottom to the top of the auditorium. In some theatres, as at Epidaurus, extra passages were inserted in the upper belt of the auditorium. In other theatres the vertical passages in the upper belt were arranged alternately with those in the lower belt, and not in the same straight line. But the ordinary practice was to construct single passages in the same straight line from bottom to top[3]. This is especially likely to have been the case at Athens, as the theatre was not divided into symmetrical belts or sections, and would not therefore naturally lend itself to the other kinds of arrangement. It was the fashion in Roman theatres to erect a portico along the top of the auditorium, following the line of the uppermost tier of seats. But there are no traces of

---

[1] The copy is taken from Wieseler's Denkmäler des Bühnenwesens, i. 1.
[2] See the plan on p. 130.
[3] Müller's Bühnenalt. p. 33.

such a portico in the theatre at Athens, or in any other theatre of purely Greek origin[1].

The following facts and measurements will give some idea of the size and capacity of the Athenian theatre. The distance between the inside corners of the auditorium was 72 feet. The distance between the outside corners was 288 feet. In the centre of the auditorium, from north to south, it is calculated by Strack that there must have been about 100 tiers of seats[2]. Of course on each of the two wings the number of tiers would be considerably less than half that amount. The arrangements throughout were designed with the view of bringing together the largest possible number of people within the smallest possible compass. The passages were little over two feet in width. The seats were of the simplest construction, so that the spectators could be packed tightly together, without any space being wasted. As the theatre was in the open air the close crowding of the audience was of course much less intolerable than it would have been in a covered building. At the same time the situation of the spectator cannot have been a very comfortable one. He had to remain cramped up in one position, with no back to lean against, and with very little opportunity of moving his limbs. That the Athenians were willing to put up with such inconveniences for several days in succession is a proof of their enthusiastic devotion to music and the drama. The total number of people which could be accommodated in the theatre at Athens is said by Plato to have been 'more than thirty thousand.' Modern investigations, based on the existing remains, lead to the conclusion that the number was 27,500. In any case the theatre was not so capacious as that of Megalopolis, which is calculated to have held 44,000 people. It was however one of the four largest theatres in Greece proper. The other three were those of Megalopolis, Epidaurus, and Sparta[3].

---

[1] Vitruv. v. 6. 4; Müller's Bühnenalt. p. 36.
[2] Strack's Altgriech. Theatergebäude, p. 2.
[3] Plat. Symp. 175 E; Zeitschrift für bild. Kunst, xiii. p. 202; Strack's Altgriech. Theatergebäude, p. 2; Müller's Bühnenalt. p. 47.

THE AUDITORIUM.

There still remains the question as to the date of the construction of the auditorium. All the authorities are agreed that the existing remains belong to the original building, and that there has been no reconstruction in later times in this part of the theatre, as there was in the case of the orchestra and the stage-buildings. But as to the date there is considerable difference of opinion. The tradition recorded by Suidas has already been referred to. It states that the construction of a stone theatre was due to the collapse of the wooden benches in 499 B.C., when Pratinas was exhibiting in the tragic contest, and his competitors were Aeschylus and Choerilus. There is a precision about the details of this tradition which gives it an appearance of authenticity and credibility. We are probably therefore justified in concluding that the construction of the auditorium was commenced early in the fifth century. Nothing is known as to the progress of the work, or the extent to which it suffered during the Persian invasion. Julius assigns its completion to the middle of the fifth century. Others put it about fifty years later. They refer to a certain slab with an inscription upon it, which is built into the south-western wall of the auditorium with the inscription inverted[1]. If the date of the inscription could be determined with certainty, it would fix the time before which the auditorium could not have been completed. But unfortunately on this point there is a difference of opinion. Julius, judging from the style of the inscription, ascribes it to the middle of the fifth century; Kirchhoff on the same grounds assigns it to the year 408 B.C. It is impossible therefore to base any exact conclusions on this particular piece of evidence. All that can fairly be inferred is that the greater part of the auditorium was finished in the course of the fifth century. Of course in a work of this kind, consisting simply of tiers upon tiers of stone seats, it is not by any means necessary that it should have been all built at the same time. It may have been added to at different periods. It is quite possible that it was not fully completed until the fourth century. But the probability seems to be that

---

[1] The inscription is given in Corp. Inscr. Att. i. 499.

by far the larger portion of it was constructed in the course of the fifth century.

A totally different opinion concerning the date of the auditorium has lately been propounded by Dr. Dörpfeld. He ascribes the whole building to the latter part of the fourth century, and asserts that before this time there was no such thing at Athens as a permanent stone theatre. Until the end of the fourth century the seats of the spectators consisted, according to his account, merely of rows of wooden benches. The stone theatre was begun and completed in the time of Lycurgus. His reasons for this novel theory are not however by any means conclusive[1], and are more than counterbalanced by the arguments on the other side. There is the precise statement in Suidas that the stone theatre was commenced in 499 B.C. Then again it is known that at Epidaurus and at the Peiraeeus stone theatres had been erected as early as the middle of the fourth century[2]. It is impossible to believe that Athens, the city in which the drama was originally developed, and whose theatrical representations continued to be the admiration of all the rest of Greece, should have been later than Epidaurus, and later than her own sea-port the Peiraeeus, in providing herself with a permanent theatre. It is also difficult to suppose that if the Athenian theatre had been built after that of Epidaurus, it would have been so much inferior in symmetry of design. The theatre at Athens, with

---

[1] Dr. Dörpfeld, in a letter of Nov. 7th, 1888, gives the following as his reasons for assigning the construction of the auditorium to the latter part of the fourth century—(1) The material. But Julius, Wheeler, and others make the style and general character of the work one of their reasons for assigning it to the fifth century. Where there is such difference of opinion, it is obviously difficult to place reliance upon arguments of this kind. (2) Certain stone-mason's marks, among which the letter Ω appears. But the letter Ω was formally adopted at Athens in 403 B.C., so that even if the evidence of these marks is to be relied on, it only brings us down to the end of the fifth century. (3) The inscription on the slab already referred to, the date of which is assigned variously to 450 or 408 B.C. Here again there is nothing to carry us beyond the fifth century. (4) The use of the word ἴκρια by Cratinus and Aristophanes. This argument has already been discussed on p. 107. (5) The notices concerning the work carried out in the theatre by Lycurgus. These notices, as was pointed out on p. 109, are far too vague and general to lead to any definite conclusion. There is nothing in them which is inconsistent with the supposition that the auditorium was substantially the work of the fifth century.

[2] Paus. ii. 27. 5; Corp. Inscr. Att. ii. 573.

its irregularity, and its adaptation to the natural conformation of the ground, has distinctly the appearance of being the earliest work of the kind. On every ground therefore it is difficult to resist the conclusion that the auditorium of which the remains still exist was substantially the work of the fifth century. It may have been added to by Lycurgus; the completion of every detail may have been due to him; but that the work as a whole belonged to the latter half of the fourth century is a suggestion which it is hardly possible to accept.

One point has still to be noticed, and that is the date of the marble thrones. The general opinion is that they are of later origin than the rest of the auditorium. The inscriptions upon them mostly belong to the Christian era, but in many cases half obliterated traces of older inscriptions are to be discovered underneath. Some of the inscriptions, however, are thought to be as early as the Macedonian period. The probability is that the marble thrones were erected by Lycurgus in the course of his completion of the theatre. Whether before the time of Lycurgus the front row of seats was in any way superior to the rest is uncertain. At Epidaurus the seats in the front row were all provided with backs, but otherwise were quite simple in design, and far less imposing than the marble thrones in the Athenian theatre[1]. It is possible that at Athens, before the alterations of Lycurgus, the front row was distinguished in some way from the other rows behind it, without displaying any very great magnificence.

§ 6. *The Orchestra.*

After the auditorium the next great division of the theatre is the orchestra. This was the name given to the flat surface enclosed between the stage-buildings and the inside boundary of the auditorium. It was called the orchestra, or 'dancing-place,' because in Greek theatres it was reserved for the performances of the chorus. In later times it was also called the Sigma, because its shape resembled the semicircular figure

---

[1] Πρακτικὰ τῆς ἐν Ἀθήναις ἀρχαιολ. ἐταιρίας 1883, p. 46 ff.

which was adopted in the fourth century as the symbol of the letter sigma[1]. In one place the word 'konistra' is used to denote the orchestra. Konistra means a surface of earth or sand. It is possible therefore that the term originated in the early period of the Greek drama, when the orchestras were not as yet covered with pavement, but consisted merely of the ordinary soil. On the other hand the word may be of late origin, as applied to the theatre. In Roman times the orchestras of Greek theatres were occasionally the scene of gladiatorial combats, and were probably strewn with sand for the purpose. It may be the case that the use of the word 'konistra,' as applied to the orchestra, arose in later times in consequence of this practice. As the term only occurs in one place, it is impossible to speak with any certainty on the subject[2]. In Roman theatres the orchestra was given up to the spectators, and the performances of singers and dancers took place upon the stage. The same practice was gradually adopted, under the Roman Empire, in the Greek theatres also. Hence the later Greek commentators and grammarians often use the word 'orchestra' improperly to denote the stage, which in their time was the actual dancing-place. This later signification of the term has given rise to much confusion. When a Greek scholiast speaks of the orchestra, it is necessary to look carefully to the context, to see whether he means the stage, or the orchestra in its proper sense[3].

In the early Greek theatres, as already pointed out, the orchestra was the most important part. The stage-buildings

---

[1] Phot. v. ὀρχήστρα (1), πρῶτον ἐκλήθη ἐν τῇ ἀγορᾷ· εἶτα καὶ τοῦ θεάτρου τὸ κάτω ἡμικύκλιον, οὗ καὶ οἱ χοροὶ ᾖδον καὶ ὠρχοῦντο. Bekk. Anecd. p. 286 ὀρχήστρα τοῦ θεάτρου τὸ νῦν λεγόμενον σίγμα· ὠνομάσθη δὲ οὕτως ἐπεὶ (ἐκεῖ) ὠρχοῦντο οἱ χοροί.

[2] Suidas v. σκηνή . . . ἡ κονίστρα, τουτέστι τὸ κάτω ἔδαφος τοῦ θεάτρου. The same scholium is repeated in Schol. Gregor. Nazianz. laud. patr. 355 B (see Hermes, vi. p. 492), and in Etym. Mag. In the former the word κονίστρα again appears; in the latter ὀρχήστρα is substituted.

[3] E. g. Schol. Aristoph. Equit. 505 (of the chorus) ἑστᾶσι μὲν γὰρ κατὰ στοῖχον οἱ πρὸς τὴν ὀρχήστραν ἀποβλέποντες· ὅταν δὲ παραβῶσιν, ἐφεξῆς ἑστῶτες καὶ πρὸς τοὺς θεατὰς βλέποντες τὸν λόγον ποιοῦνται. Here ὀρχήστρα obviously = λογεῖον. Cp. also Suidas s. v. σκηνή; Isidor. Origg. xviii. 44 'orchestra autem pulpitus erat scaenae, ubi saltator agere posset, aut duo inter se disputare.'

were a mere appendage to the orchestra. The seats of the spectators were so arranged, that while everyone had an excellent view of the orchestra, the view of the stage was in many cases a very poor one. When the Romans gave up the orchestra to the spectators, and transferred all the performances to the stage, they made considerable alterations in the arrangement and proportions of the theatre. They largely diminished the size of the orchestra, by bringing the stage several yards forward; and at the same time they cut off considerable portions from the two ends of the auditorium. In this way they were enabled to make the stage much deeper, so as to accommodate a larger number of performers. By shortening the wings of the auditorium they abolished those seats which looked away from the stage. Vitruvius gives some interesting directions for determining the proper proportions of a Greek and Roman theatre[1]. According to his figures the orchestra in a Roman theatre constituted an exact semicircle. The front line of the stage coincided precisely with the diameter of the orchestra. In a Greek theatre the stage was placed much further back. The distance between the central point of the front line of the stage, and the central point in the opposite circumference of the orchestra, was six-sevenths of the diameter of the orchestra. In a Greek theatre therefore, according to this statement, if the circumference of the orchestra was prolonged so as to form a complete circle, it would be found that the front line of the stage only intersected a very small portion of that circle. None of the existing Greek theatres coincide exactly with the rules laid down by Vitruvius; but in most cases they approximate closely. In the theatres at Epidaurus and the Peiraeeus the stage is placed a little further back than Vitruvius directs. At Athens this is still more the case. If the curve of the lowest step of the auditorium is prolonged so as to form a complete circle, the circumference of that circle does not touch the front line of the oldest existing stage. These facts enable one to realise the subordinate position occupied by the stage in early times. In the old Greek

[1] Vitruv. v. 6, 7.

theatres the original circle of the orchestra was still preserved intact, or was only encroached upon to a very small extent by the line of the stage-buildings.

The question as to the <u>character and appearance of the orchestra</u> in the Athenian theatre during the great period of the Attic drama is one of the highest interest. Unfortunately the present state of the theatre does not throw much light upon the subject. The central part of the building is mostly of very late date, and only slight traces of the original orchestra are to be discovered. It will be convenient first of all to give a brief description of the present orchestra, and then to see whether the deficiency in our information can be supplied from other sources. In the Athenian theatre the front of the auditorium consists of a broad and gently-sloping step, which rises a few inches above the level of the orchestra, and varies in width from about seven feet in the centre to about ten feet at the two sides. Along the edge of this step runs a marble balustrade, marked by the dark line in the plan. It consists of large slabs of marble, bound together by iron clamps, and 43 inches in height. On the southern side the orchestra is bounded by the stage of Phaedrus, a work of the third century A.D., which has already been referred to. About half of it is preserved, and is marked *g* in the plan. The two ends of this stage, as originally constructed, joined on to the two ends of the balustrade, so as to block up the entrances into the orchestra. Inside the balustrade there is a gutter made of limestone, 35½ inches in width. An outlet for the water runs off in a south-easterly direction. The gutter was originally open, except opposite the vertical passages, where it was bridged over with coverings of limestone. In later times it was covered over entirely with slabs of marble, with rosette-shaped openings at intervals. Some of these openings are still preserved, and are indicated in the plan. Inside the gutter is a narrow strip of Pentelic marble. Within this the orchestra is paved with slabs of different kinds of marble, arranged in lines parallel to the stage of Phaedrus. In the centre is a large rhombus-shaped figure, bounded by two strips of marble. The interior of the figure is paved with small slabs of marble, also rhombus-shaped, and of different colours. In the middle of the figure is a block of Pentelic marble, 41 inches long, and 17½ inches broad. The centre of the block contains a shallow circular depression, which may have been intended to receive an altar of Dionysus. In the south-west corner of the orchestra there formerly stood a cistern. It is marked in the plan, but has lately been removed.

Of the various portions of the orchestra which have just been described, the only one which belongs to the original building is the gutter. This was made of limestone, like the auditorium, and had no covering at first, with the exception of the bridges opposite the passages. It was intended to drain off the water from the auditorium. With the construction of the balustrade its usefulness in this respect was destroyed. The pavement of the orchestra is of excellent workmanship, and probably belongs to the time of the early Caesars. The balustrade, the stage of Phaedrus, and the marble covering of the gutter, are of later date, and are all ascribed by Dörpfeld to one period, probably the beginning of the third century A.D. The stage of Phaedrus encroaches on the orchestra in the Roman fashion. The balustrade is entirely a Roman idea. In Greek theatres there was never any obstacle between the orchestra and the auditorium. As far as one can see, the erection of the balustrade must have been due to the practice of holding gladiatorial combats in the orchestra. As for the rhombus-shaped figure, it is uncertain whether it was inserted as a mere ornament, or was intended for any particular purpose. At any rate, it throws no light upon the question of the style and appearance of the old Greek orchestras. The whole of the existing orchestra is far too late in time, and far too Roman in its character, to be of any use in this respect.

Fortunately for our knowledge of the orchestras of the early Greek theatres the recent excavations at Epidaurus have brought to light a theatre in which this portion of the building has been preserved in its original condition[1]. The theatre at

---

[1] Paus. ii. 27. 5 Ἐπιδαυρίοις δέ ἐστι θέας ἄξιον· τὰ μὲν γὰρ Ῥωμαίων πολὺ δὴ θέατρον ἐν τῷ ἱερῷ, μάλιστα ἐμοὶ δοκεῖν τι ὑπερῆρκε τῶν πανταχοῦ τῷ κόσμῳ.

Epidaurus was, according to Pausanias, the most beautiful theatre in the whole world. It was built by the younger Polycleitus in the middle of the fourth century. It did not suffer from subsequent reconstructions, like the theatre at Athens; and consequently the present remains are of the very greatest interest. The orchestra, the greater part of the auditorium, and the foundations of the stage-buildings are

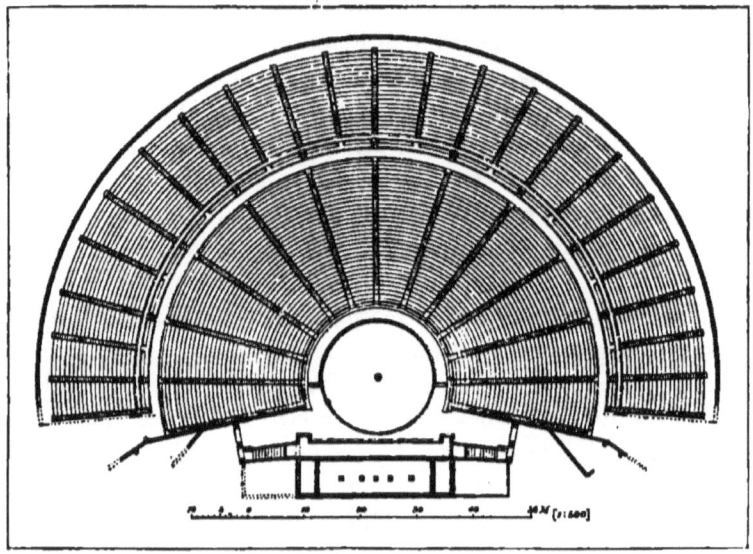

well preserved. A plan of the whole building is here inserted. The beauty of the general design is conspicuous at the first glance. The arrangement of the orchestra is as follows. Immediately in front of the lowest step of the auditorium there is a channel 6 feet 10 inches in width, and 8 inches deeper than the rest of the orchestra. The channel is paved with limestone, and reaches a little more than half way round

μεγέθει δὲ 'Αρκάδων τὸ ἐν Μεγάλῃ πόλει· ἁρμονίας δὲ ἢ κάλλους ἕνεκα ἀρχιτέκτων ποῖος ἐς ἅμιλλαν Πολυκλείτῳ γένοιτ' ἂν ἀξιόχρεως; Πολύκλειτος γὰρ καὶ θέατρον τοῦτο καὶ οἴκημα τὸ περιφερὲς ὁ ποιήσας ἦν.

The account of the present state of the theatre is derived from the Πρακτικὰ τῆς ἐν 'Αθήναις ἀρχαιολ. ἑταιρίας for 1883. The plan is from Baumeister's Denkmäler, vol. iii., v. Theatergebäude.

the orchestra, so as to be rather larger than a semicircle. At each end of it there are two holes, with outlets for water. It was obviously constructed for the purpose of draining off the water which descended from the auditorium. Inside the channel is a large circle, 66 feet in diameter. The circumference of the circle is marked by a border of stone, 15 inches wide, and on the same level as the rest of the orchestra. The interior of the circle is not paved in any way, but consists merely of earth beaten down hard and flat. In the very centre of the orchestra a circular stone, 28 inches in diameter, is sunk into the ground, so as to be on the same level as the surface round about it. In the middle of the stone is a circular hole. The purpose of the stone cannot be determined with certainty, but the most probable conjecture is that it was intended for the reception of a small stone altar. The outer border of the circle approaches within about a yard of the front line of the stage-buildings.

From the evidence afforded by these interesting remains the following conclusions may be drawn. In the first place it would appear that in the early Greek orchestras a complete circle was marked off for the performances of the chorus, slightly less in diameter than the orchestra itself. This was probably the case at Athens. On looking at the plan of the Athenian theatre it will be found that there was ample room for such a circle. The curved border of the orchestra, if prolonged so as to form an entire circle, would not reach as far as the front of the oldest proscenium, indicated in the plan by the letter *B*. Most probably, therefore, the orchestra at Athens, as at Epidaurus, had a circular dancing-place marked out for the chorus, and surrounded with a stone border. The border would run immediately inside the old limestone gutter already referred to[1]. In the second place, the evidence of the Epidaurian

---

[1] Dr. Dörpfeld writes to me as follows:—In Lykurgs Zeit war die Orchestra ein voller Kreis, weil das Skenengebäude soweit von dem Mittelpunkt des Kreises entfernt ist, dass man den ganzen Kreis zeichnen kann ... Auch das jüngere Proskenion mit den Säulen (auf dem Plane B) soweit von dem Mittelpunkt des Kreises entfernt liegt, dass die Orchestra einen ganzen Kreis bildet.

theatre seems to show that in the fifth and fourth centuries the surface of the orchestra was not paved with stone, but consisted merely of earth beaten down. There is no reason to suppose that a different plan was adopted at Athens. The statement which used to be frequently met with, that the orchestra was covered with planks, was due to ignorance of the fact that later Greek writers often used the word 'orchestra' to denote the stage[1]. In the existing Greek theatres the orchestras are, almost without exception, paved with stone. But these pavements are of comparatively late date, and do not affect the value of the evidence afforded by the theatre of Epidaurus as to the practice in the fourth and preceding centuries. Lastly, as to the position of the altar of Dionysus. That there was an altar in some part of the orchestra is proved by the express testimony of ancient writers, and by the circumstance that the dramatic performances were preceded by a sacrifice[2]. The altar probably stood in the very centre of the orchestra. This was the arrangement in the earliest times, when the drama was still a purely lyrical performance; and it is not likely that any alteration was made afterwards[3]. The evidence supplied by the theatres of Epidaurus and the Peiraeeus is distinctly in favour of the same view. In each of these theatres there is a circular hole in the centre of the orchestra. The only plausible explanation of the holes is that they were intended for the reception of small stone altars. On the above grounds therefore it seems reasonable to conclude that the position of the altar was in the centre. This would, in fact, be the most natural and appropriate place. The altar of a theatre was called the Thymele,

---

[1] Suidas v. σκηνή· ... μετὰ τὴν σκηνὴν εὐθὺς καὶ τὰ παρασκήνια ἡ ὀρχήστρα. αὕτη δέ ἐστιν ὁ τόπος ὁ ἐκ σανίδων ἔχων τὸ ἔδαφος, ἀφ' οὗ θεατρίζουσιν οἱ μῖμοι. Here the word ὀρχήστρα, as was first pointed out by Wieseler, and as the context proves, is used = λογεῖον.

[2] Suidas v. σκηνή· ... εἶτα μετὰ τὴν ὀρχήστραν (i.e. the stage) βωμὸς τοῦ Διονύσου. Poll. iv. 123 ἡ δὲ ὀρχήστρα τοῦ χοροῦ, ἐν ᾗ καὶ ἡ θυμέλη, εἴτε βῆμά τι οὖσα εἴτε βωμός. For the sacrifices in the theatre see on p. 89.

[3] Evanthius de trag. et comoed. (Gronov. Thesaur. viii. 1681), Comoedia fere vetus, ut ipsa quoque olim tragoedia, simplex carmen, quemadmodum iam diximus, fuit; quod chorus circa aras fumantes nunc spatiatus, nunc consistens, nunc revolvens gyros, cum tibicine concinebat.

because of the sacrifices offered upon it[1]. It is called by this name in a fragment of Pratinas[2]. In later times the use of the term was extended, so as to denote, not only the altar, but also the space round about it; and 'thymele' became a regular name for an orchestra[3]. By an exactly similar extension of meaning the sacred enclosure in front of a temple came to be called a 'thymele,' though the word originally denoted merely the altar which was erected there[4].

In all Greek theatres the front of the stage-buildings was separated from the wings of the auditorium by a vacant space several feet in width. Two open passages, one on the right and one on the left, led into the orchestra. The passages were closed on the outside by large gates, and these gates formed the only architectural connexion between the auditorium and the stage-buildings[5]. The passages answered a double purpose. In the first place they formed the principal entrances to the theatre for the general public. In many theatres they were the only entrances. In Athens there were two others at the upper end of the auditorium; but the main approaches in all theatres were those between the auditorium and the stage-buildings. The spectators came in by the orchestra, and then ascended the vertical passages to their proper seats. In the second place it was by these passages that the chorus entered the orchestra at the commencement of each play. In the theatre at Epidaurus the gates which led into the orchestra

---

[1] Suidas v. σκηνή· ... εἶτα μετὰ τὴν ὀρχήστραν βωμὸς τοῦ Διονύσου, ὃς καλεῖται θυμέλη παρὰ τὸ θύειν. Etym. Mag. v. θυμέλη, ἡ τοῦ θεάτρου μέχρι νῦν ἀπὸ τῆς τραπέζης ὠνόμασται, παρὰ τὸ ἐπ' αὐτῆς τὰ θύη μερίζεσθαι, τουτέστι τὰ θυόμενα ἱερεῖα.

[2] Pratinas ap. Athen. p. 617 B τίς ὁ θόρυβος ὅδε; τί τάδε τὰ χορεύματα; | τίς ὕβρις ἔμολεν ἐπὶ Διονυσιάδα πολυπάταγα θυμέλαν; cp. Hesych. v. θυμέλη; Schol. Lucian. Salt. § 76.

[3] Phrynich. p. 163 (Lob.) θυμέλην· τοῦτο οἱ μὲν ἀρχαῖοι ἀντὶ τοῦ θυσίαν ἐτίθουν, οἱ δὲ νῦν ἐπὶ τοῦ τόπου ἐν τῷ θεάτρῳ, ἐν ᾧ αὐληταὶ καὶ κιθαρῳδοὶ καὶ ἄλλοι τινὲς ἀγωνίζονται· σὺ μέντοι ἔνθα μὲν κωμῳδοὶ καὶ τραγῳδοὶ ἀγωνίζονται λογεῖον· ἐρεῖς, ἔνθα δὲ οἱ αὐληταὶ καὶ οἱ χοροὶ ὀρχήστραν, μὴ λέγε δὲ θυμέλην.

[4] θυμέλη denotes the altar before a temple in Aesch. Suppl. 666 καὶ γεραροῖσι πρεσβυτοδόκοι γερόντων θυμέλαι φλεγόντων. It is used of the sacred enclosure before the temple in Eur. Ion 46 ὑπὲρ δὲ θυμέλας διορίσαι πρόθυμος ἦν. Cp. ibid. 114, 159, 229.

[5] Remains of such gateways are found in the theatres of Epidaurus and Pergamon. See Baumeister's Denkmäler, vol. iii. p. 1741.

stood side by side with other gates leading into the stage-buildings. Sufficient remains of the gates have been preserved to admit of a complete restoration of them. The present illustration represents the two gates on the eastern side of the

theatre. The gate to the right leads into the orchestra; that to the left leads into the stage-buildings[1]. In the theatre of Dionysus at Athens the passages into the orchestra measured nine feet across on the outside. Of course they grew gradually wider, as one approached the orchestra, owing to the oblique position of the boundary walls of the auditorium[2]. They were

---

[1] The illustration is taken from Πρακτικὰ τῆς ἐν 'Αθήν. ἀρχαιολ. ἑταιρίας for 1883.

[2] The building marked *A* in the plan on p. 112 is the oldest of the stage-buildings. From the outside corner of the wings to the boundary wall of the auditorium is a distance of about nine feet.

probably closed on the outside with gates as at Epidaurus. These passages or side-entrances into the orchestra were technically called 'parodoi' or 'eisodoi[1].' In Roman theatres they were of course done away with, as the Roman stage was brought much more forward than the Greek, and the two ends coalesced with the wings of the auditorium. In place of the old open passages the Romans built vaulted entrances underneath the auditorium, and parallel with the stage. Later Greek writers, misled by the analogy of the Roman theatres, sometimes apply the terms 'vault' and 'archway' to the open side-entrances of the Greek theatre. But such language is inaccurate[2].

Before concluding this description one or two points may be mentioned concerning Greek orchestras in general. It appears from existing remains that the level of the orchestra was mostly, as at Athens, very little below the level of the front row of seats. The intermediate space was usually occupied by a single low step. The gutter running round the edge of the orchestra, to drain away the rain-water which flowed down from the tiers of seats, was a regular feature of Greek theatres, and can be traced in most of the existing ruins[3]. It is recorded that the surface of the orchestra was marked out with lines, to assist the chorus in their evolutions[4]. Similar lines are used upon the modern stage when complicated ballets are produced. Aristotle mentions cases of orchestras being strewed with chaff, and remarks that when this was done the choruses were not heard so well. But it is uncertain to what theatres or to what occasions he is referring[5].

---

[1] Πάροδοι in Schol. Aristoph. Equit. 149; Poll. iv. 126; εἴσοδοι in Aristoph. Nub. 326, Av. 296. The word πάροδος was also used to denote the entrances on to the stage, e.g. in Plut. Demetr. p. 905 B; Poll. iv. 128; Athen. p. 622 D.

[2] Vitruv. v. 6. The side entrances are called ψαλίς in Poll. iv. 123; ἀψίς in Vit. Aristoph. (Dindf. Prolegom. de Comoed. p. 36).

[3] Müller's Bühnenalt. pp. 35, 37.

[4] Hesych. v. γραμμαί.

[5] Aristot. Prob. xi. 25 διὰ τί, ὅταν ἀχυρωθῶσιν αἱ ὀρχῆστραι, ἧττον οἱ χοροὶ γεγώνασιν;

§ 7. *The Stage-buildings.*

The third and last division of the theatre consists of the stage-buildings. Unfortunately this is a subject upon which the information supplied by the existing ruins is very defective. In all the remaining theatres of purely Greek origin merely the foundations of the stage-buildings have been preserved, and it is impossible, from such evidence, to do much more than determine the original shape of the ground-plan. Our knowledge of the upper part of the structure has to be derived mainly from casual notices in the old grammarians. It will be convenient, before proceeding to the consideration of the stage-buildings in general, to give a brief account of the present state of the ruins in the Theatre of Dionysus at Athens. The stage-buildings at Athens were very frequently altered and reconstructed in the course of their history, and the task of distinguishing between the confused remains of the different periods has been by no means an easy one. The recent investigations of Dr. Dörpfeld in 1886 have for the first time placed the matter in a fairly clear light. The results of his discoveries are indicated in the plan of the theatre already given [1]. It is now possible to trace out with some degree of accuracy the foundations of the oldest stone building. These foundations are denoted in the plan by the letter *A*, and by the darker shading. It will be observed, on consulting the plan, that the first permanent stage-buildings at Athens consisted of a rectangular structure, very narrow in comparison with its length. In the front, towards each end, were two projecting side-wings. Between the side-wings, and some distance to the rear, stood the wall at the back of the stage. According to Dörpfeld no traces are to be found in this early building of a permanent stage resting on a stone foundation. The line marked *B* denotes a

---

[1] The description of this portion of the theatre of Dionysus is mainly derived from Baumeister's Denkmäler, art. Theatergebäude, in which the results of Dörpfeld's excavations are incorporated. Previous descriptions of the stage-buildings have been more or less superseded by Dörpfeld's discoveries.

stage belonging to a much later period. Of course it is obviously impossible, in the case of buildings which have undergone so many alterations in later centuries as the old stage-buildings of the Athenian theatre, to speak with absolute certainty about the original design. But if Dörpfeld's conclusions are correct, it would follow that when permanent stage-buildings were first erected at Athens, there was no stone proscenium. All that was permanent was the rectangular building with the projecting side-wings. The stage must have been at that time a temporary wooden erection, put up between the wings for the annual performances. This old wooden stage would no doubt coincide more or less closely in position with the later stage marked *B* in the plan.

The date of the erection of the first permanent stage-building is a matter of some uncertainty. Dörpfeld ascribes it to the time of Lycurgus, on the ground that it is similar to the auditorium in material and construction[1]. If this supposition were correct, we should have to assume that the Athenians had no permanent stage-buildings until the latter part of the fourth century, and that they were contented with mere temporary erections of wood during the whole of the great period of the Attic drama. This is in itself a most improbable hypothesis. It is obvious that in the time of the great Attic dramatists stage-buildings of some strength and solidity were required. That such was the case is proved by the constant use of the mêchanê, an appliance by which gods and heroes were exhibited floating through the air, and were lowered down from heaven on to the stage, and *vice versa*. Contrivances of this kind would have been impossible unless the wings and back part of the stage had been firm and substantial in construction. It seems therefore most unlikely that during this period the Athenians should have been contented with a wooden building, which would be in constant need of repair, and would never be

---

[1] In a letter of Nov. 7, 1888, Dr. Dörpfeld states that the oldest stage-building, marked *A* in the plan, 'stammt sicher aus dem 4. Jahrhundert, denn es ist gleichzeitig mit dem Zuschauerraum, wie Material und Construction beweisen.'

as safe and convenient as one of stone. It has already been shown that there is every reason to believe that the auditorium belongs to the fifth century. As the earliest stage-building is similar in style and construction it should in all likelihood be ascribed to this date also. It is very probable that the whole stage-building was renovated or reconstructed by Lycurgus in the course of his completion of the theatre. But nothing short of overwhelming evidence would induce one to believe that before his time there was no permanent stage-building at Athens.

As to the subsequent history of this part of the building, it appears that the first great alteration was the erection of a permanent stage, adorned with columns in front. At the same time the side-wings were brought further back, and also adorned with columns in the same manner as the stage. The line of the stage and side-wings in the new arrangement is denoted by the letter B. The exact date of these innovations is uncertain. Further alterations, of which the precise nature is unknown, were carried out in the time of the early Caesars, as is proved by the existence of certain fragments of columns and arches obviously belonging to that period. Lastly, in the course of the third century A. D., the theatre was completely Romanised by a certain Phaedrus. The old stage was done away with, and a new stage was erected about eight yards further to the front. This stage was only 4 feet 7 inches high, after the Roman fashion. The front part of it, facing the orchestra, was adorned with groups of figures carved in bold relief. In the centre a flight of five stone steps led down from the stage into the orchestra. The two ends of the stage, as already mentioned, joined on to the two ends of the balustrade, so as to block up the side entrances into the orchestra. About half of the stage of Phaedrus has been preserved, and is denoted by the letter g in the plan.

Such is the history of the stage-buildings in the Athenian theatre, from the wooden erection in which Aeschylus brought out his earliest tragedies to the Romanised proscenium built by Phaedrus nearly eight hundred years afterwards. Our information concerning the construction of this portion of a Greek theatre is derived partly from existing remains, partly from the notices in the grammarians and commentators. The general name for the stage-buildings in Greek was 'skēnē,' a word which properly means a booth[1]. As to their shape, they formed a long and narrow rectangular building facing the auditorium. For instance the oldest stage-buildings at Athens were about 55 yards in length, and only 11 yards in depth. In this respect the difference between an ancient and a modern theatre is very striking. In a modern theatre the depth of the stage-buildings is usually greater than their width. The distance from the front of the stage to the back of the stage-buildings is as great as the distance from the front of the stage to the furthest seats of the auditorium. The reason of the difference is easy to discover. In a modern theatre all the performers are upon the stage, which must therefore be of considerable depth. But in a Greek theatre, as the majority of the performers stood in the orchestra, and the only occupants of the stage were the three actors, with occasional supernumeraries, a narrow stage was sufficient. Then again, in a modern theatre the frequent changes of scene, and the elaborate spectacular effects, require complicated mechanical appliances, for which room has to be found at the back of the buildings. But as changes of scene were almost unknown in the Greek drama, the scenic appliances were of the simplest character, and took up very little room. Further than this, a deep stage would have been inconsistent with the general arrangement of a Greek theatre. The auditorium of a Greek

[1] The word σκηνή, from having originally denoted the booth to which the actor used to retire between his performances, came to have the following various meanings, as applied to the theatre:—(1) The stage-buildings as a whole; e. g. Hesych. v. λογεῖον· ὁ τῆς σκηνῆς τόπος ἐφ' οὗ οἱ ὑποκριταὶ λέγουσιν. (2) The wall at the back of the stage; e. g. Suidas v. προσκήνιον· τὸ πρὸ τῆς σκηνῆς παραπέτασμα. (3) The decoration or painted scenery in front of the back-wall; e. g. Plut. Demetr. p. 900 D ἔλεγε νῦν πρῶτον ἑωρακέναι πόρνην προερχομένην ἐκ τραγικῆς σκηνῆς. (4) The stage; e. g. Xen. Inst. Cyr. vi. 1. 54 τοῦ δὲ πύργου, ὥσπερ τραγικῆς σκηνῆς τῶν ξύλων πάχος ἐχόντων κ.τ.λ. When the Schol. on Soph. Ajax 330, 719 speaks of the chorus 'leaving the σκηνή,' he is probably confusing the ancient orchestra with the stage of Roman times. (5). 'The theatre' in a general sense, as we speak of 'the stage' in English; e.g. Dem. de Cor. § 180 μηδ' ἥρω τὸν τυχόντα, ἀλλὰ τούτων τινὰ τῶν ἀπὸ τῆς σκηνῆς, 'a stage hero.'

theatre consisted of a semicircle with the two ends produced. The result was that every one had an excellent view of the orchestra, and the performers there; but a large proportion of the audience had only a side view upon the stage. If therefore the stage had been of any great depth, as in modern times, the back part would have been invisible to the spectators sitting in the wings of the auditorium. For these various reasons the stage-buildings of a Greek theatre were very long and very narrow. In Roman theatres the arrangement was less unlike that in modern times. When the Romans abolished the choral performances in the orchestra, and transferred the whole spectacle to the stage, they were necessarily compelled to add to the depth of the stage, and in consequence to the depth of the stage-buildings.

The back of the stage-buildings was probably adorned with architectural embellishments, so as to form a beautiful and striking façade. Such decorations were common in Roman theatres, as is proved by the existing remains of the theatre at Orange; and the Greeks would naturally beautify their buildings in the same way. At the back would also be the principal entrances into the stage-buildings for the actors and other performers. Thus there are three large doors at the back of the stage-buildings at Orange[1]. There must also have been doors leading from the stage-buildings into the side-entrances to the orchestra, to enable the chorus to enter the orchestra. These doors are clearly visible in the ground-plan of the theatre at Epidaurus, and are placed immediately beyond the slight projections which mark the termination of the stage at each side. In one respect the theatre at Epidaurus is peculiar. It has three doors leading from beneath the stage itself on to the orchestra. One of them is exactly in the centre; the two others are at each end. No traces of similar doors are to be found in the remains of other theatres.

[1] Wieseler's Denkmäler des Bühnenwesens, iii. 3.

§ 8. *The Stage, &c.*

The different portions of the stage-buildings have next to be considered in detail. To begin with the stage itself. The usual name for the stage in Greek was the 'logeion,' or 'speaking-place,' because the actors stood there and carried on the dialogue. It was opposed to the orchestra, or dancing-place, in which the chorus went through their performances. The stage was also called the 'proskēnion,' from its position in front of the 'skēnē,' or back-wall; and the 'okribas,' because its surface consisted of a wooden platform[1]. The height of the logeion in the Greek theatre was, according to Vitruvius, from ten to twelve feet above the level of the orchestra[2]. This statement, though often called in question, has lately been confirmed by the excavations at Epidaurus. It has been found that the stage in the theatre at Epidaurus was almost exactly twelve feet high; and the holes or sockets in the wall, which were intended to receive the wooden beams of the stage, are still distinctly visible. As the proscenium at Epidaurus is probably of the same date as the rest of the theatre, it would appear that the height of the Greek stage had already been fixed at about twelve feet as early as the fourth century[3]. The question as to its height during the period from Aeschylus to Aristophanes will be discussed later on. The Greek stage, as already pointed out, con-

---

[1] Phryn. p. 163 (Lob.) σὺ μέντοι, ἔνθα μὲν κωμῳδοὶ καὶ τραγῳδοὶ ἀγωνίζονται, λογεῖον ἐρεῖς. Phot. v. τρίτος ἀριστεροῦ· ... ὁ μὲν ἀριστερὸς στοῖχος ὁ πρὸς τῷ θεάτρῳ ἦν, ὁ δὲ δεξιὸς πρὸς τῷ προσκηνίῳ. Hesych. v. ὀκρίβας· τὸ λογεῖον, ἐφ' οὗ οἱ τραγῳδοὶ ἠγωνίζοντο. Other names for the stage were (1) σκηνή, see above, p. 139. (2) βῆμα, cp. the inscription on the stage of Phaedrus, Corp. Inscr. Att. iii. 239 βῆμα θεήτρου. (3) ὀρχήστρα, an improper sense of the word, only found in later writers, e. g. Suidas v. σκηνή. (4) θυμέλη, also a late use of the word; e. g. Bekk. Anecd. p. 42 νῦν μὲν θυμέλην καλοῦμεν τὴν τοῦ θεάτρου σκηνήν.

[2] Vitruvius, v. 7.

[3] Πρακτικὰ τῆς ἐν Ἀθήναις ἀρχαιολ. ἑταιρίας for 1883. Kawerau, in Baumeister's Denkmäler, vol. iii. p. 1739, suggests that perhaps the proscenium in the theatre at Epidaurus was built later than the rest of the stage-buildings. But there do not appear to be any grounds for the supposition. On the contrary, the relative arrangement of orchestra and proscenium seems to show that both were constructed at the same time. See Kabbadias' article in the Πρακτικά for 1881.

sisted of a long and narrow platform, bounded at the back and on each side by the walls of the stage-buildings. Vitruvius gives some interesting rules for determining the size of the stage in Greek and Roman theatres respectively. According to his statements the depth of a Roman stage should be ⅕th of the diameter of the orchestra, its length should be twice the diameter. A Greek stage ought to be rather shorter and considerably narrower. Its depth should be ⅒th of the diameter of the orchestra, its length 1⅚th of the diameter[1]. These rules are more or less confirmed by the remains of the later Greek theatres, but hardly apply to the earlier ones, the stages of which are a great deal shorter, and rather less deep, than Vitruvius requires. For instance, the original stage at Athens was hardly so long as one diameter of the orchestra, instead of being nearly equal to two. The depth of the original stage cannot be determined, since it was made entirely of wood, and the foundations have disappeared. Then again, the stage at Epidaurus was about 78 feet long by 8 feet deep. According to Vitruvius it should have been about 137 feet by 11. The stage in the theatre at the Peiraeeus was about 97 feet long by 10 feet deep. It should have been 146 feet by 13[2]. From these figures it appears that in the earliest times the length of the Greek stage was not usually greater than the diameter of the orchestra. It was only in later times that the stage was extended on each side so as to project beyond the inside corners of the auditorium. The average depth of the early Greek stage seems to have been not more than ten feet. This extreme narrowness, which appears surprising to our modern notions, has already been explained as due, partly to the fact that the majority of the performers were in the orchestra, partly to the shape of the Greek auditorium, which made a deep stage impossible.

Within the last few years a novel theory has been propounded in reference to the logeion or stage. It has been suggested that during the early period of the Attic drama the stage was never intended for the actors to perform on. The

[1] Vitruv. v. 6, 7.   [2] Müller's Bühnenalt. pp. 16, 19, 23.

actors stood in the orchestra on the same level as the chorus. The background consisted of the wall, ten or twelve feet high, on which the stage was supported. The stage itself was merely used to hold various theatrical contrivances and pieces of machinery. Such is the theory put forward by Höpken and Dörpfeld[1]. Now it is certain that at any rate as early as the third century B.C. the actors were accustomed to appear upon an elevated platform, and not in the orchestra. This is proved by the numerous vase-paintings from Magna Graecia, belonging to the third century, in which comic actors are frequently represented as standing on a raised platform, with a flight of steps leading up from the orchestra[2]. Also the various notices of the grammarians, which describe the logeion as the place for the actors, were doubtless derived ultimately from Alexandrine

---

[1] See Höpken's De Theatro Attico. He bases his theory on certain passages in the extant dramas. But his arguments are of no value, and their worthlessness has been clearly demonstrated by Albert Müller in Philol. Anzeig. xv. p. 525 ff. One specimen will suffice. Höpken argues that when Dionysus in the Frogs (v. 297) appeals to the priest of Dionysus to save him, this proves that the actor and the priest must have been standing on the same level! Dr. Dörpfeld has adopted the same theory, but on altogether different grounds. See Müller's Bühnenalt. p. 109; Baumeister's Denkmäler, v. Theatergebäude. His reasons are (1) the great height of the logeion or stage. The plain answer is that in the time of Vitruvius a height of twelve feet was not considered excessive. Yet in the time of Vitruvius it is a matter of certainty that the actors occupied the stage, the chorus standing in the orchestra (Vitruv. v. 7). There is therefore no reason for asserting that a stage twelve feet high was an impossibility at an earlier period. (2) The shallowness of the stage, that at Epidaurus being only about eight feet deep. But there is nothing very abnormal in this. Even according to Vitruvius' rules the stage at Epidaurus would only have been eleven feet deep; and Vitruvius was of course describing a stage intended for actors to perform on. It is obvious that if the stage was twelve feet high, it must have been very shallow, or else the spectators in the front rows would have been unable to see down to the end of it. (3) The absence of connexion between logeion and orchestra. For example, at Epidaurus there are no traces of stone steps leading up to the stage. But when a connexion was required, it was effected by means of temporary wooden steps placed against the front of the proscenium. See on p. 148. For a discussion of the whole question of the connexion between the stage and the orchestra see below pp. 150–158. As far as the oldest stage-buildings at Athens are concerned, there is nothing to decide the question about the logeion one way or the other. Dörpfeld supposes that a temporary wooden background was put up between the side-wings. It is just as plausible to suppose that a wooden stage was erected there.

[2] See Heydemann's article, Die Phlyakendarstellungen auf bemalten Vasen, in Jahrb. des Kais. Deutsch. Archäol. Inst. 1886, p. 260 ff.

sources, and may be considered to settle the matter as far as the third century is concerned. But it may be contended that they prove nothing as to the practice which prevailed at Athens during the fourth and fifth centuries. It is necessary therefore to consider the question, whether there is any positive proof that during the great period of the Attic drama the actors were raised above the level of the chorus, and occupied an elevated stage. In a matter of this kind no evidence could be more convincing than that supplied by the extant dramas themselves. Now we are told by one of the scholiasts that in old theatrical phraseology, when an actor made his entrance he was said to 'ascend;' and when he made his exit he was said to 'descend.' The two words are actually used in this sense by Aristophanes. It is difficult to see how the usage can be accounted for, except on the supposition that the actors had been accustomed to stand on an elevated platform[1]. Then again in the Wasps, when Philocleon comes out of his house in a drunken condition, and sees the sons of Carcinus dancing in the orchestra, he exclaims, 'I must go down to them,' and forthwith proceeds into the orchestra to compete with them in the dance[2]. Also in the Birds, when Peisthetaerus wishes to point out to the Epops the aerial kingdom of the birds, he tells him to 'look down,' then to 'look up,' then to look 'round about him.' If the Epops had been standing on the floor of the orchestra, the request to look down would have been meaningless, as it would have shown him nothing but the ground at his feet[3]. It appears,

---

[1] Schol. Aristoph. Equit. 149 λεκτέον οὖν ὅτι ἀναβαίνειν ἐλέγετο τὸ ἐπὶ τὸ λογεῖον εἰσιέναι ... λέγεται γὰρ καταβαίνειν τὸ ἀπαλλάττεσθαι ἐντεῦθεν ἀπὸ τοῦ παλαιοῦ ἔθους. Aristoph. Equit. 148, 149 δεῦρο δεῦρ', ὦ φίλτατε, | ἀνάβαινε σωτὴρ τῇ πόλει καὶ νῷν φανείς, Vesp. 1342 ἀνάβαινε δεῦρο χρυσομηλολόνθιον, Eccles. 1151-1153 τί δῆτα διατρίβεις ἔχων, ἀλλ' οὐκ ἄγεις | τασδὶ λαβών; ἐν ὅσῳ δὲ καταβαίνεις, ἐγὼ | ἐπᾴσομαι μέλος τι μελλοδειπνικόν. In all these passages there is nothing in the particular circumstances of the drama to account for the usage of the words.

[2] Aristoph. Vesp. 1514 ἀτὰρ καταβατέον γ' ἐπ' αὐτούς. It might be suggested that καταβατέον here means simply 'I must contend with them.' But the literal meaning is much the more probable.

[3] Aristoph. Av. 175-178 ΠΕ. βλέψον κάτω. ΕΠ. καὶ δὴ βλέπω. ΠΕ. βλέπε νῦν ἄνω. | ΕΠ. βλέπω. ΠΕ. περίαγε τὸν τράχηλον. ΕΠ. νὴ Δία, | ἀπολαύσομαί τι δ', εἰ διαστραφήσομαι. | ΠΕ. εἶδές τι; ΕΠ. τὰς νεφέλας γε καὶ τὸν οὐρανόν.

therefore, that the testimony of Aristophanes points decisively to the existence of a stage for the actors in the fifth century. Besides this we are told that even before the time of Thespis the choreutes who carried on the dialogue with the rest of the chorus used to mount upon a sort of platform for the purpose. The practice shows that from the earliest times the necessity of raising the speaker above the level of the chorus had been felt[1]. Again, in the Symposium, Agathon, the tragic poet, is said to have 'mounted the stage along with his actors,' and confronted the audience without flinching. The passage no doubt refers to the Proagon, which took place in the Odeum. But as the Odeum was built 'like a theatre,' it is only natural to conclude that there was a similar stage in the theatre, and that it was used by the actors during the dramatic performances[2]. But apart from the various positive proofs which might be alleged, there are intrinsic improbabilities in Dörpfeld's theory which make it very difficult of acceptance. In the first place, it is hardly credible that a platform, which was erected originally to serve as a background and hold the machinery, should have been converted into a stage for the actors in later times, and yet that not a single reference to the transformation should be found in any ancient writer. Again, if the plan of the theatre at Epidaurus is consulted, it will be found that the stone border of the circular orchestra reaches to within two or three feet of the front of the proscenium. If the actors had stood in front of the proscenium, they would have been sometimes inside the stone border and sometimes outside of it; and the whole arrangement strikes one as awkward and unsymmetrical. But the most fatal objection is the following. In a Greek theatre the front row of seats was nearly on the same level as the orchestra, and the tiers of seats behind ascended in a very gradual incline. If therefore the actors had stood on the floor

[1] Poll. iv. 123 ἐλεὸς δ' ἦν τράπεζα ἀρχαία, ἐφ' ἧν πρὸ Θέσπιδος εἷς τις ἀναβὰς τοῖς χορευταῖς ἀπεκρίνατο.
[2] Plat. Symp. 194 A ἐπιλήσμων μέντ' ἂν εἴην, ὦ 'Αγάθων, εἰπεῖν τὸν Σωκράτη, εἰ ἰδὼν τὴν σὴν ἀνδρείαν καὶ μεγαλοφροσύνην ἀναβαίνοντος ἐπὶ τὸν ὀκρίβαντα μετὰ τῶν ὑποκριτῶν καὶ βλέψαντος ἐναντία τοσούτῳ θεάτρῳ κ.τ.λ. Schol. Aristoph. Vesp. 1104 (of the ᾠδεῖον) ἔστι τόπος θεατροειδὴς κ.τ.λ.

L

of the orchestra, with the chorus in front of them, they would have been hardly visible to the majority of the audience. An occasional glimpse of them might have been caught, as the chorus in the foreground moved to and fro, but that would have been all. It is difficult to believe that the Athenians should have been contented with this arrangement for more than two hundred years, and should not have resorted to the simple device of raising the actors upon an elevated platform. This difficulty becomes all the more striking, when we remember that the principal tendency of the Greek drama during the fifth and fourth centuries was to increase the importance of the actors, and to diminish the importance of the chorus. For these various reasons it is impossible to accept Dörpfeld's theory. The inherent improbabilities of the suggestion are extremely great; and the passages in Aristophanes appear to prove decisively that in the fifth century the actors stood on a considerably higher level than the chorus.

The wall which supported the stage in front was called the hyposkenion. In the original stage-buildings at Athens there was no permanent hyposkenion of stone, but a temporary wooden stage was erected each year. In later times the hyposkenion was always built of stone. According to Pollux it was decorated with pillars and small statues [1]. This statement is confirmed by existing remains. The front of the stage of Phaedrus at Athens is ornamented with a series of bas-reliefs. The hyposkenion at Epidaurus, which is very well preserved, consists of a simple wall, twelve feet high, with eighteen pilasters supporting an entablature. The illustration represents a restoration of one end of this hyposkenion [2]. The letter *a* denotes the door leading from the end of the hyposkenion into the orchestra. It has been remarked already that the presence of

---

[1] Poll. iv. 124 τὸ δὲ ὑποσκήνιον κίοσι καὶ ἀγαλματίοις κεκόσμητο πρὸς τὸ θέατρον τετραμμένοις, ὑπὸ τὸ λογεῖον κείμενον. When Athenaeus (631 E) speaks of a flute-player 'waiting in the hyposkenion,' till his turn came to perform, it is uncertain whether the word there denotes a room under the stage, or is used generally for the whole of the stage-buildings.

[2] The illustration is taken from Baumeister's Denkmäler, vol. iii. v. Theatergebäude.

doors leading through the hyposkenion into the orchestra appears to have been a peculiarity of the theatre at Epidaurus. The door marked *b* stands further back, and opens into the side-entrance. It would be by this door, or the corresponding one at the other end, that the chorus made their entrance into the orchestra.

Usually the actors stood on the stage, and the chorus in the orchestra. But sometimes the actors descended into the orchestra; and still more frequently the chorus ascended the stage. It was therefore necessary to have a means of communication between those two parts of the theatre. For this purpose steps were erected against the centre of the hyposkenion[1]. No traces of such steps have been preserved in any of the Greek theatres. In Roman theatres they are occasionally met with. For instance, the stage of Phaedrus at Athens, which is entirely Roman in style, has a flight of five stone steps in the centre leading down into the orchestra. But though there are no actual remains of these steps in any of the Greek theatres, they are expressly mentioned by ancient writers, and frequently occur in the vase-paintings of the third century B.C. from Magna Graecia, in which comic scenes are represented. A copy of one of the scenes is inserted on the next page, to show the style and formation of the steps[2]. It is probable that in the Greek theatres they were made of wood, and did not form a permanent part of

---

[1] Poll. iv. 127 εἰσελθόντες δὲ κατὰ τὴν ὀρχήστραν ἐπὶ τὴν σκηνὴν ἀναβαίνουσι διὰ κλιμάκων· τῆς δὲ κλίμακος οἱ βαθμοὶ κλιμακτῆρες καλοῦνται. Athen. de Mach. p. 29 (Wesch.) κατεσκεύασαν δέ τινες ἐν πολιορκίᾳ κλιμάκων γένη παραπλήσια τοῖς τιθεμένοις ἐν τοῖς θεάτροις πρὸς τὰ προσκήνια τοῖς ὑποκριταῖς.

[2] The illustration is from Wieseler's Denkmäler des Bühnenwesens, ix. 14.

the hyposkenion, but were merely set up when required. In the first place, there are not only no traces of such steps at Epidaurus, but the architectural character of the hyposkenion makes it clear that permanent stone steps could never have been affixed to it. In the second place, several of the vase-paintings from Magna Graecia depict stages with no such steps attached. In the third place, there is a wall painting at Herculaneum representing one of these flights of steps standing by itself, with an actor's mask at the top[1]. For these reasons

it seems fairly certain that the steps in the Greek theatres were not permanently affixed to the stage, but could be placed there or removed at pleasure.

Usually in Greek theatres the stage was terminated at each end by projecting portions of the stage-buildings, called side-wings. A door led from the stage into each of these side-wings. When this arrangement was adopted the stage practically consisted of a long narrow strip cut out of the stage-buildings. Such was the case in the theatres at Athens and the Peiraeeus. But side-wings were not an invariable feature of Greek theatres. In some cases the stage was erected in front of the stage-buildings, and was merely terminated by a wall at each end.

[1] Wieseler Denkmäl. ix. 15, iv. 5.

An examination of the ground-plan of the theatre at Epidaurus will illustrate this statement. The small projections at each end of the stage there are not side-wings, but form part of the stage itself. The stage is terminated at each side by a wall, and beyond this wall there is merely a flight of steps leading down to the ground outside. These flights of steps were probably covered over, so that persons ascending them would not be seen by the spectators in the auditorium. Where side-wings existed, it is probable that they were denoted by the word 'paraskênia,' being so called because they lay on each side of the skênê or stage [1].

In the later Greek theatres the wall at the back of the stage was built in an elaborate architectural design, and ornamented with pillars and statues. Specimens of back walls of this character are still to be seen in the theatres at Tauromenion and elsewhere, and Vitruvius gives minute directions for their construction [2]. Of course, when dramas were being performed the wall at the back of the stage was covered with painted scenery, and its architectural beauty was concealed from the spectators. But theatres in later times were regularly used for meetings of the people, as well as for dramatic performances. On such occasions, when the stage was without scenic decorations, the architectural elegance of the back-wall would add greatly to the beauty of the stage-buildings, and form a pleasing object to the eye. Speaking of the height of the back-wall, Vitruvius directs that its top should be exactly on a level with the uppermost part of the auditorium, as it was found that if this proportion was observed, the acoustic properties of the audi-

---

[1] The word παρασκήνια is explained in two ways by the commentators. (1) as a place beside the stage, used for storing stage-properties. Theophrastus is mentioned as the authority for this explanation. (2) As the side-entrances leading on to the stage. See Harp., Phot., and Etym. Mag. s. v. παρασκήνια; Bekk. Anecd. p. 292; Ulpian on Demosth. Meid. § 17. Demosthenes (l. c.) accuses Meidias of 'nailing up the paraskenia,' and so hindering his chorus from making its appearance. As we do not know in what way the dithyrambic choruses entered the orchestra, it is difficult to decide on the exact meaning of the word paraskenia. Most likely they entered in the same way as the dramatic choruses; and Meidias nailed up the doors in the side-wings which led out into the parodoi. See Meineke Frag. Com. Gr. vol. iv. p. 722.

[2] Vitruv. v. 6; Wieseler Denkmäler, iii. 6.

torium were much improved[1]. It is not known for certain whether the stage in the early Greek theatres was covered with a roof or not. At the Roman theatres of Aspendos and Orange the existing remains prove that the theatre was originally roofed over; but there is no sufficient ground for concluding that the same was the case in Greek theatres of the early period[2]. Both Vitruvius and Pollux, in describing the scenery used in a Greek theatre, speak of three doors at the back of the stage. As a matter of fact, in all the later Greek theatres, the wall at the back of the stage invariably has five doors[3]. It is obvious, therefore, that all these doors cannot have been used during dramatic representations. When the stage was prepared for the performance of a play, the two doors on the outside must have been covered up by the scenery; or else, as Albert Müller suggests, temporary side-wings must have been erected in front of them. This latter supposition is all the more probable, as the stages of the later Greek theatres were of enormous length, and might have been slightly shortened with advantage. The rooms at the back of the stage, as already pointed out, were not of any great depth, owing to the simplicity of the scenic appliances used in the Greek drama. At Athens the distance from the back of the stage to the back of the stage-buildings is little more than twenty-four feet; at Epidaurus it is rather less than twenty.

§ 9. *Relative position of Actors and Chorus.*

The different portions of the theatre have now been discussed in detail. There is still an important question to be considered, which is closely connected with the construction of the theatre, and that is the question as to the relative position occupied by actors and chorus during a dramatic performance. The ancient authorities are perfectly clear upon the subject. According to them the actors stood upon the stage, the chorus performed in

---

[1] Vitruv. v. 6.
[2] Müller's Bühnenalt. p. 28; Baumeister's Denkmäler, iii. p. 1747.
[3] Vitruv. v. 6; Poll. iv. 124; Müller's Bühnenalt. pp. 120, 121.

the orchestra underneath. If it was necessary to ascend from the orchestra to the stage, there were steps erected for that very purpose. While the actors were upon the stage, and the dialogue was proceeding, the chorus stood with their backs towards the audience, and their faces towards the stage[1]. This last fact places prominently before us the radical difference between the Greek chorus, and that of a modern opera. It proves conclusively that in the grouping of the actors and chorus in a Greek theatre there could be none of that realistic imitation of ordinary life which is sometimes to be seen upon the modern stage. To produce effects of this kind would be absolutely impossible, when the chorus were standing some distance below the actors, and with their backs towards the audience. It is most necessary therefore, in discussing the external features of a Greek dramatic performance, not to judge them by a modern standard, but to remember that the whole arrangement was entirely different. The position of the chorus in a Greek theatre was not due to any abstract considerations of propriety, but was merely the result of the peculiar circumstances under which the Greek drama was developed. Originally the performance was almost entirely lyrical, and the stage and the actors were a mere appendage. The chorus, being the principal performers, and the most prominent object of attention, occupied the central position in the orchestra. The actors were placed on a stage behind them, so as to be visible to the spectators. Eventually the dialogue between the actors completely overshadowed the songs of the chorus, and the lyrical element in the performance faded into insignificance. But the

---

[1] Pollux iv. 123 καὶ σκηνὴ μὲν ὑποκριτῶν ἴδιον, ἡ δὲ ὀρχήστρα τοῦ χοροῦ. Vitruv. v. 7 ampliorem habent orchestram Graeci et scaenam recessiorem, minoreque latitudine pulpitum, quod λογεῖον appellant, ideo quod eo tragici et comici actores in scaena peragunt, reliqui autem artifices suas per orchestram praestant actiones. Dindorf Prolegom. de Comoed. p. 29 καὶ ὅτε μὲν πρὸς τοὺς ὑποκριτὰς διελέγετο (ὁ χορὸς ὁ κωμικός), πρὸς τὴν σκηνὴν ἀφεώρα, ὅτε δὲ ἀπελθόντων τῶν ὑποκριτῶν τοὺς ἀναπαίστους διεξῄει, πρὸς τὸν δῆμον ἀπεστρέφετο. Ibid. p. 36 εἰσῄει (ὁ χορὸς ὁ κωμικὸς) ἐν τετραγώνῳ σχήματι, ἀφορῶν εἰς τοὺς ὑποκριτάς. Dübner Prolegom. de Comoed. p. 20 εἰσελθὼν οὖν ὁ χορὸς εἰς τὴν ὀρχήστραν μέτροις τισὶ διελέγετο τοῖς ὑποκριταῖς, καὶ πρὸς τὴν σκηνὴν ἑώρα τῆς κωμῳδίας. Cp. Schol. Arist. Equit. 505; Dindf. Prolegom. de Com. p. 21.

chorus still continued to occupy that prominent position in the theatre which its original importance had assigned to it.

Nevertheless, great difficulties have been raised in connexion with this subject. It has been urged that if the stage was from ten to twelve feet high, and the chorus stood in the orchestra underneath, any intercourse between the actors and the chorus would have been out of the question. Before considering this point it will be useful to collect the evidence which is supplied by the extant Greek dramas as to the relations between actors and chorus in the course of a dramatic performance. In the first place in every Greek play conversations are frequent between the actors and the chorus, or between the actors and the leader of the chorus. Then again actors and chorus often join together in the performance of musical passages, each singing alternate portions. Besides this there are a few animated scenes, in which the chorus, or the leader of the chorus, ascends the stage, and comes into actual physical contact with the actors. For instance, in the Helen of Euripides, when Theoclymenus is rushing back to the palace to kill his sister, the leader of the chorus forcibly detains him. In the Oedipus Coloneus, when Creon is attempting to carry off Antigone, he is held back by the chorus. In the Knights of Aristophanes the coryphaeus hands the sausage-seller an oil-flask and some garlic, to assist him in his contest with Cleon[1]. In addition to these momentary appearances of the chorus upon the stage, there are occasional scenes in which the chorus occupies the stage for some length of time. In the Prometheus Vinctus the Oceanidae enter by the stage, and only descend into the orchestra some time afterwards. The opening scene of the Eumenides represents the Erinyes as sleeping in the temple of Apollo, from whence they are subsequently driven. The Supplices of Euripides opens with Aethra standing in front of the temple of Demeter, and the chorus of matrons kneeling round her, and encircling her with suppliant boughs. It is not till the end of the first scene that

---

[1] Eur. Hel. 1621–1641; Soph. O. C. 856, 857; Arist. Equit. 490–494. Other examples of the same sort of thing occur in Arist. Acharn. 324–327, Av. 353–400.

they descend into the orchestra. In the Peace of Aristophanes the chorus of farmers comes on the stage to help in hauling up the statue of Peace, and remains there for a considerable time[1]. Still the instances of the chorus appearing upon the stage, either momentarily, or for a length of time, are comparatively rare. In all the forty-four Greek plays which have come down to us hardly fifteen certain examples are to be found. On the other hand the cases are not infrequent, in which the chorus might naturally be expected to ascend the stage, and take part in the action; but while they are hesitating about doing so, their attention is diverted by some unforeseen incident, or by the advent of some new personage[2]. Instances of this kind, in which the poet seems to be at especial pains to avoid the necessity of bringing the chorus on the stage, appear to show that there were certain obstacles in the way of a free and easy intercourse between the actors and the chorus. The general result then of these investigations is as follows. The actors and the chorus were able to converse together without difficulty. If necessary the chorus could ascend the stage, and join in the action. But they very seldom do so, even when it might naturally be expected that they would. There must therefore have been some difficulty about the appearance of the chorus upon the stage. Their presence there must have been felt to be an anomaly.

This conclusion tallies exactly with the facts already stated, that the chorus stood in the orchestra underneath the stage, with their faces towards the actors, and that the communication between orchestra and stage was by means of steps. Under such circumstances it is obvious that it must have been impossible for the Greek chorus to take a prominent part in the proceedings upon the stage. A further question still arises, whether, granting that the actors stood on the stage, and the chorus in the orchestra, it is possible that the stage should have

---

[1] Aesch. Prom. Vinct. 128, 279; Eum. 179 ff.; Eur. Suppl. 8, 359; Arist. Pax 426–550. Cp. also Aesch. Suppl. 222–506; Eur. Hel. 327–515; Orest. 132–206; Arist. Vesp. 403–456.

[2] E. g. Soph. Ajax 328 ff.; Eur. Hec. 1042 ff., Androm. 817 ff., &c.

been as high as ten or twelve feet. If the stage was of this abnormal height, how, it is asked, could actors and chorus even converse together with any appearance of fidelity to nature? In order to meet this difficulty it has been suggested that the chorus did not stand upon the level of the orchestra, but upon a platform erected immediately in front of the stage. This platform, it is said, must have been some distance lower than the stage, or else the persons of the actors would have been concealed from view by the chorus standing in front of them. At the same time it must have been high enough to bring the chorus into moderate proximity to the actors, so as to enable them to converse together without any great violation of probability. This platform for the chorus has been rather a favourite conception with the writers upon the subject of the Greek drama. Its existence is defended partly upon general grounds, partly by an appeal to certain passages in ancient authors. To take the ancient authorities first. G. Hermann supposed that the platform was called 'orchestra' in a narrower sense. He cited a passage in Suidas, where the orchestra is described as coming after the skênê, and as being a wooden platform on which mimes performed. But in this passage the context clearly proves that the word 'orchestra' is used in its later sense as 'the stage.' Hermann's view has therefore been very generally discarded[1].

[1] G. Hermann Opusc. vi. 2, p. 152 ff. The passage occurs in Suidas and Etym. Mag. v. σκηνή, and also in Schol. Greg. Nazianz. 355 B (see Hermes for 1872, p. 490). In all three places it is corrupt and mutilated, but the last version of the three is the most complete, and runs as follows:—σκηνή ἐστιν ἡ μέση θύρα τοῦ θεάτρου, παρασκήνια δὲ τὰ ἔνθεν καὶ ἔνθεν τῆς μέσης θύρας χαλκᾶ κάγκελλα· ὧν τὰ ἐντὸς καὶ τῆς μέσης θύρας ἢ ἵνα σαφέστερον εἴπω, σκηνή. μετὰ τὴν σκηνὴν εὐθὺς καὶ τὰ παρασκήνια ἡ ὀρχήστρα· αὕτη δέ ἐστιν ὁ τόπος ὁ ἐκ σανίδων ἔχων τὸ ἔδαφος, ἐφ' οὗ θεατρίζουσιν οἱ μῖμοι. εἶτα μετὰ τὴν ὀρχήστραν βωμὸς ἦν τοῦ Διονύσου, τετράγωνον οἰκοδόμημα κενόν, ἐπὶ τοῦ μέσου, ὃ καλεῖται θυμέλη παρὰ τοῦ θύειν. μετὰ τὴν θυμέλην ἡ κονίστρα, τουτέστι τὸ κάτω ἔδαφος τοῦ θεάτρου. The passage is very corrupt, and little reliance can be placed on any inferences derived from it. The description of σκηνή as the 'middle door,' the χαλκᾶ κάγκελλα, and the statement that the konistra comes *after* the thymele, are all astonishing. But it is clear that ὀρχήστρα here means the stage. This appears not only from the context, but also from the fact that it is said to have been the place for the μῖμοι. Wieseler bases upon the above passage his peculiar theory that the thymele was the platform for the chorus, and not an altar at all. He relies on the words τετράγωνον οἰκοδύμημα κενόν. It is true that the passage is obscure. But if it proves one thing more than another, it proves that the thymele was the altar of Dionysus, and stood in the orchestra.

III.] RELATIVE POSITION OF ACTORS AND CHORUS. 155

Wieseler has endeavoured to prove that this platform for the chorus was denoted by the word 'thymele.' Now 'thymele' was a word which had a great many meanings in ancient times. At present we are only concerned with those which had reference to the theatre. As applied to the theatre it meant originally the altar of Dionysus in the centre of the orchestra. Subsequently it was extended to denote the orchestra, or space surrounding the altar. In later times, when the Roman fashion of transferring all performances to the stage very generally prevailed, the two words 'orchestra' and 'thymele' were both of them used to denote 'the stage.' Hence we have three distinct and recognised meanings for the word 'thymele' as applied to the theatre. It denoted, firstly, the altar of Dionysus, secondly, the orchestra, thirdly, the stage. If the passages are carefully examined, in which it is asserted that 'thymele' denotes a platform for the chorus in front of the stage, it will be found that in the majority of them the word is much more naturally explained as meaning the stage itself, or the orchestra. In one or two cases the language used is apparently due to a confusion between the different meanings of the term. In no case is there a clear and definite description of a platform standing half way up between the orchestra and the stage[1]. If such a platform had really existed, it seems incredible that there should have been

---

[1] For θυμέλη = the altar of Dionysus in the orchestra see the passages quoted on p. 133. For θυμέλη = ὀρχήστρα see p. 133. For θυμέλη = λογεῖον see Bekk. Anecd. p. 292 σκηνὴ δ' ἐστὶν ἡ νῦν λεγομένη θυμέλη, Schol. Arist. Equit. 149 ὡς δ' ἐν θυμέλῃ δὲ τὸ ἀνάβαινε. In addition to the Scholium quoted in the preceding note, the following passages are cited to prove that θυμέλη sometimes = the special platform for the chorus, between the orchestra and the stage, (1) Anth. Pal. vii. 21 πολλάκις ἐν θυμέλῃσι καὶ ἐν σκηνῇσι τεθηλὼς | βλαισὸς Ἀχαρνίτης κισσὸς κ.τ.λ. (2) Corp. Inscr. Gr. 6750 δόξαν φωνήεσσαν ἐνὶ σκηναῖσι λαβοῦσαν | παντοίης ἀρετῆς ἐν μείμοις, εἶτα χοροῖσι | πολλάκις ἐν θυμέλαις. (3) Schol. Aristid. iii. p. 536 (Dindf.) ὁ χορὸς ὅτε εἰσῄει ἐν τῇ ὀρχήστρᾳ ᾗ (MS. ἡ) ἐστι θυμέλη. (4) Poll. iv. 123 καὶ σκηνὴ μὲν ὑποκριτῶν ἴδιον, ἡ δὲ ὀρχήστρα τοῦ χοροῦ, ἐν ᾗ καὶ ἡ θυμέλη, εἴτε βῆμά τι οὖσα εἴτε βωμός. (5) Isidor. Origg. xviii. 47 et dicti thymelici, quod olim in orchestra stantes cantabant super pulpitum quod thymele vocabatur. In the first and second passages θυμέλη obviously = ὀρχήστρα. In the third passage it = ὀρχήστρα or βωμὸς Διονύσου, according as ἡ or ᾗ is read. In the fourth passage there is apparently a confusion of the two meanings of θυμέλη as 'a stage' and 'an altar.' In the fifth passage the two meanings of 'orchestra' and 'stage' are confused.

no mention of it. The language of Vitruvius in particular is hardly explicable on the supposition that such a platform was in use. He says that in a Roman theatre the stage was much deeper than among the Greeks, because it had to contain all the performers, chorus as well as actors. It was only five feet high, in order that the senators sitting in the orchestra might be able to see down to the end of it. In a Greek theatre on the other hand the chorus performed in the orchestra, the actors upon the stage. The stage was therefore much narrower, and was from ten to twelve feet high[1]. It is hardly credible that Vitruvius would have expressed himself in this way, if the Greek chorus had occupied a platform five or six feet below the level of the stage. As far then as ancient authorities are concerned, the theory as to the existence of a platform for the chorus finds absolutely no support.

On general grounds there are several fatal objections to the theory. In the first place, if it were correct, we should have to believe that the Greeks first of all constructed an orchestra for the chorus to perform in; then built a stage twelve feet high; then, finding they had made their stage a great deal too lofty, got out of the difficulty by erecting a platform each year, to bring the chorus within reach of the actors. To suppose that the Greeks acted in this way would be to suppose that they were altogether deficient in common sense. In the second place it must not be forgotten that the performances at the City Dionysia consisted of dithyrambs as well as dramas. The dithyrambic choruses contained fifty members, and stood in a circular position. They must therefore have required a very considerable space for their performances. The oblong platform in front of the stage would not have been large enough to accommodate them, but would have been large enough to encroach very extensively upon the orchestra, and to drive the dithyrambic choruses into one end of it. That such was the case is most improbable. In the third place, in the theatre at Epidaurus there are no traces of any appliances for the erection of the

---

[1] Vitruv. v. 6, 7.

supposed platform. We should have expected to find holes in the floor of the orchestra, and sockets in the hyposkenion, for the reception of the beams by which the platform was supported. But neither at Epidaurus nor elsewhere are any such traces to be found. Fourthly, on the floor of the orchestra at Epidaurus a large circle is marked out with a stone border immediately in front of the stage. It is difficult to resist the conclusion that this circle was intended for the performances of the chorus. Fifthly, at the end of the Wasps the chorus make their exit dancing, headed by Philocleon and the sons of Carcinus. If they had occupied an elevated platform in the orchestra, this form of exit would have been impossible. For these reasons, combined with the silence of ancient writers, there appears to be no doubt that the platform for the chorus in front of the stage must be regarded as a fiction of modern times.

As to the enormous height of the Greek stage, and the difference in altitude between the position of the chorus and that of the actors, perhaps it will not appear so incongruous, if we carefully dismiss from our minds all associations derived from the modern stage, and if we remember the vast size of the ancient theatres. We should regard the chorus in the foreground, with its carefully arranged groups, as the prominent feature in the spectacle; while the actors on the long and narrow stage behind formed a picturesque background, after the fashion of a frieze or bas-relief. Still there is no doubt some difficulty in imagining a conversation between persons in the orchestra and persons on a stage twelve feet above them. Perhaps during the fifth century the stage was not so high as at a subsequent period, and this may be the solution of the difficulty. It was only in the plays of the fifth century that there was any very close connexion and intercourse between chorus and actors, orchestra and stage. In the fourth century the chorus disappeared almost entirely from comedy, and in tragedy its functions came to be confined to the duty of merely singing interludes. It is true that there were frequent revivals of the tragedies of Aeschylus, Sophocles, and Euripides. But the number of such revivals was small, compared with the number of original plays produced at that time. Later on, even in the plays of the great tragedians, the choral parts were curtailed or omitted[1]. Speaking roughly therefore it may be said that it was only in the drama of the fifth century that the chorus took a prominent part in the progress of each piece, and it was only at that period that a close connexion between the orchestra and the stage was desirable. Now the evidence as to the height of the Greek stage depends upon two sources, the statement of Vitruvius, and the remains of the theatre at Epidaurus. This evidence, at the earliest, does not bring us any further back than the middle of the fourth century[2]. All we know as to the stage in the Athenian theatre during the fifth century is that it was not a permanent erection at all, but merely a temporary structure of wood. There is no need to suppose that its height was definitely fixed at that time. It may have varied at different periods, and the average height may have been six or seven feet instead of ten or twelve. The subsequent raising of the stage may have been connected with the curtailment of the chorus. Of course all this is mere conjecture. At any rate the suggestion that there was a special platform for the chorus has been shown to be utterly improbable and unsupported. The other theory, that during the fifth century actors and chorus were both in the orchestra and on the same level, appears to be conclusively disproved by certain passages in Aristophanes, as well as by other considerations. All that can be regarded as fairly well established is that from the earliest period the chorus performed in the orchestra, and the actors upon an elevated stage. From the middle of the fourth century onwards this stage was from ten to twelve feet high. As to its height during the fifth century, this is a point upon which it is impossible to speak with certainty.

§ 10. *Various details.*

To return to the subject of the construction of the theatre in general. It is obvious that, considering the enormous size of

[1] Dio Chrysost. or. xix. p. 288, Dindf.   [2] See above, p. 142.

the building, and the immense number of spectators which it was intended to accommodate, the greatest attention must have been bestowed upon its acoustic properties. Vitruvius is most emphatic upon the necessity of keeping this object in view, when choosing a site for a theatre. The situation against the side of a hill, and the gentle and symmetrical upward slope of the tiers of seats, are mentioned as qualities by which acoustic excellence was ensured. The height of the stage-buildings was also of great importance. It was found that the best results were obtained by making them exactly the same height as the uppermost parts of the auditorium[1]. The wooden stage also contributed to make the voices of the actors more audible. When Alexander the Great wished to have a stage built entirely of bronze, it was pointed out to him that this material would be fatal from the acoustic point of view[2]. Vitruvius mentions a peculiar practice which was adopted for the purpose of adding resonance to the voices of the actors. Hollow vessels of bronze, of different tones, were suspended in niches in various parts of the auditorium. When a sound was uttered of the same tone as that of any of the vessels, its resonance was increased. He states that this custom, though not adopted in Rome, existed in many Greek and Italian theatres; and that Mummius, after his capture of Corinth, brought back several of these vessels from the theatre there. In the remains of the existing theatres no traces are to be found of the niches he describes[3]. It is probable that the whole plan was merely an experiment adopted in a few special cases. As far as Athens was concerned, no such extraneous assistance to the voice was necessary. Experiments at the present day have shown that the acoustic properties of the theatre of Dionysus are excellent; and this must have been still more the case when the stage-buildings were standing. Probably therefore, in spite of the vast numbers of the audience, the persons in the back rows could hear the words spoken in the orchestra and upon the

---

[1]. Vitruv. v. 6.
[2] Plut. Non posse suaviter &c., 1096 C.
[3] Vitruv. v. 5; Baumeister's Denkmäler, vol. iii. p. 1741.

stage much more clearly than might at first sight have been supposed.

Another point mentioned by Vitruvius in connexion with the theatre is the advantage of erecting porticoes in the rear of the stage-buildings, to serve as a shelter for the people in case of a sudden shower of rain, and also for the convenience of the choregi. He adds that at Athens there were three buildings close to the theatre, which served admirably for this purpose. These were the Odeum, the temple of Dionysus, and the Portico of Eumenes[1]. The Odeum here referred to must be that built by Pericles, since the only other one existing in the time of Vitruvius was close to the spring called Enneakrounos[2]. The exact position of the Odeum of Pericles has not been determined with certainty. The temple of Dionysus mentioned by Vitruvius is apparently the older of the two temples, marked D in the plan, and lying to the south-west of the original stage-buildings. The Portico of Eumenes is supposed to have been built by Eumenes II in the beginning of the second century B.C., and it is thought that traces of it are to be found stretching westwards from the theatre[3]. Immediately to the south of the stage-buildings are the foundations of a hall of late date, marked C in the plan. Possibly this may have been some erection in connexion with the theatre, built for the purposes described by Vitruvius. In the theatre itself there was no protection for the people either from the sun or from the rain. The huge canvass awnings, suspended upon masts, which the Latin writers refer to, were an invention of the Italians, and were only adopted in Greek theatres at a very late period[4].

The interior of the theatre at Athens was decorated with the statues of various public persons, some distinguished, others not. In the time of Lycurgus bronze statues were erected in honour of Aeschylus, Sophocles, and Euripides[5]. Pausanias

---

[1] Vitruv. v. 9.
[2] Plut. Pericles, p. 160 A; Pausan. i. 14. 1.
[3] Wheeler, in Papers of the American School at Athens, vol. i. p. 127.
[4] Val. Max. ii. 4. 6; Corp. Inscr. Gr. 4283.
[5] Plut. X orat. p. 841 F.

mentions that in his time there were several statues of dramatic poets in the theatre, but, with the exception of Sophocles, Euripides, and Menander, they were all very obscure individuals[1]. Astydamas, the tragic poet, was voted a statue in the theatre on account of the excellence of his tragedy called Parthenopaeus. He wrote an epigram to be inscribed upon the base, regretting that he had not been born in the time of the great tragic writers, so as to be able to compete with worthy antagonists. The Athenians were so disgusted with his conceit, that they refused to allow the epigram to be inscribed, and the expression 'to praise one's self like Astydamas' passed into a proverb[2]. In addition to the statues of the dramatic poets there were also statues of Themistocles and Miltiades, each with a captured Persian standing beside him[3]. In later times it is stated that a statue of Eurycleides the conjuror was erected in the theatre[4]. It is probable that during the reign of Hadrian thirteen statues of him were placed in the thirteen different blocks of the auditorium. The inscriptions on the bases of four of these statues have been found in the existing remains of the theatre[5]. Besides the statues there were also various inscriptions and tablets connected with theatrical affairs. A copy of the decree of the Amphictyonic Council, conferring certain privileges upon the Athenian actors, was inscribed in stone and put up in the theatre[6]. Numerous records of dramatic and dithyrambic contests were erected either in the theatre, or the immediate neighbourhood. There were lists of the victors in all the competitions at the Lenaea and City Dionysia. There were lists of all the tragedies and comedies ever produced in the theatre at Athens. There were lists of all the poets and actors who had competed there, with the number of their victories appended to each name. A complete account of these various records has already been given at the end of the first chapter[7].

[1] Pausan. i. 21. 1.
[2] Suidas v. σαυτὴν ἐπαινεῖς.
[3] Schol. Aristid. iii. p. 535, ed. Dindorf.
[4] Athen. p. 19 E.
[5] Corp. Inscr. Att. iii. 464, 46–4668.
[6] Corp. Inscr. Att. ii. 551.
[7] See chap. i. pp. 59–62.

Before concluding this description of the theatre of Dionysus it may be interesting to give some account of the various other purposes for which it was used at different times, in addition to its primary object as a place for dramatic representations. From the earliest period the contests between the dithyrambic choruses were held in the theatre. The recitations of the rhapsodists and the competitions between the harp-players were also transferred to the same place from the Odeum in which they had been held previously[1]. Besides this various ceremonies unconnected with art took place in the theatre during the festivals of Dionysus. The large audiences attracted by the dramatic performances at the City Dionysia made it a suitable occasion for displays of various kinds. It was in the theatre at the City Dionysia that the orphan sons of soldiers, after being educated by the state, were publicly paraded, before being dismissed from state control. On the same occasion the tribute collected from the allies was exhibited in the orchestra, as a proof of the power and magnificence of the Athenian empire. When crowns were bestowed upon deserving citizens, it was a special mark of honour for the fact to be proclaimed in the theatre at the City Dionysia[2]. The annual cock-fight in commemoration of the Persian invasion was held in the theatre[3]. But the most important of the non-dramatic purposes for which the theatre came to be used was that of meeting-place for the assemblies of the people. In the fifth and fourth centuries the regular place of assembly was the Pnyx. But already at a very early period special assemblies used to be held in the theatre after each festival of Dionysus, to discuss matters connected with the festival. These semi-religious meetings probably paved the way to the later practice of holding ordinary meetings there. As early as the year 411, on the occasion of the overthrow of the Four Hundred,

---

[1] Hesych. v. ᾠδεῖον.
[2] See chap. ii. p. 89.
[3] Aelian. Var. Hist. ii. 28. On the outside of the arms, in the throne of the priest of Dionysus, there are two bas-reliefs, in which kneeling Cupids are depicted in the act of setting cocks to fight. The significance of the reliefs is explained by the fact that the annual cock-fight was held in the theatre. See Julius in Zeitschrift für bildende Kunst, vol. xiii. p. 198.

Thucydides mentions that an assembly of the people was held in the theatre. It was in the theatre that the meeting was convened which condemned Phocion and his friends to death in 317 B.C. In 295 B.C. Demetrius, after capturing the city, summoned a gathering of the people in the theatre[1]. These meetings were all of a special character, and were not regular assemblies of the people; but they served as precedents for the use of the theatre for political, as opposed to religious and artistic, purposes. Similarly we are told on the authority of Aristotle that the Ephebi received their shields and spears from the state at assemblies of the people in the theatre[2]. After the middle of the third century the theatre became the regular meeting-place. The Pnyx henceforward was only used for assemblies for the election of magistrates[3]. In this later period the theatre was also used for various exhibitions which seemed unworthy of its character as a temple of Dionysus. Sword-swallowers, conjurors, and exhibitors of puppet-shows are mentioned among the entertainers who occupied the stage which had formerly been dignified by Euripides[4]. But the greatest degradation which the theatre at Athens ever suffered was when, under the influence of Roman custom, it was given up to gladiatorial combats. This was a pollution which called forth indignant protests from writers such as Philostratus and Dio Chrysostom[5].

[1] Demosth. Meid. § 9; Thucyd. viii. 93, 94; Plut. Phoc. p. 757 D, Demetr. p. 905 A; Müller (Bühnenalt. p. 74) is mistaken in stating, on the authority of Diod. xvi. 84, that on the news of the capture of Elatea in 339, the Athenians hastily assembled in the theatre. The description in Diodorus is merely a paraphrase of the celebrated description in Demosth. de Cor. § 169. Demosthenes says that at daybreak, before the Senate had transacted the preliminary business, the people had already taken their seats in the Pnyx (ἄνω καθῆτο). When Diodorus says that they met in the theatre, he is merely using the language of his own time, the theatre being then the regular meeting-place.

[2] Harpocrat. v. περίπολος.

[3] Poll. viii. 132.

[4] Plut. Lycurg. p. 51 E; Athen. p. 19 E; Alciphron iii. 20.

[5] Dio Chrysost. or. xxxi. p. 386, Dindf.; Philostrat. vit. Apoll. iv. 22 (vol. i. p. 142, ed. Kayser).

CHAPTER IV.

THE SCENERY.

§ 1. *General character of the Scenery.*

THE scenery in use upon the Attic stage was simple in character and limited in amount, compared with that employed in a modern theatre. Elaborate set pieces and gorgeous spectacular effects were entirely unknown. The principal expense in the production of a play was the training of the chorus, the payment of the actors, and the supply of suitable dresses. The scenery was never made the prominent feature of the exhibition. All that was desired was an appropriate background to show off to advantage the figures of the performers. The simplicity in the character of the ancient scenery was a necessary result of the peculiar construction of the stage. The Attic stage was a long and narrow strip, little more than ten feet in depth, and bounded in the rear by an immovable wall, which could neither be drawn asunder, nor pushed backwards or forwards. Under these circumstances any representation of the interior of a building was quite out of the question. All those elaborate spectacular illusions, which are rendered practicable by the great depth of the modern stage, were impossible in an ancient theatre. Nothing more was required than to cover over the permanent wall at the back with a suitable view. Then again, in addition to the simplicity of the mechanical arrangements, the number of scenes in use upon the Attic stage was very limited in amount. Not only was a change of scene in the course of the same play practically unknown, but there was often very little difference between one play and another as regards the character of the scenery required. Each of the three great branches of the drama had a background of a conventional type specially appropriated to itself, and this typical background was the one usually adopted. When therefore a series of tragedies was being exhibited, or a series of comedies, it must often have happened that the same scenery would do duty for two or three plays in succession. Thus the question of the scenery was one of the smallest of the difficulties which the Attic stage-manager had to contend with. Very little variety was necessary, and the mechanical arrangements were simple in the extreme.

At the same time it would be a mistake to suppose that there was anything poor or mean in the scenery of the Athenian theatre. The greatest period of the Attic drama corresponded with the greatest period of Attic art. Poets like Aeschylus and Sophocles personally superintended the mounting of their plays. It is safe therefore to conclude that the scenery was thoroughly in harmony with the rest of the performance, and was as elaborate as the nature of the Greek drama required. It would have been alien to the simplicity of the Attic taste to have allowed the poetry and the acting to be overshadowed by gorgeous spectacles and magnificent decorations. The prominent feature in an Athenian dramatic performance was the chorus in the foreground, with its graceful arrangement and picturesque dresses. Above the chorus, on the narrow stage, stood the actors and mute figures, arranged in line, and dressed in brilliant colours. The long scene in the rear formed a pleasing background, and showed off the persons of the actors to advantage. It presented a broad expanse to the eye; but not much attempt was made to convey the ideas of depth and of distance. In its general effect the scene upon the stage resembled a long frieze or bas-relief painted in brilliant colours, rather than a picture with a distant perspective.

It was only by a process of very gradual development that the scenic arrangements and general mounting of a play were brought to that pitch of excellence which they displayed during the latter part of the fifth century and afterwards.

The art of stage decoration among the Greeks grew out of very small beginnings. During the earliest period of the drama the background to the actor's platform consisted merely of some booth or covered erection for the performer to change his dress in. Out of this booth and platform were developed the stage and stage-buildings of a later period. At first the whole structure was of wood, and the background to the stage consisted of a bare hoarding, with doors for the actors to enter by. There was no painted scenery, and no attempt was made to give an actual representation of the scene in which the action was supposed to be taking place. Everything was left to the imagination of the spectators. In this respect the early Attic stage resembled our own Elizabethan drama, in which scenery was practically unknown, and the back of the stage consisted merely of a bare wall. When Aeschylus made his first appearance as a tragic writer things were still in this primitive condition. The progress of the art of stage decoration can be distinctly traced in the extant plays of Aeschylus. In the Supplices, the earliest of his tragedies, there is no mention of any scenery in the background, no clear definition of the exact spot where the action is taking place. The only thing that is distinctly referred to is the altar of the gods at which the suppliants take shelter. In this respect, in the total absence of local colouring, the Supplices differs from all the other Greek plays which have been preserved. It may therefore be concluded with certainty that at the time when the Supplices was produced the scenic art was still in its infancy. The back of the stage was merely a bare wall, and the only attempt at decoration consisted in placing upon the stage such properties as were required by the particular play. In the Supplices there was an altar, and that was all[1]. In the Prometheus Vinctus the scene of the action is clearly defined as a rocky region of the Caucasus. But in all probability the rock to which Prometheus is chained was merely built up upon the stage, and no attempt was made to give an elaborate representation of the view. The scene of the Persae is before the palace of King Xerxes, and the

[1] Aesch. Suppl. 189.

palace is distinctly referred to in the course of the play[1]. But in the Seven against Thebes, which was produced five years after the Persae, there is again very little local colouring. All is vague and indistinct. The scene of the play is not far from the Acropolis at Thebes, but there is no mention of any palace or other building from which the actors make their entrance[2]. In the Oresteia, the last dramatic production of Aeschylus, a great advance is noticeable in the art of scenic decoration. In all the three plays of which the trilogy is composed the scene of the action is very clearly defined, and very frequently referred to. The first two tragedies take place in front of the palace of Agamemnon at Argos; the scene of the third is partly before the temple of Apollo at Delphi, partly before that of Athênê at Athens[3]. By this time painted scenery had been invented, and was doubtless used in the Oresteia. The contrast between the earliest and the latest of the tragedies of Aeschylus, as regards local colouring and allusions to the scene of action, is very marked and conspicuous, and clearly denotes the advance which had been made in the manner of mounting a play. It is also noticeable that in all the three tragedies of the Oresteia the machine called the ekkyklêma is employed[4]. It is obvious, therefore, that by this time the stage-buildings had reached a certain degree of elaboration, else such an appliance could hardly have been used. Whether they were still of wood, or had already been built of stone, in any case they probably resembled in their general character and arrangement the stage-buildings of a later period.

By the middle of the fifth century the use of painted scenery had fully established itself. After this period no great change was made in the general system of mounting a play. There was still, no doubt, much room for improvement in the manner in which the work was carried out. The art of scene-painting was brought to greater perfection by succeeding generations, and

---

[1] Aesch. Pers. 159, 160.
[2] Aesch. Theb. 240.
[3] Aesch. Agam. 3, Choeph. 22, Eum. 35, 242.
[4] Aesch. Agam. 1372 ff., Choeph. 973 ff., Eum. 40 ff.

various mechanical appliances and devices were introduced. But by the middle of the fifth century the general method of stage decoration had been finally settled, and was only modified in details at a subsequent period. Taking this date as our starting-point, it will be interesting to consider the question as to the number and character of the scenes most in use upon the Attic stage. Our principal authority will be the Greek plays still in existence.

Vitruvius divides scenery into three classes—tragic, comic, and satyric. According to his description the salient features in a tragic scene were columns, pediments, statues, and other signs of regal magnificence. In comedy the scene represented a private house, with projecting balconies, and windows looking out upon the stage. The scenery in the satyric drama consisted of a rustic region, with trees, caverns, mountains, and other objects of the same kind[1]. The above list is not intended to be an exhaustive one. It merely describes in general outline the type of scene which was most characteristic of each of the three great branches of the drama. At the same time it is more exhaustive than might at first sight be supposed. If the extant Greek dramas are examined, it will be found that in the great majority of cases the scenery conforms to the general type described by Vitruvius. To take the tragic poets first. Twenty-five tragedies by Sophocles and Euripides have been preserved. In no less than seventeen out of the twenty-five the scene is laid in front of a palace or a temple[2]. In all these cases the general character of the scenery would be exactly such as Vitruvius describes. The prominent feature would be a magnificent building, with columns, pediments, and statues. Of the remaining eight tragedies, there are four in which the scene consists of an encampment, with tents in the background[3]. The other four all require special scenery. In the Philoctetes the scene is laid in front of a cavern in a desert

---

[1] Vitruv. v. 6.
[2] Viz. Soph. O. R., Antig., Electr., Trach.; Eur. Alc., Med., Hipp., Herc. Fur., Phoen., Hel., Orest., Bacch., Ion, Iph. Taur., Andr., Suppl., Heraclid.
[3] Viz. Eur. Hec., Troad., Iph. Aul., Rhesus.

island. In the Ajax it is laid partly before the tent of Ajax, partly in a solitary quarter by the sea-shore. The background in the Oedipus Coloneus consists of a country region, with the sacred enclosure of the Eumenides in the centre. Finally, the Electra of Euripides is altogether exceptional in having its scene laid before a humble country cottage. On the whole the evidence of the extant tragedies tends to confirm the statement of Vitruvius, and exemplifies the conventional character of Greek tragic scenery. In the great majority of instances the background would be an imposing pile of buildings, adorned with various architectural embellishments. As to the satyric drama, the Cyclops of Euripides is the only specimen of this class of composition which has been preserved. The scene there corresponds exactly to the description of Vitruvius, and consists of a country region, with the cave of Polyphemus in the centre. There can be little doubt that in all satyric dramas the background was of much the same character. As the chorus always consisted of satyrs, whose dwelling was in the forest, the scene of the play would naturally be laid in some deserted country district. In regard to comedy, it is necessary to distinguish between the Old Comedy and the New. The scene in the New Comedy was almost invariably laid in front of an ordinary private house, as is proved by the adaptations of Plautus and Terence. In the Old Comedy, to judge from the extant plays of Aristophanes, the same was generally the case. In six out of the eleven comedies of Aristophanes, the background consists merely of a house, or of houses standing side by side[1]. In four others the principal part of the action takes place before a house. In the Thesmophoriazusae the scene consists of a house and a temple standing side by side. In the Lysistrata there is a private house, and near it the entrance to the Acropolis. In the Acharnians the opening scene takes place in the Pnyx; the rest of the action is carried on before the houses of Dicaeopolis, Euripides, and Lamachus. The scene in the Knights is laid partly before the

[1] Viz. the Wasps, Peace, Clouds, Frogs, Ecclesiazusae, Plutus.

house of Demos, and partly in the Pnyx. The only comedy in which the scenery is of an altogether exceptional character is the Birds, in which the background consists of a wild country region, filled with rocks, and trees, and bushes. It appears, therefore, that even in the Old Comedy there was not much variety in the scenery.

The result of this examination of the extant plays is to prove that the number of scenes required on the Attic stage was not very large. In most plays the action took place before a palace, or a temple, or a private house. In such cases it is probable that the same scenes were used over and over again; and if it was necessary to make any distinction between the scenes in different plays, a rearrangement of the ornaments and properties upon the stage would suffice for all practical purposes. On the Athenian stage the scenery was entirely subordinated to the music and the acting. It helped to carry out the illusion, but was never allowed to predominate. To make spectacular effects the prominent feature in a dramatic performance would have been utterly foreign to the taste of the Athenians.

§ 2. *Mechanical arrangements for the Scenery.*

The scenery consisted of painted curtains or boards, which were affixed to the wall at the back of the stage. The ordinary name for a scene was skênê or proskênion [1]. According to Aristotle the invention of scene-painting was due to Sophocles. Vitruvius on the other hand assigns it to Aeschylus [2]. His

---

[1] Poll. iv. 131 καταβλήματα δὲ ὑφάσματα ἢ πίνακες ἦσαν ἔχοντες γραφὰς τῇ χρείᾳ τῶν δραμάτων προσφόρους· κατεβάλλετο δ' ἐπὶ τὰς περιάκτους ὄρος δεικνύντα ἢ θάλατταν ἢ ποταμὸν ἢ ἄλλο τι τοιοῦτον. Suid. v. προσκήνιον· τὸ πρὸ τῆς σκηνῆς παραπέτασμα. For the use of σκηνή = the painted scenery at the back of the stage, see chap. iii. p. 139. Nannio the courtesan was called 'proskênion' because of the deceptive character of her beauty (Athen. p. 587 B).

[2] Aristol. Poet. c. 4 καὶ τό τε τῶν ὑποκριτῶν πλῆθος ἐξ ἑνὸς εἰς δύο πρῶτος Αἰσχύλος ἤγαγε καὶ τὰ τοῦ χοροῦ ἠλάττωσε καὶ τὸν λόγον πρωταγωνιστὴν παρεσκεύασεν. τρεῖς δὲ καὶ σκηνογραφίαν Σοφοκλῆς. Vitruv. vii. praef. § 11. Vitruvius' account is supported by the statement in the Life of Aeschylus that γραφαί were first introduced by him.

account of the matter is precise and full of detail. He says that the first tragic scene ever painted was made by a certain Agatharchus under the superintendence of Aeschylus, and that Agatharchus wrote a book upon the subject. His example was followed by Democritus and Anaxagoras, who composed similar treatises. In these works they laid down the rules of perspective, and pointed out the proper method of producing upon the flat surface of a scene the effect of gradations of distance. The account in Vitruvius has a great appearance of accuracy, and it is probable that he is correct in ascribing the introduction of scene-painting to Aeschylus. But it is clear that it cannot have come into use much before the middle of the fifth century; otherwise there would have been no grounds for assigning the invention to Sophocles, who only began to exhibit in 468. The statements of Vitruvius prove that the art was rapidly brought by the Greeks to a very considerable degree of perfection.

As the mechanical arrangements for fixing up the scenery have not been described by any of the ancient writers, a detailed account of the matter is impossible. But several facts of a general character can be deduced from the testimony of the existing plays. It is therefore not difficult to form a rough conception of the arrangements which must have been adopted in preparing the back of the stage for a dramatic representation. In all Greek plays the action was supposed to take place in the open air. The scene was generally laid before some building or tent, or in a country district with a rock or cavern in the background. The upper portion of the painted scene represented merely the sky, and was probably the same in all dramas. The lower portion was separable from the upper, and on it was delineated the building or landscape which the particular play required. This lower portion of the scene must have stood some small distance in front of the upper portion. It is impossible that the whole scene should have been in one piece, and have ascended in a straight line from the bottom to the top of the stage. If this had been the case there would have been no room for the narrow ledge or platform, which Pollux calls the 'distegia[1].' The distegia was a contrivance which enabled actors to take their stand upon the roof of a palace or private house. Several instances of its use are to be found in the existing Greek plays. For example, the Agamemnon of Aeschylus opens with the watchman sitting upon the roof of the palace at Argos, and waiting for the beacon's signal. In the Phoenissae of Euripides Antigone and the attendant mount upon the roof to get a view of the army encamped outside the city. In the concluding scene of the Orestes Hermione and Orestes are seen standing upon the roof of the palace. Examples are also not infrequent in comedy. In the Acharnians the wife of Dicaeopolis views the procession from the roof of the house. At the commencement of the Wasps Bdelycleon is seen sleeping upon the roof, and his father Philocleon tries to escape through the chimney. At the end of the Clouds Strepsiades climbs up by a ladder to the roof of the phrontisterion, in order to set it on fire. The distegia must also have been used in such scenes as that in which Evadne appears upon the summit of a cliff, and that in which Lysistrata and Myrrhina are seen upon the battlements of the Acropolis[2]. It follows from these examples that there must have been room enough between the top of the palace or other building, and the surface of the scene behind it, to allow a narrow ledge or platform to be inserted. The arrangements for the purpose could hardly have been carried out in any other way than that described above. The scene must have consisted of two portions, the upper and the lower. The upper portion, representing the sky, must have been affixed to the permanent wall at the back of the stage, and probably remained the same in all dramas. The lower portion, representing the building or landscape, would be fastened to a wooden frame a short distance in front of the permanent back-wall. There

[1] Poll. iv. 129 ἡ δὲ διστεγία ποτὲ μὲν ἐν οἴκῳ βασιλείῳ διῆρες δωμάτιον, οἷον ἀφ' οὗ ἐν Φοινίσσαις ἡ 'Αντιγόνη βλέπει τὸν στρατόν, ποτὲ δὲ καὶ κέραμος, ἀφ' οὗ βάλλουσι τῷ κεράμῳ· ἐν δὲ κωμῳδίᾳ ἀπὸ τῆς διστεγίας πορνοβοσκοί τι κατοπτεύ-ουσιν ἢ γρᾴδια ἢ γύναια καταβλέπει.

[2] Aesch. Agam. 3; Eur. Phoen. 89, 193, Orestes 1567–1575; Aristoph. Acharn. 262, Vesp. 68, 144, Nub. 1485–1503, Lysist. 864, 874, 883.

would thus be room for the erection of the ledge or distegia between the wooden frame and the wall at the back.

If the scene represented a dwelling-house, there were windows in the upper storey, out of which the characters could peer upon the stage. Such windows are mentioned by Vitruvius, and instances of their use occur in the extant comedies. For example Philocleon in the Wasps tries to escape out of an upper window, and in the Ecclesiazusae the old woman and the young girl are seen looking out of one[1]. It need hardly be remarked that the doors of the building represented by the painted scenery would correspond more or less closely with the permanent doors in the back-wall, so as to admit of easy ingress and egress to the actors. In the same way if the scene was a cavern in a country region, the entrance to the cavern would be made to correspond with the central door in the wall at the back. Concerning the manner in which the scenery was finished off at the top nothing can be laid down for certain. It is not even known whether the stage itself was covered with a roof or not. The fact that there was a roof to the stage in Roman theatres is hardly sufficient ground for forming any definite conclusion as to the Athenian theatre of the earliest period[2].

§ 3. *The entrances to the Stage.*

The question as to the number and the character of the entrances leading upon the stage is one of some importance in connexion with the Greek drama. In order to avoid confusion in dealing with this subject it is necessary to carefully distinguish between the permanent doors in the walls surrounding the stage, and the temporary doors or entrances which were left when the scenery had been put up. First, as to the permanent doors. It will be evident from what follows that every Greek theatre must have had at least five such doors. There must have been three doors in the stone wall

[1] Vitruv. v. 6; Arist. Vesp. 379, Eccles. 924, 930, 961–963.   [2] See chap. iii. p. 150.

at the back of the stage, and two doors at the sides, one leading from each of the wings. Probably this was the plan adopted in the earliest stage-buildings at Athens. In the later theatres the stage was much longer than at Athens, and there were always five doors in the wall at the back. But it has been pointed out in the last chapter that in all probability only three of these doors were used in the course of the actual performances, and that the two outer ones were either covered over by the scenery or concealed by temporary side-wings of wood[1].

The next point to be considered is the number of the entrances which had to be provided when the scenery was erected, and the stage was made ready for a dramatic performance. Pollux and Vitruvius, in speaking of the scenery and stage-decorations, agree in saying that there were three doors at the back of the stage[2]. But this statement is much too universal. In the majority of cases no doubt there were three such doors. When the scene represented a palace, or temple, or dwelling-house, three doors appear to have been always used. But when the scene was of an exceptional character, the number of the entrances from the back of the stage would vary according to the requirements of the play. For instance in the Philoctetes there would only be a single entrance, that from the cavern. In the first part of the Ajax the only entrance would be that leading out of the tent; in the second part there would be no entrance at all, the background consisting merely of a solitary region by the sea-shore. In the Cyclops the only opening at the back of the stage was the mouth of Polyphemus' cave. In such plays as the Prometheus of Aeschylus, and the Andromeda of Euripides, the background consisted of rocks and cliffs, and there was no entrance from that quarter. It is clear therefore that the statement that a Greek scene was provided with three doors or entrances at the back is not universally true, but only applies to the majority of cases.

Some details concerning the character of the three doors may be gathered from the statements in Pollux and Vitruvius[3].

[1] See chap. iii. p. 150.
[2] Poll. iv. 124, 126; Vitruv. v. 6.
[3] Vitruv. v. 6 ipsae autem scaenae suas habent rationes explicatas ita uti

When the scene was a palace, the central door was decorated with regal grandeur. The side-doors were supposed to lead to the guest-chambers. Occasionally one of the side-doors led to a guest-chamber, the other to a slaves' prison. In comedy the character and arrangement of the doors would vary considerably, according as the scene was laid in front of one, or two, or three dwelling-houses. In the last case, of which an example is supplied by the Acharnians, there would be one door for each of the three houses. Sometimes one of the side-doors represented the way into an outhouse, or workshop, or stable. Sometimes it led into a temple, as in the Thesmophoriazusae. In comedy, no doubt, there was much greater diversity as to scenic details than in tragedy.

In addition to the entrances at the back of the stage, which varied in number and character according to circumstances, there were also, according to Pollux and Vitruvius, two side-entrances on to the stage in every Greek play. There was one entrance from each of the side-wings[1]. That this must have been the case is proved by the evidence of the existing plays, apart from the statements of ancient writers. For instance in the Philoctetes it is obvious that Odysseus and Neoptolemus cannot have entered from the back of the stage. The only opening here was the cave of Philoctetes. Odysseus and his companion, who are supposed to have just landed on the island, could not have entered from any other direction but the side of the stage. Similarly in the Cyclops, where the scene represents the cave of Polyphemus, Odysseus and his mariners could only make

mediae valvae ornatus habeant aulae regiae, dextra ac sinistra hospitalia. Poll. iv. 124, 125 τριῶν δὲ τῶν κατὰ τὴν σκηνὴν θυρῶν ἡ μέση μὲν βασίλειον ἢ σπήλαιον ἢ οἶκος ἔνδοξος ἢ πᾶν τοῦ πρωταγωνιστοῦ τοῦ δράματος, ἡ δὲ δεξιὰ τοῦ δευτεραγωνιστοῦντος καταγώγιον· ἡ δὲ ἀριστερὰ τὸ εὐτελέστατον ἔχει πρόσωπον ἢ ἱερὸν ἐξηρημωμένον, ἢ ἄοικός ἐστιν· ἐν δὲ τραγῳδίᾳ ἡ μὲν δεξιὰ θύρα ξενών ἐστιν, εἱρκτὴ δὲ ἡ λαία. τὸ δὲ κλίσιον ἐν κωμῳδίᾳ παράκειται παρὰ τὴν οἰκίαν, παραπετάσματι δηλούμενον. καὶ ἔστι μὲν σταθμὸς ὑποζυγίων ... ἐν δὲ Ἀντιφάνους Ἀκεστρίᾳ καὶ ἐργαστήριον γέγονεν. Throughout this passage Pollux is guilty of his usual fault of converting particular cases into general rules.

[1] Poll. iv. 126 παρ' ἑκάτερα δὲ τῶν δύο θυρῶν τῶν περὶ τὴν μέσην ἄλλαι δύο εἶεν ἄν, μία ἑκατέρωθεν, πρὸς ἃς αἱ περίακτοι συμπεπήγασιν. Vitruv. v. 6 secundum ea loca versurae sunt procurrentes, quae efficiunt una a foro, altera a peregre, aditus in scaenam. Phot. v. παρασκήνια· αἱ εἴσοδοι αἱ εἰς τὴν σκηνήν.

their entrance from the side. Then again there are such scenes as that at the end of the Seven against Thebes, where the corpses of the two brothers are borne away to burial, and Antigone and Ismene follow slowly after. It is impossible to suppose that the procession retired into the palace. It must therefore have made its exit by a side-entrance.

The mode of using the different entrances was regulated by certain conventional rules such as were common among the Athenians. The openings at the back of the stage always led out of some building, or tent, or cavern, or other dwelling-place. They could only therefore be used by persons who were supposed to be inside the dwelling-place. People coming from the immediate neighbourhood, as well as people coming from a distance, had to enter the stage by one of the side-approaches. This arrangement was an obvious one, and could hardly have been otherwise. But as regards the use of the side-entrances the Athenians had a special regulation which was due entirely to local causes. The theatre at Athens was situated in such a position that the western side looked towards the city and the harbour, the eastern side towards the open country. In consequence of this fact the side-entrances upon the Athenian stage came to acquire a peculiar significance. If a man entered by the western side, it was understood that he was coming from the city where the scene of the action was laid, or from the immediate neighbourhood; or else that he had arrived from distant parts by sea, and was coming from the harbour. The eastern entrance was reserved for people who had journeyed from a distance by land. The same regulation was applied to the entrances to the orchestra. If a chorus came from the city, or the harbour, or the suburbs, it used the western parodos; if it came by land from a distance, it used the eastern[1]. It is obvious that at Athens, where play-bills

---

[1] Vitruv. v. 6 secundum ea loca versurae sunt procurrentes, quae efficiunt una a foro, altera a peregre, aditus in scaenam. Vit. Aristoph. (Dindf. Prolegom. de Com. p. 36) ὁ κωμικὸς χορὸς συνέστηκεν ἐξ ἀνδρῶν κδ΄. καὶ εἰ μὲν ὡς ἀπὸ τῆς πόλεως ἤρχετο ἐπὶ τὸ θέατρον, διὰ τῆς ἀριστερᾶς ἀψῖδος εἰσῄει, εἰ δὲ ὡς ἀπὸ ἀγροῦ, διὰ τῆς δεξιᾶς. Poll. iv. 126 τῶν μέντοι παρόδων ἡ μὲν δεξιὰ ἀγρόθεν ἢ ἐκ λιμένος ἢ ἐκ πόλεως ἄγει· οἱ δὲ ἀλλαχόθεν πεζοὶ ἀφικνούμενοι κατὰ τὴν

were unknown, a conventional arrangement of this kind would be of great assistance to the audience, and would enable them to follow the action of the piece with greater ease and intelligence than they could otherwise have done. The custom originated in the topographical situation of the Athenian theatre, but was afterwards adopted in all other Greek theatres, and became a conventional rule of the Greek stage. The entrances to the right of the audience were used by persons from the neighbourhood; the entrances to the left by persons from a distance.

Another regulation concerning the entrances upon the stage is mentioned by Pollux. It refers to the three doors at the back of the stage. According to Pollux the central door was reserved for the principal character, the door to the right for the secondary characters, the door to the left for those of least significance[1]. It is plain that this statement must be taken with very considerable deductions. In the first place it only applies to tragedy, and only to those plays in which the background represented a palace or similar building. Even then it cannot have been by any means universal. Pollux has here been following his favourite practice of making a general rule out of an occasional occurrence. His statement in fact only applies to dramas of the type of the Oedipus Tyrannus, in which the principal character is at the same time a person of the highest rank. In such cases it is very likely that his rule about the doors was observed. It would be in harmony with the statuesque and conventional character of Greek tragedy. But there are many plays in which it would be absurd to suppose that any such regulation was adopted. For in-

ἑτέραν εἰσίασιν. In the Life the words ἀπὸ ἀγροῦ denote 'from a distance.' In Pollux ἀγρόθεν means 'from the country in the suburbs.' As applied to the *stage* the words 'right' and 'left' were always used from the point of view of the actors: cp. the account of the periaktoi in Poll. iv. 126. But as applied to the *orchestra* they were sometimes used from the point of view of the actors, sometimes from that of the audience. Hence the eastern parodos might be called the right or the left parodos, according to the point of view from which it was regarded. This is the reason of the apparent discrepancy between the statements in the Life and in Pollux. The author of the Life is looking at the orchestra from the point of view of the actors, Pollux from the point of view of the audience.

[1] Poll. iv. 124.

stance, in the Antigone it can hardly be imagined that the tyrant Creon entered only by a side-door, while the central door, with its regal splendour, was reserved for the oppressed heroine Antigone. Similarly in the Electra it is ridiculous to suppose that Clytaemnestra entered from the inferior part of the palace, Electra from the more magnificent. There can be no doubt that Pollux, in his statement about the doors, has converted a few special instances into a general law.

The entrances to the stage were of course intended for the actors. They were also sometimes used by the chorus. For instance in the Helena the chorus ascends the stage, and disappears within the palace-doors. After a time it reappears from the palace, and descends once more into the orchestra[1]. But such cases are of very rare occurrence. The question has been raised whether in the same way the actors ever made their exits and entrances by the passages into the orchestra. The only example of an actor entering by the orchestra is in the Plutus of Aristophanes. When Carion is sent to fetch the chorus of farmers, the language of the play certainly seems to imply that he returns into the orchestra at the head of them, and afterwards ascends on to the stage[2]. But as this is the only example of such a proceeding, the matter must be considered doubtful. On the other hand there is no doubt that the actors occasionally made their exit by the orchestra. In the Eumenides Athênê and the Propompi descend into the orchestra, and retire at the head of the procession. At the end of the Wasps Philocleon comes down into the orchestra, and dances off followed by the chorus[3]. Such instances are however only rarely to be met with.

§ 4. *Changes of Scene.*

A change of scene during the actual progress of a play was a practice almost unknown upon the Greek stage during the classical period. In the extant tragedies only two instances

[1] Eur. Hel. 327, 515.
[2] Aristoph. Plut. 223–318.
[3] Aesch. Eum. 1003 ff.; Aristoph. Vesp. 1514 ff.
cf. Ar. Eccl.

are to be found, one in the Eumenides of Aeschylus, the other in the Ajax of Sophocles. It does not appear that in either case very much alteration in the scenery was required. In the Eumenides the earlier part of the action takes place in front of the temple of Apollo at Delphi, the latter part before the temple of Athênê at Athens. All that was here necessary was to change the statue in front of the temple. The background doubtless remained the same during both portions of the play. There is not the least reason to suppose that any attempt was made to depict the actual scenery of Delphi or of Athens. Such a supposition would be inconsistent with the rude and undeveloped state of scenic decoration during the Aeschylean period, and moreover minute accuracy of that kind was utterly foreign to the Athenian taste. The other example of a change of scene is in the Ajax of Sophocles. The play begins in front of the tent of Ajax, but ends in a solitary region by the sea-shore. Here again a very slight alteration in the scenery would have been sufficient. Probably the opening scene represented a coast view, with the tent of Ajax in the centre. During the latter part of the play the tent was made to disappear, and only the coast view was left behind. A change of this kind could have been easily carried out, without much mechanical elaboration. It is to be noticed that in each of the above cases, while the scenery was being changed, both orchestra and stage were deserted by the performers. In the Eumenides it was not until Apollo had retired into the temple, and the Erinyes had set out in pursuit of Orestes, that the change from Delphi to Athens took place. Similarly in the Ajax both Tecmessa and the chorus had disappeared in search of Ajax before the scene was transferred to the sea-shore. It appears then that as far as tragedy is concerned changes of scene were very rarely resorted to during the fifth century, and even then were of the slightest possible description.

In comedy they were equally unusual. The Old Comedy was a creation of the wildest fancy, utterly unfettered by any limitations of fact or probability. In the plays of the Old Comedy the scene of the action shifts about from one place to another in the most irregular fashion. All considerations of time and space are disregarded. But it may be taken for certain that on the actual stage no attempt was made to represent these changes of scene in a realistic manner. The scenery was no doubt of the simplest and most unpretending character, corresponding to the economical manner in which comedies were put upon the stage. In all the extant plays of Aristophanes a single background would have been sufficient. For instance in the Frogs the action takes place partly before the house of Hercules, partly in Hades before the house of Pluto. The background probably represented the houses standing side by side, or a single house may have done duty for that of Hercules and that of Pluto in turn. The opening scene of the Acharnians takes place in the Pnyx; the rest of the play is carried on before the houses of Dicaeopolis, Euripides, and Lamachus. Most likely the three houses stood in a row, the Pnyx being sufficiently represented by a few benches upon the stage. The fact that the house of Dicaeopolis was supposed to be sometimes in the town, and sometimes in the country, would be of very little moment in a performance like the Old Comedy, where the realities of existence were totally disregarded. In the Lysistrata the action is rapidly transferred from the front of a house to the front of the Acropolis. In the Thesmophoriazusae it takes place partly before a house, partly before the temple of Demeter. It is not necessary, in either of these plays, to suppose any change in the scenery. The house and the Acropolis in the one case, and the house and temple in the other, would be depicted as standing side by side. In the Knights the background throughout the play consisted of the house of Demos; and the Pnyx, as in the Acharnians, was represented by a few benches. As far then as the Old Comedy is concerned it is probable that changes of scenery in the course of a play were seldom or never resorted to. In the New Comedy, to judge from the adaptations of Plautus and Terence, they appear to have been equally infrequent. On the whole it may be said that elaborate changes of scene during a play were practically unknown throughout the classical period.

The only appliances for changing scenery that are mentioned by the ancient Greek writers are the 'periaktoi [1].' These were huge triangular prisms, revolving upon a socket at their base. Each of the three sides of the prism consisted of a large flat surface, shaped like an upright parallelogram. One of these prisms was placed at each end of the stage, in such a manner as to fit in exactly with the scene at the back, and continue it in the direction of the side-wings. Each of the three sides was painted to represent a different view, but care was taken that in every case the painting coincided exactly with the painting in the back-scene. As the periaktos or prism was turned round, it presented a different surface to the spectators. Accordingly it was possible, by revolving both the periaktoi, to make a change in the character of the scenery at each end of the stage, while the scene in the background remained the same as before. The periaktos to the right of the audience depicted views in the immediate neighbourhood of the city where the action was taking place. The periaktos to the left represented a more remote country. This fact corresponds exactly with the regulation already referred to, that the entrances to the right of the audience were reserved for people from the immediate neighbourhood, while people from a distance came in by the left.

[1] Poll. iv. 126 παρ' ἑκάτερα δὲ τῶν δύο θυρῶν τῶν περὶ τὴν μέσην ἄλλαι δύο εἶεν ἄν, μία ἑκατέρωθεν, πρὸς ἃς αἱ περίακτοι συμπεπήγασιν, ἡ μὲν δεξιὰ τὰ ἔξω πόλεως δηλοῦσα, ἡ δ' ἑτέρα τὰ ἐκ πόλεως, μάλιστα τὰ ἐκ λιμένος· καὶ θεούς τε θαλαττίους ἐπάγει, καὶ πάνθ' ὅσα ἐπαχθέστερα ὄντα ἡ μηχανὴ φέρειν ἀδυνατεῖ. εἰ δ' ἐπιστραφεῖεν αἱ περίακτοι, ἡ δεξιὰ μὲν ἀμείβει τόπον (a. l. τὸ πᾶν), ἀμφότεραι δὲ χώραν ὑπαλλάττουσιν. Vitruv. v. 6 secundum autem spatia ad ornatus comparata, quae loca Graeci περιάκτους dicunt, ab eo quod machinae sunt in his locis versatiles trigonoe habentes singulae tres species orna- tionis, quae, cum aut fabularum muta- tiones sunt futurae, seu deorum adventus cum tonitribus repentinis, versentur mutentque speciem ornationis in fronte, &c. Serv. on Verg. Georg. iii. 24 scaena quae fiebat aut versilis erat aut ductilis erat. Versilis tum erat cum subito tota machinis quibusdam convertebatur, et aliam picturae faciem ostendebat. How the periaktoi introduced sea-gods, and other objects too heavy for the mêchanê, is as yet an unsolved problem. A change of τόπος means a change from one part of the same district to another: a change of χώρα means an entire change of district.

The principal use of the periaktoi must have been to produce a change of scene in cases where the prominent feature of the background remained the same. For instance, if the action had been taking place in front of a temple or palace, and was to be transferred to a temple or palace in a different country, the requisite alteration might easily be carried out by means of the periaktoi. The building in the background would remain the same, but the scenery on each side would be altered. Occasions for using the periaktoi might occur, either in the course of the same play, or between different plays. Most Greek tragedies and comedies took place before a temple, a palace, or a private house. If therefore a series of plays was being exhibited, it might be convenient to retain the same scene in the background, and produce the necessary distinction between the different plays by altering the scenery at each side. The usage of the periaktoi was regulated by a curious conventional custom. If only one periaktos was turned round, the alteration in the scenery was of course confined to one end of the stage. This was done when the change of scene was supposed to be a slight one, and was merely from one part of the same district to another. But when the action was transferred to an entirely new district, then both the periaktoi were turned round, and the scenery was changed at each end. Besides their use in producing a change of scene, the periaktoi were also employed to introduce gods upon the stage in the midst of a thunderstorm. It is not said how this was managed; but the most probable explanation seems to be that when the god appeared at one end of the stage, the periaktos was turned round so as to change the blue sky into a dark and gloomy atmosphere. The sound of thunder would be imitated from within.

It is difficult to say when the periaktoi were first introduced, or whether they were used at all during the classical period of the Greek drama. They are mentioned by one grammarian among a list of stage appliances which might be ascribed to Aeschylus[1]. But it is most unlikely that contrivances of

---

[1] Cramer, Anecd. Par. i. 19 εἰ μὲν δὴ πάντα τις Αἰσχύλῳ βούλεται τὰ περὶ τὴν σκηνὴν εὑρήματα προσνέμειν, ἐκκυκλήματα· καὶ περιάκτους καὶ μηχανὰς ...

such complexity existed at that early period. It is true that they might have been used in producing the change of scene in the Eumenides from the temple at Delphi to the temple at Athens. But they could have been perfectly well dispensed with. In fact, as far as the extant Greek dramas are concerned, there are no occasions on which it is necessary to suppose that they were used, and there are no passages in which they are referred to. It may therefore reasonably be doubted whether they existed at all during the great period of the Attic drama, and whether their invention is not rather to be ascribed to a much later period.

The periaktoi, as stated above, are the only appliances for changing scenery that are mentioned in Greek writings. Servius describes another kind of contrivance, by means of which the scene was parted asunder in the middle, and then drawn aside in both directions, so as to disclose a new scene behind¹. But it is probable that this invention dated from comparatively late times. There is nothing in the existing Greek dramas to suggest that such a contrivance was in use during the classical period.

§ 5. *Stage Properties, etc.*

In addition to the scenery in the background the stage was of course decorated with such objects and properties as were required by the particular play. Aeschylus is said to have been the first to adorn the stage in this manner². If the scene was a palace or a temple, statues of the gods were generally placed in front of it, and are frequently referred to in the course of the drama. For instance there was the statue of Athênê in front of her temple in the Eumenides, and the statues of the tutelary deities before the palace of the Atreidae in the Electra of

ἡ καὶ Σοφοκλῆς ἐστιν ἃ τούτων προσεμη-χανήσατο καὶ προσεξεῦρεν, ἔστι τοῖς βουλομένοις ὑπὲρ τούτων ἐρίζειν καὶ ἕλκειν ἐπ' ἄμφω τὴν φήμην τοῦ λόγου.

¹ Serv. on Verg. Georg. iii. 24 scaena quae fiebat aut versilis erat aut ductilis erat ... ductilis tum cum tractis tabu-latis huc atque illuc species picturae nudabatur interior.

² Vit. Aesch. p. 6 Dindf. καὶ τὴν ὄψιν τῶν θεωμένων κατέπληξε τῇ λαμ-πρότητι, γραφαῖς καὶ μηχαναῖς, βωμοῖς τε καὶ τάφοις, σάλπιγξιν, εἰδώλοις, Ἐρινύσι κ.τ.λ.

Sophocles. In the Hippolytus there were two statues in front of the palace of Theseus, one of Artemis the huntress, and the other of Cypris the goddess of love. When Hippolytus returns from the hunt, he offers a garland of flowers to the statue of Artemis, but refuses to pay the slightest homage to the statue of Cypris, in spite of the remonstrances of his attendant. Again, in the country region depicted in the Oedipus Coloneus the statue of the hero Colonus stood in a conspicuous position[1]. Other examples of the practice of decorating the stage with statues are frequently to be met with both in tragedy and in comedy. Altars again were very common objects upon the Greek stage. In the Supplices of Aeschylus the fugitive maidens take refuge round an altar. The Oedipus Tyrannus opens with the spectacle of a group of Thebans kneeling in supplication before the altar of Apollo[2]. Another very ordinary feature in the stage-decoration was the stone obelisk in honour of Apollo of the Highways. It was an ordinary practice among the Greeks to place such obelisks in front of their houses. Their presence upon the stage is frequently referred to both in tragedy and in comedy[3]. Various other objects were occasionally required by particular plays. There was the tomb of Darius in front of the palace of Xerxes in the Persae, and the tomb of Agamemnon in front of the palace of the Atreidae in the Choephori. In the Oedipus Coloneus a rocky ledge was required for Oedipus to rest himself upon. In the Acharnians and the Knights a few benches must have been erected upon the stage to serve as a rude imitation of the Pnyx. Walls, watch-towers, and beacon-towers are mentioned by Pollux; and the presence of other similar decorations and erections can be inferred from the extant tragedies and comedies[4].

There was one piece of realism which the Greeks were not averse to, and that was the presence of horses and chariots upon the stage. There are many instances in tragedy of per-

---

[1] Aesch. Eum. 242; Soph. Electr. 1373, O. C. 59; Eur. Hipp. 70-106.
[2] Aesch. Suppl. 188-200; Soph. O. R. 1-3, 142.
[3] Poll. iv. 123; Aesch. Agam. 1080 ff.; Schol. Eur. Phoen. 631; Arist. Vesp. 875.
[4] Aesch. Pers. 684, Choeph. 4; Soph. O. C. 19; Poll. iv. 127.

sons from a distance arriving in a chariot drawn by horses or mules. The vast size of the Greek theatre, and the length and narrowness of the stage, made it peculiarly suitable for displays of this character. In the Agamemnon of Aeschylus Agamemnon and Cassandra approach the palace in a chariot; Agamemnon remains seated there for a considerable time, while he converses with Clytaemnestra; he then dismounts and enters the palace, leaving Cassandra still in the chariot. In the Prometheus the chorus of the Oceanidae enter the stage in a car. In the Electra of Euripides, when Clytaemnestra comes to visit her daughter at the country cottage, she arrives in a chariot, accompanied by Trojan maidens, who assist her to dismount. Several other instances might be mentioned. Animals for riding were also introduced upon the stage. In the Prometheus there is the winged steed upon which Prometheus makes his entrance; and finally in the Frogs of Aristophanes Xanthias rides in upon a donkey[1].

§ 6. *The Ekkyklêma.*

Several mechanical contrivances are mentioned in connexion with the Greek stage. The most peculiar of these, and the one most alien to all our modern notions of stage illusion, was the ekkyklêma[2]. It has already been pointed out that, owing to

---

[1] Aesch. Agam. 782–1054, Prom. 135, 279, 284; Eur. Electr. 998, 999; Arist. Ran. 27.

[2] The ekkyklêma is described in the following passages:—Poll. iv. 128 καὶ τὸ μὲν ἐκκύκλημα ἐπὶ ξύλων ὑψηλὸν βάθρον, ᾧ ἐπίκειται θρόνος· δείκνυσι δὲ τὰ ὑπὸ σκηνὴν ἐν ταῖς οἰκίαις ἀπόρρητα πραχθέντα. καὶ τὸ ῥῆμα τοῦ ἔργου καλεῖται ἐκκυκλεῖν. ἐφ' οὗ δὲ εἰσάγεται τὸ ἐκκύκλημα, εἰσκύκλημα ὀνομάζεται, καὶ χρὴ τοῦτο νοεῖσθαι καθ' ἑκάστην θύραν, οἱονεὶ καθ' ἑκάστην οἰκίαν. (The θρόνος mentioned by Pollux must be derived from some particular instance of the use of the ekkyklêma. The epithet ὑψηλόν may be corrupt: it is certainly not correct.) Schol. Arist. Acharn. 408 ἐκκύκλημα δὲ λέγεται μηχάνημα ξύλινον τροχοὺς ἔχον, ὅπερ περιστρεφόμενον τὰ δοκοῦντα ἔνδον ὡς ἐν οἰκίᾳ πράττεσθαι καὶ τοῖς ἔξω ἐδείκνυε, λέγω δὴ τοῖς θεαταῖς. Eustath. Il. 976. 15 τὸ ἐγκύκλημα, ὃ καὶ ἐγκύκληθρον λέγεται, μηχάνημα ἦν ὑπότροχον, ὑφ' οὗ ἐδείκνυτο τὰ ἐν τῇ σκευῇ ἢ σκηνῇ. Schol. Aesch. Choeph. 973 ἀνοίγεται ἡ σκηνὴ καὶ ἐπὶ ἐκκυκλήματος ὁρᾶται τὰ σώματα. Schol. Aesch. Eum. 64 καὶ δευτέρα δὲ γίγνεται φαντασία· στραφέντα γὰρ μηχανήματα ἔνδηλα ποιεῖ τὰ κατὰ τὸ μαντεῖον ὡς ἔχει. Schol. Soph. Aj. 346 ἐνταῦθα ἐκκύκλημά τι γίνεται, ἵνα φανῇ ἐν μέσοις ὁ Αἴας ποιμνίοις. Schol. Aristoph. Nub. 184 ὁρᾷ δὲ ὡς φιλοσόφους κομῶντας, στραφέντος τοῦ ἐγκυκλήματος.

the arrangement of the auditorium, it was impossible upon the Greek stage to represent the interior of a building. If the back-scene had been drawn apart, and an attempt made to exhibit the inside of a palace, the great majority of the spectators would have been unable to see what was going on. Under these circumstances, if a dramatist wished to bring before the eyes of the audience a deed which had been perpetrated inside a house or palace, he had recourse to the ekkyklêma. It was a small wooden platform, rolling upon wheels, and was kept inside the stage-buildings. When it was required to be used, one of the doors in the background was thrown open, and it was rolled forward on to the stage. Upon it was arranged a group of figures, representing in a sort of tableau the deed or occurrence which had just taken place inside the building. It was <u>mostly used in cases where a mur</u>der had <u>been committed.</u> The ekkyklêma was rolled out upon the stage, and on it were seen the corpses of the murdered persons, with the murderers standing beside them with the bloody weapons in their hands. It might be rolled through any of the three doors at the back of the stage. The contrivance was of course a purely conventional one, and had to be adopted owing to the peculiar construction of the Greek theatre. All pretence of realism and illusion was abandoned. But this was a point upon which the Greeks did not lay very much stress. And when they had once habituated themselves to the use of the ekkyklêma as a conventional contrivance for exhibiting interiors, it is obvious that the scene must have been a very impressive one. The sudden spectacle of the murderer standing beside his victim's body, with the instrument of death in his hand, must have formed a most effective tableau.

In the extant Greek tragedies there are several instances of the use of the ekkyklêma. In the Hercules Furens the platform is rolled out, and exhibits Hercules lying prostrate between the bodies of his wife and children, with his limbs in chains, and his face covered up. Amphitryon then comes out of the palace and loosens his chains. Later on Theseus comes out and uncovers his face, and helps him to rise. He then descends to the stage, and the ekkyklêma is rolled back into the palace. In the Hippolytus, after the suicide of Phaedra, her dead body is displayed upon the ekkyklêma, and Theseus takes from it the letter in which she makes her charge against Hippolytus. In the Agamemnon the platform rolls out and reveals the person of Clytaemnestra standing beside the dead bodies of Agamemnon and Cassandra. In a similar manner in the Choephori Orestes is brought to view standing over the bodies of Aegisthus and Clytaemnestra, and pointing to the net with which his father had been murdered many years ago. After a time he is seized with frenzy, and descends from the ekkyklêma, and hastens away to the temple of Apollo at Delphi. The platform is then rolled back into the palace. In the Electra of Sophocles the door is thrown open at the command of Aegisthus, and the platform rolls out and exhibits Orestes and Pylades standing beside the corpse of Clytaemnestra, which is covered with a cloth. Aegisthus himself removes the cloth, and then Orestes and Pylades descend to the stage, and the platform is drawn back again. The same contrivance is used for exhibiting the body of Eurydice at the end of the Antigone, and for revealing the interior of the tent of Ajax in the play of the same name. Finally in the Eumenides the interior of the Pythian temple is displayed, with Orestes crouching beside the altar, and the Erinyes asleep on seats round about him. Orestes, at the command of Apollo, leaves the platform, and starts on his way to Athens. Soon afterwards the Erinyes are awakened by the ghost of Clytaemnestra, and descend to the stage, and so into the orchestra[1]. Besides the above instances from tragedy the ekkyklêma is also parodied on two occasions by Aristophanes. In the Thesmophoriazusae Euripides and Mnesilochus call at the house of Agathon to borrow some female clothing. Agathon is 'rolled out' on the ekkyklêma, hands them some articles which are brought to him from inside the house, and then, when he is tired of their importunity, orders himself to be 'rolled in again as fast as possible.' In the Acharnians Dicaeopolis goes

---

[1] Eur. H. F. 1029–1402, Hipp. 806–865; Aesch. Agam. 1379, 1404, 1440, Choeph. 973, 981, Eum. 64–180; Soph. El. 1458 ff., Ant. 1293, Ajax 346 ff.

to the house of Euripides to borrow a tragic dress. Euripides is upstairs in his study writing tragedies, and cannot come down, but allows himself to be 'rolled out,' and supplies the necessary dresses[1]. The two passages in Aristophanes, where the mechanism of the apparatus is carefully emphasised in order to add to the ridicule, are very valuable as evidence. They confirm the statements of the scholiasts, and prove that the description of the ekkyklema previously given is a correct one.

From the examples of the use of the ekkyklema in tragedy the following further particulars as to its character and construction may be inferred. It appears that persons upon the ekkyklema could easily descend to the stage, and persons on the stage could easily touch those on the ekkyklema. It follows, therefore, that the ekkyklema must have been a low platform, not much above the level of the stage. In the Acharnians, when Euripides is rolled out, he is represented as still sitting in his room upstairs. Probably in this case a tall erection, something like a pedestal, was employed, to produce a ludicrous effect. As to the dimensions of the ekkyklema, it is plain that it must have been large enough to support several persons. At the same time it cannot have been of any very great size. Its width must have been less than the width of the doors in the background, to permit of its being rolled through them. Its depth cannot have been very great, because of the narrowness of the Greek stage. Hence there is some difficulty as to its use in the Eumenides. It is hard to see how it could have been large enough to support the twelve or fifteen members of the chorus of the Eumenides, together with Orestes in the centre. There can scarcely be any doubt that the ekkyklema was used on this occasion. The supposition that the back-scene was rolled apart, and disclosed the interior of the

---

[1] Arist. Acharn. 408, 409 ΔΙ. ἀλλ' ἐκκυκλήθητ'. ΕΥ. ἀλλ' ἀδύνατον. ΔΙ. ἀλλ' ὅμως. | ΕΥ. ἀλλ' ἐκκυκλήσομαι· καταβαίνειν δ' οὐ σχολή. Id. Thesmoph. 95, 96 ΕΥ. σίγα. ΜΝ. τί δ' ἐστιν; ΕΥ. Ἀγάθων ἐξέρχεται. | ΜΝ. καὶ ποῖός ἐστιν; ΕΥ. οὗτος οὑκκυκλούμενος, 238 ἐνεγκάτω τις ἔνδοθεν δᾷδ' ἢ λύχνον, 265 εἴσω τις ὡς τάχιστά μ' εἰσκυκλησάτω. The ekkyklema is also used in the Clouds (v. 185 ff.) to show the interior of the phrontisterion, with the disciples of Socrates at work.

temple, is inconsistent with the practice of the Greek stage, and quite incompatible with the construction of the Greek theatre. It is possible that only a few of the Eumenides were displayed upon the ekkyklêma, and that the rest of them came out of the temple afterwards. But the question is one of some difficulty, and has not yet been satisfactorily solved.

A contrivance called the exostra is occasionally referred to. The name implies that it was something which was 'pushed out' upon the stage. The metaphorical use of the word in Polybius and Cicero proves it to have been a platform on which objects were exhibited in a conspicuous manner. It is probable therefore that the statement of the grammarians is correct, and that the exostra was merely the ekkyklêma under another name[1].

§ 7. *The Mêchanê.*

Another appliance of even greater importance than the ekkyklêma, and one very frequently employed upon the Greek stage, was the mêchanê or Machine[2]. It consisted of a sort of crane with a pulley attached, by which weights could be raised or lowered. It was placed in the left or western corner of the stage, up at the very top of the back-wall. It was used in case the characters in a play had to appear or disappear in a supernatural manner. By its means a god or hero could be lowered

---

[1] Poll. iv. 129 τὴν δὲ ἐξώστραν ταυτὸν τῷ ἐκκυκλήματι νομίζουσιν. Hesych. v. ἐξώστρα· ἐπὶ τῆς σκηνῆς τὸ ἐκκύκλημα. Polyb. xi. 6. 8 τῆς τύχης ὥσπερ ἐπίτηδες ἐπὶ τὴν ἐξώστραν ἀναβιβαζούσης τὴν ὑμετέραν ἄγνοιαν. Cic. de Prov. Cons. § 14 iam in exostra belluatur, antea post siparium solebat.

[2] Poll. iv. 128 ἡ μηχανὴ δὲ θεοὺς δείκνυσι καὶ ἥρως τοὺς ἐν ἀέρι, Βελλεροφόντας ἢ Περσέας, καὶ κεῖται κατὰ τὴν ἀριστερὰν πάροδον, ὑπὲρ τὴν σκηνὴν τὸ ὕψος. Schol. Luc. Philops. vii. p. 357 Lehmann ἄνωθεν ὑπὲρ τὰς παρ' ἑκάτερα τῆς μέσης τοῦ θεάτρου θύρας (αὗται δὲ πρὸς τὴν εὐθείαν τοῦ θεάτρου πλευρὰν ἀνεῴγεσαν, οὗ καὶ ἡ σκηνὴ καὶ τὸ προσκήνιόν ἐστι) μηχανῶν δύο μετεωριζομένων ἢ ἐξ ἀριστερῶν θεοὺς καὶ ἥρωας ἐνεφάνιζε παρευθύ, ὥσπερ λύσιν φέροντας τῶν ἀμηχάνων καὶ τούτου παραδηλουμένου, ὡς οὐ χρὴ ἀπιστεῖν τοῖς δρωμένοις, ἐπεὶ θεὸς πάρεστι τῷ ἔργῳ. Aristoph. Daedal. fr. 9 (Meineke) ὁ μηχανοποιός, ὁπότε βούλει τὸν τροχὸν | ἐλᾶν ἀνεκάς, λέγε, χαῖρε φέγγος ἡλίου. The μηχανὴ was also called ἐώρημα, Suidas s. v. The ropes by which the actor was suspended were called αἰῶραι; Poll. iv. 131 αἰώρας δ' ἂν εἴποις τοὺς κάλως οἱ κατήρτηνται ἐξ ὕψους ἀνέχειν τοὺς ἐπὶ τοῦ ἀέρος φέρεσθαι δοκοῦντας ἥρως ἢ θεούς. The word ἀριστερά in Pollux and the Scholiast, being applied to the stage, means the left from the point of view of the actors. In the Athenian theatre this would be the western side.

from heaven down to earth, or raised up from earth to heaven, or exhibited motionless in mid-air. In most cases a car was used for the purpose, and was attached to the pulley by a rope or chain. In this car the god or hero took his stand. But any other form of vehicle might be substituted for the car, according to the requirements of the particular play. Euripides went so far as to exhibit his hero Bellerophon ascending up to heaven on the winged steed Pegasus. Trygaeus, in the Peace of Aristophanes, was represented as riding through the air upon a beetle. As to the strength of the mêchanê, it must at any rate have been powerful enough to support two or three people at the same time. Thus in the Helen of Euripides the twin Dioscuri descend from heaven by this contrivance. Again, in the Medea of Euripides both Medea and her slaughtered children are borne through the air in a chariot. But the old notion that the mêchanê was capable of lowering a whole tragic chorus of twelve or fifteen members down from the sky is absurd on the face of it. The notion was derived from the Prometheus of Aeschylus. It was supposed that the winged car in which the Oceanidae made their appearance was gently lowered through the air, and suspended in front of Prometheus, while about a hundred and fifty lines of the play were being spoken. But the supposition is ridiculous and quite unnecessary. The car of the Oceanidae was simply drawn on to the stage, and the maidens sat there for a time conversing with Prometheus, and then dismounted from it and descended into the orchestra. As to the way in which the mêchanê was worked, and the manner in which the gods and heroes were made to disappear from view at the top of the stage, there is no information. Unfortunately the construction of the upper part of the stage-buildings is a subject about which we are entirely ignorant. It is useless therefore to hazard conjectures concerning the exact nature of the arrangements adopted.

The mêchanê was used under various circumstances; but the most ordinary occasion for its employment was to introduce the 'deus ex machina' at the end of a play, when affairs had reached such a complicated condition that only divine interference could put them right again. Under ordinary circumstances the gods and goddesses of the Greek stage walked about like mortal beings [1]. But when they were introduced, in the manner described, to untie the knots at the conclusion of a play, the supernatural character of their intervention was emphasised by their appearance in the sky. The god so introduced was called the 'deus ex machina,' or 'god from the machine'; and the phrase became a proverbial one to denote an unexpected benefactor [2]. The 'deus ex machina' was a favourite device with Euripides. It is never used by Aeschylus in his extant tragedies, and only once by Sophocles, at the end of the Philoctetes. But Euripides has recourse to it on several occasions. The Andromache, Orestes, Electra, Ion, Helena, Supplices, and Iphigenia in Tauris are all brought to a conclusion by the appearance of a god from heaven. The practice is strongly censured by Aristotle, who points out that in a well-constructed plot there should be no need of supernatural agencies, and the conclusion should be the inevitable result of the preceding incidents. He considers that the only proper occasion for the employment of the 'deus ex machina' is when a god is to be brought down from heaven to give information about the past or future, which no mere human being could be supposed to be acquainted with [3]. It will be found that some of the uses of the 'deus ex machina' in Euripides answer to this description of Aristotle, and would not incur his censure. In several cases the god is introduced, not so much to set matters right, as to inform the characters of the destiny which awaits them in the future. In the Andromache, the Electra, and the Supplices the plot has already been brought to a conclusion before the god appears. His function is confined to announcing the future course of events. These therefore are what Aristotle would call permissible uses of the 'deus ex machina.'

The principal purpose then of the mêchanê was to bring

---

[1] Eur. Hipp. 53 ἔξω τῶνδε βήσομαι τόπων (of Aphrodite, who is speaking the prologue). Cp. Aesch. Prom. 941–943.

[2] Suid. v. ἀπὸ μηχανῆς. Luc. Philops. 29 θεὸν ἀπὸ μηχανῆς. Plat. Cratyl. p. 425 D.

[3] Aristot. Poet. c. 15.

down a god from heaven at the conclusion of a play. But it was also occasionally employed under various other circumstances, when a god or hero had to be lowered from heaven, or lifted up from earth. For example Medea, in the play of Euripides, escapes from Jason with her slaughtered children upon an aerial car. In the Hercules Furens Iris and Lyssa are sent down by Hêra to drive Hercules to madness. They appear for a time suspended in the air above the palace; and then Iris reascends to heaven, Lyssa goes down into the palace to execute her purpose. Other instances are to be met with in the lost plays of Euripides. Perseus was exhibited as gliding down through the air in front of the cliff where Andromeda had been chained. Bellerophon made his ascent to heaven on the winged Pegasus[1]. The ascent of Trygaeus upon the beetle was intended by Aristophanes as a parody on the Bellerophon of Euripides. His speech in the course of his aerial journey consists of a ludicrous mixture of phrases from the Bellerophon, shouts to the beetle to keep his head straight, and terrified appeals to the stage-manager to look after the security of the pulley[2].

§ 8. *Other Mechanical Contrivances.*

Two other contrivances for moving people through the air are mentioned by the ancient writers; but the information concerning them is very defective. The Fig-Branch was a sort of hook, from which the actors were suspended by means of ropes and bands. The Crane was an instrument by which the bodies of dead heroes were caught up and conveyed into the sky. It was used by Aeschylus in the Psychostasia, when Dawn carried away the body of her son Memnon. The notices about the Crane and Fig-Branch are too brief and contradictory to enable their exact character, and their relationship with the mêchanê,

---

[1] Eur. Med. 1317 ff., Herc. Fur. 815 ff.; Nauck, Trag. Græc. Frag. pp. 316, 358; Poll. iv. 128.

[2] Arist. Pax 154 ff. ἀλλ' ἄγε, Πήγασε, χώρει χαίρων, | χρυσοχάλινον πάταγον ψαλίων | διακίνησας φαιδροῖς ὠσίν. | τί ποιεῖς; τί ποιεῖς; ποῖ παρακλίνεις | τοὺς μυκτῆρας πρὸς τὰς λαύρας; | ... ὦ μηχανοποιέ, πρόσεχε τὸν νοῦν ὡς ἐμέ.

to be defined with accuracy[1]. Another appliance for exhibiting gods in a supernatural manner was the theologeion. It was a narrow platform high up at the back of the stage, upon which the gods made their appearance when they were to be represented as actually in heaven. Probably it was similar in construction to the ekkyklēma, and was usually invisible, but was pushed forward through an opening at the back when required. The most celebrated instance of its employment was in the Psychostasia of Aeschylus. Zeus was there represented as sitting in heaven, holding scales in his hands, in which were placed the destinies of Achilles and Memnon respectively. On each side of him stood Thetis and Dawn, supplicating for the lives of their sons. The scene was in imitation of that in the Iliad, where Zeus weighs the fates of Achilles and Hector[2]. It is possible that the scene in the Peace between Hermes and Trygaeus took place upon the theologeion. Sometimes the contrivance was used in place of the ordinary mēchanē to introduce the 'deus ex machina' at the end of a play. The god, instead of being lowered from heaven, was displayed suddenly upon the platform high up in the background[3].

Several other devices in use upon the Attic stage are briefly mentioned by Pollux, but his descriptions are so meagre and obscure that little or nothing can be inferred as to their exact character. Charon's Steps was a contrivance for bringing ghosts and spectres upon the stage, such as the ghost of Darius in the Persae, and the ghost of Clytaemnestra in the Aga-

---

[1] Poll. iv. 130 ἡ δὲ γέρανος μηχάνημά ἐστιν ἐκ μετεώρου καταφερόμενον ἐφ' ἁρπαγῇ σώματος, ᾧ κέχρηται Ἠὼς ἁρπάζουσα τὸ σῶμα τὸ Μέμνονος. Plut. Prov. 116 (Paroemiogr. Gotting. i. p. 338) κράδης ῥαγείσης· νῦν οὐχ ὁ σύκινος κλάδος, ἀλλ' ἡ ἀγκυρίς, ἀφ' ἧς οἱ ὑποκριταὶ ἐν ταῖς τραγικαῖς σκηναῖς ἐξαρτῶνται θεοῦ μιμούμενοι ἐπιφάνειαν ζωστῆρσι καὶ ταινίαις κατειλημμένοι. So also Hesych. v. κράδη. Pollux (iv. 128) makes the κράδη the comic counterpart of the μηχανή; but this is utterly improbable.

[2] Poll. iv. 130 ἀπὸ δὲ τοῦ θεολογείου ὄντος ὑπὲρ τὴν σκηνὴν ἐν ὕψει ἐπιφαίνονται θεοί, ὡς ὁ Ζεὺς καὶ οἱ περὶ αὐτὸν ἐν Ψυχοστασίᾳ. Plut. Aud. Poet. p. 17 A.

[3] Luc. Philops. 29 θεὸν ἀπὸ μηχανῆς ἐπεισκυκληθῆναί μοι. Bekker, Anecd. p. 208. 9 ἀπὸ μηχανῆς· μηχανή ἐστι παρὰ τοῖς κωμικοῖς ἐγκυκλήματός τι εἶδος ἀπὸ συνθήκης πρὸς ὃ φέρεται (ὁ) εἰς τὴν σκηνὴν δείξεως χάριν θεοῦ ἢ ἄλλου τινὸς ἥρωος. Trygaeus probably mounted to the theologeion. But Niejahr (Quaest. Scaen. p. 20 ff.) suggests that he only rose a short distance upon the beetle, then descended to earth again, and that his own house then did duty as the house of Zeus.

memnon. It can hardly have been anything else than a flight of steps leading out upon the stage from underneath. The 'anapiesma' was used by river-gods, Furies, and other subterranean beings for the purpose of appearing above ground. The word 'anapiesma' seems to mean something which was pushed back. It is probable therefore that the contrivance was merely the ordinary trap-door of the modern theatre, through which the spectral being was raised on to the stage[1]. The 'bronteion' was a device for imitating the noise of thunder behind the scenes, and was of a very simple character. Pebbles were poured out of a jar into a large brazen vessel, or else bags were filled with stones and flung against a metal surface. The 'keraunoskopeion' was obviously intended to imitate lightning, but the description in Pollux is unintelligible. The 'stropheion' was some sort of revolving machinery, by which heroes were exhibited in heaven, or deaths at sea and in battle were represented. The 'hemikyklion' was semicircular in shape, and gave a distant view of a city, or of a person swimming in the sea. The 'hemistrophion' is merely mentioned by name, and no description of it is appended [2].

The question whether a drop-scene was used in the Athenian theatre during the great period of the drama is one which has not yet been satisfactorily settled. In Roman theatres a drop-scene was invariably used between the different plays, the mechanism being exactly the reverse of that employed in modern times. When the play was going to begin, the curtain was let down into a narrow crevice in the front of the stage, and at the end of the performance was drawn up again [3]. There can be no doubt that similar curtains were used in Greek theatres at a later period; but the question is whether they were used at Athens during the fifth and fourth centuries. There are no references to anything of the kind in the extant Greek dramas, and there are no passages in ancient writers

---

[1] Poll. iv. 132 αἱ δὲ χαρώνιοι κλίμακες, κατὰ τὰς ἐκ τῶν εἰδωλίων καθόδους κείμεναι, τὰ εἴδωλα ἀπ' αὐτῶν ἀναπέμπουσιν. τὰ δὲ ἀναπιέσματα, τὸ μέν ἐστιν ἐν τῇ σκηνῇ ὡς ποταμὸν ἀνελθεῖν ἢ τοιοῦτόν τι πρόσωπον, τὸ δὲ περὶ τοὺς ἀναβαθμούς, ἀφ' ὧν ἀνέβαινον Ἐρινύες.

[2] Poll. iv. 127–132; Suid. v. βροντή.

[3] Ovid. Met. iii. 111; Hor. Ep. ii. 1. 189.

which can be held to prove the existence of a drop-scene in the early Athenian theatre[1]. The question must therefore be discussed on general grounds. To our modern notions a drop-scene appears to be almost a necessity in the case of plays which commence with the actors already in position upon the stage. In the Greek drama such plays are not infrequent. For instance, in the opening scene of the Oedipus Tyrannus the Thebans are discovered kneeling at the altar before the palace of the king. In the Troades, when Poseidon comes forward to speak the prologue, he sees Hecuba stretched upon the ground in an attitude of despair. The Orestes of Euripides opens with Orestes stretched upon a bed in front of the palace, and his sister Electra watching beside him. Many other examples might be cited of plays which begin with the actors already in a fixed position. Unless therefore a drop-scene was used between the plays, it would have to be supposed that the actors came on the stage in full view of the people, took up the required position, and then began the dialogue. There would be a great sacrifice of illusion in such a mode of commencement. Besides this the drop-scene would of course be the natural and obvious mode of concealing the stage from view while the scenery was being altered between the different plays. For

[1] The following passages are cited in proof of the existence of a drop-scene:
—(1) Athen. p. 536 A γενομένων δὲ τῶν Δημητρίων Ἀθήνησιν ἐγράφετο ἐπὶ τοῦ προσκηνίου (ὁ Δημήτριος) ἐπὶ τῆς οἰκουμένης ὀχούμενος. Here προσκήνιον more probably denotes the scene at the back of the stage. (2) Suid. v. προσκήνιον· τὸ πρὸ τῆς σκηνῆς παραπέτασμα· ἡ δὲ τύχη παρελκομένη τὴν πρόφασιν καθάπερ ἐπὶ προσκήνιον παρεγύμνωσε τὰς ἀληθεῖς ἐπινοίας. Suidas has here mistaken the meaning of the passage he quotes, in which προσκήνιον = 'the stage.' (3) Synesius (flor. about 400 A. D.), Aegypt. p. 128 C εἰ δέ τις ... κυνοφθαλμίζοιτο διὰ τοῦ προσκηνίου. Even if προσκήνιον means 'the drop-scene' in this passage, it would be no proof of the existence of a drop-scene in classical times. (4) Poll. iv. 122 (speaking of the theatre) ἔξεστι δὲ καὶ τὸ παραπέτασμα αὐλαίαν καλεῖν, Ὑπερείδου εἰπόντος ἐν τῷ κατὰ Πατροκλέους· οἱ δὲ ἐννέα ἄρχοντες εἱστιῶντο ἐν τῇ στοᾷ, περιφραξάμενοί τι μέρος αὐτῆς αὐλαίᾳ. Suid. v. αὐλαία, and Bekk. Anecd. p. 463 αὐλαία τὸ τῆς σκηνῆς παραπέτασμα· κέχρηται δὲ αὐτῷ Ὑπερείδης ἐν τῷ κατὰ Πατροκλέους. Hesych. v. αὐλαία ... τὸ τῆς σκηνῆς παραπέτασμα. Et. Mag. p. 170 λέγονται δὲ αὐλαῖαι καὶ τὰ παραπετάσματα τῆς σκηνῆς, ὡς παρὰ τῷ θεολόγῳ. It is obvious that the grammarians here cited were thinking of a drop-scene. But the passage they refer to in Hypereides has nothing to do with a drop-scene. It is doubtful, therefore, whether this testimony is of any value except for the practice of their own times. It can hardly be considered decisive for the classical period.

these reasons it has been inferred that the Athenians cannot have done without one. But on the other hand it has already been pointed out that it is a great mistake to apply our modern notions of propriety to an ancient dramatic performance. The Athenian drama was quite unlike any modern exhibition, and one point of difference may have been the absence of the drop-scene. On the Athenian stage, where the changes of scenery required between the different plays were usually of the slightest character, it was not nearly so necessary as in modern times. Its chief advantage would have been in the case of plays which open with the actors already arranged in a sort of tableau. To judge by our modern ideas, the effect in such cases would have been greatly heightened, and the illusion much more fully carried out, by the use of a drop-scene. But the Greeks did not lay very much stress upon realism and illusion in their scenic arrangements. They were satisfied with simple and conventional methods of representing events upon the stage. Such devices as the ekkyklēma and the periaktoi would never have been tolerated, if the object had been to produce an illusion by the accurate imitation of real objects. It is therefore very likely that in the dramas just referred to the Athenians were quite content for the actors to come forward and take up their position in full view of the audience, before the play actually commenced. Custom in such cases is everything. What might appear ludicrous to a modern audience would pass unnoticed to an audience that was used to it. An illustration of this fact may be found in the early history of the English drama, in which there was little or no attempt at scenery, and the illusion was spoiled by the presence of spectators sitting upon the stage. Yet the audience of those days was not dissatisfied. It is therefore easy to imagine that the Athenians did perfectly well without a drop-scene. At the same time there is no evidence to prove that such was the case. And the drop-scene is a very convenient device, and one that would naturally suggest itself from the very first. On the whole therefore it seems safest, until further evidence is forthcoming, to regard the question as an open one.

CHAPTER V.

THE ACTORS.

§ 1. *Rise of the Actor's Profession.*

BEFORE proceeding to give an account of the actors in the ancient Greek drama, there are one or two points which ought to be made clear, in order to avoid possible misconceptions. In the first place the actors and the chorus were entirely distinct from one another. The chorus was chosen and paid by the choregus, and performed in the orchestra. The actors were hired by the state, and their proper place was upon the stage. The term 'hypokritês,' or 'actor,' was never applied to the members of the chorus. It was not even applied to all the performers upon the stage, but only to such of them as took a prominent part in the dialogue. The various mute characters, such as the soldiers and attendants, and also the subordinate characters who had only a few words to say, were not dignified with the title of 'actor.' In the second place it should be remembered that the Greek actors invariably wore masks, and were consequently able to appear in several parts in the course of the same performance. When, therefore, it is said that in the early history of Greek tragedy only a single actor was employed in each play, this does not imply that the number of characters was limited to one. All it implies is that only one character could appear at a time. The number of actors in a Greek play never exceeded three, even in the latest period. But the effect of this regulation upon the capacities of the Greek drama was less cramping and restrictive than might have been supposed. There was no limitation to the number of mute and subordinate characters which might be introduced at any time upon the stage. There was no restriction upon the number of the more prominent characters, provided they were not brought upon the stage simultaneously. The only limitation was this—that not more than three of the more prominent characters could take part in the dialogue in the course of the same scene.

The principal function of the actors was to carry on the dialogue and work out the action of the play. The principal function of the chorus was to sing the odes which filled up the pauses in the action. Of course very frequently the chorus took part in the dialogue; but, speaking in general terms, the dialogue was the business of the actors. Such was the condition of things during the best period of the Attic drama. But in former times the case had been very different. At first the whole performance was a choral one, and consisted simply of the songs and hymns chanted at the festivals of Dionysus. There were no actors and there was no dialogue. The history of the early development of the drama is in other words the history of the gradual introduction of actors and dialogue into a choral entertainment, and the gradual increase in the importance of the dialogue, until eventually it overshadowed the choral part altogether. The first step in the process by which a lyrical performance was converted into a dramatic one was as follows. The custom arose of filling up the intervals between the different portions of the choral songs with recitations by the leader of the chorus, and dialogues between him and the other members. For this purpose the leader of the chorus used to mount upon a small table. The subject of the recitations and the dialogues would be the same as the subject of the ode, and would in most cases refer to the adventures of the god Dionysus. In these interludes by the leader of the chorus lay the germ of the drama. The performance as a whole was still essentially lyrical, but the practice of inserting dialogue had been established[1]. In the case of tragedy the next step forward

[1] Poll. iv. 123 ἐλεὸς δ' ἦν τράπεζα ἀρχαία, ἐφ' ἧν πρὸ Θέσπιδος εἷς τις ἀναβὰς τοῖς χορευταῖς ἀπεκρίνατο. Arist. Poet. c. 4 καὶ ἡ μὲν (τραγῳδία ἐγένετο) ἀπὸ τῶν ἐξαρχόντων τὸν διθύραμβον, ἡ δὲ (κωμῳδία) ἀπὸ τῶν τὰ φαλλικά.

was taken by Thespis. He introduced a single actor, who took the part which had previously been taken by the leader of the chorus, and filled up the pauses in the choral odes either with monologues or with dialogues between himself and the leader[1]. Not much is known about the drama of Thespis except that it was still essentially lyrical. But as he is said to have employed masks, it is clear that the single actor might appear in different characters in successive scenes, and in this way some approach might be made to a dramatic representation of a story[2]. The decisive innovation was due to Aeschylus. He introduced a second actor, and effected a total change in the character of the performance. Henceforward the intervals between the choral odes were filled with dialogues between the two actors upon the stage, instead of dialogues between the single actor and the leader of the chorus. At the same time Aeschylus cut down the length of the choral odes, and made the dialogue the essential and prominent feature of the performance[3]. The result was a radical change in the nature of tragedy: it became a dramatic instead of a lyrical form of art. During the greater part of his career Aeschylus was contented with two actors. Three at least out of his seven extant plays are written for performance by two actors only[4]. This limitation upon the number of the performers necessitated great simplicity in the construction of the play, since it was impossible for more than two personages to take part in the dialogue at the same time. Hence the earlier plays of Aeschylus, though essentially dramatic in comparison with anything which preceded them, are simple in plot and lyrical in tone when compared with the tragedies of his

---

[1] Diog. Laert. iii. 56 ὥσπερ δὲ τὸ παλαιὸν ἐν τῇ τραγῳδίᾳ πρότερον μὲν μόνος ὁ χορὸς διεδραμάτιζεν, ὕστερον δὲ Θέσπις ἕνα ὑποκριτὴν ἐξεῦρεν ὑπὲρ τοῦ διαναπαύεσθαι τὸν χορόν.

[2] Suidas v. Θέσπις.

[3] Aristot. Poet. c. 4 καὶ τό τε τῶν ὑποκριτῶν πλῆθος ἐξ ἑνὸς εἰς δύο πρῶτος Αἰσχύλος ἤγαγε, καὶ τὰ τοῦ χοροῦ ἠλάττωσε, καὶ τὸν λόγον πρωταγωνιστὴν παρεσκεύασεν.

[4] Viz. the Supplices, Persae, and Seven against Thebes. In the concluding scene of the Seven the part of Ismene would not be taken by a regular actor. Apparently the opening scene of the Prometheus requires three actors, unless we are to adopt the very improbable supposition that the person of Prometheus was represented by a wooden figure, which was nailed to the rock, and from behind which the protagonist spoke the part.

successors. The different scenes rather serve to unfold a series of pictures than to develop a complicated plot. Descriptive speeches take the place of animated dialogue. Sophocles added greatly to the capacities of the drama by introducing a third actor[1]. He was thus enabled to give much greater variety and spirit to the dialogue. In his hands for the first time tragedy became essentially dramatic, and the lyrical element was thrust still further into the background. The innovation of Sophocles was adopted by Aeschylus in his later years, and the Orestean trilogy—the last and most elaborate of his works—requires three actors. Under Sophocles tragedy received its full development. The number of actors in tragedy was henceforward limited to three.

The satyric drama was intimately connected with tragedy, and the number of actors was apparently the same. Thus the Cyclops of Euripides, the only extant satyric play, requires three actors. In an ancient vase-painting, which represents the performers in a satyric play, three actors are depicted[2]. It is true that the Alcestis of Euripides, which was performed in place of the usual satyric drama, only requires two actors. But the number in this case was probably due to the choice of the poet, and not to any official regulation. In regard to comedy, very little is known as to the steps by which it was developed. The source of comedy lay in the phallic songs performed at the festivals of Dionysus. The dramatic element originated in the interludes by the leader of the chorus. The process of development must have been much the same as in tragedy; but the names of the persons who introduced actors and dialogue into comedy were forgotten even in Aristotle's

---

[1] Aristot. Poet. c. 4; Diog. Laert. iii. 56; vit. Soph.; Suidas v. Σοφοκλῆς. The Life of Aeschylus assigns the introduction of the third actor to Aeschylus, but adds that Dicaearchus ascribed it to Sophocles. The passage in Themistius (xxvi. p. 316 D καὶ οὐ προσέχομεν Ἀριστοτέλει ὅτι τὸ μὲν πρῶτον ὁ χορὸς εἰσιὼν ᾖδεν εἰς τοὺς θεούς, Θέσπις δὲ πρόλογόν τε καὶ ῥῆσιν ἐξεῦρεν, Αἰσχύλος δὲ τρίτον ὑποκριτὴν (a. l. τρίτον ὑποκριτάς) is doubtful, and cannot weigh against Aristotle's definite statement in the Poetics. The balance of evidence is distinctly in favour of the conclusion that the third actor was first introduced by Sophocles.

[2] Wieseler, Denkmäler, vi. 2; Eur. Cyclops 197 foll.

time. The only piece of information upon the subject is to the effect that Cratinus was the first to limit the number of actors to three, and that before his time there was no regulation as to the number of persons introduced upon the stage. After the time of Cratinus there were no further innovations, and the number of the actors in comedy was permanently fixed at three [1].

This number was never exceeded either in comedy or in tragedy. All the extant Greek plays could be performed by three actors. It is sometimes said that the Oedipus Coloneus of Sophocles requires four actors; but this is not the case. Although there are several occasions on which Ismene appears upon the stage simultaneously with three other personages, still on each of these occasions she does not say a word, but is merely a mute figure. It is evident therefore that during this portion of the play her part was taken by a 'super,' while at the beginning and end of the play, where she had speeches to make, the part was acted by the tritagonist [2]. It might at first sight appear that the comedies of Aristophanes require more than three actors; but investigations have shown that there is not one of his plays which could not be performed by this number, assisted by a supply of 'supers [3].'

The smallness in the number of the actors necessarily limited the capacities of the Greek drama. It made it impossible for life to be represented upon the stage with the realism of a modern play. Mute personages—such as officers, soldiers, and servants—might be introduced in any number; but the characters taking part in the dialogue could never at any one time exceed three. The realistic effect produced by a promiscuous conversation between a large group of persons was impossible upon the Greek stage. Sometimes a certain awkwardness was caused by the limitation in the number of the performers. In the extant Greek dramas occasions are not infrequent where a fourth actor might have been a great advantage. For instance,

---

[1] Arist. Poet. cc. 4, 5; Anon. de Comoed. (Dindf. Prolegom. de Comoed. p. 27); Diomedes, p. 490 K.
[2] Soph. O. C. 1117 ff., 1249 ff., 1500 ff.
[3] Cp. Beer, über die Zahl der Schauspieler bei Aristophanes, Leipz. 1844.

there is the exciting scene at the end of the Orestes of Euripides. Orestes is seen upon the roof of the palace threatening to kill Hermione, and Pylades is standing beside him. Menelaus from below makes a piteous appeal to Pylades, but Pylades says not a single word in reply, but leaves Orestes to answer for him. His silence is very unnatural, and is only to be accounted for by the fact that there was no actor to spare, and therefore the poet could not put any words in his mouth. Two of the actors were already employed in playing the parts of Orestes and Menelaus, and the third was required for Apollo, who comes on the scene immediately afterwards. Consequently the part of Pylades had to be taken by a mute personage. Then again there is the scene at the end of the Electra of Euripides. Orestes has heard his fate, and as he leaves the stage he bids farewell to Pylades, and urges him to marry his sister Electra. Pylades maintains a stolid silence, and the Dioscuri reply on his behalf. Here again his silence is due to the necessities of the case. The three actors with whom the poet was supplied were all employed, and Pylades was merely a dumb figure. Similar instances of awkward and almost ludicrous silence on the part of certain characters will occur to all readers of the Greek drama. But they are not so numerous as might have been expected, and it is astonishing to find how successfully the Greek drama, keeping within its own peculiar limits, was able to accomplish its ends with three actors only.

There were several advantages in the smallness of the number. In the first place the dialogue gained in clearness and simplicity, owing to the fewness of the persons taking part in it. This simplicity was especially well suited to the severe and statuesque character of Greek tragedy, in which the rapid movement of a dialogue between a large number of persons would have been altogether inappropriate. In the extant Greek tragedies even the three actors permitted by custom are used with considerable reserve. They are never allowed to join promiscuously in the dialogue for any length of time. Whenever three characters are upon the stage, it will be found that in most cases one of them stands by in silence, while the other two carry on the dialogue. The two change from time to time, but it is only on rare occasions and for brief periods, that all three converse promiscuously together. It appears, therefore, that the Greek tragic writers, so far from feeling the restriction upon the number of the actors as an impediment, did not even employ the number allowed by custom with as much freedom as they might have done. There was another obvious advantage in the restriction. As only three actors were needed, it was easy to ensure that they should all be performers of first-rate excellence. In modern times the large number of actors required constitutes a great difficulty. It is rare to see the subordinate characters in a play of Shakespeare even tolerably performed. The effect of the piece is spoiled by the feebleness of the princes, dukes, lords, and ladies who crowd the stage. In the Greek drama, owing to the limitation upon the number of the performers, this difficulty was avoided, and a high standard of excellence maintained throughout the play. It was all the more necessary, among the Greeks, to take some precaution of this kind, since the size of the theatre demanded unusual powers in the actor. In a modern theatre an actor, however poor, can at any rate usually be heard. But in the vast open-air theatre at Athens it required a man with an exceptionally clear and powerful voice to make himself audible to the vast multitude of spectators. It cannot have been an easy task to find actors who combined histrionic talent with voices of sufficient power, and if a large number had been required, there would have been great difficulty in meeting the demand. This consideration doubtless helped to ensure the continued observance of the rule as to the number of the actors.

The original Greek word for an actor was 'hypokritês.' Etymologically the word seems to have meant 'one who answers[1].' According to the old grammarians the origin of the term was due to the fact that in the early drama, when the chorus played

---

[1] Phot. v. ὑποκρίνεσθαι· τὸ ἀποκρίνεσθαι οἱ παλαιοί· καὶ ὁ ὑποκριτὴς ἐντεῦθεν, ὁ ἀποκρινόμενος τῷ χορῷ. So also Hesych. v. ὑποκρίνοιτο, and Poll. iv. 123. Apollon. Lex. Hom. v. ὑποκρίναιτο· πρωταγωνιστοῦντος γὰρ τοῦ χοροῦ τὸ παλαιὸν οὗτοι ὥσπερ ἀποκριταὶ ἦσαν, ἀποκρινόμενοι πρὸς τὸν χορόν.

the principal part, the main function of the actor was to 'reply to the chorus.' This derivation of the word is very likely the correct one. In the times before Aeschylus, when there was only one actor, all the dialogue was necessarily carried on between the actor and the chorus. It is therefore not improbable that the duty of replying to the questions and remarks of the chorus may have been regarded as the salient feature in the performance of the actor, and have given rise to his name. In the course of the fourth century the old Attic word for an actor went out of use, and a new one was substituted. Henceforward actors were generally called 'artists,' or 'artists of Dionysus[1].'

As far as tragedy is concerned the art of acting may be said to have commenced in the time of Thespis. But actors did not come into existence as a separate class until many years afterwards. Before the period of Aeschylus, when only a single actor was required, his part was taken by the poet. It is expressly said that Thespis was 'himself acting, according to ancient custom,' at that performance which excited the disapproval of Solon[2]. But when a second actor was introduced by Aeschylus, then the actor's profession became of necessity distinct from that of the poet. For some time afterwards the poets continued to act occasionally in their own tragedies, side by side with the professional actors. But the practice went gradually out of fashion in the course of the earlier part of the fifth century. Aeschylus appears, from the statement in his Life, to have abandoned the stage even before the introduction of a second actor[3]. Sophocles was prevented from appearing as an actor by the weakness of his voice. It is true that he sometimes performed in public. In the Thamyris

---

[1] Demosth. Fals. Leg. § 192 πάντας τοὺς τεχνίτας συνήγαγεν; Aristot. Prob. xxx. 10 οἱ περὶ τὸν Διόνυσον τεχνῖται; Polyb. xvi. 21.

[2] Plut. Solon p. 95 C; Aristot. Rhet. iii. 1 ὑπεκρίνοντο γὰρ αὐτοὶ τὰς τραγῳδίας οἱ ποιηταὶ τὸ πρῶτον.

[3] The words in the Life are ἐχρήσατο δ' ὑποκριτῇ πρώτῳ μὲν Κλεάνδρῳ, ἔπειτα καὶ τὸν δεύτερον αὐτῷ προσῆψε Μυννίσκον τὸν Χαλκιδέα· τὸν δὲ τρίτον ὑποκριτὴν αὐτὸς ἐξεῦρεν, ὡς δὲ Δικαίαρχος ὁ Μεσσήνιος, Σοφοκλῆς. These words imply that he employed Mynniscus for the first time on the occasion of his introduction of a second actor; and that previously to this innovation, when only one actor was required, he had

he played the harp, and in the Nausicaa he delighted the spectators by his skill with the ball. But it is not likely that on either of these occasions he took a regular actor's part. He probably appeared upon the scene merely as a mute character, in order to show his skill with the harp and the ball[1]. After the time of Sophocles there are no further instances of tragic poets performing in their own plays[2]. As to the early history of comic acting very little is known. Cratinus is mentioned as one of the old poets who were called 'dancers,' and it is therefore probable that he acted in his own comedies[3]. But after his time there is no certain instance of a comic poet appearing upon the stage. The professional actor was universally employed. The statement that Aristophanes acted the part of Cleon in the Knights is due to a misconception on the part of the scholiast[4].

It appears then that it was in the beginning of the fifth century that the profession of the actor came into existence as a distinct occupation. It grew very rapidly in importance. At first the

been accustomed to employ Cleander, instead of acting himself. He must, therefore, have given up acting before the production of the Supplices, and considerably before the first appearance of Sophocles. The statement that Sophocles was the *first* dramatic poet to abandon acting in person can only be true to the extent that he was the first poet who never acted at all.

[1] Vit. Soph. πρῶτον μὲν καταλύσας τὴν ὑπόκρισιν τοῦ ποιητοῦ διὰ τὴν ἰδίαν μικροφωνίαν; Athen. p. 20 F; Eustath. Od. p. 1533.

[2] Müller (die Griech. Bühnen. p. 184) states, on the authority of Zenob. Prov. v. 100, that Astydamas the Elder acted in his own tragedy, the Parthenopaeus. The words in Zenobius are εὐημερήσας ἐν τῇ ὑποκρίσει Παρθενοπαίου. But this is merely a carelessness of expression, on which no stress can be laid. In the account given by Suidas (v. σαυτὴν ἐπαινεῖς) of the same occurrence the expression is εὐημερήσαντι ἐπὶ τραγῳδίας διδασκαλίᾳ Παρθενοπαίου. The whole story about Astydamas the Elder receiv-

ing a statue on account of the success of his Parthenopaeus is rather dubious, since the inscription in Corp. Inscr. Att. ii. 973 shows that Astydamas the Younger produced a Parthenopaeus in 340 B.C. It is possible that in the story about the Parthenopaeus the elder and the younger Astydamas have been confused.

[3] Athen. p. 22 A.

[4] The story about Aristophanes acting the part of Cleon in the Knights was due to a misunderstanding of the phrase καθίεναι τὸ δρᾶμα δι' ἑαυτοῦ. The Knights was the first play Aristophanes produced in his own name. See Meineke, Frag. Com. Gr. ii. 928 ff. Antiphanes is said (Müller, Griech. Bühnen. p. 184) to have acted one of his own comedies, the evidence being the inscription in Corp. Inscr. Att. ii. 972 ['Αντιφάνη]ς πέμ(πτος) 'Ανασῳ(ζομένοις)· [ὑπεκρίνετο 'Αντ]ιφάνης. But it is by no means certain that the name of the poet is rightly filled in as Antiphanes. Even if it is, it does not follow that the actor Antiphanes was the same person.

actors were so little regarded that their names were not thought worthy of a place in the notices of dramatic victories. But in the records of the latter half of the century a change is observable, and the names of the actors regularly appear side by side with those of the poets and choregi. About the same time a prize was instituted for the best actor at the different contests, as well as for the best poet[1]. In the fourth century the actors sprang into still greater prominence. The art of acting tended to outshine the art of dramatic writing. An age of great actors succeeded to an age of great poets. The same phenomenon is not uncommon in the theatrical history of other nations. In England, for instance, a period of dramatic productiveness was followed by a period of sterility and insignificance, and from the time of Garrick downwards the names of the great actors, who have made themselves famous by interpreting the masterpieces of Shakespeare, are more conspicuous than the names of dramatic authors. In Athens the fourth century was the period when acting was brought to the greatest perfection. To such an extent had the importance of the actor's profession increased, that in Aristotle's time a play depended more for its success upon the skill of the actor than upon the genius of the poet. The effect upon dramatic writing was most pernicious. The poets began to write their plays with a view to exhibiting the capacities of the actors. Scenes which had no connexion with the plot were introduced for the sole purpose of enabling an actor to make a display of his talents[2]. Sophocles is said by one of the old grammarians to have been guilty of the same sort of practice. But if there is any truth in the statement, the evil effects are not very apparent in the extant tragedies[3]. The charge might be brought with more plausibility against the monodies of Euripides, which are feeble from a literary point of view, but would enable an actor with a fine voice to make a great impression. However it was not until the fourth century that the influence of the actors became so

[1] See chap. i. p. 54.
[2] Aristot. Poet. c. 9 λέγω δ' ἐπεισοδιώδη μῦθον ἐν ᾧ τὰ ἐπεισόδια μετ' ἄλληλα οὔτ' εἰκὸς οὔτ' ἀνάγκη εἶναι. τοιαῦται δὲ ποιοῦνται ὑπὸ μὲν τῶν φαύλων ποιητῶν δι' αὐτούς, ὑπὸ δὲ τῶν ἀγαθῶν διὰ τοὺς ὑποκριτάς: Rhet. iii. 1 μεῖζον δύνανται νῦν τῶν ποιητῶν οἱ ὑποκριταί.
[3] Vit. Soph. p. 3 Dindf.

universal as to inflict distinct injury upon the art of dramatic writing.

The selection of the necessary number of actors for each dramatic performance was, except in very early times, undertaken by the state. The details in connexion with this arrangement have already been discussed in a previous chapter[1]. The main points may be recapitulated here. During the early part of the fifth century the poets chose their own actors. Certain poets and certain actors were permanently associated together. But as the actors increased in importance, they were placed on the same footing as the poets and choregi, and were appointed by the state. They were then distributed among the poets by lot. In the course of the fourth century the use of the lot was discontinued in the case of tragedy, and a new arrangement was adopted, which was rendered possible by the fact that each tragic poet exhibited several tragedies at the same time. Under the new system each tragedy was performed by a different actor, and in this way all the competing poets enjoyed in turn the services of all the actors. In comedy, as each poet exhibited only a single play, the old system of distribution by lot was retained. If an actor was engaged for one of the great Athenian festivals, and failed to put in an appearance, he was fined by the state. On one occasion Athenodorus, the great tragic actor, was hired to perform at the City Dionysia. But he failed to keep his engagement, as he preferred to be present and perform at the festivities held by Alexander the Great in Phoenicia, after his return from Egypt. A heavy fine was inflicted upon him in consequence, but the fine was paid by Alexander[2].

§ 2. *The distribution of the Parts among the Actors.*

It has already been shown that the number of the actors in a Greek play was limited to three. These three actors had distinctive names, according to the prominence of the parts which they took. The principal actor was called the protagonist; next in importance came the deuteragonist; the tritagonist

---

[1] See chap. ii. pp. 74–77.   [2] Plut. Alex. p. 681 E.

played the inferior characters[1]. The importance of the protagonist on the Greek stage has been pointed out in previous chapters[2]. In the ordinary theatrical language of the time a play was said to be 'acted by the protagonist,' as if the other actors were of no account. The protagonist was publicly appointed by the state, but was allowed to choose the second and third actor at his own discretion. In the same way the prize for acting at each festival was confined to the protagonists. The other performers had nothing to do with it. In tragedy more especially the protagonist was a person of the greatest importance; the deuteragonist and tritagonist were placed in a very subordinate position. The whole structure of a Greek tragedy was designed with the object of fixing the interest upon some grand central figure. The significance of the other characters consisted simply in their capacity to excite the passions and draw forth the sentiments of the leading personage. This being so, it was essential that the protagonist should concentrate the interest upon himself; otherwise the harmony and balance of the play would have been destroyed. Hence the subordinate actors were strictly forbidden to attempt to outshine the protagonist. They were called upon to exercise the greatest self-denial. Even if they had finer voices than the protagonist, they were made to moderate and restrain their powers, so as to allow the protagonist to retain the superiority, and rivet the attention of the spectators upon the central figure[3]. The jealousy of protagonists towards their fellow-actors is well exemplified by the story about Theodorus, who had a theory that the first speaker in a play always attracted the sympathies of the audience, and therefore would never allow any other actor, however inferior, to appear upon the stage before himself[4].

[1] Plut. Rep. Ger. 817 A; Dem. Fals. Leg. § 10; Suidas v. Σοφοκλῆς.

[2] See chap. i. p. 55, ch. ii. p. 75.

[3] Cic. Div. in Caecil. § 48 ut in actoribus Graecis fieri videmus saepe illum, qui est secundarum aut tertiarum partium, quum possit aliquanto clarius dicere, quam ipse primarum, multum summittere, ut ille princeps quam maxime excellat, &c.

[4] Aristot. Pol. vii. 17. The story about Theodorus has caused some difficulty. Does it mean that Theodorus, besides taking the principal character, also played the part of the person who made the first speech in the tragedy?

The distribution of the different parts among the actors was undertaken by the poet if the play was a new one[1]. But if an old play was being reproduced, the matter would be arranged by the protagonist who had the management of the performance. The three actors between them filled all the parts in a play, appearing in various characters successively. Such a practice was rendered possible by the use of masks. An actor had only to change his mask and his dress, and he could then re-appear in a new character. Changes of this kind could be effected in a very few moments, as is shown by the one or two traditions on the subject which have been preserved by the ancient scholiasts. For example, in the opening scene of the Phoenissae Jocasta speaks the prologue, and then leaves the stage. Thereupon Antigone and an old attendant mount by a staircase on to the roof of the palace, in order to view the Argive army encamped outside the walls. The scholiast tells us that the protagonist played the parts both of Jocasta and of Antigone. It was necessary, therefore, after Jocasta had left the stage, that there should be a slight interval before Antigone appeared upon the palace roof, to give the actor time to change his mask and dress. Euripides managed this by making the attendant come out alone upon the roof at first, and look about him to see that the coast is clear, while he addresses a few words to Antigone, who is still inside the

[1] If so, he would have been debarred from acting some of the most popular tragedies of the time. For instance, the actor who took the part of Electra in the play of Sophocles could not act the part of the paedagogus, since Electra comes on the stage as soon as the paedagogus leaves it. There would be the same difficulty about the Orestes, the Medea, and many other plays. It has been suggested that the reference is to some preliminary announcement of the title of the play, which Theodorus preferred to make himself, instead of leaving it to a subordinate. Such announcements were made in Greek theatres in later times (cp. Lucian, Pseudolog. 19; Heliod. Aethiop. viii. 17; Synesius, περὶ προνοίας p. 128 D), and may have been customary in Athens, or in other parts of Greece, in the time of Theodorus. But it is extremely improbable that the reference is to any such practice. The audience would hardly pay much attention to the voice of the person who announced the name of the coming play. The meaning is probably that Theodorus used to take the part of the character which spoke first, whenever it was possible to do so. In such plays as the Electra it would be impossible.
¹ Alciphron, Epist. iii. 71.

palace. When he sees that all is safe, he calls on Antigone to follow after him, and she thereupon mounts the staircase, and appears to the spectators. The speech of the attendant, while he is looking about upon the roof, consists of only fifteen iambic lines. Thus the space of time required to speak fifteen lines was enough to enable an actor to change from one character to another[1]. There is a further instance which shows that even less time was necessary. In the Choephori, when Aegisthus is murdered, a servant rushes out upon the stage and calls to Clytaemnestra. As Clytaemnestra comes out, he apparently runs back into the palace. Clytaemnestra speaks five lines, and then Orestes hastens out of the palace, followed by Pylades. In the scene which ensues Pylades has three lines to speak; and the scholiast says that his part was taken by the servant who had just left the stage, so as to avoid the necessity of four actors. The servant must therefore have changed his mask in a very few moments[2]. As such rapid changes were possible, a great variety of characters might be introduced in the course of a play, in spite of the restriction that more than three characters could not take part in the dialogue at the same time.

In the distribution of parts the protagonist took the principal character. The parts of Oedipus, Electra, and Antigone, in the plays of the same name by Sophocles, are specially mentioned as having been acted by celebrated protagonists. Orestes in the play of Euripides is also described as the part of the protagonist[3]. Usually, as in the above instances, the principal character gave the name to the piece. But this was not always the case. In the Oenomaus of Sophocles the part of Oenomaus was played by the tritagonist Aeschines. In the Cresphontes of Euripides the principal character was Merope, and was taken by Theodorus. The part of Cresphontes fell to Aeschines as tritagonist[4]. It does not therefore follow that the character which gave the name to a play was necessarily

---

[1] Schol. Eur. Phoen. 93.
[2] Schol. Aesch. Choeph. 906.
[3] Aul. Gell. vii. 5; Stob. Flor. 97. 28; Dem. Fals. Leg. § 246; Strattis ap. Meineke, Frag. Com. Gr. ii. p. 763.
[4] Hesych. v. ἀρουραῖος Οἰνόμαος; Dem. de Cor. § 180; Aelian, Var. Hist. xiv. 40.

the leading one. In the Agamemnon of Aeschylus most likely the protagonist played the part of Clytaemnestra, as this is certainly the most impressive character in the play, though not the one with which the spectators are in sympathy. Besides playing the leading part the protagonist had also to take his share of the subordinate characters when he could be spared. It has already been mentioned that in the Phoenissae of Euripides the protagonist appeared in the part of Antigone, as well as in that of Jocasta. At times he took even the smallest characters if the necessities of the play demanded it. Plutarch states that the protagonist, in the part of a messenger or an attendant, often gained more applause than the actor who bore the sceptre and the crown[1]. It was, in fact, the chief advantage of the Greek system that even the subordinate characters were played with as much excellence as the more important ones. The tritagonist took what in modern times would be called the 'heavy' parts. It was his special privilege, as Demosthenes remarks, to play the tyrant and the sceptred monarch[2]. Aeschines, in his career as tritagonist, often had to act gloomy tyrants of this kind, such as Creon, Cresphontes, and Oenomaus. Such characters did not require great powers in the actor. There was no pathos to be excited, no play of conflicting emotions to be exhibited. All that was necessary was a powerful voice, and a capacity for declaiming verses. Most likely for the same reason the tritagonist usually spoke the prologues, which also did not require much more in the actor than good powers of elocution. Thus the ghost of Polydorus, which speaks the prologue in the Hecuba of Euripides, was acted by Aeschines as tritagonist[3]. The deuteragonist took the parts which, in point of interest, were intermediate between the leading characters, and the heavy parts which fell to the tritagonist. There are not, however, any traditions as to particular characters having been played by the deuteragonist. Attempts have been made in modern times to assign the characters in the extant Greek dramas to the prot-

[1] Plut. Lysand. p. 446 D. [3] Dem. l. c., de Cor. §§ 180, 267.
[2] Dem. Fals. Leg. § 247.

agonist, deuteragonist, and tritagonist respectively. Such speculations are interesting, in so far as they show that all the existing plays could be perfectly well performed by three actors. Otherwise they are not of very great value. There is generally no difficulty in deciding which was the leading character. But it is obvious that the subordinate parts might be distributed in various ways; and no doubt the arrangement differed at different periods. There are no traditions on the subject in addition to those already mentioned. Any attempt, therefore, to reproduce the exact arrangement adopted at a particular period must depend more or less upon conjecture.

§ 3. *Extra Performers.*

For every Greek play a chorus was provided by the choregus, and three actors were supplied by the state. But in most plays a certain number of additional performers were required. The parts which these extra performers had to fill may be divided, roughly speaking, into three classes. In the first place there were the various mute personages, who simply appeared upon the stage, and did nothing more. The second class consisted of minor characters with only a few words to say. In these cases extra performers were required, either because the regular actors were already occupied, or because the part was that of a boy or girl, which the regular actor would be unable to take. Thirdly, in many cases a small subordinate chorus was required, in addition to the ordinary one. The general name for the persons who undertook these parts was 'parachorēgēmata[1].' This word obviously means something

---

[1] As there is some doubt about the meaning of the word παραχορήγημα, it will be well to quote the passages where it occurs. They are (1) Schol. Aesch. Prom. 12 ἐν παραχορηγήματι αὐτῷ εἰδωλοποιηθεῖσα Βία. (2) Schol. Aesch. Eum. 573 ἐν παραχορηγήματι αὐτῷ εἰσιν οἱ Ἀρεοπαγῖται μηδαμοῦ διαλεγόμενοι. (3) Schol. Aristoph. Ran. 211 ταῦτα καλεῖται παραχορηγήματα, ἐπειδὴ οὐχ ὁρῶνται ἐν τῷ θεάτρῳ οἱ βάτραχοι, οὐδὲ ὁ χορός, ἀλλ' ἔσωθεν μιμοῦνται τοὺς βατράχους; ὁ δὲ ἀληθῶς χορὸς ἐκ τῶν εὐσεβῶν νεκρῶν συνέστηκεν. (4) Schol. Aristoph. Pax 113 τὰ τοιαῦτα παραχορηγήματα καλοῦσιν, οἷα νῦν τὰ παιδία ποιεῖ καλοῦντα τὸν πατέρα· εἶτα πρὸς οὐδὲν ἔτι τούτοις χρήσεται. (5) Poll. iv. 109 ὁπότε μὴν ἀντὶ τετάρτου ὑποκριτοῦ δέοι τινὰ τῶν χορευτῶν εἰπεῖν ἐν

which is supplied by the choregus in addition to his ordinary expenditure. It follows therefore that the cost of the extra performers was borne by the choregus. Properly he was only responsible for the chorus; but if additional men were required, he had to supply them. This conclusion is confirmed by Plutarch's story of a certain tragic actor who was going to appear as a queen, but refused to proceed with the part, unless the choregus provided him with a train of female attendants[1]. Extra performers were especially necessary in the Old Comedy, in which a great number of characters appear upon the stage.

If songs had to be sung, or words spoken, behind the scenes, by persons out of sight of the audience, these persons were called 'paraskênia.' In many cases their part could be taken by members of the chorus, and in this way no extra expense would fall upon the choregus.

It remains to consider more in detail the three classes of 'parachorēgēmata'. The mute personages appeared most frequently in the shape of attendants, body-guards, crowds of people, and so on. The Oedipus Rex opens with a number of suppliants kneeling at the altar before the palace of the king. In the Choephori Orestes and Pylades are accompanied by attendants. The judgment scene in the Eumenides requires twelve per-

ᾠδῇ, παρασκήνιον καλεῖται τὸ πρᾶγμα, ὡς ἐν 'Αγαμέμνονι Αἰσχύλου· εἰ δὲ τέταρτος ὑποκριτής τι παραφθέγξαιτο, τοῦτο παραχορήγημα ὀνομάζεται, καὶ πεπρᾶχθαί φασιν αὐτὸ ἐν Μέμνονι Αἰσχύλου. The first and second instances refer to mute personages, the third instance refers to an extra chorus, the fourth to extra performers who say only a few words upon the stage. It is therefore quite clear that the word παραχορήγημα included all classes of extra performers, as distinct from the actors and the chorus. There are no grounds for excluding the mute personages from the class of παραχορηγήματα, as Müller (die Griech. Bühnen. p. 179) and others have done. Pollux appears to make the distinction between παρασκήνιον and παραχορήγημα lie in the fact that the former sang, the latter spoke. The distinction is a foolish one, and was probably due to Pollux's habit of generalising from one particular instance. The word παρασκήνιον, in its present sense, only occurs in the passage of Pollux. To judge from the etymology of the word, it most likely denoted performers behind the scenes. The words ἐν 'Αγαμέμνονι Αἰσχύλου in the passage of Pollux are corrupt, the corruption arising from the words ἐν Μέμνονι Αἰσχύλου which follow. There is no παρασκήνιον in the Agamemnon. The reference cannot be to the speech of Pylades in the Choephori (vv. 900–902), because (1) the Choephori could not be called the Agamemnon, (2) the part of Pylades was taken by one of the regular actors, as the scholiast ad loc. informs us.

[1] Plut. Phocion p. 750 C.

formers to play the parts of the members of the Areopagus. In the Agamemnon, when the king and Cassandra arrive in the chariot, servants stand ready to spread carpets beneath their feet [1]. Probably in many other instances great personages were accompanied by attendants, although there is no special reference to them in the play. Not unfrequently more prominent characters appeared upon the stage as mute figures. Pylades says nothing throughout the Electra of Sophocles and the Electra of Euripides. In the latter play one of the Dioscuri must also have been a dumb figure, since two actors were already upon the stage when the Dioscuri make their appearance. The person of Force in the Promethus Vinctus is another example. A very frequent occasion for the employment of mute characters was in pathetic scenes between children and their parents. The children appear as silent figures, but give occasion for touching speeches by their parents. There is an example in the Ajax of Sophocles, where Ajax addresses his son Eurysaces. But the instances in Euripides are much more frequent. There is the celebrated scene in the Medea, where Medea half relents at the sight of her children. There is the address of Megara to her children in the Hercules Furens. Other examples are to be found in the introduction of Manto, the daughter of Teiresias, in the Phoenissae, and of Polymestor's children in the Hecuba [2]. Mute figures were also very useful in occasionally personating one of the regular characters of the play, when the actor of the character was temporarily required for another purpose. It has already been pointed out that in the middle of the Oedipus Coloneus the part of Ismene is played by a dumb personage, to enable the previous actor of the part to appear in another character. One of the best instances of this practice is in the final scene of the Orestes, in which most of the prominent characters are brought upon the stage together, after the fashion of a modern drama. But only three of them can speak: Helen, Hermione, Electra, and Py-

---

[1] Aesch. Choeph. 713, Eum. 678 ff., Agam. 908. Herc. Fur. 454, Phoen. 834, Hecub. 978.
[2] Soph. Aj. 544; Eur. Med. 1021,

lades are all mute figures. The silence of Pylades is especially unnatural. In cases of this kind an attempt is made to produce effects which were hardly compatible with the limited resources of Greek tragedy.

The second class of extra performers took all those minor parts in which a certain amount of speaking or singing was required, but which it was impossible for the regular actors to take. In tragedy they were generally required for the boys' parts, which were unsuitable for grown up actors. Euripides was especially fond of introducing boys upon the stage. In the Alcestis Eumelus bewails his mother's death in a short ode. Another example is the mournful dialogue between Andromache and her little son Molossus[1]. In the Old Comedy these additional actors were frequently needed to perform small parts at times when the three regular actors were already on the stage. Examples are very numerous. There are the daughters of Trygaeus in the Peace, and the daughters of the Megarian in the Acharnians. The herald and Pseudartabas are additional examples from the Acharnians[2].

In the third place an extra chorus was sometimes required. The Propompi in the Eumenides, and the chorus of boys in the Wasps, both appear side by side with the regular chorus, and must therefore have been personated by extra performers. An additional chorus, consisting of shepherds, was also required in the Alexander of Euripides[3]. Sometimes the extra chorus was not visible to the spectators, but sang behind the scenes. In such cases the singing might be done by members of the regular chorus, if they had not yet entered the orchestra. Examples are to be found in the chorus of frogs in the Frogs of Aristophanes, and Agathon's chorus in the Thesmophoriazusae[4]. Both these choruses were behind the scenes, and would therefore come under the class called 'paraskênia.' Their part would be taken by members of the regular chorus. In the opening scene of the Hippolytus a band of huntsmen

[1] Eur. Alc. 393, Androm. 504.
[2] Aristoph. Pax 114, Acharn. 43, 94, 729.
[3] Aesch. Eum. 1032; Aristoph. Vesp. 248; Schol. Eur. Hipp. 58.
[4] Aristoph. Ran. 209, Thesm. 104.

sing a short ode to Artemis upon the stage. Immediately after their disappearance the regular chorus, consisting of women of Troezen, enters the orchestra. In this case the huntsmen cannot have been personated by members of the regular chorus; but it is possible that the singing was done by the chorus behind the scenes, while the huntsmen were represented by mute figures [1].

§ 4. *Costume of the Tragic Actors.*

To return to the subject of the actors. The next point to be discussed is their costume, and general appearance upon the stage. First, as to the tragic actors. The practice of the Greeks in regard to tragic costume was totally opposed to all modern notions upon the subject. Historical accuracy and archaeological minuteness in the mounting of a play were matters of supreme indifference to the Greeks. Though the scenes of most of their tragedies were laid in heroic times, they never made the slightest attempt to reproduce upon the stage an accurate representation of the costume of the Homeric period. On the other hand they were not content that the heroes and gods of their tragedy should appear upon the scene in the costume of ordinary life, as was formerly the case in our modern theatres. Greek tragedy was essentially ideal: the existence it depicted was far above the level of everyday life. Even when the subject of a tragedy was taken from contemporary history, as in the case of the Persae of Aeschylus, the treatment was ideal. In the Persae of Aeschylus no Greek statesmen or generals are introduced upon the stage, or even mentioned by name. The scene is laid far away in Persia; the characters are all Persian; everything common and familiar is banished out of sight. Such being the tone of Greek tragedy, the costume of ordinary life would have been out of keeping. A special dress was invented, similar to that of common life, but more flowing and dignified. The garments were dyed with every variety of brilliant colour. The

[1] Eur. Hipp. 61.

bulk of the actor was increased by padding his chest and limbs, and placing huge wooden soles under his feet. Masks were employed in which every feature was exaggerated, to give superhuman dignity and terror to the expression. In this way a conventional costume was elaborated, which continued for centuries to be the regular dress of the tragic actors. All the leading characters in a Greek tragedy were dressed in this fashion, with only slight variations and additions, such as particular circumstances required. A fairly accurate conception of the appearance presented by one of these tragic figures of the Greek stage may still be obtained in modern times. Our knowledge on the subject is derived partly from the descriptions of Pollux and others, partly from works of art. The works of art, it is true, are in most cases Italian; but Greek tragedies were commonly performed in Italy even in imperial times, and Roman tragedy was in all respects a mere reproduction of the Greek. Hence works of art depicting tragic scenes and figures, though Italian in origin, present the characteristics of the Greek stage. It would be unsafe to depend upon them for points of minute detail. But they correspond in the main with the descriptions of Pollux, and it is possible to obtain from them a fairly trustworthy picture of the general appearance of the Greek actors. The accompanying representation of a tragic actor is copied from an ivory statuette which was found in the ruins of a villa near Rieti[1].

In no respect is the difference between the ancient and the modern actor more conspicuous than in the use of masks. The invention of the tragic mask was ascribed to Thespis. At the commencement of his career as an actor Thespis is said to have merely painted his face with white lead or purslane. Later on he employed masks; but these were of a very simple character, consisting simply of linen, without paint or colouring. Choerilus introduced certain improvements which are not specified. Phrynichus set the example of using female masks[2]. Aeschylus was the first to employ painted masks, and to pourtray features

[1] The illustration is taken from Monumenti Inediti, xi. 13.

[2] Suidas vv. Θέσπις, Χοιρίλος, Φρύνιχος.

of a dreadful and awe-inspiring character. By several writers Aeschylus is regarded as the inventor of the tragic mask, and to a certain extent this view is correct, since it was Aeschylus who first gave the tragic mask that distinctive character, from which in later times it never varied except in detail[1]. After the time of Aeschylus there is no further mention of any radical alterations or improvements in the manufacture of masks.

The use of masks is indissolubly connected with the style and character of Greek tragedy. Without masks it would have been impossible for one actor to play several parts, or for men to play the parts of women. Of course the Greek actor had no opportunity of displaying those powers of facial expression which are one of the chief excellencies in modern acting. It was only by his gestures that he could emphasise the meaning of what he had to say: his features remained immovable. But niceties of facial expression would have been entirely lost in the vast expanse of a Greek theatre. The tragic mask, on which were depicted in bold and striking lines the main traits in the character represented, was really much more effective, and could be seen by the most distant spectator. Then again it must have been difficult, if not impossible, for a Greek actor to delineate finely drawn shades of individual character. The masks necessarily ran in general types, such as that of the brutal tyrant, the crafty statesman, the suffering maiden, and so on. The acting would have to correspond. It would be difficult to imagine the part of Hamlet acted in a mask. But the characters of Greek tragedy were mostly types rather than individuals. The heroes and heroines were drawn in broad general outlines, and there was little attempt at delicate strokes of character-painting. The use of masks no doubt helped to give this particular bent to Greek tragedy.

Masks were generally made of linen. Cork and wood were occasionally used[2]. The mask covered the whole of the head, both in front and behind. The white of the eye was painted on

---

[1] Suidas v. Αἰσχύλος; Hor. A. P. 278; Evanth. de trag. et com. (Gronov. Thesaur. viii. p. 1683).

[2] Poll. x. 167; Isidor. Orig. x. 119; Suidas v. Θέσπις; Verg. Georg. ii. 387; Prudent. c. Symmach. ii. 646.

the mask, but the place for the pupil was left hollow, to enable the actor to see[1]. The expression of the tragic mask was gloomy and often fierce; the mouth was opened wide, to give a clear outlet to the actor's voice. One of the most characteristic features of the tragic mask was the onkos[2]. This was a cone-shaped prolongation of the upper part of the mask above the forehead, intended to give size and impressiveness to the face. The onkos was not used in every case, but only where dignity was to be imparted. It varied in size according to the character of the personage. The onkos of the tyrant was especially large; that of women was less than that of men. A character was not necessarily represented by the same mask throughout the piece. The effects of misfortune or of accident had often to be depicted by a fresh mask. For instance, in the Helen of Euripides Helen returns upon the stage with her hair shorn off, and her cheeks pale with weeping. Oedipus, at the end of the Oedipus Tyrannus of Sophocles, is seen with blinded eyes and blood-stained face. In such cases a change of mask must have been necessary.

The number and variety of the masks used in tragedy may be seen from the accounts in Pollux. For the ordinary tragic personages there were regular masks of a stereotyped character. Pollux enumerates twenty-eight kinds[3]. His information was derived from Alexandrian sources, and his list represents the number of masks which were employed on the later Greek stage for the ordinary characters of tragedy. It is not likely that in the time of Sophocles or Euripides the use of masks was reduced so completely to a system as in the later period; but the descriptions in Pollux will give a fairly accurate idea of the style of the masks used in earlier times. Of the twenty-eight masks described by Pollux six are for old men, eight for young men, three for attendants, and eleven for women. The principal features by which the different masks are discriminated from one another are the style of the hair, the colour of the complexion, the height of the onkos, and the

---

[1] Aul. Gell. v. 7; Wieseler, Denkmäler, p. 42.
[2] Poll. iv. 133–135, 139.
[3] Poll. iv. 133–141.

expression of the eyes. To take a few examples. The strong and powerful man, such as the tyrant, has thick black hair and beard, a tall onkos, and a frown upon his brow. The man wasted by disease has fair hair, a pale complexion, and a smaller onkos. The handsome youth has fair ringlets, a light complexion, and bright eyes. The lover is distinguished by black hair and a pale complexion. The maiden in misfortune has her hair cut short in token of sorrow. The aged lady has white hair and a small onkos, and her complexion is rather pale. Attendants and messengers are marked by special characteristics. One of them wears a cap, another has a peaked beard, a third has a snub nose and hair drawn back. One sees from these examples how completely Greek tragedy was dominated by conventional rules, in this as in all other respects. As soon as a personage entered the stage, his mask alone was enough to give the spectators a very fair conception of his character and position.

The twenty-eight tragic masks enumerated by Pollux were used for the ordinary characters of tragedy, and formed a regular part of the stock of the Greek stage-manager. But special masks were required when any unusual character was introduced. Pollux gives a long list of such masks[1]. In the first place there were numbers of mythological beings with strange attributes. Actaeon had to be represented with horns, Argo with a multitude of eyes. Evippe in the play of Euripides had the head of a mare. A special mask of this kind must have been required to depict Io with the ox-horns in the Prometheus Vinctus of Aeschylus. A second class of special masks was needed to represent allegorical figures such as Justice, Persuasion, Deceit, Jealousy. Of this kind are the figures of Death in the Alcestis of Euripides, and Frenzy in the Hercules Furens. Lastly there were personifications of cities, rivers, and mountains. Five specimens of ancient tragic masks are given on the next page. The first is the mask of a youth, the fifth that of a man; the second and third are probably masks of women. The fourth is an example of one of the

[1] Poll. iv. 141, 142. Special masks were called ἔκσκευα πρόσωπα.

special masks, and depicts Perseus with the cap of darkness upon his head [1].

We now come to the dress of the tragic actors. Nothing is known as to the style of dress adopted by Thespis and his immediate successors. The tragic costume which eventually pre-

[1] Figs. 1–3 are copied from Wieseler, Denkmäler, v. 20, 24, 26. The first is a marble, the second and third are from wall-paintings at Herculaneum. Figs. 4 and 5 are copied from the Archaeol. Zeitung for 1878. They are from wall-paintings at Pompeii.

vailed upon the Greek stage dates from the time of Aeschylus. His creative spirit revolutionised every department of Greek tragedy. It was he who transformed it into an essentially dramatic species of art, and gave it the characteristics of grandeur and terror. It was necessary to make a corresponding change in the masks and dresses of the actors; and this improvement also was effected by Aeschylus. The invention of the Greek tragic costume, both in its main features and in most of its subordinate details, is invariably ascribed to Aeschylus[1]. The dress which he introduced was so well adapted to its purpose, that it continued unchanged in its principal characteristics throughout the remaining history of Greek tragedy. Subsequent generations, while making various small additions and alterations, never altogether abandoned the original design. All the later representations of tragic actors, whether found in Etruscan mosaics, or wall-paintings of Cyrene and Pompeii, obviously belong to one common type. In spite of considerable differences in point of detail, they show a distinct general resemblance to one another[2]. The tragic costume, as finally settled by Aeschylus, was in many respects not unlike that worn by the hierophants and torch-bearers who officiated at the Eleusinian mysteries. According to one tradition the similarity was due to the priests having copied the dress of the tragic actors in later times. But it is much more probable that the very reverse was the case, and that Aeschylus, in the course of his innovations, borrowed some hints from the dress of the priests[3].

The object of Aeschylus was to devise a costume that should be suitable to the heroes and gods and supernatural beings with which his stage was peopled. It was necessary to invent something more splendid than the dress of ordinary life. For this purpose he employed various devices. Among

[1] Athen. p. 21 E; vit. Aesch.; Philostrat. vit. Apoll. vi. 11 (p. 220, ed. Kayser); Cramer, Anecd. Par. i. p. 19.
[2] Wieseler, Denkmäler vii., viii., ix. 1, xiii. 2.
[3] Athen. p. 21 E καὶ Αἰσχύλος δὲ οὐ μόνον ἐξεῦρε τὴν τῆς στολῆς εὐπρέπειαν καὶ σεμνότητα, ἣν ζηλώσαντες οἱ ἱεροφάνται καὶ δᾳδοῦχοι ἀμφιέννυνται. An emendation, ζηλώσας ἦν, has been proposed. But probably the text is quite correct, and the author of the statement was mistaken in the inference which he drew from the resemblance between the dress of the tragic actors and that of the Eleusinian priests.

them was the cothurnus, or tragic boot, the aim of which was to increase the stature of the actors, and to give them an appearance of superhuman grandeur. It was a boot with a wooden sole of enormous thickness attached to it. The wooden sole was painted in various colours. According to some accounts Aeschylus invented the boot altogether; according to other accounts his innovation consisted in giving increased thickness to the sole, and so raising the height of the actors. After his time it continued to be a regular

feature in tragic costume down to the latest period of Greek and Roman tragedy[1]. The cothurnus varied in height according to the dignity and position of the wearers, a king, for instance, being provided with a larger cothurnus than a mere attendant. In this way the physical stature of the persons upon the stage was made to correspond to their social position. In the accompanying illustration, representing a tragic scene, the

---

[1] The name for the tragic boot in Greek was ἐμβάτης (Suid. v. Αἰσχύλος), ὀκρίβας (Lucian, Nero c. 9), or κόθορνος (vit. Aesch.). Cothurnus was the regular name in Latin. Pollux (iv. 115) appears to be mistaken in calling ἐμβάτης the comic boot, in opposition to the notices in other grammarians.

difference between the cothurnus of the servant and that of the hero is very conspicuous[1]. Whether the cothurnus was worn by all the characters in a tragedy, or only by the more important ones, is uncertain. There was another tragic boot called the 'krêpis,' of a white colour, which was introduced by Sophocles, and worn by the chorus as well as by the actors. Very possibly this may have been a boot more like those of ordinary life than the cothurnus, and may have been worn by the subordinate characters[2]. The illustrations show that the cothurnus was rather a clumsy contrivance, and that it must have been somewhat inconvenient to walk with. The tragic actor had to be very careful to avoid stumbling upon the stage. Lucian says that accidents were not infrequent. Aeschines met with a misfortune of this kind as he was acting the part of Oenomaus at Collytus. In the scene where Oenomaus pursues Pelops he tripped up and fell, and had to be lifted up again by the chorus-trainer Sannio[3]. The use of the cothurnus, combined with the onkos, or prolongation of the crown of the mask, added greatly to the stature of the tragic actor. To prevent his seeming thin in comparison with his height, it was found necessary to increase his bulk by padding. His figure was thus made to appear of uniformly large proportions[4].

The garments of the tragic actor were the same as the ordinary Greek dress, but their style and colour were more magnificent. They consisted of an under-garment or tunic, and an over-garment or mantle. The tunic was brilliantly variegated in colour. Sometimes it was adorned with stripes, at other

The sole of the cothurnus was of wood, as appears from Schol. Lucian, Epist. Saturn. 19. Works of art show that it was painted: see Wieseler, Denkmäler, vii., viii.; and cp. Ovid. Am. ii. 18. 13 risit Amor pallamque meam pictosque cothurnos. According to Suidas (v. Αἰσχύλος), Aristot. (ap. Themist. or. xxvi. p. 316), Philostrat. (vit. Apoll. vi. 11, p. 220 Kayser) the cothurnus was invented by Aeschylus: the Life says that it was only enlarged by him. For the use of the cothurnus in late times see Lucian, Nero c. 9, Necyom. c. 16, Iup. Trag. c. 41, de Salt. c. 27; Martial, viii. 3. 13, &c., &c.

[1] The illustration is from Wieseler, Denkmäler, ix. 1. The original is a wall-painting from Pompeii or Herculaneum.

[2] Vit. Soph. p. 2 Dindf.

[3] Lucian, Somnium vel Gallus 26; vit. Aeschin.

[4] Phot. v. σωμάτια; Lucian, de Salt. 27.

times with the figures of animals and flowers, or similar ornamentation. A special tunic of purple was worn by queens. The ordinary tragic tunic reached down to the feet, in accordance with the old Athenian custom, the shorter tunic not having been generally adopted at Athens until after the time of Pericles. The tunics worn by females upon the stage were sometimes longer than those worn by men, and trailed upon the ground, as the name 'syrtos' implies. On the other hand, it appears from various illustrations that shorter ones were occasionally provided for attendants and other minor characters. The tunic of the tragic actor was fastened with a broad girdle high up under the breast, and flowed down in long and graceful folds, giving an appearance of height and dignity. It was also supplied with long sleeves reaching to the waist. In ordinary life sleeves of this kind were considered effeminate by the European Greeks, and were mostly confined to the Greeks of Asia. The general character and appearance of the tragic tunic is well exemplified in the illustrations already given [1].

The over-garments were the same in shape as those worn off the stage, and consisted of two varieties. The 'himation' was a long mantle passing round the right shoulder, and covering the greater part of the body. The chlamys was a short cloak flung across the left shoulder. As far as shape was concerned all the tragic mantles belonged to one or the other of these two classes, but they differed in colour and material. Pollux gives a list of several of them, but does not append any description [2]. The mere names prove that they were very gorgeous in colour. There were mantles of saffron, of frog-green, of gold, and of purple. Queens wore a white mantle with purple borders. These were the colours worn by tragic personages under ordinary circumstances. But if they were in misfortune or in exile,

---

[1] For the general account of the χιτών or tunic see Pollux iv. 115-118. The name ποικίλον shows that it was brilliantly coloured. As to the length of the tunic see Lucian, Iup. Trag. c. 41, Eustath. Il. p. 954. 47, and the illustrations in Wieseler's Denkmäler, &c. For the ornamentation see Wieseler, Denkmäl. vi. 2, vii., viii. The girdle is clearly shown in many of the works of art. The sleeves were called χειρίδες (vit. Aesch.; Lucian, Iup. Trag. c. 41).

[2] Poll. iv. 116-118.

the fact was signified to the spectators from the very first by dressing them in the garb of mourning. In such cases the colours used were black, dun, grey, yellow, or dirty white.

Coverings for the head were not usually worn by the Greeks except when they were on a journey. The same practice was observed upon the stage. Thus in the Oedipus Coloneus Ismene arrives from Thebes wearing a 'Thessalian hat.' Ladies also wore a mitra, or band for binding the hair. In the scene in the Bacchae, where Pentheus is dressed up as a female, one of the articles mentioned is the hair-band[1].

Such was the tragic costume invented by Aeschylus, and universally adopted upon the Greek stage. No stress was laid upon historical accuracy; no attempt was made to discriminate one rank from another by marked variety in the costume. The same dress in its main features was worn by nearly all the characters of a Greek tragedy. In some instances special costumes were invented for particular classes of men. Soothsayers such as Teiresias always wore a woollen garment of network, which covered the whole of the body. Shepherds were provided with a short leathern tunic. Occasionally also heroes in great misfortune, such as Telephus and Philoctetes, were dressed in rags[2]. But the majority of the characters wore the regular tragic costume, with slight additions and variations; and the only means by which the spectators were enabled to identify the well-known personages of mythology, and to discriminate between the different ranks of the characters, was by the presence of small conventional emblems. For instance, the gods and goddesses always appeared with the particular weapon or article of dress with which their names were associated. Apollo carried his bow, and Hermes his magic wand. Athênê wore the aegis[3]. In the same way the well-known heroes of antiquity had generally some speciality in their costume which enabled the spectators to recognise them as soon as they came upon the stage. Hercules was always con-

---

[1] Poll. iv. 116; Soph. O. C. 314; ii. 11.
Eur. Bacch. 833. [3] Aesch. Eum. 181, 404; Poll. iv. 117.
[2] Poll. iv. 116, 117; Varro, Res Rust.

spicuous by means of his club and lion's skin; Perseus wore the cap of darkness, as depicted in the illustration already given[1]. Kings in a similar manner were distinguished by the crown upon their head, and the sceptre in their hand. They also had a special article of dress, consisting of a short tunic with a swelling bosom, worn over the ordinary tunic[2]. Foreigners were discriminated by some one particular attribute, rather than by a complete variety in their costume. For example, Darius wore the Persian turban; otherwise he was probably dressed in the ordinary tragic style[3]. Warriors were equipped with complete armour, and occasionally had a short cloak of scarlet or purple wrapped round the hand and elbow for protection[4]. Old men usually carried a staff in their hands. The staff with a curved handle, which occurs not infrequently in ancient works of art, was said to be an invention of Sophocles[5]. Crowns of olive or laurel were worn by messengers who brought good tidings; crowns of myrtle were a sign of festivity[6]. The above examples illustrate the mode in which the different characters and classes were discriminated upon the Greek stage by small varieties in their equipment. But in its main features the dress of the majority of the characters was the same, and consisted of the elaborate costume designed by Aeschylus.

Concerning the tragic costume as a whole a few observations may be made. The devotion to conventional rules is as conspicuous here as in Greek art generally. Persons in misfortune wear clothes of a particular colour. Soothsayers have garments of network. Gods and heroes are denoted by special symbols. The tragic dress, after having been once elaborated, is retained for centuries without any important innovation. As to the appearance which the tragic actor presented upon the stage, it is obvious that he must have been an impressive, though rather unnatural, figure. His large stature and bulky limbs, his harsh

[1] Poll. iv. 117. See above, p. 222.
[2] Lucian, Somn. vel Gall. 26; Poll. iv. 116. The special tunic was called κόλπωμα.
[3] Aesch. Pers. 661.
[4] Poll. iv. 116, 117. The cloak was called ἐφαπτίς.
[5] Eur. Ion 743; Vit. Soph. p. 2 Dindf.
[6] Aesch. Agam. 493; Soph. O. R. 83; Eur. Alc. 759.

and strongly-marked features, his tunic with its long folds and brilliantly variegated pattern, his mantle with its gorgeous colours, must have combined to produce a spectacle of some magnificence. In criticising his appearance we must always remember that he was intended to be seen in theatres of vast dimensions, in which even the front rows of spectators were a considerable distance from the stage, while the more distant part of the audience could only discern general effects. For such theatres the tragic costume of the Greeks was admirably adapted, however unwieldy and unnatural it may have appeared on a closer inspection. Its magnificence and dignity were especially appropriate to the ideal figures which move in the dramas of Aeschylus and Sophocles. In the Frogs of Aristophanes Aeschylus is humorously made to declare that it was only right that the demigods of tragedy should wear finer clothes, and use longer words, than ordinary mortals. The tragedy of Euripides was altogether more human in tone, and a more ordinary costume would have been better suited to it. But the Greeks, with their strong feeling of conservatism in matters of art, clung to the form of dress already established. The result was not altogether satisfactory. The attempt to exhibit human nature pure and simple upon the Greek stage was bound to appear somewhat incongruous. It often happened that the speeches and actions of the heroes in Euripides were highly inconsistent with the superhuman grandeur of their personal appearance. In any case the step from the sublime to the ridiculous was a very short one in the case of the Greek tragic actor. The play had to be elevated in tone, and the performance of a high standard, to carry off the magnificence of the actor's appearance. Otherwise his unwieldy bulk and gloomy features excited laughter rather than tears. Lucian is especially fond of ridiculing the tragic actors of the time. He laughs at their 'chest-paddings and stomach-paddings,' 'their cavernous mouths that look as if they were going to swallow up the spectators,' and the 'huge boots on which they are mounted.' He wonders how they can walk across the stage in safety[1]. In

[1] Lucian, de Salt. 27, Anachar. 23.

Philostratus there is an amusing story of the extraordinary effect produced upon a country audience in Spain by the appearance of a tragic actor before them for the first time. It is said that

as soon as he came upon the stage they began to be rather alarmed at his wide mouth, his long strides, his huge figure, and his unearthly dress. But when he lifted up his voice and commenced his speech in the loud and sonorous clang of the tragic stage, there was a general panic, and they all fled out of the theatre as if he had been a demon[1]. Such stories and criticisms bring clearly before us the unnatural character of the Greek tragic costume. It was well suited to an ideal drama and a theatre of enormous size. Under other conditions it was inevitable that it should appear ridiculous. In order to give an idea of the style and character of Greek tragic acting, two representations of tragic scenes are inserted, the first of which obviously represents Medea hesitating about the murder of her children[2].

§ 5. *Costume of Satyric Actors.*

The costume of the actors in the satyric drama naturally comes next for consideration. Tragedy and the satyric drama were sister forms of art, descended from the same original. But while tragedy advanced in dignity and magnificence, the satyric drama retained all the wild licence and merriment which in early times had characterised the dithyrambic performances in honour of Dionysus. Its chorus invariably consisted of satyrs. As to the characters upon the stage, with which we are at present concerned, one of them was always Silenus, the drunken old follower of Dionysus; the rest were mainly heroes out of mythology, or other legendary beings. Thus in the Cyclops of Euripides, the only extant specimen of a satyric play, the characters upon the stage consist of Silenus on the one hand, and Odysseus and the Cyclops on the other. Concerning the costume of the actors the notices of Pollux are exceedingly brief. But it is possible to obtain fairly clear conceptions on the subject from several works of art, and more especially from the well-known vase-painting at Naples, which depicts all the persons concerned in the production of a satyric play, from the poet down to the flute-player[3]. From this painting we see

---

[1] Philostrat. vit. Apoll. v. 9 (p. 171 Kayser).
[2] The illustrations are taken from Monumenti Inediti, xi. 31, 32. The originals are wall-paintings at Pompeii.
[3] Wieseler, Denkmäl. vi. 1-10.

that the characters in a satyric drama, with the exception of Silenus, were dressed in much the same way as in tragedy. Their masks exhibit the same features, and their garments are of the same general description. The tunic appears to have been rather shorter, to facilitate ease of movement, as the acting in a satyric play was no doubt less dignified and statuesque than in tragedy. For the same reason the tall cothurnus of tragedy does not appear to have been worn. It is not depicted in the works of art; and although this fact in itself is perhaps hardly decisive, since even in representations of tragic scenes the cothurnus is occasionally left out, still on general grounds

it appears to be most improbable that the cothurnus should have been worn in the satyric drama. But on the whole the heroic characters in satyric plays were dressed in much the same fashion as in tragedy. As to Silenus, his mask always represents a drunken old man, with a half-bestial expression. His under-garments, as depicted in works of art, are of two kinds. Sometimes he wears a tight-fitting dress, encasing the whole of his body with the exception of his head, hands, and feet. At other times he wears close-fitting trousers, and a tunic reaching to the knees. All these garments are made of shaggy materials, to resemble the hide of animals[1]. Certain over-garments are also mentioned by Pollux as having been worn by Silenus, such as fawn-skins, goat-skins, imitation panther-skins, mantles of purple, and mantles inwoven with flowers or animals[2]. The figures in the accompanying illustration, which is taken from the vase-painting already referred to, represent the three actors in a satyric drama. The first is playing the part of some unknown hero of mythology. His tunic is rather short, and he has no cothurnus; otherwise he exhibits the usual features of the tragic actor. The second figure represents Hercules. His tunic is still shorter, and barely reaches to the knees. The third figure is that of Silenus. His body is covered with a single close-fitting garment, and he carries a panther-skin over his shoulders. All these figures are holding their masks in their hands.

§ 6. *Costume of Comic Actors.*

The inquiry into the costume of the actors in Athenian comedy falls into two divisions. There is the Old Comedy and the New. The Middle Comedy was merely a state of transition between the two, and presented no very distinctive characteristics of its own. The Old Comedy was essentially the product of a particular time and place. With its local allusions and personal satire it was unsuited for reproduction or imitation among later generations. Consequently very few traditions were preserved concerning the style of the masks and dresses used in it. The information on the subject to be found among later writers is extremely scanty. Attempts have been made to illustrate the costumes of the Old Attic comedy by the light of certain vase-paintings from Magna Graecia, which depict scenes out of the comedies of the Phly-

---

[1] Specimens of the first kind of dress are to be found in Wieseler, Denkmäl. vi. 2, 6, 7, 10; specimens of the second kind in vi. 8, 9. The tunic was called χιτὼν χορταῖος, μαλλωτός, ἀμφίμαλλος, and was apparently made of wool: cp. Poll. iv. 118; Hesych. and Suid. v. χορταῖος; Dion. Hal. A. R. vii. 72; Ael. Var. Hist. iii. 40.

[2] Poll. iv. 118. These articles are part of the dress of Silenus. The other actors were dressed quite differently. The dress of the chorus is described in the next chapter.

akes, and belong mostly to the third century B.C.[1] The Phlyakes were the comedians of the Italian Greeks, and represented one branch of the old Doric comedy. This comedy had much in common with the phallic exhibitions, out of which Attic comedy was developed. It is probable therefore that there was a considerable resemblance, as far as the costume of the actors was concerned, between the performances of the Phlyakes and the Old Comedy at Athens. Hence the vase-paintings referred to, of which a specimen is here inserted, may be of assistance in helping us to form some

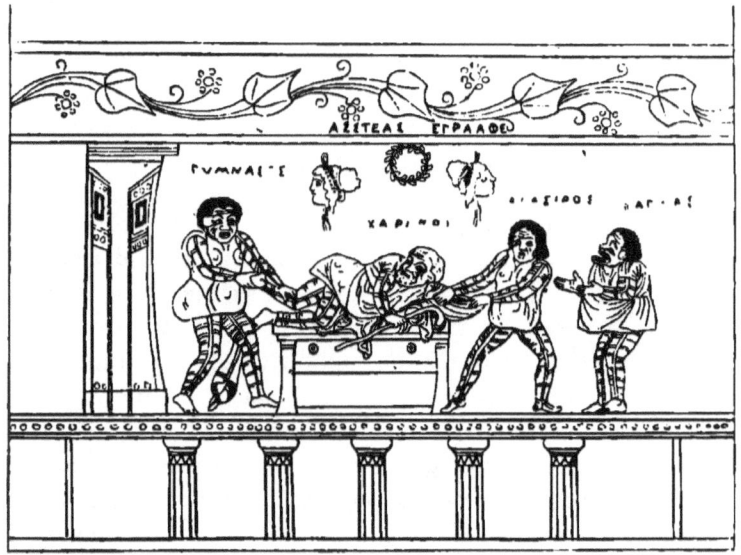

general picture of the external features of the Old Comedy. But the connexion is too remote to lead to any very definite conclusions. Our principal source of information as to the costumes of the actors in the Old Comedy must be the extant plays of Aristophanes, together with the few casual notices of the Scholiasts upon the subject.

[1] See Heydemann's article, Die Phlyakendarstellungen auf bemalten Vasen, in Jahrb. d. Kais. Deutsch. Archäol. Inst. 1886, p. 260 foll. Specimens are given in Wieseler's Denkmäl. iii. 18, ix. 7-15, A. 25, 26. The illustration is taken from Wieseler, ix. 15.

The Old Comedy was the direct descendant of the boisterous phallic performances at the festivals of Dionysus. Coarseness and indecency were an essential part of it. The actors therefore regularly wore the phallus, as appears to have been also the case among the Phlyakes. Aristophanes in the Clouds takes credit to himself for having discarded this piece of indecency, and for having introduced a more refined style of wit into his comedy. But whatever his practice in the Clouds may have been, there are numerous passages to show that he reverted to the old custom in his later plays[1]. Possibly in addition to wearing the phallus the actors were also stuffed and padded in the grotesque fashion which is apparent in the representations of the Phlyakes. Apart from these special features the dresses in the Old Comedy resembled those of ordinary life, as may be shown from numerous passages in Aristophanes. As far as the masks were concerned, when particular individuals were introduced upon the stage, such as Socrates or Euripides, the masks were portraits or caricatures of the actual persons. Before a word was spoken the character was recognised by the audience. When Aristophanes brought out the Knights, the general terror inspired by Cleon was so great that the mask-makers refused to make a portrait-mask of him, and an ordinary mask had to be worn. Socrates, during the performance of the Clouds, is said to have stood up in his place in the theatre, to enable the strangers present to identify him with the character upon the stage[2]. As to the masks of the fictitious characters there is no definite information; but they were doubtless grotesque and extravagant in type, like those worn by the chorus, and those depicted in the vase-paintings from Magna Graecia. Not unfrequently in the Old Comedy figures of a fanciful and extravagant character were introduced upon the stage. Thus Pseudartabas, the King's Eye, had a mask with one huge eye in the centre of it. The trochilus in the Birds created laughter

---

[1] Schol. Arist. Nub. 538 εἰσῄεσαν γὰρ οἱ κωμικοὶ διεζωσμένοι δερμάτινα αἰδοῖα γελοίου χάριν. Arist. Nub. 537–539. That the phallus was worn in the later comedies of Aristophanes is proved by such passages as Thesmoph. 62, 643, Lysist. 985, 1073, 1085, &c.

[2] Poll. iv. 143; Platon. de Comoed. (Dindf. Proll. de Comoed. p. 21); Arist. Equit. 230; Ael. Var. Hist. ii. 13.

by its immense beak. The epops was provided with a ridiculously large crest, but seems otherwise to have been dressed like a human figure. Iris in the Birds came on the stage with outspread wings, swelling tunic, and a head-covering of enormous size, so as to cause Peisthetaerus to ask her whether she was a ship or a hat. Prometheus with his umbrella, and Lamachus with his nodding crests, are further examples of grotesque costume[1]. It has already been shown that the production of a comedy was a comparatively cheap affair, and cost about the same as a chorus of boys. It is not therefore probable that the costumes in the Old Comedy were very expensive or elaborate.

The New Comedy was of much longer duration than the Old Comedy, and was much more widely spread. It continued to flourish at Athens itself as late as the second century, and was transferred to Rome in the translations of Plautus and Terence and the other comic writers. There is no lack of information as to the costumes generally in use. In the first place all the actors wore masks, just as in the other branches of the Greek drama. As far as abstract fitness goes, the masks might well have been dispensed with. As the New Comedy was essentially a comedy of manners and every-day life, and its chief excellence lay in the accurate delineation of ordinary human character, it is probable that a style of representation after the fashion of the modern stage would have been much more appropriate to it. In a theatre of moderate size, with actors untrammelled by the use of masks, all the finer shades in the character-painting might have been exhibited clearly to the spectators. But in ancient times such a thing was impossible. To the Greek mind the use of masks was inseparably associated with the stage; and the Greeks were in such matters extremely tenacious of ancient custom. It is also very questionable whether in their enormous theatres masks could possibly have been dispensed with. At any rate they were invariably retained in the New Comedy. But it is a strange

[1] Schol. Aristoph. Acharn. 97; Aristoph. Av. 62, 94, 104, 1203 (with Schol. ad loc.), 1508, Acharn. 575 ff.

thing that, although in all other respects the New Comedy was a faithful representation of ordinary life and manners, the masks employed should have been of the most ludicrous and grotesque character. The fact is expressly stated by Platonius, and is borne out by the evidence of numerous works of art[1]. There was a total disregard for realism and fidelity to nature. The exaggerated eyebrows and distorted mouths gave an utterly unnatural expression to the features. Such masks were perfectly in keeping with the tone of the Old Comedy, in which parody and caricature predominated. But it is strange that they should have been adopted in the New Comedy, which otherwise was praised for holding the mirror up to nature. The reason probably lay in the size of the theatres. The excellence and humour of a finely-drawn mask would have been lost upon an audience seated at a great distance from the stage. Of course the statement of Platonius has to be taken with some qualification. The masks were not invariably distorted. Some of the young men and women were depicted with handsome, though strongly-marked, features, as in tragedy. But the comic characters always wore masks of the grotesque kind just referred to. Copies of four comic masks are given on the next page[2].

Pollux supplies a long list of the masks in ordinary use in the New Comedy, with accurate descriptions of each of them[3]. His list comprises masks for nine old men, eleven young men, seven slaves, three old women, and fourteen young women. In this list are included all the stock characters of the New Comedy, such as the harsh father, the benevolent old man, the prodigal son, the rustic youth, the heiress, the bully, the pimp, the procuress, and the courtesan. For all these characters there

[1] Platon. ap. Dindf. Proll. de Com. p. 21 ἐν δὲ τῇ μέσῃ καὶ νέᾳ κωμῳδίᾳ ἐπίτηδες τὰ προσωπεῖα πρὸς τὸ γελοιότερον ἐδημιούργησαν ... ὁρῶμεν γοῦν τὰ προσωπεῖα τῆς Μενάνδρου κωμῳδίας τὰς ὀφρῦς ὁποίας ἔχει, καὶ ὅπως ἐξεστραμμένον τὸ στόμα καὶ οὐδὲ κατ' ἀνθρώπων φύσιν. See Wieseler, Denkmäl. v. 27-52.

[2] The first illustration is taken from Archaeol. Zeitung, 1878, Taf. 4, and represents the masks of a girl and a slave. The original is a wall-painting at Pompeii. The second illustration, which is taken from Monumenti Inediti, xi. 32, contains two copies of terra cottas found at Pompeii. It will be seen that the mask of the girl is not unlike a tragic mask in general character.

[3] Poll. iv. 143-154. Cp. Quint. Inst. xi. 3. 74.

238   THE ACTORS.   [Ch.

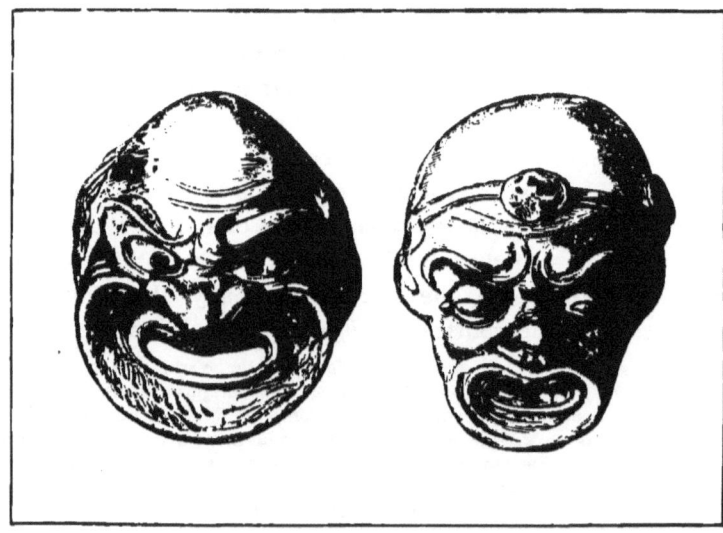

are regular masks with strongly characteristic features. In the plays of the New Comedy, as each personage stepped upon the stage, he must have been recognised at once by the audience as an old friend. Constant repetition must have rendered them familiar with the typical features of each sort of character. Certain kinds of complexion, and certain styles of hair and eyebrow, were appropriated to particular classes. White or grey hair was of course the regular sign of old age. Red hair was the mark of a roguish slave. Thick curly hair denoted strength and vigour. Miserly old men wore their hair close-cropped, while soldiers were distinguished by great shaggy manes. The hair of the courtesans was bound up with golden ornaments, or brilliantly-coloured bands. Beards were distinctive of manhood or middle age, and were not used in the masks of youths or old men. The complexion was always a prominent feature in the mask. A dark sun-burnt complexion was the sign of rude health, and was given to soldiers, country youths, or young men who frequented the palaestra. A white complexion denoted effeminacy; pallor was the result of love or ill-health. Red cheeks, as well as red hair, were given to rogues. The eye-brows were strongly-marked and highly characteristic. When drawn up they denoted pride or impudence, and were used in the masks of young men and of parasites. The hot-tempered old father, who alternated between fits of passion and fits of affection, had one eye-brow drawn up and the other in its natural position, and he used to turn that side of his face to the audience which was best in keeping with his temper at the moment. Noses were generally of the straight Greek type; but old men and parasites occasionally had hook noses, and the country youth was provided with a snub nose. Sometimes the ears showed signs of bruises, to denote that the person had frequented the boxing-school. The modern equivalent would be a broken nose, but among Greek boxers the ear was the part principally aimed at. The above abstract of the account in Pollux, together with the illustrations on the previous page, will give some idea of the different styles of mask employed in the later comedy.

The costume of the actors in the New Comedy was the same as that of ordinary life. The covering for the foot was a light sort of shoe, which was merely drawn on, without being tied in any way[1]. Pollux gives a short account of the dresses used in the New Comedy, from which it appears that particular colours were appropriated to particular classes[2]. White was worn by old men and slaves, purple by young men, black or grey by parasites. Pimps had a bright-coloured tunic, and a variegated mantle. Old women were dressed in yellow or

light blue, young women and priestesses in white. Procuresses wore a purple band round the head. The above statements are to a certain extent corroborated by the testimony of the works of art, but there are numerous exceptions. They cannot therefore be regarded as an exhaustive account of the subject. Other details of dress and costume are mentioned by Pollux. Old men carried a staff with a bent handle. Rustics were

---

[1] This shoe was called ἐμβάς in Greek, and soccus in Latin: see Ammon. de diff. vocab. p. 49; Aristoph. Nub. 858.
[2] Poll. iv. 119–120.

dressed in a leather tunic, and bore a wallet and staff, and occasionally a hunting-net. Pimps had a straight staff, and carried an oil flask and a flesh-scraper. Heiresses were distinguished by fringes to their dress. Considered as a whole the costume of the New Comedy seems to have been even more conventional than that of tragedy. The colour of a person's dress, the features of his mask, and small details in his equipment, would tell the spectators at once what sort of a character he was intended to represent. A scene from a wall-painting is here inserted, as a specimen of the style and outward appearance of the New Comedy[1].

§ 7. *Speech, Song, and Recitative.*

The profession of acting in ancient times required a great variety of accomplishments. The words of a play were partly spoken and partly sung, and it was necessary that the actor should have a knowledge of music, and a carefully cultivated voice. He had to combine the qualities of a modern actor with those of an operatic singer. In fact the Greek drama was not unlike a modern comic opera in this particular respect, that it consisted of a mixture of speaking and of singing. The question as to the mode in which the different portions of the dialogue were delivered, and the proportion which speech bore to song in the parts of the actors, is a matter of very great interest. In the first place there can be little doubt that, with few exceptions, all that portion of the dialogue which was written in the ordinary iambic trimeter was merely spoken or declaimed, with no musical accompaniment whatsoever. This of course constituted by far the larger part of the dialogue. Some remarks of Aristotle in the Poetics may be cited in proof of the above statement. Aristotle expressly says that in certain portions of the drama there was no music at all. In another place he remarks that when dialogue was introduced into tragedy, the iambic trimeter was naturally adopted as the most suitable metre, since

---

[1] The illustration is from Monumenti Inediti, xi. 32.

it is 'better adapted for being spoken' than any other[1]. A second argument is to be found in the practice of the Roman stage. In two of the manuscripts of Plautus there are marks in the margin to discriminate between the portions of the play which were spoken, and the portions which were sung. The result is to show that, while the rest of the play was sung, the iambic trimeters were always spoken[2]. As Roman comedy was a close and faithful imitation of the Greek, it follows almost as a matter of certainty that the iambic trimeters were spoken in the Greek drama also. It is true that in one place Lucian contemptuously remarks about the tragic actor, that he 'occasionally even sings the iambic lines[3].' But this statement, at the very most, cannot be held to prove more than that in Lucian's time iambic passages were sometimes sung or chanted. It is no proof that such a practice ever existed in the classical period. It is quite possible that in the second century A.D., when the chorus had either disappeared from tragedy, or been very much curtailed, some of the more emotional portions of the iambic dialogue may have been sung or chanted as a sort of equivalent. But Lucian himself speaks of the practice with disapproval, as a sign of bad taste and degeneracy. There can be little doubt that in the classical period the ordinary iambic dialogue was spoken. The only exception was in cases where iambic lines occurred in close connexion with lyrical metres. For instance, iambics are sometimes inserted in the midst of a lyrical passage. At other times speeches in iambics alternate with speeches in a lyrical metre, and the pairs of speeches are

---

[1] Aristot. Poet. c. 6 τὸ δὲ χωρὶς τοῖς εἴδεσι τὸ διὰ μέτρων ἔνια μόνον περαίνεσθαι καὶ πάλιν ἕτερα διὰ μέλους, c. 4 τό τε μέτρον ἐκ τετραμέτρου ἰαμβεῖον ἐγένετο· τὸ μὲν γὰρ πρῶτον τετραμέτρῳ ἐχρῶντο διὰ τὸ σατυρικὴν καὶ ὀρχηστικωτέραν εἶναι τὴν ποίησιν, λέξεως δὲ γενομένης αὐτὴ ἡ φύσις τὸ οἰκεῖον μέτρον εὗρε, μάλιστα γὰρ λεκτικὸν τῶν μέτρων τὸ ἰαμβεῖόν ἐστιν· σημεῖον δὲ τούτου, πλεῖστα γὰρ ἰαμβεῖα λέγομεν ἐν τῇ διαλέκτῳ τῇ πρὸς ἀλλήλους, ἑξάμετρα δὲ ὀλιγάκις καὶ ἐκβαίνοντες τῆς λεκτικῆς ἁρμονίας.

[2] The mark C (canticum) denotes the part which was sung, DV (diverbium) the part which was spoken. These marks are found in cod. vetus (B), and cod. decurtatus (C), and the plays in which they occur are the Trinummus, Paenolus, Pseudolus, Truculentus, and parts of others. See Christ, Metrik p. 677 ff.

[3] Lucian, de Salt. 27 ἐνίοτε καὶ περιᾴδων τὰ ἰαμβεῖα.

bound up into one metrical system[1]. In such cases no doubt the iambics were sung, or given in recitative. But the ordinary iambic dialogue, and in consequence the greater part of the play, was spoken without musical accompaniment.

The only portions of a play which the actors had to sing were the lyrical passages. In an actor's part the lyrical passages consisted, in most cases, either of solos, or of joint performances in which actors and chorus took part alternately. These solos and musical duets were in tragedy confined mainly to lamentations and outbursts of grief[2]. In general it may be said that, both in tragedy and comedy, song was substituted for speech in those scenes where the emotions were deeply roused, and found their fittest expression in music.

In addition to the declamation of the ordinary dialogue, and the singing of the lyrical passages, there was also a third mode of enunciation in use upon the Greek stage. It was called 'parakataloge,' and came half-way between speech on the one hand, and song on the other. Its name was due to the fact that it was allied in character to 'kataloge,' or ordinary declamation. It corresponded closely to what is called recitative in modern music, and consisted in delivering the words in a sort of chant, to the accompaniment of a musical instrument. On account of its intermediate character it was sometimes called 'speech,' and sometimes 'song.' It was first invented by Archilochus, and employed by him in the delivery of his iambics, which were partly sung, and partly given in recitative. A special kind of harp, called the klepsiambos, was originally employed for the purpose of the accompaniment. Recitative was subsequently introduced into the drama, as Plutarch expressly states[3]. It

---

[1] Instances of iambics in the midst of lyrical passages are to be found in Aesch. Agam. 1160, 1171, Aristoph. Acharn. 492. Iambic passages in strophic arrangement with lyrics appear in Aesch. Theb. 203-244, Soph. O. C. 1448-1504.

[2] Songs by the actors were called τὰ ἀπὸ τῆς σκηνῆς, or (in tragedy) μονῳδίαι. Musical duets between actors and chorus were in tragedy called κόμμοι. Suidas vv. μονῳδεῖν, μονῳδία; Aristot. Poet. c. 12.

[3] Plut. Mus. p. 1140 F ἀλλὰ μὴν καὶ Ἀρχίλοχος τὴν τῶν τριμέτρων ῥυθμοποιίαν προσεξεῦρε ... καὶ τὴν παρακαταλογήν. καὶ τὴν περὶ ταῦτα κροῦσιν ... ἔτι δὲ τῶν ἰαμβείων τὸ τὰ μὲν λέγεσθαι παρὰ τὴν κροῦσιν, τὰ δ' ᾄδεσθαι, Ἀρχίλοχόν φασι καταδεῖξαι, εἶθ' οὕτω χρήσασθαι τοὺς τραγικοὺς ποιητάς. Athen. p. 636 B ἐν οἷς γάρ (φησὶ) τοὺς ἰάμβους

is not easy to determine, by means of the slight and hazy notices upon the subject, what were the particular portions of a play in which recitative was employed. But there are certain indications which seem to show that it was used in the delivery of iambic, trochaic, and anapaestic tetrameters, and of regular anapaestic dimeters. Thus it is distinctly recorded of the actor Nicostratus that he gave trochaic tetrameters in recitative to the accompaniment of the flute[1]. Then again, the two sets of trochaic tetrameters, which came at the end of the parabasis, cannot have been sung, as their very name implies. The probability therefore is that they were given in recitative[2]. Thirdly, there is a passage in the Peace where the metre changes abruptly from lyrics to trochaic tetrameters without any break in the sentence[3]. It is difficult to suppose that in such a case a transition was made suddenly from song to mere speech. But the transition from song to recitative would have been quite feasible. Fourthly, it is asserted that on those occasions when the speech of an actor was accompanied by dancing on the part of the chorus, the metres employed were mostly iambic and anapaestic tetrameters[4]. But as it is impossible, in the case of Greek performers, to imagine dancing without a musical accompaniment, the verses must have been given in recitative. Fifthly, in the parabasis to the Birds the nightingale is asked to lead off the anapaests with the flute; and the scholiast remarks that 'the parabasis was often spoken to the accompaniment of the flute[5].' This statement means that the anapaestic tetrameters, which constitute the parabasis proper, were given in recitative. Lastly, there is the fact that

---

ᾖδον, ἰαμβύκας ἐκάλουν· ἐν οἷς δὲ παρελογίζοντο τὰ ἐν τοῖς μέτροις, κλεψιάμβους. Hesych. v. καταλογή· τὸ τὰ ᾄσματα μὴ ὑπὸ μέλει λέγειν.

[1] Xen. Symp. vi. 6 ὥσπερ Νικόστρατος ὁ ὑποκριτὴς τετράμετρα πρὸς τὸν αὐλὸν κατέλεγεν.

[2] The two groups of trochaic tetrameters in the parabasis were called ἐπίρρημα and ἀντεπίρρημα. See Platon. in Dindf. Prolegom. de Comoed. p. 21.

[3] Arist. Pax 1171, 1172.

[4] Schol. Arist. Nub. 1355 οὕτως ἔλεγον πρὸς χορὸν λέγειν, ὅτε τοῦ ὑποκριτοῦ διατιθεμένου τὴν ῥῆσιν, ὁ χορὸς ὠρχεῖτο. διὸ καὶ ἐκλέγονται ὡς ἐπιτοπλεῖστον ἐν τοῖς τοιούτοις τὰ τετράμετρα, ἢ τὰ ἀναπαιστικά, ἢ τὰ ἰαμβικά, διὰ τὸ ῥᾳδίως ἐμπίπτειν ἐν τούτοις τὸν τοιοῦτον ῥυθμόν.

[5] Aristoph. Av. 682-684 ἀλλ', ὦ καλλιβόαν κρέκουσ' | αὐλὸν φθέγμασιν ἠρινοῖς, | ἄρχου τῶν ἀναπαίστων, and Schol. ad loc. πολλάκις πρὸς αὐλὸν λέγουσι τὰς παραβάσεις.

the terms 'speech' and 'song' are both used of anapaests, implying that they occupied an intermediate position [1]. For these and other similar reasons it appears probable that recitative was employed in passages written in the metres already specified, that is to say, in iambic, trochaic, and anapaestic tetrameters, and in regular anapaestic dimeters. It seems too that on certain rare occasions it was used in lyrical passages [2]. The instrument employed, in dramatic performances, for the accompaniment of the recitative, as well as for the accompaniment of the singing generally, was the flute [3]. The harp had formerly been used very frequently [4]. But it was found that the flute, being a wind-instrument, harmonised better with the human voice [5]. However, the harp was occasionally introduced. In the Frogs Aeschylus calls for the harp, when he is going to give a specimen of the lyrics of Euripides. Similarly, in the parody of the choruses of Aeschylus, the recurrence of the refrain 'phlattothrat' points to an accompaniment on the harp [6].

§ 8. *Importance of the Voice in Greek Acting.*

In ancient acting the possession of a fine musical voice was a matter of absolute necessity. Several considerations will make it evident that the voice of the actor, upon the Greek stage, must have been far more important than it is at present. In the first place a considerable portion of the words in every Greek play were either sung, or delivered in recitative. In the second place each actor had to play several parts in succession, and to appear sometimes as a man, and sometimes as a woman. It would be essential, therefore, to mark the difference between

---

[1] The exodos, mostly consisting of anapaests, is described as ἅπερ ἐπὶ τῇ ἐξόδῳ τοῦ δράματος ᾄδεται in Schol. Arist. Vesp. 270, and as ὃ ἐξιόντες ᾖδον in Poll. iv. 108. But in Dindf. Proll. de Com. p. 37 it is called τὸ ἐπὶ τέλει λεγόμενον τοῦ χοροῦ. As far as the anapaestic tetrameters are concerned, the word ᾄδοντας in Aristoph. Plut. 1209, and Hesych.'s definition of ἀνάπαιστα as τὰ ἐν ταῖς παραβάσεσι τῶν χορῶν ᾄσματα,

show that they were not merely spoken: the expression λέγοντας ἔπη in Aristoph. Equit. 508 proves that they were not sung. See Christ, Metrik p. 680 ff.

[2] Aristot. Probl. xix. 6 διὰ τί ἡ παρακαταλογὴ ἐν ταῖς ᾠδαῖς τραγικόν;

[3] Schol. Arist. Nub. 312, Vesp. 580; Arist. Eccles. 890–892.

[4] Sext. Empir. p. 751, 21.

[5] Aristot. Probl. xix. 43.

[6] Aristoph. Ran. 1304, 1286.

the various personages by a corresponding variety in the tone of voice employed; and for this purpose an organ of great flexibility and compass must have been required. In the third place the whole character of Greek acting was largely modified by the costume of the performers. A modern actor adds force and emphasis to his speeches by means of the variety of his facial expression. A single glance, a slight movement of the features, is often enough to produce a very great effect. But to the Greek actor this mode of impressing the spectators was denied, owing to the use of masks. His features bore the same settled expression throughout the play. Even his gestures, in the case of tragedy, must have been very much restricted, owing to the cumbersome dress which he had to wear. On account of these limitations he was compelled to rely mainly upon his voice for the purpose of expressing all the fleeting emotions of the character he represented. Great skill and variety in the modulation of his tones were needed to counterbalance the absence of facial movement. Lastly, the Greek actor required a voice of enormous power, in order to make himself heard. When it is remembered that the theatre of Dionysus was in the open air, and was capable of holding from twenty to thirty thousand spectators, it will easily be seen that, in spite of the excellence of the acoustic arrangements, the demands upon the actor's voice must have been excessively great. For these various reasons the first and most essential requisite in a Greek actor was a powerful and expressive voice.

As a matter of fact, whenever an actor is mentioned by an ancient author, he is referred to in language which at the present day would seem much more appropriate to a notice of an operatic singer. It is always the excellence of the voice which is emphasised, little regard being paid to other accomplishments. And it is not so much the quality as the strength of the voice which is commended. The highest merit, on the Greek stage, was to have a voice that could fill the whole theatre. Numberless passages from ancient authors might be quoted in proof of this assertion, but a few specimens will suffice. Of Neoptolemus, the great tragic actor, it is said that 'his powerful voice' had raised him to the head of his profession[1]. Licymnius, the actor mentioned in one of the letters of Alciphron, won the prize for acting at a tragic contest on account of 'his clear and resonant utterance[2].' Dionysius, the tyrant of Syracuse, on a certain occasion, being covetous of distinction as a dramatic writer, despatched a company of actors to the Olympic festival, to give a performance of one of his tragedies. As he wished to ensure that the exhibition should be of the highest excellence, he was careful to choose 'actors with the best voices[3].' In a similar manner the emperor Nero prided himself on his talents as an actor. He instituted a tragic contest at the Isthmian festival, in order to display his powers. At this contest the actor Epeirotes 'was in splendid voice, and as his tones were more magnificent than ever, he won the greatest applause[4].' The above passages are in reference to particular actors. Remarks about acting in general are of the same type. Demosthenes is reported to have said that 'actors should be judged by their voices, politicians by their wisdom.' According to Zeno an actor was bound to have 'a powerful voice and great strength.' Aristotle defines the science of acting as being 'concerned with the voice, and the mode of adapting it to the expression of the different passions.' Lucian remarks that the actor is 'responsible for his voice only.' Plato would expel 'the actors with their beautiful voices' from his ideal state[5]. Finally there is the curious fact recorded by Cicero, that in the performance of a Greek play, when the actors of the second and third parts 'had louder voices' than the protagonist, they used to moderate and restrain their tones, in order to leave him the

---

[1] Diod. Sic. xvi. 92 Νεοπτόλεμος ὁ τραγῳδός, πρωτεύων τῇ μεγαλοφωνίᾳ καὶ τῇ δόξῃ.

[2] Alciph. iii. 48 τορῷ τινι καὶ γεγωνοτέρῳ φωνήματι χρησάμενος.

[3] Diod. Sic. xv. 7 ἐξαπέστειλε τοὺς εὐφωνοτάτους τῶν ὑποκριτῶν ... οὗτοι δὲ τὸ μὲν πρῶτον διὰ τὴν εὐφωνίαν ἐξέπληττον τοὺς ἀκούοντας.

[4] Lucian, Nero 9 ὁ δ' Ἠπειρώτης ἄριστα φωνῆς ἔχων, εὐδοκιμῶν δ' ἐπ' αὐτῇ καὶ θαυμαζόμενος λαμπροτέρᾳ τοῦ εἰωθότος.

[5] Plut. X orat. p. 848 B τοὺς ὑποκριτὰς ἔφη δεῖν κρίνειν ἐκ τῆς φωνῆς. Diog. Laert. vii. 20 τὴν μὲν φωνὴν καὶ τὴν δύναμιν μεγάλην ἔχειν. Aristot. Rhet. iii. 1. Lucian, de Salt. 27 μόνης τῆς φωνῆς ὑπεύθυνον παρέχων ἑαυτόν. Plat. Legg. 817 C καλλίφωνοι ὑποκριταί.

pre-eminence[1]. These passages, and others of the same kind which might be quoted, read like notices about operatic singers and musical performances, and prove conclusively the supreme importance of the voice among the ancient Greek actors. The principal reason was the immense size of the theatres, which could only be filled by voices of great power. Hence in critical notices of actors the strength of the voice is more regarded than its quality.

Such being the requirements of the Greek stage, it was necessary that the actors should receive a musical education as elaborate as that of a professional singer in modern times. Cicero informs us that the Greek tragic actors spent many years in the training of their voices, and used to test them, before each performance, by running over all their notes from the highest to the lowest[2]. They had to be careful and abstemious in their diet, as excess in eating and drinking was found to be inconsistent with the possession of a good voice[3]. The importance attached to this particular quality in the actor's art was not always beneficial in its results. Actors were sometimes inclined to violate good taste by intruding into their performances mere exhibitions of skill in the manipulation of the voice. They were ready to catch the applause of the populace by startling effects, such as imitations of the rushing of streams, the roaring of seas, and the cries of animals[4]. Moreover, it was a common fault among the ancient actors that, as a result of excessive training, their voices sounded artificial and unnatural. There was a special term to denote the forced tone of voice which was caused by too much exercise. Aristotle remarks that one of the principal excellencies of the tragic actor Theodorus was the thoroughly natural character of his delivery. Unlike other actors he seemed to speak with his own voice[5].

---

[1] Cic. div. in Caecil. § 48 quum possit aliquanto clarius dicere... multum summittere, ut ille princeps quam maxime excellat.

[2] Cic. de Orat. i. § 251.

[3] Aristot. Probl. xi. 22; Athen. p. 343 E.

[4] Plut. Aud. Poet. 18 B.

[5] Aristot. Rhet. iii. 2 διὸ δεῖ λανθάνειν ποιοῦντας, καὶ μὴ δοκεῖν λέγειν πεπλασμένως ἀλλὰ πεφυκότως... οἷον ἡ Θεοδώρου φωνὴ πέπονθε πρὸς τὴν τῶν ἄλλων ὑποκριτῶν· ἡ μὲν γὰρ τοῦ λέγοντος ἔοικεν εἶναι, αἱ δ' ἀλλότριαι.

§ 9. *Style of Greek Acting.*

Both in tragic and comic acting a loud and exceedingly distinct utterance must have been a matter of necessity. But in comedy the tone of voice adopted appears, as was only natural, to have been much less sonorous than that of the tragic actors, and to have approached much more closely to the style of ordinary conversation[1]. In tragedy on the other hand it was the conventional practice to declaim the verses with a loud and ringing intonation, and to fill the theatre with a deep volume of sound. Ancient authors often refer to the sonorous utterances of the tragic stage[2]. With bad actors the practice would easily degenerate into mere bombast. Pollux mentions a series of epithets such as 'booming' and 'bellowing,' which were applied to actors guilty of such exaggeration. Socrates and Simylus, the tragic actors with whom Aeschines went on tour in the country districts of Attica, derived their nickname of 'the Ranters' from a fault of this kind[3].

Another point which was required from ancient actors was great distinctness in the articulation of the separate words, and a careful observance of the rhythm and metre of the verses. In this respect the Athenians were a most exacting audience. Cicero speaks of their 'refined and scrupulous ear,' their 'sound and uncorrupted taste[4].' Ancient audiences in general had a much keener ear for the melody of verse than is to be found in a modern theatre. A slovenly recitation of poetry, and a failure to emphasise the metre, would not have been tolerated by them. Cicero remarks on the fact that, though the mass of the people knew nothing about the

---

[1] Lucian, Anachar. c. 23 αὐτοὶ δέ (οἱ τραγῳδοὶ) μεγάλα τε ἐκεκράγεσαν καὶ διέβαινον οὐκ οἶδ' ὅπως ἀσφαλῶς ἐν τοῖς ὑποδήμασι ... οἱ δὲ κωμῳδοὶ βραχύτεροι μὲν ἐκείνων καὶ πεζοὶ καὶ ἀνθρωπινώτεροι καὶ ἧττον ἐβόων.

[2] Philostrat. vit. Apoll. v. 8 (p. 171 Kayser) ἐπεὶ δὲ ἐξάρας τὴν φωνὴν γεγωνὸν ἐφθέγξατο: Alciphron, iii. 48 τορῷ τινι καὶ γεγωνοτέρῳ φωνήματι χρησάμενος: Lucian, l. c. See also the passages quoted on p. 247.

[3] Pollux (iv. 114), speaking of tragic acting, says εἴποις δ' ἂν βαρύστονος ὑποκριτής, βομβῶν, περιβομβῶν, ληκυθίζων, λαρυγγίζων, φαρυγγίζων. Dem. de Cor. § 262.

[4] Cic. Orat. §§ 25, 27.

theory of versification, their instinctive feeling for rhythmical utterance was wonderfully keen. He says that if an actor should spoil the metre in the slightest degree, by making a mistake about a quantity, or by dropping or inserting a syllable, there would be a storm of disapproval from the audience[1]. No such sensitiveness is to be found in modern theatres. It is common enough at the present day to hear blank verse declaimed as if it were prose. But among the ancient Greeks the feeling for correctness of rhythm in poetical recitations was just as instinctive as is the feeling for correctness of tune among ordinary musical audiences at the present time. If an actor in a Greek theatre made a slip in the metre of his verses, it was regarded in much the same way as a note out of tune would be regarded in a modern concert-room. As a consequence the mode of declamation practised on the ancient stage must have been much more rhythmical than anything we are now accustomed to, and the pauses and movements of the metre must have been much more clearly emphasised.

The use of appropriate gesture, in the case of Greek acting, was especially important, since facial expression was prevented by the mask, and the actor had to depend solely on the tones of his voice, and the effectiveness of his movements. In comedy, as might be expected, the gesticulation was of a free and unconstrained character, and is exemplified in numerous works of art. In tragedy, on the other hand, the nature of the actor's dress made rapid and violent movements impossible. Even if they had been possible, they would have been inconsistent with the tone of the tragic stage. The world of Greek tragedy was an ideal world of heroes and demigods, whose nature was grander and nobler than that of human beings. The realistic portrayal of ordinary human passions was foreign to the purpose of Greek tragedy. Scenes of physical violence, such as the forcible seizure of Antigone by Creon, were of rare occurrence. To be in harmony with this elevation of tone it was necessary that the acting should be dignified and

---

[1] Cic. de Orat. iii. §§ 195, 196, Parad. § 26.

self-restrained. Violent movements were avoided. A certain statuesque simplicity and gracefulness of pose accompanied all the gestures of the tragic actor. On the long and narrow stage the figures were arranged in picturesque and striking groups, and the successive scenes in the play presented to the eye of the spectator a series of artistic tableaux. The representations of tragic scenes and personages in ancient works of art are characterised by a certain dignity and repose which call to mind the creations of the sculptor. This sober and restrained style of acting was developed under the influence of Aeschylus and Sophocles during the great period of Attic tragedy. In later times a certain tendency to realism and exaggeration in the gestures and the movements began to show itself. The actors of the fourth century were censured by many critics for having degraded the art of acting from its former high level, and for having introduced a style which was unworthy of the dignity of the tragic stage. Callippides was called an ape by the old actor Mynniscus because of the exaggerated vehemence of his manner[1]. But as the tragic costume, with its unwieldy accompaniments, was retained with little alteration, it must have prevented any great advance in the direction of realism and freedom of movement. The statuesque style of acting continued on the whole to be characteristic of the tragic stage, and was indeed the only proper style for Greek tragedy.

§ 10. *The Actors' Guild.*

In the course of the fourth century the members of the theatrical profession at Athens formed themselves into a guild, for the purpose of protecting their interests and increasing their importance. The members of the guild were called The Artists of Dionysus. Poets, actors, and chorus-singers, trainers, and musicians all belonged to the guild. When it first came into

---

[1] Aristot. Poet. c. 26 ἡ μὲν οὖν τραγῳδία τοιαύτη ἐστίν, ὡς καὶ οἱ πρότερον τοὺς ὑστέρους αὐτῶν ᾤοντο ὑποκριτάς, ὡς λίαν γὰρ ὑπερβάλλοντα πίθηκον ὁ Μυννίσκος τὸν Καλλιππίδην ἐκάλει, τοιαύτη δὲ δόξα καὶ περὶ Πινδάρου ἦν ... εἶτα οὐδὲ κίνησις ἅπασα ἀποδοκιμαστέα, εἴπερ μηδ' ὄρχησις, ἀλλ' ἡ φαύλων, ὅπερ καὶ Καλλιππίδῃ ἐπετιμᾶτο καὶ νῦν ἄλλοις ὡς οὐκ ἐλευθέρας γυναῖκας μιμουμένων.

existence is not known for certain. Sophocles is said to have formed a sort of literary club, which may have been the prototype of the guild; but it is possible that there was no connexion between the two. At any rate it was fully established in the time of Aristotle, by whom it is mentioned [1].

The guild was of great value in maintaining and enforcing the various privileges of the members of the theatrical profession. These were of two kinds. In the first place actors were permitted to travel through foreign and hostile states for the purpose of giving dramatic performances. Even in time of war their persons and property were ensured from violation. Owing to this custom the actors Aristodemus and Neoptolemus were able to travel frequently to and fro between Athens and Macedonia during the height of the war, and to assist materially in the negotiation of the peace [2]. In the second place actors claimed to be exempt from naval and military service, in order to pursue their professional avocations in Athens and elsewhere. In the time of Demosthenes this immunity from service was occasionally granted, but had not yet hardened into an invariable custom. Demosthenes mentions the cases of two members of the theatrical profession who were severely punished for avoiding military service. One of them was Sannio the chorus-trainer, and the other was Aristides the chorus-singer. Meidias also is said to have used the most strenuous exertions to prevent the chorus of Demosthenes from being exempted from service [3]. At this time therefore it seems that such immunity was sometimes granted and sometimes not. Later on the Guild of Artists of Dionysus succeeded in getting the Amphictyonic Council to pass a decree, by which the Athenians were bound as a religious obligation to grant exemption from military service to all members of the theatrical profession. In the same decree the duty of allowing them a safe passage through their territories was enforced upon the Greek nation generally. This decree was renewed towards the beginning of the third century at the

---

[1] Vit. Soph. ταῖς δὲ Μούσαις θίασον ἐκ τῶν πεπαιδευμένων συναγαγεῖν τεχνῖται. Aristot. Probl. xxx. 10 οἱ Διονυσιακοὶ
[2] Dem. Fals. Leg. § 315.
[3] Dem. Meid. §§ 15, 58-60.

request of the Guild. A copy of the decree was engraved on stone and erected in the theatre at Athens, and has fortunately been preserved[1]. A translation of the more important passages will be of interest, as throwing light upon the position of the theatrical profession at Athens. It ran as follows: 'It was resolved by the Amphictyonic Council that security of person and property, and exemption from arrest during peace and war, be ensured to the artists of Dionysus at Athens; . . . . that they enjoy that exemption from military service and that personal security which has previously been granted to them by the whole Greek nation; that the artists of Dionysus be exempt from naval and military service, in order that they may hold the appointed celebrations in honour of the gods at the proper seasons, and be released from other business, and consecrated to the service of the gods; that it be unlawful to arrest or seize an artist of Dionysus in time of war or peace, unless for debt due to a city or a private person; that if an artist be arrested in violation of these conditions, the person who arrests him, and the city in which the violation of the law occurs, be brought to account before the Amphictyonic Council; that the immunity from service and personal security which is granted by the Amphictyonic Council to the artists of Dionysus at Athens be perpetual; that the secretaries cause a copy of this decree to be engraved on a stone pillar and erected in the temple, and another sealed copy of the same to be sent to Athens, in order to show the Athenians that the Amphictyonic Council are deeply concerned in the observance of religious duties at Athens, and are ready to accede to the requests of the artists of Dionysus, and to ratify their present privileges, and confer such other benefits upon them as may be possible.' In this decree it is very noticeable that dramatic performances are treated throughout as religious observances in honour of the gods, and the members of the theatrical profession are regarded as ministers consecrated to the service of the gods. The maintenance of their privileges is therefore a religious obligation in which the Amphictyonic Council is deeply interested. The religious

[1] Corp. Inscr. Att. ii. 551.

character of the old Greek drama has already been pointed out at the commencement of the first chapter.

Another inscription has been preserved referring to the Athenian Guild of Artists of Dionysus[1]. It appears that the Guild had a sacred enclosure and altar at Eleusis, where they were accustomed to offer libations to Demeter and Korê at the time of the Eleusinian mysteries. During the disturbances of the Sullan campaigns the altar was dismantled, and the yearly celebrations discontinued. The inscription is a decree of the Guild thanking a certain Philemon for his exertions in restoring the altar and renewing the annual ceremonies.

From the time of the fourth century onwards guilds of actors similar to that at Athens were rapidly formed in various places throughout the Greek-speaking world. In this way the masterpieces of Greek tragedy were made familiar to the most remote districts to which Greek civilisation had penetrated. But it is beyond the scope of the present work to trace the progress of the Greek drama outside the limits of Athens and Attica.

§ 11. *Social position of Actors.*

In Greece the profession of the actor was an honourable one, and there was no suspicion of degradation about it, as there was in Rome[2]. Actors and other dramatic performers were regarded as ministers of religion. In the dramatic exhibitions at Athens the actors were placed on the same level as the poets and choregi. Their names were recorded in the public archives, and in commemorative tablets; and competitions in acting were established side by side with the competitions between the poets. It is true that Aeschines is very frequently taunted by Demosthenes with his theatrical career, but the taunts are due to the fact, not that he was an actor, but that he was an unsuccessful one. Actors at the head of their pro-

---

[1] Corp. Inscr. Att. ii. 552.
[2] Corn. Nep. praef. 5 in scaenam vero prodire et populo esse spectaculo nemini in iisdem gentibus fuit turpidudini. Livy xxiv. 24 (of Ariston the tragic actor) huic genus et fortuna honesta erant; nec ars, quia nihil tale apud Graecos pudori est, ea deformabat.

fession occupied a very distinguished position. Aristodemus, the tragic actor, was on two occasions sent as ambassador to Macedon by the Athenians, and was largely instrumental in negotiating the peace[1]. The great Athenian actors were much sought after by the monarchs of the time. Aristodemus and Neoptolemus were frequently at the court of Philip, and Thessalus and Athenodorus at the court of Alexander[2]. Thessalus was a great favourite with Alexander, and was employed by him on delicate missions[3]. The leading actors seem to have made large incomes. For instance, Polus told Demosthenes that he was paid a talent for acting during two days only[4]. It is not stated whether the performance to which he refers took place at Athens, or elsewhere; but in all probability it was in some foreign state. There is no evidence to show what salaries were paid to the actors at the great Athenian festivals.

As for the lower ranks of the profession, the tritagonists, chorus-singers, musicians, and so on, though there was nothing dishonourable about their calling, their reputation does not seem to have been very high. Their strolling and uncertain manner of life seems to have had a bad effect upon their character. Aristotle, in his Problems, asks the question why it is that the artists of Dionysus are generally men of bad character? He thinks the reason is partly due to the vicissitudes in their fortunes, and the rapid alternations between luxury and poverty, partly to the fact that their professional duties left them no time for general culture[5]. His remarks of course apply mainly to the lower grades of the profession.

§ 12. *Celebrated Athenian Actors.*

Before concluding this account of Greek acting some notice of the principal Greek actors may not be out of place. Unfortu-

---

[1] Aesch. Fals. Leg. §§ 15-19; Dem. de Cor. § 21.
[2] Dem. Fals. Leg. § 315, de Pace § 6; Diod. Sic. xvi. 92; Plut. Alex. 681 D.
[3] Plut. Alex. 669 D.
[4] Plut. X orat. p. 848 B. Gellius, N. A. xi. 9, gives the same story about Aristodemus.
[5] Aristot. Probl. xxx. 10.

nately in most cases little more is known about them than their names. Several tragic actors of the fifth century are referred to by ancient writers, such as Cleander and Mynniscus, the actors of Aeschylus, and Cleidemides and Tlepolemus, the actors of Sophocles[1]. But no details are recorded as to their individual characteristics and different styles. One interesting fact is known about Mynniscus, to the effect that he considered the acting of his successors as deficient in dignity and over-realistic. He was especially severe upon Callippides, the representative of the younger generation of actors[2]. This Callippides was notorious for his conceit. On one occasion, when he was giving himself airs in the presence of Agesilaus the Spartan, he was considerably disconcerted by being asked by the latter whether he was 'Callippides the pantaloon[3].' Another tragic actor of the same period was Nicostratus, who was especially excellent in his delivery of the long narrative speeches of the messengers. His style was so perfect that to 'do a thing like Nicostratus' came to be a proverbial expression for doing it rightly[4].

But it was in the age of Demosthenes that the most celebrated group of tragic actors flourished. Among them was Polus of Aegina, who was considered to be the greatest actor of his time, and whose name is very frequently referred to by later writers. He was one of the actors who had the credit of having taught elocution to Demosthenes[5]. At the age of seventy, and shortly before his death, he performed the feat of acting eight tragedies in four days[6]. A well-known story is told about him to the following effect. Soon after the death of a favourite son, he happened to be acting the part of Electra in the play of Sophocles. In the scene in which Electra takes in her hands the urn supposed to contain the ashes of Orestes, and pours forth a lamentation over his death, Polus came upon the stage with the urn containing the ashes of his own son, and holding it in his hands proceeded to

[1] Vit. Aesch.; Schol. Aristoph. Ran. 803, Nub. 1267.
[2] Aristot. Poet. c. 26.
[3] Xen. Symp. iii. 11; Plut. Ages. p. 607 D ἀλλὰ οὐ σύγε ἐσσὶ Καλλιππίδας ὁ δεικηλίκτας;
[4] Macar. Cent. iii. 46; Prov. Coisl. 124.
[5] Rhet. Graec. vi. p. 35 (Walz).
[6] Plut. an sen. 785 C.

act the scene with such profound depth of feeling as to produce the greatest impression upon the audience. As Gellius remarks, the acting in this case was no fiction, but a reality[1]. Another of the great actors of this time was Theodorus, about whom a few facts are recorded. The exceedingly natural tone of his delivery, and his habit of never permitting any of the subordinate actors to appear upon the stage before himself, have already been referred to. He considered that tragedy was much more difficult to act in than comedy, and once told the comic actor Satyrus that it was easy enough to make an audience laugh, but to make them weep was the difficulty[2]. His own powers in this respect were very great. Once when acting in Thessaly he produced such an effect upon the brutal tyrant Alexander of Pherae, that Alexander was compelled to leave the theatre, because, as he afterwards told Theodorus, he was ashamed to be seen weeping over the sufferings of an actor, while he was perfectly callous about those of his countrymen[3]. The tomb of Theodorus, close to the banks of the Cephisus, was still to be seen in the time of Pausanias[4].

The other leading tragic actors of this period were Aristodemus, Neoptolemus, Thessalus, and Athenodorus. The two former were frequently at the court of Philip, and took a large part in bringing about the peace of Philocrates. They are therefore denounced by Demosthenes as traitors to their country, and advocates of Philip's interests[5]. Neoptolemus was the actor who, at the banquet held in Philip's palace on the day before his assassination, recited a passage out of a tragedy bearing upon the uncertainty of human fortune, and the inexorable power of death. The fact was afterwards remembered as an ominous coincidence[6]. Thessalus and Athenodorus were often rivals. At Tyre, after the return of Alexander from Egypt, they were the principal competitors in the great tragic contest, in which the kings of Cyprus were the choregi, and the chief generals of the army acted as judges.

[1] Gell. N. A. vii. 5.
[2] Plut. de se laud. 545 F.
[3] Ael. Var. Hist. xiv. 40.
[4] Pausan. i. 37. 3.
[5] See above, p. 255.
[6] Diod. Sic. xvi. 92.

On this occasion Athenodorus won, to the great grief of Alexander, who said he would have given a part of his kingdom to have ensured the victory of Thessalus[1]. The same two actors were also competitors at the City Dionysia in the year 341, but both of them were then beaten by Neoptolemus[2].

Among the Greeks the distinction between the tragic and the comic actors was as complete as that between the tragic and comic poets[3]. There are no instances during the classical period of an actor attempting both branches of the profession. Still less is recorded about the great comic actors than about the actors of tragedy. A few names are mentioned, but there is almost a total absence of details concerning their style and mannerisms. We are told that one of Hermon's jests was to knock the heads of his fellow-actors with a stick, and that Parmenon was celebrated for his skill in imitating the grunting of a hog[4]. Interesting criticisms on the acting and the actors in comedy are unfortunately nowhere to be found.

---

[1] Plut. Alex. 681 D.
[2] Corp. Inscr. Att. ii. 973.
[3] Plat. Rep. 395 B ἀλλ' οὐδέ τοι ὑπο- κριταὶ κωμῳδοῖς τε καὶ τραγῳδοῖς οἱ αὐτοί.
[4] Schol. Aristoph. Nub. 542; Plut. Aud. Poet. 18 B.

CHAPTER VI.

THE CHORUS.

§ 1. *History of the Chorus.*

THE history of the chorus in the Greek drama is a history of gradual decay. In the earliest period, when both tragedy and comedy were mainly lyrical, the members of the chorus were the sole performers. After the introduction of actors and dialogue the chorus still continued for a time to play the leading part. But from the beginning of the fifth century it began slowly to dwindle in importance, until at length it disappeared almost entirely from comedy, and sank even in tragedy to the position of the band in a modern theatre. As far as tragedy is concerned the process of decline can be traced with clearness in the existing dramas. It takes two distinct forms. In the first place there is a gradual diminution in the length of the part assigned to the chorus; in the second place there is a tendency to withdraw the chorus from all active participation in the plot. First, as to the length of the choral part. In the Supplices, the oldest of existing Greek tragedies, the part of the chorus forms no less than three-fifths of the whole composition. In the other plays of Aeschylus, with the exception of the Prometheus, the average length of the choral part is nearly a half. In the tragedies of Sophocles the size is very much reduced. The choral part in Sophocles varies from about a quarter of the whole in the Ajax and the Antigone to about a seventh in the

Electra and Philoctetes. In Euripides it varies from about a quarter in such plays as the Bacchae and Alcestis to about a ninth in the Orestes. It appears therefore that in the course of the fifth century the part of the chorus was gradually but continuously reduced in size. In the second place, side by side with the diminution in bulk, there was a constant tendency to diminish the importance of the chorus by severing its connexion with the plot. In the lyrical tragedies of the earliest period the chorus was no doubt on most occasions the principal object of interest, and took the leading part in the conduct of the piece. This is still the case in some of the extant tragedies of Aeschylus. In the Supplices, for instance, the whole subject of the plot is the destiny of the fugitive maidens who form the chorus. It is their adventures which excite the sympathy of the audience; the other characters are of very little significance. Again in the Eumenides the interest centres chiefly round the conduct and feelings of the chorus of Erinyes. But in the other plays of Aeschylus the chorus begins to take very much the same position as it occupies in the plays of Sophocles, and the earlier plays of Euripides. It was at this period that Attic tragedy was brought to its highest perfection, and the question as to the proper place of the chorus in the plot was solved in the manner most consistent with the genius of the Greek drama. In Sophocles, in most of the later plays of Aeschylus, and the earlier plays of Euripides, the chorus performs two distinct functions. During the progress of the dialogue it plays the part of a sympathetic witness, following the course of the action with the keenest interest, but seldom actively interfering. Its general character is that of the better class of ordinary citizens. But during the choral odes which fill up the pauses in the action it takes an altogether higher tone. It then becomes the mouthpiece of the poet, uttering in sublime language reflexions upon the events which have just taken place, and expounding the hidden purposes of the gods. Such is the position of the chorus in the best period of Greek tragedy. It is altogether subordinated to the actors, and seldom takes a prominent part in the incidents of the play.

But at the same time, whether it is acting the part of a sympathetic spectator, or serving merely as the mouthpiece of the poet, all its utterances have a distinct reference to the plot which is being worked out upon the stage. Nothing irrelevant is introduced. The dialogue and the choral element are skilfully interwoven into one harmonious whole. But in the later tragedies of Euripides the position of the chorus is altered very much for the worse. A tendency is observable to sever all connexion between the chorus and the action of the play. Choral odes are introduced, which have no particular reference to the individual tragedy, but consist merely of picturesque descriptions of scenes from the ancient mythology. This tendency was carried still further by Agathon, whose choral odes were professedly mere interludes, and might be transferred from one play to another. His example was followed by the later tragic poets, so that in the course of the fourth century the tragic chorus came to occupy the position of the band in modern times [1]. Its functions were limited to the duty of providing music and singing between the several acts of a tragedy. The history of the comic chorus was very similar; but the steps of the process cannot be traced in detail, since the works of only one comic poet have been preserved. In the Plutus, the last of the extant comedies of Aristophanes, the chorus is already reduced to the very slightest proportions. Soon afterwards it practically disappeared. In the New Comedy, which was essentially a comedy of every-day life, a chorus would have been altogether out of place [2].

---

[1] Aristot. Poet. c. 18.
[2] Platonius ap. Dindf. Prolegom. de Comoed. p. 20 τῶν γὰρ χορηγῶν μὴ χειροτονουμένων καὶ τῶν χορευτῶν οὐκ ἐχόντων τὰς τροφὰς ὑπεξῃρέθη τῆς κωμῳδίας τὰ χορικὰ μέλη, καὶ τῶν ὑποθέσεων ὁ τρόπος μετεβλήθη, p. 21 καὶ τὰς παραβάσεις παρῃτήσαντο, διὰ τὸ τοὺς χοροὺς ἐπιλείψαι, χορηγῶν οὐκ ὄντων. Anon. de Comoed. ap. Dindf. l.c. p. 27 τήν τε γὰρ ὑπόθεσιν οὐκ ἀληθῆ ἔχει, καὶ χορῶν ἐστέρηται, ὅπερ τῆς νεωτέρας ὑπῆρχε κωμῳδίας. Apparently, however, some sort of a chorus was occasionally introduced in the New Comedy, but its position was altogether subordinate and insignificant. See vit. Aristoph. (Dindf. Proll. de Com. p. 36) πάλιν δὲ ἐκλελοιπότος καὶ τοῦ χορηγεῖν τὸν Πλοῦτον γράψας εἰς τὸ διαναπαύεσθαι τὰ σκηνικὰ πρόσωπα καὶ μετεσκευάσθαι, ἐπιγράφει χοροῦ, φθεγγόμενος ἐν ἐκείνοις ἃ καὶ ὁρῶμεν τοὺς νέους οὕτως ἐπιγράφοντας ζήλῳ Ἀριστοφάνους.

§ 2. *Size of the Chorus.*

The tragic chorus, being a direct descendant of the old dithyrambic choruses, originally consisted of fifty members[1]. After all connexion between tragedy and the dithyramb had been severed, the number of the choreutae in a tragic chorus was reduced to twelve. It has been suggested that this number was due to the practice of each poet exhibiting four tragedies at a time. It is supposed that the original chorus of fifty was divided as equally as possible among the four tragedies, so that each chorus came to consist of twelve members. The conjecture is a plausible one, but cannot be regarded as certain, owing to the scantiness of our information concerning the early history of tragedy. The size of the tragic chorus remained unaltered until the time of Sophocles, and in all the earlier plays of Aeschylus twelve choreutae are employed. Sophocles raised the number from twelve to fifteen[2]. After his time there was no further change, and during the remaining period of the Attic drama the tragic chorus was always composed of fifteen persons. The various technical terms which refer to the arrangement of the tragic chorus are all based on the supposition that it is a chorus of fifteen. It is not quite certain whether the innovation of Sophocles was adopted by Aeschylus in his later plays. The Oresteia of Aeschylus was brought out ten years after the first appearance of Sophocles; and it has been contended that the chorus in this trilogy contained fifteen members. But there is hardly sufficient evidence to determine the matter with any certainty[3]. However on general

---

[1] Poll. iv. 110. Pollux further states that the number continued to be fifty until the Eumenides of Aeschylus was produced; and that the people were so alarmed at the sight of the fifty Erinyes that they passed a law reducing the number of the tragic chorus. The story is of course a fiction, on a par with the statement in the Life, that Aeschylus was banished to Sicily as a punishment for terrifying the people with his Eumenides.

[2] Suid. v. Σοφοκλῆς; Vit. Soph. p. 2 Dindf.

[3] The decision of the question depends on the passage in the Agamemnon, vv. 1344-1371. There is no doubt that the twelve iambic couplets, 1348-1371, were delivered by twelve choreutae. The difficulty is to decide whether the three trochaic tetrameters, 1344, 1346, and 1347, were delivered by three additional

grounds it seems probable that Aeschylus should have followed the example of Sophocles. At any rate there is no doubt that after the middle of the fifth century the number of the choreutae was fixed at fifteen [1]. The satyric chorus was of the same size as the tragic—a natural result of the intimate connexion between tragedy and the satyric drama [2]. The comic chorus, throughout all the period with which we are acquainted, invariably consisted of twenty-four members. All the authorities are unanimous on the subject [3].

The size of the chorus in the Greek drama was regulated by invariable custom, and no alteration was ever made to suit the requirements of a particular play. For instance, in the Supplices of Aeschylus the number of the Danaides was fifty, but the chorus consisted of only twelve maidens, who did duty for the fifty. Again, in the Eumenides the proper number of the chorus should have been three, if the legend had been accurately adhered to. But the number of Erinyes was raised from three to twelve or fifteen in order to keep up the ordinary size of the chorus. In this respect, as usual, the Greeks were careless about minute accuracy.

§ 3. *Costume of the Chorus.*

The costume of the chorus is a subject in regard to which the information is not very copious. Masks were universally worn by choreutae, or by the coryphaeus. Either view is plausible, and it seems impossible to determine the matter without further evidence. The statement of Schol. Arist. Equit. 586, that the chorus in the Agamemnon was fifteen in number, is merely an inference from the passage just referred to. · The statement of Schol. Aesch. Eum. 585, that the chorus in the Eumenides consisted of fifteen persons, is simply grounded on the assumption that the number was the same as in later times. In neither case is the evidence of any independent value.

[1] Fifteen is the number given in Poll. iv. 109; Suid. v. χορός; Schol. Arist. Av. 298, Equit. 586; Schol. Aesch. Eum.

585. The number is given as fourteen in Vit. Aesch.; Bekk. Anecd. p. 746; Tzetzes, Prolegom. ad Lycophron, p. 254 M. The explanation of the discrepancy lies in the fact that when the chorus is said to consist of fourteen members the coryphaeus is not included.

[2] Tzetzes l. c. τὴν δὲ τραγῳδίαν καὶ τοὺς σατύρους ἐπίσης μὲν ἔχειν χορευτὰς ιαʹ (? ιδʹ). Id. apud Dübner, Prolegom. de Com. p. xxiv. ἑκκαίδεκα δὲ σατύρων, τραγῳδίας. Though the numbers are wrong in both passages, it is plain that the tragic and satyric choruses were of the same size.

[3] Poll. iv. 109; Schol. Arist. Av. 298, Acharn. 210; Bekk. Anecd. p. 746, &c., &c.

the chorus, as well as by the actors upon the stage[1]. The tragic chorus was usually composed of old men, or women, or maidens. In such cases they wore the ordinary Greek dress, consisting of a tunic and a mantle. No attempt was made to give them an impressive appearance by the use of strange and magnificent costumes, similar to those worn by the actors. Such costumes were perfectly appropriate to the heroes and gods upon the stage, but would have been out of place in the chorus, which was generally supposed to represent the ordinary public. The masks of the tragic chorus would of course be suitable to the age and sex of the persons represented. A special kind of white shoe, said to be the invention of Sophocles, was worn by the tragic chorus[2]. Old men usually carried a staff[3]. Various little details in dress and equipment would be added according to circumstances. Thus the chorus of bereaved matrons in the Supplices of Euripides were dressed in black garments, and had their hair cut short, as a sign of mourning, and carried branches twined with wool, the symbol of supplication, in their hands. The chorus of maidens in the Choephori, who had come to offer libations at the tomb of Agamemnon, were also dressed in black[4]. In some cases the tragic chorus was altogether of an exceptional character, and required a special costume. In the Supplices of Aeschylus the daughters of the Aegyptian Danaus appear to have been dressed as foreigners. Probably the same was the case with the Persian Elders in the Persae. The Bacchantes in the play of Euripides carried tambourines in their hands, and were doubtless also provided with fawn-skins and wands of ivy[5]. But no tragic chorus ever caused a greater sensation than the chorus of Erinyes in the Eumenides of Aeschylus. Their costume was designed by Aeschylus himself, and the snakes in the hair, which afterwards became one of their regular attributes, were specially invented for the occasion. As they rushed into the

---

[1] Pausan. i. 28. 6; Schol. Arist. Clouds 343; Wieseler, Denkmäl. vi. 2.
[2] Vit. Soph.
[3] Aesch. Agam. 75; Eur. Herc. Fur. 108.
[4] Eur. Suppl. 10, 97; Aesch. Choeph. 10, 11.
[5] Aesch. Suppl. 234–236 ἀνέλληνα στόλον | πέπλοισι βαρβάροισι καὶ πυκνώμασι | χλίοντα; Eur. Bacch. 58.

COSTUME OF THE CHORUS.

orchestra, their black dresses, distorted features, and snaky locks, are said to have inspired the spectators with terror[1]. But this chorus was of a very exceptional kind. In most cases the tragic chorus was composed of ordinary men and women, and their dress was that of every-day life.

The dress of the satyrs in the chorus of the satyric drama was of a very simple character. It is depicted in several works of art, and the accuracy of the delineation is confirmed by the descriptions in ancient writers. The present illustration represents three members of a satyric chorus, and is taken from the

vase-painting referred to in previous chapters[2]. The only dress of the satyrs was a rough goat-skin round the loins, with a tail hanging down behind. The phallus was invariably worn. The mask was provided with a shock of bushy hair, and exhibited coarse and lascivious features[3]. Apart from the goat-skin the satyrs are represented as perfectly naked[4]. It has been sug-

---

[1] Aesch. Eum. 52; vit. Aesch. p. 4 Dindf.; Poll. iv. 110; Pausan. i. 28. 6.

[2] The illustration is from Wieseler, Denk. vi. 2. The original is a Greek vase-painting, with the names of the actors appended in many cases. See chap. v. p. 231.

[3] Cp. Dion. Hal. A. R. vii. 72 τοῖς δὲ εἰς Σατύρους (εἰκασθεῖσι) περιζώματα καὶ δοραὶ τράγων καὶ ὀρθότριχες ἐπὶ ταῖς κεφαλαῖς φόβαι καὶ ὅσα τούτοις ὅμοια: Eur. Cycl. 439.

[4] Cp. Hor. A. P. 221 mox etiam agrestes Satyros *nudavit*.

gested that in the theatre they wore slippers and some sort of flesh-coloured tights. But it is not necessary to suppose that this was the case. In the illustration one of the choreutae is wearing his mask upon his head, and is fully attired as a satyr; the others are carrying their masks in their hands.

The chorus of the Old Comedy, when it consisted of men and women, was dressed in the tunic and mantle of ordinary life. The mantle was laid aside for the purpose of dancing, as the dances of the Old Comedy were of a wild and energetic character, and required freedom of action [1]. The masks were of a ludicrous type, with the features distorted [2]. In addition to the ordinary choruses of men and women a great many of the choruses of the Old Comedy consisted of fanciful personifications of various kinds. Such, for example, was the chorus of Clouds in Aristophanes, the chorus of Seasons in Cratinus, the chorus of Trifles in Pherecrates, and the chorus of Towns and of Cities in Eupolis [3]. In all these cases the dress and general make-up appear to have been of a grotesque character, and only in a remote degree emblematic of the ideas and objects personified. For instance, the Clouds of Aristophanes appeared as women dressed in gaily-coloured garments, and wore masks of a ridiculous type, with long noses and other exaggerations. The only resemblance to clouds was in the colours of the dresses [4]. Probably in other similar cases the personification was carried out in the same rough and ready manner. Another large class of choruses was composed of various kinds of animals. Aristophanes had a chorus of Birds and of Wasps. Magnes, a comic poet belonging to the earlier part of the fifth century, introduced choruses of Birds, of Insects, and of Frogs. Eupolis had a chorus of Goats, and Archippus a chorus of Fishes [5]. It would be highly interesting to know how the cos-

[1] Arist. Achar. 627 ἀλλ' ἀποδύντες τοῖς ἀναπαίστοις ἐπίωμεν: Thesm. 656 τῶν θ' ἱματίων ἀποδύσας.
[2] Schol. Arist. Nub. 343.
[3] Meineke, Frag. Com. Gr. ii. pp. 162, 296, 455, 507.
[4] Schol. Arist. Nub. 289 μέλλει δὲ τὰς Νεφέλας γυναικομόρφους εἰσάγειν,
ἐσθῆτι ποικίλῃ χρωμένας, ἵνα τὰ τῶν οὐρανίων φυλάττωσι σχήματα: id. 343 εἰσεληλύθασι γὰρ οἱ τοῦ χοροῦ προσωπεῖα περικείμενοι μεγάλας ἔχοντα ῥῖνας καὶ ἄλλως γελοῖα καὶ ἀσχήμονα.
[5] Aristoph. Equit. 522, 523; Meineke, F. C. G. ii. pp. 426, 718.

tume of the chorus was managed in such cases. Fortunately a contemporary vase-painting has been discovered which throws great light upon the subject. A copy of the painting is here inserted[1]. The vase is of Athenian workmanship, and belongs to the first half of the fifth century. The scene represents a chorus of men dressed as birds, dancing to the accompaniment of the flute. The bodies of the choreutae are covered with a close-fitting dress, made in rough imitation of feathers. Two long ends hang down from each side of the waist, and a bunch of feathers is affixed to each knee. The arms are provided with

wings. A row of upright feathers is attached to the crown of the head, and the mask is made with a long and pointed nose, suggestive of the beak of a bird. This painting has the unique advantage of being a piece of contemporary workmanship. Whether it is intended to represent one of the old comic choruses, or merely some mimetic dance unconnected with the drama, there can be no doubt that it affords a very clear indication of the manner in which animals were imitated in the choruses of the Old Comedy. There appears to have been

[1] The illustration is taken, by permission of the Council of the Hellenic Society, from the Journal of Hellenic Studies, vol. ii. no. 2, plate xiv. B. See Mr. Cecil Smith's interesting article on the subject.

none of the realism one meets with in a modern pantomime. The imitation was only carried so far as to be generally suggestive of the animal intended. The body and legs were left unfettered, to allow of free movement in the dance. At the same time, to judge from the specimen before us, the costumes seem to have been designed with a great deal of spirit and humour, and to have been extremely well adapted to the purpose for which they were intended.

§ 4. *Arrangement of the Chorus.*

Except on rare occasions the dramatic choruses were drawn up in formations of military regularity, both on their first entrance, and during the progress of the play. They presented a perfectly symmetrical appearance in the orchestra. In this respect they offer a contrast to the choruses in a modern opera, and to the crowds which are introduced upon the modern stage. As a rule no attempt was made to imitate the fluctuating movements and haphazard grouping of an ordinary crowd. The chorus marched into the orchestra, and took up its position before the stage, with the regularity and precision of a body of soldiers. In all dramatic choruses—tragic, comic, and satyric— the rectangular formation was invariably adopted, as opposed to the circular arrangement of the dithyrambic choruses[1]. Every dramatic chorus, when drawn up in this way, consisted of a certain number of 'ranks,' and a certain number of 'files.' For instance, the tragic chorus, with its fifteen members, contained five ranks of three men each, and three files of five men each. Similarly the comic chorus, which was composed of twenty-four persons, contained six ranks of four men each, and four files of six men each. According to the Attic phraseology a chorus was said to be drawn up 'by ranks,' when the different members of the same rank stood one behind the other. It was said to be drawn up 'by files' when the members of the same

---

[1] Tzetzes, Prolegom. ad Lycophron, p. 254 M, τραγικῶν δὲ καὶ σατυρικῶν καὶ κωμικῶν ποιητῶν κοινὸν μὲν τὸ τετραγώνως ἔχειν ἱστάμενον τὸν χορόν: Bekk. Anecd. p. 746; Et. Mag. v. τραγῳδία; vit. Aristoph. (Dindf. Prolegom. de Com. p. 36).

file were one behind the other. Accordingly, when a tragic chorus was drawn up 'by ranks,' the men stood five abreast and three deep. When it was drawn up 'by files,' they stood three abreast and five deep. The same regulations applied to the comic chorus. It might be arranged 'by ranks,' with the men six abreast and four deep; or 'by files,' with the men four abreast and six deep[1]. The arrangements throughout were of this military character. In fact the training of a choreutes was considered by many of the ancient writers to be an excellent preparation for warlike service[2].

In the great majority of cases the chorus was supposed to consist of persons from the neighbourhood, and therefore entered the orchestra by the western passage. Their right side was towards the stage, and their left side towards the spectators. As a consequence, the left side of the chorus was much the most conspicuous and important, and the best-trained choreutae were placed there[3]. The tragic chorus might enter five abreast and three deep, or three abreast and five deep, according as the formation was by ranks or by files. As a matter of fact the arrangement by files was the one almost invariably adopted. There are several technical terms in connexion with the tragic chorus, and they all refer to a chorus which is supposed to be entering from the western side, and to be drawn up three abreast and five deep. An oblong formation of this kind would evidently be more convenient in the narrow side-entrances, and would present a broader surface to the spectators and to the stage. A diagram is here inserted, representing a tragic chorus entering three abreast from the western parodos. It will enable the reader to follow the various technical phrases with less

---

[1] Poll. iv. 108, 109 καὶ τραγικοῦ μὲν χοροῦ ζυγὰ πέντε ἐκ τριῶν καὶ στοῖχοι τρεῖς ἐκ πέντε· πεντεκαίδεκα γὰρ ἦσαν ὁ χορός. καὶ κατὰ τρεῖς μὲν εἰσῄεσαν, εἰ κατὰ ζυγὰ γίνοιτο ἡ πάροδος· εἰ δὲ κατὰ στοίχους, ἀνὰ πέντε εἰσῄεσαν... ὁ δὲ κωμικὸς χορὸς τέτταρες καὶ εἴκοσιν ἦσαν οἱ χορευταί, ζυγὰ ἕξ, ἕκαστον δὲ ζυγὸν ἐκ τεττάρων, στοῖχοι δὲ τέτταρες, ἐξ ἄνδρας ἔχων ἕκαστος στοῖχος.

[2] Athen. p. 628 F.

[3] Schol. Aristid. iii. p. 535 Dindf. ὅτε εἰσῄεσαν οἱ χοροὶ πλαγίως βαδίζοντες ἐποιοῦντο τοὺς ὕμνους καὶ εἶχον τοὺς θεατὰς ἐν ἀριστερᾷ αὐτῶν καὶ οἱ πρῶτοι τοῦ χοροῦ ἀρ:στερὸν στοῖχον, p. 536 τοὺς οὖν καλοὺς τῶν χορευτῶν ἔταττον εἰσιόντες ἐν τοῖς τῶν ἑαυτῶν ἀριστεροῖς, ἵνα εὑρεθῶσι πρὸς τὸν δῆμον ὁρῶντες.

difficulty. When drawn up in this way the tragic chorus consisted of three files parallel to one another. As already stated, the first file was the most important, because it was nearest to the spectators. The members of this file were called 'aristerostatae,' or 'men on the left,' and consisted of the handsomest and most skilful of the choreutae. The middle file was the least important of the three, as it was most out of sight of the spectators. The worst choreutae were placed in this file, and

```
                           AUDIENCE
    5TH      4TH      3RD      2ND      1ST
    RANK     RANK     RANK     RANK     RANK

    (5)      (4)      (3)      (2)      (1)   1ST FILE

    (10)     (9)      (8)      (7)      (6)   2ND FILE  →→→

    (15)     (14)     (13)     (12)     (11)  3RD FILE

                            STAGE
```

were called 'laurostatae,' or 'men in the passage.' The third file was the one nearest to the stage. Occasionally, if the chorus wheeled completely round, it came in full view of the spectators. It was therefore of more importance than the middle file, and a better class of choreutae were placed in it. They were called the 'dexiostatae,' or 'men on the right[1].' In addition to the above technical terms there were also special names for the six men who composed the front and hindmost

---

[1] Poll. ii. 161 τάχα δὲ καὶ ὁ ἀριστεροστάτης ἐν χορῷ προσήκοι ἂν τῇ ἀριστερᾷ,
ὡς ὁ δεξιοστάτης τῇ δεξιᾷ. Phot. v.
λαυρόσταται· μέσον τοῦ χοροῦ· οἱονεὶ γὰρ ἐν στενωπῷ εἰσιν· φαυλότεροι δὲ οὗτοι.

ranks—nos. 1, 6, 11, 5, 10, and 15 in the diagram. They were styled 'kraspeditae,' or 'fringe-men¹.' Finally, the three files had different names, according to their relative proximity to the spectators. The members of the left file were called 'front-line men'; the members of the middle and right-hand files were called 'second-line men' and 'third-line men' respectively².

The first or left file, as already pointed out, was much the most important, because the members of it were in full view of the audience. The central position, no. 3 in the diagram, was occupied by the coryphaeus, or leader of the chorus³. The post of the leader was an extremely arduous one. While the dialogue was in progress, he had to carry on conversations with the actors upon the stage. During the choral odes he had to give the note to the choreutae, and superintend the dances and manœuvres. At the same time his own dancing and mimetic gestures were supposed to be a conspicuous feature in the performance. It is plain, therefore, that his position must have been a difficult one to fill. Demosthenes, speaking of dithyrambic choruses, says that the loss of the coryphaeus means the ruin of the chorus; and this must have been still more the case in a dramatic performance⁴. On the other hand the possession of a skilful leader would contribute very largely to the success of the chorus and of the drama. The choreutae on each side of the leader, nos. 2 and 4 in the diagram, were called his 'parastatae,' or 'assistants,' and were next in importance to the leader himself. The two choreutae on the outside, nos. 1 and 5 in the diagram, were called the 'third men⁵.' As already

¹ Plut. Conv. p. 678 D ὥσπερ χοροῦ, τοῦ συμποσίου τὸν κρασπεδίτην τῷ κορυφαίῳ συνήκοον ἔχοντος. The κρασπεδῖται were also called ψιλεῖς; cp. Suid. v. ψιλεύς· ἐπ' ἄκρου χοροῦ ἱστάμενος: Hesych. v. ψιλεῖς· οἱ ὕστατοι χορεύοντες.
² Hesych. v. ἀριστεροστάτης· ὁ πρωτοστάτης τοῦ χοροῦ. Poll. iv. 106 δεξιοστάτης, ἀριστεροστάτης, δευτεροστάτης, τριτοστάτης.
³ Phot. v. τρίτος ἀριστεροῦ· ἐν τοῖς τραγικοῖς χοροῖς τριῶν ὄντων στοίχων καὶ πέντε ζυγῶν, ὁ μὲν ἀριστερὸς πρὸς τῷ θεάτρῳ ἦν, ὁ δὲ δεξιὸς πρὸς τῷ προσκηνίῳ.

συνέβαινεν οὖν τὸν μέσον τοῦ ἀριστεροῦ στοίχου τὴν ἐντιμοτάτην καὶ τὴν οἷον τοῦ πρωτοστάτου χώραν ἐπέχειν καὶ στάσιν. The coryphaeus was also called χορηγός Athen. p. 633 A, χοραγός Plut. Apophth. Lac. p. 219 E, ἡγεμών and ἡγεμὼν κορυφαῖος Dem. Meid. § 60.
⁴ Dem. Meid. § 60.
⁵ Aristot. Met. iv. 11 ταῦτα δ' ἐστὶν ὅσα πρός τι ἓν ὡρισμένον διέστηκε κατὰ τὸν λόγον, οἷον παραστάτης τριτοστάτου πρότερον, καὶ παρανήτη νήτης· ἔνθα μὲν γὰρ ὁ κορυφαῖος, ἔνθα δὲ ἡ μέση ἀρχή.

remarked, the coryphaeus, together with the other four members of the left file, constituted the pick of the whole chorus.

Concerning the formation in which the comic chorus entered the orchestra there is not much information. Like the tragic chorus, it might enter either by ranks or by files; that is to say, it might come in six abreast and four deep, or four abreast and six deep. There can be no doubt that the oblong formation of four abreast and six deep was the one usually adopted. It would be more suitable from every point of view. Both the tragic and the comic choruses were probably preceded into the orchestra by the flute-player[1]. On certain rare occasions the formal entrance in a rectangular body was dispensed with, and an irregular mode of entrance was adopted, in order to produce a dramatic effect. The best example is in the Eumenides of Aeschylus. When the Erinyes made their second appearance, they came rushing into the orchestra one by one, in hot pursuit of Orestes, and created a profound sensation by their movements and appearance[2]. There is another instance in the Birds of Aristophanes. The chorus of Birds begins by entering one by one. The flamingo comes first, and its appearance is criticised by the actors upon the stage. The cock follows, and is similarly criticised. Then comes the hoopoe, and after it the glutton-bird. Finally the whole chorus of birds comes fluttering in together, so as to block up the side-entrances[3]. In the Lysistrata the chorus is divided into two halves, one consisting of men, the other of women. The chorus of men enters first; the chorus of women follows after an interval. The chorus in the Ecclesiazusae is composed of women who have been invited to a political gathering by Praxagora. They enter by twos and threes, in a perfectly irregular fashion, so as to imitate a real assemblage[4]. But instances of this kind were very rare and exceptional. Usually the chorus

---

[1] Schol. Arist. Vesp. 580 ἔθος δὲ ἦν ἐν ταῖς ἐξόδοις τῶν τῆς τραγῳδίας χορικῶν προσώπων προηγεῖσθαι αὐλητήν, ὥστε αὐλοῦντα προπέμπειν. As the flute-player preceded the chorus on its exit, it is most likely that he did the same at its entrance.

[2] Poll. iv. 109; Vit. Aesch. p. 4 Dindf.

[3] Arist. Av. 268-296.

[4] Arist. Lysist. 254, 319, Eccles. 41-60.

entered in a rectangular body, with the precision of a troop of soldiers.

In most cases the entrance of the chorus took place at the conclusion of the 'prologue,' or introductory scene upon the stage; and the march in was accompanied by a chant, which was called the 'parodos,' or entrance song[1]. However, in a considerable number of plays there was no parodos at all, but the chorus entered the orchestra in silence, while the first act of the drama was in progress, and then commenced a musical dialogue with the actors upon the stage. Instances of this mode of entrance are to be found in such tragedies as the Electra of Sophocles and the Orestes of Euripides[2]. In the vast majority of Greek plays the entrance of the chorus is managed in one or other of the two ways just specified. Either the chorus comes in at the termination of the prologue, chanting the parados; or else the parados is omitted, and the chorus enters in silence, and then proceeds to sing a musical duet with the actors. A few plays are exceptional, and do not conform to either of these two conventional types. Occasionally, for instance, there is no prologue, and the play commences with the parodos, as in the Supplices and Persae of Aeschylus. Then again, in the Eumenides the parados is sung on the second entrance of the Erinyes, after their arrival at Athens. In the Supplices of Euripides the chorus are seen kneeling upon the stage in supplication when the play commences. There they remained in silence during the performance of the prologue, and then proceeded to sing an ode, in place of the usual parodos, from their position on the stage. In the Clouds it appears that the chorus chant the first two odes behind the scenes, and then

---

[1] Arg. Aesch. Pers. τῶν δὲ χορῶν τὰ μέν ἐστι παροδικά, ὡς ὅτε λέγει δι' ἥν αἰτίαν πάρεστιν, ὡς τὸ " Τύριον οἶδμα λιποῦσα." Schol. Eur. Phoen. πάροδος δέ ἐστιν ᾠδὴ χοροῦ βαδίζοντος ᾀδομένη ἅμα τῇ εἰσόδῳ, ὡς τὸ " Σῖγα σῖγα λεπτὸν ἴχνος ἀρβύλης τίθετε." In Aristot. Poet. c. 12 the πάροδος is described as ἡ πρώτη λέξις ὅλου χοροῦ, which Westphal (Prolegom. ad Aesch. p. 57) alters to ἡ πρώτη λέξις ὅλη τοῦ χοροῦ, in order to make the word ὅλος bear the same meaning throughout the chapter. Whichever reading is adopted, the definition seems too wide.

[2] Other examples are the Prom. Vinct. of Aeschylus; the Philoctetes of Sophocles; the Medea, Heracleidae, Troades, and Electra of Euripides.

enter the orchestra silently. The Rhesus commences with a dialogue in anapaests between Hector and the chorus. Lastly, in the Ecclesiazusae there is no song of any kind. The women of the chorus drop in by twos and threes, and proceed at once to take part in an ordinary dialogue with the actors on the stage.

The next point to be considered is the position taken up by the chorus after entering the orchestra. On most occasions, as already stated, the chorus came in by the western side, drawn up in rectangular formation, with the stage on its right hand and the spectators on its left. It advanced half way into the orchestra, then came to a halt, and each member of the chorus turned round to the right, so as to face the stage. By this manœuvre the whole chorus was made to look towards the stage, and the arrangement by files was converted into one by ranks. For instance, the tragic chorus, which had entered three abreast and five deep, now stood before the stage five abreast and three deep. The coryphaeus and principal choreutae stood in the back line, and retained their position nearest to the spectators, and furthest away from the stage. This position they kept throughout the performance[1]. In a similar manner the comic chorus, after entering the orchestra four abreast and six deep, would halt in front of the stage, go through the manœuvre just described, and convert itself into a body standing six abreast and four deep. There is no information as to the position of the coryphaeus in the comic chorus. But there can be no doubt that, like the tragic coryphaeus, he stood in the back row, as near as possible to the spectators.

While the actors were upon the stage, and the dialogue was in

[1] Müller (die Griech. Bühnen. p. 214), following Hermann (Opusc. vi. 2, p. 144), supposes the whole chorus to have wheeled completely round, so that the left file came to be nearest to the stage. He thinks it more natural for the coryphaeus to have been immediately in front of the stage, where he would be in a position to converse with the actors. But he could do so equally well from the centre of the back row. And it seems most improbable that care should have been taken, during the entrance into the orchestra, to place the coryphaeus and best choreutae in the line most conspicuous to the spectators, but that throughout the rest of the performance they should have been stationed in a position where the majority of the spectators would hardly have been able to see them.

progress, the chorus continued to stand with their backs towards the spectators, and their faces towards the stage, so as to follow the course of the action[1]. This was their normal position during the play, and although it may seem strange to our modern ideas, it was a necessary consequence of the peculiar circumstances under which the Greek drama was developed. When the stage was empty, the pauses between the acts were filled up by the choral odes called stasima. There is no reliable information as to the position and movements of the chorus during the performance of the stasima. As the singing was accompanied by dancing, the choreutae must have been moving to and fro. But in the absence of evidence it seems useless to venture on conjectures as to the exact nature of the evolutions. One thing may be regarded as certain, that during the performance of the stasima the chorus did not continue to face towards the empty stage, and turn their backs upon the audience. Such a position would have been quite unnatural and unmeaning. In the Old Comedy there was a peculiar sort of interlude called the parabasis, which came during a pause in the action, and consisted of a series of lyrics and addresses, delivered by the chorus, and dealing with ordinary topics of the day. While reciting the first part of the parabasis the chorus wheeled completely round so as to face the spectators. Hence the name 'parabasis,' which means 'a turning aside.' The latter part was antistrophical in form, and during its delivery the chorus separated into two divisions, which stood facing one another. The different portions of the parabasis were then given by each division in turn[2].

---

[1] Anon. de Com. (Dindf. Prolegom. de Com. p. 29); Vit. Aristoph. (ibid. p. 36); Schol. Arist. Equit. 505.

[2] Schol. Arist. Equit. 505, Pax 733. As to the formation during the latter part of the parabasis, it is almost certain that the chorus was then divided into ἡμιχόρια. Two MSS. assign the strophe and antistrophe to ἡμιχόρια in Nubes 563, 595, Vespae 1060, 1091, Aves 737, 769, and the epirrhema and antepirrhema in Ranae 686, 717. See Arnoldt, die Chorpartieen bei Aristoph. p. 180 ff. That the half-choruses stood facing one another seems to be indicated by Hephaest. 14, p. 131 ἔστι δέ τις ἐν ταῖς κωμῳδίαις καὶ ἡ καλουμένη παράβασις, ἐπειδὰν εἰσελθόντες εἰς τὸ θέατρον καὶ ἀντιπρόσωπον ἀλλήλοις στάντες οἱ χορευταὶ παρέβαινον : Anon. de Comoed. (Dübner, Prolegom. de Com. p. xx) ἀπελθόντων δὲ τῶν ὑποκριτῶν πρὸς ἀμφότερα τὰ μέρη τοῦ δήμου ὁρῶν ἐκ τετραμέτρου δεκαὲξ στίχους ἀναπαίστους ἐφθέγγετο, καὶ τοῦτο ἐκαλεῖτο στροφή.

Sometimes, though not often, in the course of a play the chorus left the orchestra for a short period, and made a second entrance later on[1]. The instances of the practice which occur in the Eumenides and the Ajax were necessitated by the change of scene in those plays[2]. There is another example in the Helena of Euripides. Helen and the chorus retire into the palace, to enquire about the fate of Menelaus from Theonoë. In their absence Menelaus enters the stage, and recounts his adventures to the audience. Then Helen and the chorus return, and the recognition gradually takes place[3]. Similar temporary departures of the chorus are to be found in the Alcestis and the Ecclesiazusae; but they seem to have been of very rare occurrence[4]. At the end of the play the chorus retired by the passage from which it had entered, and was preceded by the flute-player[5]. In the Seven against Thebes the chorus leave the orchestra in two divisions, one following the body of Polyneices, the other that of Eteocles. But in most cases they probably marched out in the same rectangular formation in which they had entered. The position of the flute-player during the performance is unknown.

§ 5. *The Delivery of the choral part.*

As regards the delivery of the words, the chorus, like the actors, was not confined to one manner only, but used song, speech, and recitative by turns, according to the varying character of the metre. The lyrical portions of the drama were almost invariably sung. The ordinary iambic trimeters were spoken. The systems of anapaestic dimeters, and the iambic, trochaic, and anapaestic tetrameters were delivered in recitative to the accompaniment of the flute[6]. A question now arises, which is of great interest and importance in connexion with the choral part of the performance. It is obvious to any reader of a Greek play that many of the speeches and songs

---

[1] Poll. iv. 108. The temporary departure was called μετάστασις, the return ἐπιπάροδος.
[2] Aesch. Eum. 235; Soph. Ajax 815.
[3] Eur. Hel. 327 foll.
[4] Eur. Alc. 746; Arist. Eccles. 310.
[5] Schol. Arist. Vesp. 580.
[6] See chap. v. p. 241 foll.

assigned to the chorus were not intended to be delivered by the whole of the chorus, but by individual members. This fact is patent to every one. But when any attempt is made to settle the exact character of the distribution, the greatest diversity of opinion prevails. The question as to the parts which were delivered by the whole chorus, and the parts which were delivered by sections or individuals, is one of the most intricate which the Greek drama presents. Unfortunately the ancient writers supply hardly any information upon the subject. The whole matter has been discussed and investigated in recent years with the greatest diligence, and attempts have been made to portion out the choral odes between different members and sections of the chorus on the strength of indications supplied by the metre, or by the sense of the words[1]. But it is plain that inferences based on evidence of this kind must be very uncertain in character. As a matter of fact different investigators have arrived at the most contradictory conclusions. It is impossible therefore to regard their suggestions otherwise than in the light of interesting conjectures. They have no claim to absolute acceptance. Hence in the present state of our knowledge any detailed account of the matter is out of the question. It will be necessary to be content with certain general conclusions, which are based on actual evidence, or are so plausible in themselves as to be very widely accepted.

First then as to the part taken by the chorus as a whole. In ordinary circumstances the parodos and the stasima appear to have been sung by the whole chorus together. The parodos, as already explained, was the song of the chorus on its first entrance. The stasima were the long and important odes inserted between the successive divisions of the play, in order to fill up the pauses in the action. It is natural in itself to suppose

[1] See especially Arnoldt, Die Chorpartieen bei Aristophanes (Leipzig 1873), Die chorische Technik des Euripides (Halle 1878), Der Chor im Agamemnon des Aeschylos (Halle 1881); Christ, Theilung des Chors im attischen Drama (München 1877); Muff, Die chorische Technik des Sophokles (Halle 1877), De choro Persarum (Halle 1878), Der Chor in den Sieben des Aeschylos (Halle 1882); Hense, Der Chor des Sophokles (Berlin 1877), Ueber die Vortragsweise Soph. Stasima (Rhein. Museum, xxxii); Zielinski, Die Gliederung der altattischen Komödie (Leipzig 1885).

that these portions should have been sung by the whole chorus, and the supposition is borne out by the statements of Aristotle[1]. Sometimes there were exceptions. For example, the chorus in the Alcestis, on its first entrance, is divided into two half-choruses, which sing successive passages of the parodos alternately. In the Ion the parodos is obviously sung by subdivisions or by individuals, and not by the whole chorus. In the Frogs a long speech by the coryphaeus is inserted in the middle of the parodos. In the Lysistrata the chorus is divided throughout the play into two half-choruses, one of men, the other of women[2]. But in the majority of cases the parodos and the stasima were given by the whole body of the chorus. Not unfrequently, in the middle of the dialogue, small odes were inserted which resembled stasima in their general character, but differed from them in point of brevity, and from the fact that they came in the course of the dialogue, and not during a pause in the action. They were often songs of triumph or exultation, occasioned by sudden developments in the plot; in which case they appear to have been called 'hyporchêmata,' and were accompanied by a lively dance[3]. These short odes were no doubt sung by the whole chorus, in the same manner as the stasima. It has been suggested that the strophes and antistrophes in the stasima were delivered by half-choruses in succession, and that the epode was given by the whole chorus. But there is no real evidence in support of this hypothesis, and epodes are only rarely to be met with in dramatic choruses.

---

[1] Aristot. Poet. c. 12 χορικόν, καὶ τούτου τὸ μὲν πάροδος τὸ δὲ στάσιμον, κοινὰ μὲν ἁπάντων ταῦτα, ἴδια δὲ τὰ ἀπὸ τῆς σκηνῆς καὶ κόμμοι ... χορικοῦ δὲ πάροδος μὲν ἡ πρώτη λέξις ὅλου χοροῦ (Westphal, ὅλη τοῦ χόρου). It is probable, as Bergk (Griech. Literat. iii. p. 131) points out, that κοινὰ μὲν ἁπάντων (χορευτῶν) = sung by the whole chorus; cp. the expression θρῆνος κοινὸς χοροῦ καὶ ἀπὸ σκηνῆς, which occurs a little later in the same chapter. Ἴδια = sung by individuals or sections; cp. ἴδια ᾄσματα in the vit. Soph. (p. 8 Dindf.).

[2] Schol. Eur. Alc. 79 ἐκ γερόντων Φεραίων ὁ χορός, διαιρεῖται δὲ εἰς δύο ἡμιχόρια. That the anapaests in Ranae 354-371, which come in the middle of the parodos, were spoken by the coryphaeus is proved by the concluding lines (ὑμεῖς δ' ἀνεγείρετε μολπὴν κ.τ.λ.), in which the rest of the chorus is commanded to begin.

[3] Cramer, Anecd. Paris. i. p. 19 τῆς τραγικῆς ποιήσεως εἴδη εἰσὶ δέκα, πρόλογος ... ὑπορχηματικός. Athen. p. 631 C ἡ ὑπορχηματικὴ ὄρχησίς ἐστιν, ἐν ᾗ ᾄδων ὁ χορὸς ὀρχεῖται. Examples are

In the second place some of the words assigned to the chorus were actually delivered by the coryphaeus. There is no direct testimony to this effect, but the matter hardly admits of doubt. On a great many occasions the chorus drops the tone of lyrical exaltation, and converses with the persons on the stage in an easy and familiar manner. It plays the part of an ordinary actor. In all such cases it is evident that the chorus must have been represented by the coryphaeus alone. The dialogues between the actors and the coryphaeus were a peculiar and distinctive feature of the old Greek drama. They were, in fact, a direct survival from the early period, when there was only a single actor upon the stage, and when the dramatic element in a play was necessarily confined to conversations between the actor and the chorus. In addition to the dialogues just mentioned, there are several other portions of the chorus which may be assigned to the coryphaeus with a fair amount of certainty. Such are the anapaests with which the approach of a new personage is announced at the end of a choral ode in tragedy. These anapaests, being delivered in recitative, would make a gentle transition from the song of the chorus to the speech of the actors. Then again, it is probable that in comedy all the anapaestic tetrameters were spoken by the coryphaeus, including the speech to the people at the commencement of the parabasis, and speeches such as that which is inserted in the parodos of the Frogs[1]. In comedy also the coryphaeus had frequently to address words of exhortation and remonstrance to the rest of the chorus[2]. Finally, the anapaests with which most Greek plays conclude were in all likelihood spoken by the coryphaeus as the chorus marched out of the orchestra. It was the old fashion in tragedy for the entrance song of the chorus to commence with a series of anapaests. The custom is retained in the Persae, Supplices, and Agamemnon of Aeschylus, and the Ajax of Sophocles. It has been suggested

to be found in Aesch. Suppl. 418–437, Soph. Trach. 205–225, Ajax 693–717. Cp. Schol. Soph. Trach. 216 τὸ γὰρ μελιδάριον οὐκ ἔστι στάσιμον, ἀλλ' ὑπὸ τῆς ἡδονῆς ὀρχοῦνται.

[1] See above, p. 278.
[2] E. g. Arist. Ran. 382, Vesp. 1516, Thesmoph. 655, &c.

that these introductory anapaests were also delivered by the coryphaeus; but the suggestion is hardly a plausible one. If chanted in combination by the whole body of the chorus they would make the first entrance of the chorus infinitely more impressive. It need hardly be remarked that when the chorus was divided into half-choruses, the part generally taken by the coryphaeus was in this case taken by the leaders of the two halves. For example, throughout the Lysistrata the chorus of men and the chorus of women were represented in the dialogue by their respective leaders. In the Seven against Thebes the concluding anapaests would be spoken by the leaders of the hemichoria. It is also highly probable that the two sets of trochaic tetrameters, which come at the end of the parabasis, were recited, not by the half-choruses, but by their leaders.

Thirdly, certain portions of the chorus were occasionally spoken or sung by individual choreutae. The best known example is in the Agamemnon, during the murder of the king, when the chorus stands outside the palace, debating helplessly as to what it ought to do, and each of the old men pronounces his opinion in turn. There is another instance in the lyrical ode at the commencement of the Eumenides. The Erinyes wake up, find that Orestes is gone, and reproach Apollo in a series of brief, detached sentences, each being sung by one member of the chorus[1]. The above examples admit of no doubt. Whether the practice was a common one, and whether the choral parts were frequently distributed among individual choreutae, is a matter of great uncertainty. It is manifestly unsafe to infer that it was done in all cases where the choral passage is full of mutual exhortations and addresses, and the language is broken up into disconnected sentences. For example, in the parodoi in Aristophanes the members of the chorus often address one another by name, and exhort one another to greater activity. But it does

---

[1] Aesch. Agam. 1344 ff., Eum. 140 ff., Schol. ad loc. ἀναστήσει αὐτὰς οὐκ ἀθρόως, μιμούμενος ἐμφατικῶς τὴν ἀλήθειαν, ἀλλ' ἐγείρεταί τις πρώτη, ὥστε μὴ ἀθρόως τὸν χορὸν φθέγξασθαι. Müller (Griech. Bühnenalt. p. 218) is mistaken in citing the passage in the Lysistrata, 727–780, as an example of the delivery of words by individual choreutae. The three women who take part in the dialogue are not members of the chorus, but performers upon the stage.

not therefore follow, as has been suggested, that these passages were delivered in portions by individuals. A chorus might be perfectly well chanted by the whole body, though written in vivid and dramatic style[1]. It is hardly safe therefore to distribute choral passages among individual choreutae except on very strong evidence. The extent to which the practice prevailed in the ancient drama must be regarded as an open question.

Fourthly, the division into half-choruses was not infrequent[2]. It might be done in two ways. In the first place the chorus throughout the whole play might be composed of two separate divisions, differing from one another in point of age, sex, or position. The chorus in the Lysistrata, consisting of one body of men, and one body of women, is an example. In the second place the chorus might be divided temporarily into half-choruses, either because of the special requirements of the play, or merely for purposes of singing and recitation. There are several certain examples in tragedy. In the Ajax of Sophocles the sailors hasten off, some to the east and some to the west, in search of Ajax. They return after a time from opposite sides of the orchestra, bringing word that they have not found him. In the Orestes, while Helen is being attacked within the palace, Electra keeps watch outside, and posts the chorus in two divisions at each end of the orchestra, to guard against surprise[3]. The examples in the Alcestis and the Seven against Thebes have already been referred to. In comedy the practice was not at all uncommon, if the testimony of certain manuscripts is to be accepted. Various choral passages in the comedies of Aristophanes are distributed between half-choruses, including

---

[1] Cp. the sensible remarks of the Schol. on Arist. Ran. 375 ἐντεῦθεν Ἀρίσταρχος ὑπενόησε μὴ ὅλου τοῦ χοροῦ εἶναι τὰ πρῶτα· τοῦτο δὲ οὐκ ἀξιόπιστον. πολλάκις γὰρ ἀλλήλοις οὕτω παρακελεύονται οἱ περὶ τὸν χορόν.

[2] Poll. iv. 107 καὶ ἡμιχόριον δὲ καὶ διχορία καὶ ἀντιχόρια. ἔοικε δὲ ταὐτὸν εἶναι ταυτὶ τὰ τρία ὀνόματα· ὁπόταν γὰρ ὁ χορὸς εἰς δύο μέρη τμηθῇ, τὸ μὲν πρᾶγμα καλεῖται διχορία, ἑκατέρα δὲ ἡ μοῖρα ἡμιχόριον, ἃ δ' ἀντᾴδουσιν, ἀντιχόρια. The Schol. on Arist. Equit. 589 has a curious note to the effect that when the chorus was divided into two halves of different sex or age, the older or stronger half was always slightly more numerous. In a comic chorus there would be 13 men to 11 women, 13 women to 11 boys, and so on.

[3] Soph. Ajax 866 ff.; Eur. Orest. 1258 ff.

the two odes at the end of the parabasis, and other lyrical pieces of an antistrophic character[1].

The general result then is as follows. The words assigned to the chorus were delivered, sometimes by the whole chorus, sometimes by half-choruses, sometimes by the coryphaeus, and sometimes by individual choreutae. Whether there were any further subdivisions is uncertain. It has been suggested that the divisions into ranks and files were utilised for musical purposes; that in tragedy, for instance, successive passages were delivered in turns by ranks of three men, or files of five men; and that the ranks and files of the comic chorus were used in the same manner. All this is pure conjecture. It may or may not have been the case; but there is no evidence one way or the other. The portions of the choral part which were generally given by the whole chorus were the parodoi, or entrance-songs, and the stasima, or odes during the pauses in the dialogue. The portions assigned to the coryphaeus were principally those in which the chorus abandoned its lyrical elevation of tone, and spoke like one of the actors upon the stage. The various lyrical passages which occur in the course of the actual dialogue have still to be accounted for. These consist chiefly of short odes not unlike stasima, or of musical duets between the actors and the chorus. The odes were probably sung by the whole chorus. As to the musical duets it is impossible to speak with certainty. All that is known in regard to them is the fact that they were not sung by the whole chorus[2]. Whether they were mostly given by half-choruses, or smaller subdivisions, or by individual choreutae, or by the coryphaeus, is a matter concerning which there is no trustworthy information. Such indications as are supplied by varieties in metre, grammar, or subject, are too vague and uncertain to lead to any definite conclusion. Unless, therefore, further evidence of a distinct character is discovered, this par-

---

[1] See Arnoldt, Die Chorpartieen bei Aristophanes, p. 180 ff., where a list is given of the passages which are assigned to half-choruses by Rav. and Ven., e. g. Acharn. 1150, 1162, Nub. 563, 595,

Vesp. 1060, 1091, Av. 737, 769, 1058, 1088, Eccles. 290, 301, Thesmoph. 659, Lysist. 321.

[2] See above, p. 278, note 1.

ticular question will have to be regarded as an unsettled problem.

§ 6. *The Dancing.*

In the ancient Greek drama, as in modern opera, the three sister arts of Music, Poetry, and Dancing, were all brought into requisition. But there was this difference—in the Greek drama the poetry was the principal feature of the performance; the music and the dancing were subordinate. Moreover dancing was seldom introduced by itself as a mere spectacle; it was mainly used in combination with singing, to interpret and add vividness to the words of the song. The music, the poetry, and the dancing were blended together into one harmonious whole, each part gaining an advantage by its combination with the other two. The dancing of the chorus is the subject which we have now to consider. It was an element of great importance in the old Greek drama. Most, if not all, of the choral songs were accompanied by dances of one sort or another. To the Greek mind there was an inseparable connexion between song and dance, and the notion of choral singing unaccompanied by dancing would have appeared strange and unusual. The two arts had grown and developed simultaneously, as appears from the fact that many of the technical terms in metrical phraseology referred originally to the movements of the dance. For instance, the smallest division of a verse was called a 'foot.' A verse of two feet was styled a 'basis,' or 'stepping.' The words arsis and thesis, which denoted the varying stress of the voice in singing, originally referred to the raising up and placing down of the foot in marching and dancing. These terms show how closely the two arts of dancing and singing were associated together in ancient Greece. A choreutes who was unable to accompany a song with expressive dance-movements, was looked down upon as an inferior performer[1]. Dancing therefore, as might have been expected, played a

---

[1] Athen. p. 628 E εἰ δέ τις ... ταῖς ᾠδαῖς ἐπιτυγχάνων μηδὲν λέγοι κατὰ τὴν ὄρχησιν, οὗτος δ᾽ ἦν ἀδόκιμος.

most important part in tragedy, comedy, and the satyric drama. It was held among the Greeks in the greatest estimation, and there was none of that feeling of degradation about it which was common among the Romans. A man might dance in public without any loss of dignity, provided the dance was of a graceful and becoming character. Sophocles himself, the great tragic poet and fellow general of Pericles, was not ashamed to appear in a dance in one of his own tragedies [1].

At the same time it should be remembered that dancing in ancient Greece was a very different thing from dancing in modern times. It included a great deal more. The word 'dancing' in English necessarily implies movement with the feet. It would be impossible in English to say that a man was dancing, if he continued to stand in the same position. But in Greek dancing this was not necessarily the case. The word 'orchêsis,' which we translate as 'dancing,' had in reality a much wider meaning. Greek dancing originated, according to Plato, in the instinctive tendency of mankind to accompany speech and song with explanatory movements of the body [2]. It was essentially a mimetic performance. It included, not only all such motions as are denoted by dancing in the modern sense of the word, but also every kind of gesture and posture by which various objects and events can be represented in dumb show. Its principal function was to interpret and illustrate the words of poetry. For this purpose nothing could be more important than appropriate gesticulation. Hence in Greek dancing the movements of the hands and arms played a larger part than the movements of the feet. The same was the case in Roman dancing also. A few quotations will illustrate this fact. Telestes, the celebrated dancer employed by Aeschylus, was said to be able to 'depict events with his hands in the most skilful manner [3].' Ovid, in his Art of Love, when advising a lover to show off his best qualities before his mistress, tells him to sing if he has a good voice, to

---

[1] Athen. p. 20 F.
[2] Plat. Seqq. 816 A.
[3] Athen. p. 21 F καὶ Τέλεσις δὲ ἡ

Τελέστης, ὁ ὀρχηστοδιδάσκαλος, πολλὰ ἐξεύρηκε σχήματα, ἄκρως ταῖς χερσὶ τὰ λεγόμενα δεικνυούσαις.

dance 'if his arms are flexible[1].' The flourishes and gesticulations with which a professional carver cut up a hare were called 'dancing' by the ancients[2]. Quintilian, speaking of the gestures used in oratory, gravely says that there ought to be a considerable difference between the orator and the dancer; that the gestures of the orator should represent the general sense of the words, rather than the particular objects mentioned[3]. The bare fact of his comparing an orator with a dancer is a proof of the vital difference between ancient and modern dancing, and the importance of mere gesticulation in the former.

The purpose, then, of ancient dancing was to represent various objects and events by means of gestures, postures, and attitudes. In this kind of mimicry the nations of southern Europe are particularly skilful, as may be seen at the present day. The art was carried by the Greeks to the highest perfection, and a good dancer was able to accompany a song with such expressive pantomime as to create a visible picture of the things described. Aristotle defines dancing as an imitation of 'actions, characters, and passions by means of postures and rhythmical movements[4].' His language indicates very clearly the unlimited capabilities of Greek dancing. Its general character will be well exemplified by the following account from Plutarch's Symposiaca. Dancing, it is there stated, might be divided into Motions, Postures, and Indications. Motions were of the greatest use in depicting actions and passions. Postures were the attitudes in which each motion terminated. For example, a dancer might halt in such a posture as to suggest Apollo, or Pan, or a Bacchante. Indications were not mimetic at all, but consisted in merely pointing out certain objects, such as the heaven, the earth, the bystanders.

---

[1] Ovid, Ars Am. i. 595 si vox est, canta; si mollia brachia, salta.

[2] Juv. v. 120 structorem interea, ne qua indignatio desit, | saltantem spectes et chironomunta volanti | cultello.

[3] Quint. Inst. xi. 3. 89 abesse enim plurimum a saltatore debet orator, ut sit gestus ad sensum magis quam ad verba accommodatus, &c.

[4] Arist. Poet. c. 1 καὶ γὰρ οὗτοι (οἱ ὀρχησταί) διὰ τῶν σχηματιζομένων ῥυθμῶν μιμοῦνται καὶ ἤθη καὶ πάθη καὶ πράξεις.

Dancing might be defined as poetry without words. The combination of poetry and dancing, of words and gestures, produced a perfect imitation[1]. In the above account from Plutarch we have a clear exposition of the Greek conception of dancing as the handmaid of poetry. Its function was to delineate and to emphasise the creations of the poet. This was the part which it played in the Greek drama. It is most important therefore, when speaking of dancing in connexion with the old dramatic performances, to remember the vital difference between the ancient and modern meaning of the words.

Some few facts have been recorded concerning the history of dancing in connexion with the drama. In the earliest times it consisted mainly of movements with the feet. The use of the hands and arms in dancing, and the introduction of elaborate gesticulation, was a development due to a later period[2]. In the old-fashioned dramas of Thespis and his immediate successors dancing necessarily played a very important part. Both tragedy and comedy were at that time mainly lyrical, and the long choral odes were accompanied throughout by dances. The early dramatists, such as Thespis, Phrynichus, Pratinas, and Cratinus, were called 'dancers' as well as poets, because one of their principal duties consisted in training their choruses in the art of dancing[3]. Phrynichus, in an epigram of which two verses are still preserved, boasts of having discovered more figures in dancing than there are waves in a stormy sea[4]. The tragic dance of the sixth century, to judge from the specimens given by Philocleon at the end of the Wasps, was of a wild and lively character[5]. The tone of solemnity, by which it was afterwards distinguished, was due to the innovations of Aeschylus. It was probably in the time of Aeschylus that dancing in tragedy

---

[1] Plut. Symp. 747 B fol. The three divisions of dancing are φοραί, σχήματα, δείξεις.

[2] Athen. p. 630 B πρώτη δὲ εὕρηται ἡ περὶ τοὺς πόδας κίνησις τῆς διὰ τῶν χειρῶν. οἱ γὰρ παλαιοὶ τοὺς πόδας μᾶλλον ἐγυμνάζοντο ἐν τοῖς ἀγῶσι.

[3] Athen. p. 22 A.

[4] Plut. Symp. 732 F καίτοι καὶ Φρύνιχος, ὁ τῶν τραγῳδιῶν ποιητής, περὶ αὑτοῦ φησιν ὅτι Σχήματα δ' ὄρχησις τόσα μοι πόρεν, ὅσσ' ἐνὶ πόντῳ | κύματα ποιεῖται χείματι νὺξ ὀλοή.

[5] Arist. Vesp. 1474 ff.

reached its highest pitch of excellence. His long choruses gave ample opportunities for the display of the dancer's skill. Moreover, the training of the chorus was personally superintended by Aeschylus, and he is said to have himself invented a great number of postures and attitudes to be used in dancing[1]. Towards the end of the fifth century the art appears to have declined in significance, along with the general decrease in the importance of the chorus. It began to lose something of its mimetic character. Plato, the comic poet, who flourished at the end of the fifth century, contrasts the mediocrity of the choral dancing in his day with the excellence of that of a former period. In old times, he says, a good dancer was a sight worth seeing; but the choreutae of the present day stand in a row, like so many cripples, and bawl out their songs, without any attempt at appropriate motions and gestures[2]. This deterioration was a necessary consequence of the tendency to thrust the chorus more and more into the background.

The general character of the dancing in the Greek drama has already been described. As far as details are concerned our information is very defective, and only slight indications are to be obtained from the existing plays. It is probable that when the parodoi commenced with a series of anapaests, the chorus only marched in, without dancing. But all parodoi written in lyrical metres were undoubtedly accompanied with a dance. The iambic and trochaic tetrameters, in which many of the parodoi in Aristophanes are written, seem to have been generally intended for choruses which entered running, and with an appearance of great haste[3]. The stasima, or long choral odes between the acts, are said by many of the scholiasts to have been unaccompanied by dancing, and to have been de-

---

[1] Athen. p. 21 E.
[2] Athen. p. 628 E ὥστ' εἴ τις ὀρχοῖτ' εὖ, θέαμ' ἦν· νῦν δὲ δρῶσιν οὐδέν, | ἀλλ' ὥσπερ ἀπόπληκτοι στάδην ἑστῶτες ὠρύονται.
[3] Aristoph. Acharn. 204 τῇδε πᾶς ἔπου, δίωκε, καὶ τὸν ἄνδρα πυνθάνου κ.τ.λ.,

Schol. ad loc. γέγραπται δὲ τὸ μέτρον τροχαϊκόν, πρόσφορον τῇ τῶν διωκόντων γερόντων σπουδῇ. ταῦτα δὲ ποιεῖν εἰώθασιν οἱ τῶν δραμάτων ποιηταὶ κωμικοὶ καὶ τραγικοί, ἐπειδὰν δρομαίως εἰσάγωσι τοὺς χορούς, ἵνα ὁ λόγος συντρέχῃ τῷ δράματι. Cp. Pax 301, 325, Plutus 257.

livered by the chorus standing perfectly still[1]. The statement is no doubt an error, due to false etymology. The stasima, or 'stationary songs,' was so called, not because the chorus stood still during their delivery, but because it remained all the time in the orchestra. They were therefore opposed to the parodoi, which were delivered while the chorus was coming in, and to the exodoi, which were delivered while it was going out. That the stasima were accompanied by dancing is proved by several references to dancing which they contain, and also by Aristotle's definition of them, in which nothing is said as to the absence of dancing[2]. Only one piece of information has been preserved concerning the manœuvres of the chorus during the stasima. It is said that while singing the strophe they moved to the right, and while singing the antistrophe they moved back again to the left; and that during the epode they remained standing in the same position as at first[3]. Sometimes, as was previously pointed out, lively odes called hyporchemata were inserted in the middle of the dialogue to mark the joy of the chorus at an unexpected turn of fortune. The dances by which they were accompanied were extremely brisk and energetic, in tragedy as well as in comedy[4]. The exodoi, or concluding utterances of the chorus, were not usually attended with dancing, but were delivered in recitative as the chorus marched out. There is an exception in the Wasps and the Ecclesiazusae, which are terminated by the chorus dancing out of the orchestra. But Aristophanes himself remarks that this was an innovation[5]. There is no reason to suppose that in tragedy the kommoi, or musical dialogues between actors and chorus, were

---

[1] Schol. Eur. Phoen. 202; Suidas v. στάσιμον, &c.

[2] Aristot. Poet. c. 12 στάσιμον δὲ μέλος χοροῦ τὸ ἄνευ ἀναπαίστου καὶ τροχαίου. Aesch. Eum. 307 ἄγε δὴ χορὸν ἄψωμεν. Arist. Thesmoph. 953 ὅρμα, χώρει | κοῦφα ποσίν, ἄγ' ἐς κύκλον, | χειρὶ σύναπτε χεῖρα. Other passages of the same kind are not infrequent.

[3] Schol. Eur. Hec. 647.

[4] The liveliness of the hyporchematic dances, even in tragedy, is proved by such expressions as the following: Eur. Troad. 325 πάλλε πόδ' αἰθέριον, Electra 859 θὲς ἐς χορόν, ὦ φίλα, ἴχνος: Soph. Ajax 693 ἔφριξ' ἔρωτι, περιχαρὴς δ' ἀνεπτόμαν.

[5] Arist. Vesp. 1536 τοῦτο γὰρ οὐδεὶς πω πάρος δέδρακεν, | ὀρχούμενον ὅστις ἀπήλλαξεν χορὸν τρυγῳδῶν, Schol. ad loc. εἰσέρχεται γὰρ ὁ χορὸς ὀρχούμενος, οὐδαμῶς δὲ ἐξέρχεται: Eccles. 1179 αἴρεσθ' ἄνω, ἰαί, εὐαί.

unaccompanied with dancing. But naturally, if this was the case, the dance would be of a quiet and sober kind, consisting more of appropriate gestures and motions, than of dancing in the modern sense of the word.

During a large part of every Greek play the chorus had nothing to say or sing, but merely stood watching the actors, and listening to the dialogue. It would be absurd to imagine that they remained stolid and indifferent during all this period. Chorus and actors were supposed to form one harmonious group, and no doubt the chorus followed the events upon the stage with a keen appearance of interest, and expressed their sympathy with the different characters by every kind of gesture and by-play. Occasionally the long descriptive speeches delivered from the stage were accompanied with a mimetic dance on the part of the chorus[1]. The events described by the actor were represented in dumb show by the choreutae. In comedy it was a regular practice to introduce descriptive speeches of this sort, the metres used being iambic or anapaestic tetrameters, which were especially suitable for dancing to. There is an example in the Clouds, where Strepsiades describes his quarrel with Pheidippides. The various phases of the quarrel were represented in dumb show by the chorus, keeping time with the recitative of the actor[2]. Again, we are told that Telestes, the dancer employed by Aeschylus, 'danced the Seven against Thebes' so successfully as to bring the various events before the very eyes of the spectators. The statement no doubt refers to the dumb show with which he accompanied the long descriptive speeches that abound in that play[3].

Each of the three different species of the drama had its own special kind of dance. The tragic dance was called the 'emmeleia.' It was grave and majestic in its motions, and was one of the two dances approved of by Plato, and admitted into his

---

[1] Schol. Arist. Ran. 924 ἡ πρὸς τὰς ῥήσεις ὑπόρχησις.
[2] Schol. Arist. Nub. 1355 οὕτως ἔλεγον πρὸς χορὸν λέγειν, ὅτε τοῦ ὑποκριτοῦ διατιθεμένου τὴν ῥῆσιν, ὁ χορὸς ὠρχεῖτο.
[3] Athen. p. 22 A Ἀριστοκλῆς γοῦν φησιν ὅτι Τελέστης, ὁ Αἰσχύλου ὀρχηστής, οὕτως ἦν τεχνίτης, ὥστε ἐν τῷ ὀρχεῖσθαι τοὺς Ἑπτὰ ἐπὶ Θήβας φανερὰ ποιῆσαι τὰ πράγματα δι' ὀρχήσεως.

ideal republic[1]. Some of the postures or figures in the tragic dance are mentioned by the ancient writers. One of them represented a man in the act of thrusting with the sword; another depicted a man in an attitude of menace, with clenched fist. The rest are a mere list of names, of which the meaning is uncertain. But it is plain from the existence of such lists that the art of tragic dancing was reduced to a regular system, and that the various attitudes and postures were taught in a methodical manner[2]. We can hardly be mistaken in assuming that as a rule the movements of the tragic dance were slow and deliberate, and more like walking than dancing in the modern sense. The hyporchematic style, with its wild and lively motions, was only adopted in tragedy on special occasions, to show the excessive joy of the choreutae. The kommos at the conclusion of the Persae gives us a vivid picture of the general style of a tragic dance. The Persian Elders follow Xerxes into the palace, bewailing the ruin of the empire in mournful strains. At each fresh exclamation of grief they fall into some new posture, first beating their breasts, then plucking their beards, then rending their garments, then tearing their hair; and in this manner they move slowly on through the palace doors[3].

The comic dance was called the kordax. Its movements were coarse and lascivious, and its general style was suggestive of the phallic songs out of which comedy had been developed. It was a dance for drunken people, and no one but a man without any sense of shame would dance it when he was sober. It was considered vulgar and disgraceful by Plato, and excluded from his commonwealth[4]. Aristophanes, in the Clouds, takes credit to himself for having abandoned it in that play; but, as the scholiast remarks, he frequently introduces it elsewhere[5]. In the comic dances the wildest movements were admissible. The

---

[1] Plat. Legg. 816 A.
[2] Suid. v. ξιφισμός; Hesych. v. ξιφίζειν; Poll. iv. 105 καὶ μὴν τραγικῆς ὀρχήσεως σχήματα σιμὴ χείρ, καλαθίσκος, χεὶρ καταπρηνής, ξύλου παράληψις, διπλῆ, θερμαυστρίς, κυβίστησις, παραβῆναι τέτταρα.
[3] Aesch. Pers. 1038 foll.
[4] Schol. Arist. Nub. 542 κόρδαξ κωμική, ἥτις αἰσχρῶς κινεῖ τὴν ὀσφῦν. Hesych. v. κόρδαξ; Plat. Legg. p. 816 A; Theoph. Char. 6.
[5] Arist. Nub. 540 οὐδὲ κόρδαχ' εἴλκυσεν.

chorus, at the end of the Wasps, when encouraging the sons of Carcinus to fresh exertions, bid them 'whirl round like tops, and fling their legs up into the sky.' Occasionally the circular dance of the dithyrambic chorus was adopted in comedy[1].

The dance used in the satyric drama was called the 'sikinnis.' It was mainly a parody and caricature of noble and graceful dances, and was very violent and rapid in its movements. One of the postures used in the satyric dance was called the owl, and is variously explained by the old grammarians as having consisted in shading the eyes with the hands, or in turning the head to and fro like an owl[2].

§ 7. *The Music.*

The music of a Greek play was simple in its character, and altogether subordinate to the poetry. As Plutarch remarks, it was a sort of seasoning or relish, the words being the main attraction[3]. Any comparison therefore between a Greek play and a modern opera, as far as the music is concerned, must be entirely illusive. In the first place all Greek choral singing was in unison. The use of harmony in musical compositions was unknown to the Greeks. Even in modern times Greek Church Music has retained the practice of chanting in unison. Consequently the general style of the music in a Greek drama must have been exceedingly simple and severe compared with the intricate combinations of modern music. In the second place, the music was fitted to the words, instead of the words being subordinated to the music. Each note of the music corresponded to a separate syllable of the verse, and the time of the music was determined entirely by the metre of the verse. The ode was chanted in unison, syllable after syllable, by the whole body of the choreutae. The modern practice of adapting

---

[1] Arist. Vesp. 1529 στρόβει, παράβαινε κύκλῳ καὶ γάστρισον σεαυτόν, | ῥῖπτε σκέλος οὐράνιον· βέμβικες ἐγγενέσθων, Thesm. 953 ὅρμα, χώρει | κοῦφα ποσίν, ἄγ' ἐς κύκλον, | χειρὶ σύναπτε χεῖρα.

[2] Poll. iv. 99, 103; Athen. p. 629 F–630 A; Dion. Hal. A. R. vii. 72; Phot. v. σκώπευμα.

[3] Plut. Symp. 713 C τὸ δὲ μέλος καὶ τὸν ῥυθμὸν ὥσπερ ὄψον ἐπὶ τῷ λόγῳ, καὶ μὴ καθ' αὑτὰ προσφέρεσθαι.

the words to the exigencies of the music, and making different parts of the chorus sing different words at the same time, was altogether unknown. Hence it is probable that the words of a Greek chorus were heard with considerable distinctness by the whole audience. When all the singing was in unison, and the notes of the music corresponded to the syllables of the verse, there was no reason why this should not be the case. In modern choral singing the poetry is so far sacrificed to the music, that even the general drift of the words cannot usually be distinguished with much clearness. But this could never have been the case in the ancient drama, where the lyrical portions of the play often contained the finest poetry and the profoundest thoughts of the whole composition. The choreutae were doubtless made to sing with great precision and distinctness of utterance; and this training, combined with the simple character of the music, would make it possible for the words of an ancient chorus to be heard without difficulty. In the third place, the instrumental accompaniment was limited in amount, and was never allowed to predominate. The flute or harp simply gave the note, but otherwise was kept quite in the background. In lyrical, as opposed to dramatic, poetry there was a tendency for the flute to overpower the voices. Pratinas, in a lyrical fragment still preserved, complains of this practice, saying that 'the Muse has made Poetry the mistress: let the flute play the second part; it is but the servant of Poetry[1]!' These words, which only refer to a tendency in the lyrical poets of the time, are significant as showing the Greek conception of the relative position of instrument and voice in choral singing. In the Greek drama, as already remarked, the instrumental portion of the music was altogether subordinate; and the music as a whole was made subservient to the words and the poetry.

The scales in which Greek music was written were called Modes or Harmonies, and differed from one another, not only according to the intervals between the notes, but also in respect

[1] Pratinas apud Athen. p. 617 B τὰν δοιδὰν κατέστασε Πιερὶς βασίλειαν· ὁ δ' αὐλὸς | ὕστερον χορευέτω· καὶ γὰρ ἐσθ' ὑπηρέτας.

of the particular style of music with which they were respectively associated. This was a peculiar feature of the Greek musical system. Every Mode had a special kind of metre and of melody appropriated to itself, and a composition in a given Mode was necessarily of a certain well-defined character. The difference between the several Modes was very much the same as that between various kinds of national music in modern times. For example, an air in the Phrygian Mode bore the same sort of relation to one in the Lydian as a lively Swiss song bears to a plaintive Irish melody. Of the various Modes used in Greek music the tragic poets selected those which were most suited to their purpose. The Dorian and the Mixolydian Modes were the two most commonly employed in tragedy. The Dorian was majestic and dignified in style; the Mixolydian was pathetic. The one was used in the solemn and profound choral odes, the other in cases where deep emotion had to be expressed[1]. Besides these two principal Modes, certain others were occasionally employed. The old Ionic Mode was severe and sober, before the degeneracy of the Ionic nation had altered its character. It was therefore well adapted to tragedy, and was used by Aeschylus[2]. The music of the Phrygian Mode was passionate and enthusiastic, and was first introduced into tragedy by Sophocles[3]. The Hypodorian and the Hypophrygian Modes were only employed in the songs of the actors upon the stage, and not in choral odes. The reason was that the style of their music was better suited to realistic acting, than to choral singing[4]. Sometimes a few notes of instrumental music were inserted by themselves, at intervals in the choral songs, as a sort of refrain. The 'phlattothrat,' which recurs in the parody of Aeschylus' lyrics in the Frogs, is an instance of such a refrain, the instrument used being the harp. The flute was also employed in the same way. Such refrains were called 'diaulia'[5].

[1] Plut. Mus. 1136 D-F.
[2] Heracleid. ap. Athen. p. 625 B; Aesch. Suppl. 69 'Ιαονίοισι νόμοισι.
[3] Vit. Soph. p. 8 Dindf.
[4] Aristot. Prob. xix. 30. 48.

[5] Arist. Ran. 1286 ff.; Hesych. v. διαύλιον· ὁπόταν ἐν τοῖς μέλεσι μεταξὺ παραβάλλῃ μέλος τι ὁ ποιητὴς παρασιωπήσαντος τοῦ χοροῦ.

During the latter part of the fifth century the character of Greek music underwent a considerable change. The severity and simplicity of the music of the Aeschylean period was succeeded by a style in which softness, variety, and flexibility were the prominent features. The author of the movement was the celebrated musician Timotheus[1]. His innovations were regarded by the philosophers and old-fashioned critics as so many corruptions of the art of music, and as a proof of the growing effeminacy of the age[2]. In one of the comedies of Pherecrates the person of Music is made to complain of the treatment she has received at the hands of various composers, and ends her complaint by charging Timotheus with having outraged and insulted her more than any one else had done, and compares his florid melodies to the 'intricate movements of ants in a nest[3].' The new kind of music was very generally adopted by the later tragic poets, such as Euripides and Agathon, and is frequently ridiculed by Aristophanes[4]. Euripides appears to have foreseen from the first that the new style would soon become popular. On a certain occasion, when a novel composition by Timotheus was loudly hissed in the theatre, he told him not to be discouraged by his temporary want of success, as in a few years he would be sure to have every audience at his feet[5]. The prediction was verified by the result.

---

[1] Suid. v. Τιμόθεος. Plut. Mus. 1135 D.
[2] Suid. l. c. τὴν ἀρχαίαν μουσικὴν ἐπὶ τὸ μαλακώτερον μετήγαγεν.
[3] Pherecrat. Cheiron. frag. 1 (Meineke, F. C. G. ii. p. 326) ᾄδων ἐκτραπέλους μυρμηκίας.
[4] Arist. Ran. 1301 foll., Thesm. 100 μύρμηκος ἀτραπούς, ἢ τί διαμινύρεται; Schol. ad loc. ὡς λεπτὰ καὶ ἀγκύλα ἀνακρουομένου μέλη τοῦ Ἀγάθωνος· τοιαῦται γὰρ αἱ τῶν μυρμήκων ὁδοί.
[5] Plut. an seni etc. 795 C.

CHAPTER VII.

THE AUDIENCE.

§ 1. *Composition of the Audience.*

THE theatre of Dionysus at Athens, during the period of the Lenaea and the City Dionysia, presented a spectacle which for interest and significance has few parallels in the ancient or the modern world. On these occasions the city kept universal holiday. Business and politics were forgotten; the law-courts were closed; even prisoners were released from gaol, to enable them to partake in the general rejoicings. The deity in honour of whom the festivals had been established was Dionysus, the god of wine, and the type of the productive power of nature. The various proceedings were in reality so many religious celebrations. But there was nothing of an austere character about the worship of Dionysus. To give freedom from care was his special attribute, and the sincerest mode of paying homage to his power was by a genial enjoyment of the various pleasures of life. At this time of universal merriment the dramatic performances formed the principal attraction. Each day soon after sunrise the great majority of the citizens made their way to the southern slopes of the Acropolis, where the theatre of Dionysus was situated. The tiers of seats rising up the side of the hill were speedily filled with a crowd of nearly thirty thousand persons. The sight of such a vast multitude of people, gathered together at daybreak in the huge open amphitheatre, and dressed for the most part in white, or in red, brown, yellow, and other rich colours, must have been exceedingly striking and picturesque. The performances which brought them together were not unworthy of the occasion. The plays exhibited at the festivals of Dionysus rank among the very noblest achievements of Greek genius. For beauty of form, depth of meaning, and poetical inspiration they have never been surpassed. The point of unique interest about the Greek drama is the superlative excellence of its productions, combined with the fact that it was essentially a national amusement, designed for the entertainment of the great mass of the citizens. It would be difficult to point to any similar example of the whole population of a city meeting together each year to enjoy works of the highest artistic beauty. It is seldom that art and poetry have penetrated so deeply into the life of the ordinary citizens. Our curiosity is naturally excited in regard to the tone and composition of the audiences before which a drama of such an exceptional character was exhibited. The object of the following chapter will be to bring together and present in one view all the available information upon this subject.

At the Lenaea, which was held in the winter, when travelling was difficult, the audience consisted almost exclusively of natives of Athens. The City Dionysia came about two months later, at the commencement of the spring, and attracted great crowds of strangers from various parts of Greece. Representatives from the allied states came to pay the annual tribute at this season of the year. It was also a favourite time for the arrival of ambassadors from foreign cities; and it was considered a mere matter of politeness to provide them with front seats in the theatre, if they happened to be in Athens during the celebration of the City Dionysia[1]. In addition to these visitors of a representative character, there were also great numbers of private individuals, attracted to Athens from all parts of Greece by the magnificence of the festival, and the fame of the dramatic exhibitions. Altogether the visitors formed a considerable portion of the audience at the City Dionysia. One of the great aggravations of the offence of Meidias was that his assault upon

[1] Dem. de Cor. § 28.

Demosthenes was committed in the presence of 'large multitudes of strangers[1].' Apparently the natives of foreign states were not allowed to purchase tickets for the theatre in their own name, but had to get them through an Athenian citizen[2].

The composition of the purely Athenian part of the audience is a subject upon which a great deal has been written, the principal difficulty being the question as to the admittance of boys and women to the dramatic performances. In the treatment of this matter scholars appear to have been unduly biassed by a preconceived opinion as to what was right and proper. Undoubtedly Athenian women were kept in a state of almost Oriental seclusion. And the old Attic comedy was pervaded by a coarseness which seems to make it utterly unfit for boys and women. For these reasons some writers have gone so far as to assert that they were never present at any dramatic performances whatsoever[3]. Others, while not excluding them from tragedy, have declared that it was an impossibility that they should have been present at the performances of comedy[4]. But the attempt to draw a distinction between tragedy and comedy, in regard to the admission of boys and women to the theatre, will not bear examination. If they were present at one, they must have been present at both. The tragic and the comic competitions frequently took place upon the same days, and succeeded one another without any interval; and it is difficult to suppose that, after the tragedies were over, a large part of the audience had to be turned out before the comedies could begin. Moreover, if women and boys had been present at the tragedies, they would of necessity have been spectators of the satyric dramas, which were nearly as coarse as the comedies. It is useless therefore to endeavour to separate tragedy from comedy in the consideration of this question.

As a matter of fact the evidence upon the subject, if con-

[1] Dem. Meid. § 74.
[2] Theophrast. Char. 9 καὶ ξένοις δὲ αὑτοῦ θέαν ἀγοράσας μὴ δοὺς τὸ μέρος θεωρεῖν.
[3] E. g. Böttiger, Kleine Schriften i. p. 295 ff.; Wachsmuth, Hellen. Alterthumskunde ii. p. 391; Bergk, Griech. Literatur. iii. p. 49.
[4] E. g. Bernhardy, Griech. Litterat. ii. 2. p. 132; Böckh, Trag. Princip. p. 37; Meineke, Menand. et Philem. Reliq. p. 345.

sidered without prejudice, makes it practically certain that there were no restrictions of the kind suggested. The audience at the dramatic performances, whether tragic or comic, was drawn from every class of the population. Men, women, boys, and slaves were all allowed to be present. The evidence from ancient authors is too copious to be accounted for on any other supposition. There are three passages in Plato which in themselves are almost enough to decide the question. In one place, speaking of poetry in general, and more especially of tragedy, Plato says it is a kind of rhetoric addressed to 'boys, women, and men, slaves, and free citizens without distinction.' In another place, where he is treating of the management of his ideal republic, he says there will be no great readiness to allow the tragic poets to 'erect their stages in the market-place, and perform before women and children, and the general public.' A passage of this kind would have very little point, unless it was intended as a condemnation of the prevailing practice. In a third place he declares that if there was a general exhibition of all kinds of public amusements, and the audience were called upon to state what they were most pleased with, the little children would vote for the conjuror, the boys for the comic poet, the young men and the more refined sort of women for the tragic poet[1]. These three passages of Plato are hardly consistent with the supposition that the drama was a spectacle which boys and women were never allowed to witness.

In addition to the above evidence there are also several places in Aristophanes where boys and women are referred to as forming part of the audience. They must therefore have been present at the performances of the Old Comedy. For instance, in the Clouds Aristophanes prides himself on having refrained from introducing the phallus 'to make the boys laugh.' In the Peace he says that 'both the boys and the men' ought to wish for his victory in the contest, because of his boldness in attacking Cleon. In another part of the Peace, when some barley is thrown among the male part of the spectators,

---

[1] Plat. Gorg. 502 B–E, Legg. 817 A–C, 658 A–D.

Trygaeus remarks that the women have not got any[1]. Other passages of the same kind might be quoted. That women were present at the New Comedy is proved conclusively by a letter of Alciphron, in which Menander is supposed to be writing to his mistress Glycera. In this letter he says that nothing is dearer to him than to be crowned with the ivy of Dionysus, as victor in the comic contest, 'while Glycera is sitting in the theatre and looking on[2].' Other pieces of evidence are as follows. In Lucian's dialogue Solon tells Anacharsis that the Athenians educate their sons by taking them to tragedies and comedies, and showing them examples of virtue and vice, so as to teach them what to imitate and what to avoid[3]. In the Frogs there is the well-known passage in which Aeschylus taunts Euripides with the immorality of his plays, which have caused women of refinement to commit suicide from very shame. If women were never present at the performance of the tragedies of Euripides, there would be very little meaning in the reproach[4]. Then again we are told that when Alcibiades was choregus, and 'entered the theatre' dressed in a splendid purple robe, he was admired 'not only by the men, but also by the women[5].' The shameless person in Theophrastus smuggles his sons into the theatre with a ticket which belongs to some one else. The miser never takes his sons to the theatre except when the entrance is free[6]. The regulation of Sphyromachus, providing that men, women, and courtesans should sit apart from one another, can hardly have referred to any place but the theatre[7]. The cumulative effect of all these passages is difficult to resist. It is impossible to explain them all away by far-fetched interpretations. Even the story of the effect produced by the Eumenides of Aeschylus upon the audience—of the boys dying of fright and the women having miscarriages—such a story, though in itself a foolish

---

[1] Aristoph. Nub. 537-539, Pax 765, 766, 962-967. Cp. also Arist. Pax 50 ἐγὼ δὲ τὸν λόγον γε τοῖσι παιδίοις ... φράσω; Eupolis, Προσπάλτιοι, fr. 2 (Meineke, Frag. Com. Gr. ii. p. 521) 'Ἡράκλεις, τοῦτ' ἔστι σοι | τὸ σκῶμμ' ἀσελγὲς καὶ Μεγαρικὸν καὶ σφόδρα |

ψυχρόν, γελῶσιν, ὡς ὁρᾷς, τὰ παιδία.
[2] Alciphron, Epist. ii. 3.
[3] Lucian, Anachar. 22.
[4] Aristoph. Ran. 1050, 1051.
[5] Athen. p. 534 C.
[6] Theophrast. Char. 9 and 13.
[7] Schol. Aristoph. Eccles. 22.

invention, could hardly have originated unless women and boys had been regularly present at the theatre[1]. That they were admitted at a later period is proved by the direct evidence of inscriptions in the theatre of Dionysus, which show that in Hadrian's time seats were specially reserved for priestesses and other women[2]. This fact would not of course be conclusive evidence as to the custom which prevailed in the classical period of Athenian history. But as far as it goes, it tends to confirm the conclusions based upon the evidence of ancient authors.

No doubt at first sight it appears a very startling fact that women and boys should have been spectators of the Old Comedy. But it should always be remembered that the comedies performed at the festivals of Dionysus were a portion of a religious celebration, which it was a pious duty to take part in. Ribaldry and coarseness were a traditional element in the worship of Dionysus, handed down from rude and primitive times, and were not lightly to be dispensed with. The Greeks in such matters were thoroughly conservative. It was a feeling of this kind which caused the satyric drama to be developed side by side with tragedy, in order that the old licentious merriment of the satyrs might not be utterly forgotten. The coarseness of the Old Comedy, being a regular part of the celebrations in honour of Dionysus, might be witnessed by boys and women without degradation, though their presence at similar scenes in real life would have been regarded in a very different manner. Where the worship of the gods was concerned, the practice of keeping women in strict seclusion was allowed to drop into abeyance. Women and even girls were present at the phallic processions in honour of Dionysus[3]. Their appearance on such occasions were regarded as a mere matter of course. It need not therefore surprise us that women and boys should have been present in the theatre at the performances of the Old Comedy.

Whether they were ever present in large numbers is a further question. Even those writers who admit that their presence

---

[1] Vit. Aeschyli, p. 4 Dindf.
[2] Corp. Inscr. Att. iii. 282, 313, 315, 316, 321, 322, 324, 325, 333, 342, 343, 345, 350, 351, 354, 361, &c.
[3] Aristoph. Achar. 241–246; Menand. Frag. Incert. 32 (Meineke, Frag. Com. Gr. iv. p. 243).

was not prohibited by law, generally add that the more respectable women would in all probability keep away[1]. But the only authority for such a notion is to be found in a couple of passages in Aristophanes, which represent the husband as present in the theatre, while the wife was at home[2]. There is nothing so unusual in an occurrence of this kind as to warrant any sweeping conclusions. Some people must necessarily have remained at home, from the mere fact that the theatre would not have been large enough to contain the whole population of Athens, if men, women, and children had all been present. But it is hardly probable, for the reasons already stated, that there was anything disreputable in a woman visiting the theatre. Reformers like Aristotle were in advance of ordinary public opinion in their feelings about such matters. There is a passage in Aristotle's Politics which is of great interest as showing the general sentiment on the subject[3]. Aristotle expresses a strong opinion that boys should be prevented from seeing or hearing any piece of coarseness or indecency. Even if such ribaldry is an essential feature in the worship of any particular deity, he says that only men should be allowed to be present. The men should pay the proper homage to gods of this character on behalf of themselves, their wives, and their children; but boys should not be permitted to be witnesses of comedies and similar spectacles. This passage, in which Aristotle is combating the prevailing practice of the times, is an additional proof that boys were present at the performance of comedies, and shows clearly that when the worship of the gods was concerned ordinary public opinion did not consider such spectacles improper.

[1] E. g. Müller, die Griech. Bühnenalterthümer p. 291.
[2] Aristoph. Av. 793-796 εἴ τε μοιχεύων τις ὑμῶν ἐστιν ὅστις τυγχάνει, | κᾆθ' ὁρᾷ τὸν ἄνδρα τῆς γυναικὸς ἐν βουλευτικῷ, | οὗτος ἂν πάλιν παρ' ὑμῶν πτερυγίσας ἀνέπτατο, | εἶτα βινήσας ἐκεῖθεν αὖθις αὖ καθέζετο. Thesm. 395-397 ὥστ' εὐθὺς εἰσιόντες ἀπὸ τῶν ἰκρίων | ὑποβλέπουσ' ἡμᾶς, σκοπούνταί τ' εὐθέως | μὴ μοιχὸς ἔνδον ᾖ τις ἀποκεκρυμμένος.

[3] Aristot. Pol. vii. 17 ἐπιμελὲς μὲν οὖν ἔστω τοῖς ἄρχουσι μηθὲν μήτε ἄγαλμα μήτε γραφὴν εἶναι τοιούτων πράξεων μίμησιν, εἰ μὴ παρά τισι θεοῖς τοιούτοις οἷς καὶ τὸν τωθασμὸν ἀποδίδωσιν ὁ νόμος· πρὸς δὲ τούτοις ἀφίησιν ὁ νόμος τοὺς ἔχοντας ἡλικίαν πλέον προσηκουσαν καὶ ὑπὲρ αὐτῶν καὶ τέκνων καὶ γυναικῶν τιμαλφεῖν τοὺς θεούς. τοὺς δὲ νεωτέρους οὔτ' ἰάμβων οὔτε κωμῳδίας θεατὰς νομοθετητέον.

Besides women and children it appears that slaves were occasionally present at the theatre. Plato in the Gorgias mentions slaves as one of the classes before which the tragic poets will not be allowed to perform in his ideal commonwealth[1]. The shameless man described by Theophrastus takes the 'paedagogus' to the theatre, along with his sons, and crowds them all into seats which did not really belong to him[2]. It is not however probable that the number of slaves among the audience was ever very great. Their presence would depend upon the kindness of their masters. But the two passages just quoted prove that there was no law to prevent their attendance.

§ 2. *Price of Admission.*

The dramatic entertainments at Athens were provided by the state for the benefit of the whole people. The entrance was originally free, and every man was allowed to get the best seat he could. But as the drama was extremely popular from the very first, the struggle for seats caused great disturbances. People used to come and secure places the night before the performance began; citizens complained that they were crowded out of the theatre by foreigners; blows and fights were of frequent occurrence. It was therefore decided to charge a small entrance fee, and to sell all the seats in advance. In this way the crush of people was avoided, and as each man's seat was secured for him, he was able to go to the theatre at a more reasonable hour[3]. The price of a seat for one day's performance was two obols. The same price appears to have been charged for all the different parts of the theatre, with the exception of the reserved seats for priests, officials, and other distinguished persons[4]. A gradation of prices, according to the goodness and badness of the seat, would probably not have been

---

[1] Plat. Gorg. 502 D.
[2] Theophrast. Char. 9.
[3] Schol. Lucian. Tim. 49; Suidas v. θεωρικόν.
[4] Dem. de Cor. § 28 ἀλλ' ἐν τοῖν δυοῖν ὀβολοῖν ἐθεώρουν ἄν. This passage shows that there was no alternative between the reserved seats for distinguished persons, and the ordinary two-obol seats. The passage in Plat. Apol. 26 D, which has often been quoted to prove that some seats cost a drachma, has probably no reference to the theatre. See above, chap. iii. p. 106.

tolerated by the democracy, as giving the rich too great an advantage over the poor.

Until the time of Pericles every man had to pay for his place, although the charge was a very small one. But the poorer classes began to complain that the expense was too great for them, and that the rich citizens bought up all the seats. Pericles therefore, in order to gratify the democracy, passed a measure directing that every citizen should have the price of the entrance to the dramatic performances paid to him by the state. The sum given in this way was called 'theoric' money. The law is described as if it was of universal application, but it is probable that in Pericles' time, and for many years afterwards, only the needy citizens applied for the theoric grant[1]. The amount given to each man is sometimes said to have been a drachma, sometimes two obols. There is no doubt that the entrance fee for one day's performance was two obols. If therefore a drachma was given, it must have been for a festival at which the performances in the theatre lasted three days. The amount of the theoric grant would of course vary according to the length of the festival[2]. It is well known that in later times this system of theoric donations developed into the most scandalous abuse. Grants of money were given to the citizens, not merely at the Dionysia, but at all the other Athenian festivals, to provide them with banquets and means of enjoyment. The rich claimed the grant with quite as much eagerness as the poor. The military revenues were impoverished in order to supply the theoric fund[3]. At first, however, the donations were limited to the dramatic performances at the Dionysia.

---

[1] Ulpian. ad Dem. Olynth. i. p. 13; Plut. Pericles p. 157 A.

[2] The amount of the grant is given as two obols by Suidas, Photius, and Etym. Mag. v. θεωρικόν; by Libanius, Hypoth. ad Dem. Olynth. i. p. 8; and by Schol. Aristoph. Vesp. 1118. It is given as a drachma by Schol. Lucian. Tim. 49; and by Photius, Suidas, and Harpocrat. s.v. θεωρικά. That the amount was two obols for a single day is proved by the passage in Dem. de Cor. § 28 ἐν τοῖν δυοῖν ὀβολοῖν ἐθεώρουν ἄν. Ulpian, on Dem. Olynth. i. p. 13, is mistaken in asserting that of the two obols one was for admission to the theatre, the other for refreshments. The Schol. on Dem. de Cor. § 28 also erroneously states that the price of admission was one obol.

[3] Liban. Hypoth. ad Dem. Olynth. i. p. 8; Ammonius, de diff. vocab. v. θεωρός; Dem. de Cor. § 118, Philipp. iv. § 38.

The receipts from the sale of places in the theatre went to the lessee. The arrangement in this matter was a peculiar one. The lessee was a person who entered into a contract with the state, by which he undertook to keep the fabric of the theatre in good repair, and in return was allowed to take all the entrance money. If he failed to keep the theatre in good condition, the state did the necessary repairs itself, and made him pay the expenses. He had to provide reserved seats in the front rows for distinguished persons, and it is uncertain whether the state paid him for these seats or not. For all the other portions of the theatre he was allowed to charge two obols and no more [1].

§ 3. *The Distribution of the Seats.*

When the theatre was full the audience numbered close on thirty thousand persons [2]. As to the arrangement of this enormous mass of people some few facts are known, and some inferences may be made; but the information is not very complete. The great distinction was between the dignitaries who had reserved seats in the front, and the occupants of the ordinary two-obol seats at the back. A gradation of seats with descending prices was, as previously stated, unknown to the ancient Athenians. The privilege of having a reserved seat in the theatre was called 'proedria,' and was conferred by the state [3]. From the large number of persons who enjoyed the distinction it is clear that several of the front rows must have been reserved; and this conclusion is confirmed by the inscriptions in the theatre, which show that seats were assigned to particular in-

---

[1] The lessee was generally called ἀρχιτέκτων (Dem. de Cor. § 28), because part of his contract was to look after the buildings of the theatre. He was also called θεατροπώλης (Poll. vii. 199), from the fact of his selling seats; and θεατρώνης (Theophrast. Char. 11), from the fact of his having taken the theatre on lease. The nature of the arrangement with the lessee may be gathered from (1) Corp. Inscr. Att. ii. 573, in which the lessees of the theatre at the Peiraeeus engage to keep the fabric in good repair; (2) Dem. de Cor. § 28 ἡ θέαν μὴ καταvεῖμαι τὸν ἀρχιτέκτονα αὐτοῖς κελεῦσαι; (3) Ulpian. ad Dem. Olynth. i. p. 13 ὥστε λαμβάνειν ... δύο ὀβολούς, ἵνα ... τὸν δ' ἄλλον παρέχειν ἔχωσι τῷ ἀρχιτέκτονι τοῦ θεάτρου.

[2] See above, chap. iii. p. 122.

[3] Schol. Aristoph. Equit. 572. Pollux. iv. 121, states rather doubtfully that the προεδρία in the theatre might also be called πρῶτον ξύλον.

dividuals as far back as the twenty-fourth tier from the front[1]. The recipients of the honour, or at any rate the more prominent of them, were conducted in a solemn procession to the theatre each morning by one of the state officials[2].

Foremost among the persons who had seats in the front rows were the priests and religious officers connected with the different divinities. That they should be distinguished in this manner was only in keeping with the essentially religious character of the ancient Greek drama. An inscription referring to the theatre at the Peiraeeus, and belonging to the third or fourth century B.C., mentions the priests specially by name as the most conspicuous members of the class who had the 'proedria'[3]. The inscriptions upon the seats in the theatre at Athens, which represent for the most part the arrangement that existed during the reign of Hadrian, place the matter in a very clear light. They enable us to determine the occupants of fifty-four out of sixty-seven seats in the front row; and it is found that of these fifty-four persons no less than forty-five were priests, or ministers connected with religion. Similarly, in the rows immediately behind the front row, a large number of places were set apart for the different priests and priestesses[4]. Such was the arrangement in the time of Hadrian, and there can be little doubt that it was much the same in its general character during the period of the Athenian democracy.

Among state officials the nine archons and the ten generals had distinguished places in the theatre. In Hadrian's time the archons occupied seats in the front row, and it is probable that this position was assigned to them from the earliest period. The generals were in some prominent part of the theatre, but the

---

[1] Corp. Inscr. Att. iii. 303-384.
[2] Corp. Inscr. Att. ii. 589 shows that in the Peiraeeus the demarch used to conduct the persons honoured with proedria to the theatre. A similar practice was no doubt observed at Athens.
[3] Corp. Inscr. Att. ii. 589 καὶ εἰσαγέτω αὐτὸν ὁ δήμαρχος εἰς τὸ θέατρον καθάπερ ἱερεῖς καὶ τοὺς ἄλλους οἷς δέδοται ἡ προεδρία παρὰ Πειραιέων. Cp. also

Hesych. v. νεμήσεις θέας· 'Αθηναῖοι τὰς ἐν τῷ θεάτρῳ καθέδρας, ψηφίσματι νενεμημένας προεδρίας ἱερεῦσιν.
[4] Corp. Inscr. Att. iii. 240-298. Fifty-two thrones in the front row have been preserved, with the inscriptions upon them; and it is quite clear that two other thrones must have been reserved for the two remaining Thesmothetae.

exact place is not known. The snob in Theophrastus was always anxious to sit as near to them as possible[1]. Ambassadors from foreign states, as was previously pointed out, were generally provided with front seats, on the motion of some member of the Council. Demosthenes is taunted by Aeschines for the excessive politeness which he showed to Philip's ambassadors on an occasion of this kind. The lessee of the theatre at the Peiraeeus, as appears from an inscription still extant, was ordered to provide the ambassadors from Colophon with reserved places at the Dionysia. The Spartan ambassadors were sitting in 'a most distinguished part of the theatre' when they considerately gave up a place to an old man for whom no one else would make room[2]. The judges of the various contests sat together in a body, and would naturally be provided with one of the best places in the theatre[3]. The orphan sons of men who had fallen in battle received from the state, in addition to other honours, the distinction of 'proedria.' The same privilege was frequently conferred by decree upon great public benefactors, and was generally made hereditary in the family, descending by succession to the eldest male representative. An honour of this kind was bestowed upon Demosthenes[4].

With the exception of the reserved places in the front rows, the rest of the auditorium consisted of the ordinary two-obol seats. Concerning the arrangements adopted in this part of the theatre a few details have been recorded. It appears that special portions of the auditorium were set apart for the different classes of the community. There was a particular place for the members of the Council of Five Hundred, and another place for the Ephebi, or youths between the age of eighteen and twenty[5]. The women were separated from the men, and the courtesans sat apart from the other women[6]. It is probable that all the

---

[1] Corp. Inscr. Att. iii. 254-260; Aristoph. Equit. 573-576; Theophrast. Char. 5.

[2] Aeschin. Fals. Leg. § 111, Ctesiph. § 76; Dem. de Cor. § 28; Corp. Inscr. Att. ii. 164; Cic. de Senect. § 63; Val. Max. iii. 5.

[3] See chap. i. p. 46.

[4] Aeschin. Ctesiph. § 154; Plut. X Orat., prephisms I and II, p. 851 A-F.

[5] Schol. Aristoph. Av. 795; Poll. iv. 122 βουλευτικὸν μέρος τοῦ θεάτρου καὶ ἐφηβικόν.

[6] Schol. Aristoph. Eccles. 22.

women sat at the back of the theatre, at a long distance from the stage. Foreigners also seem usually to have been confined to the back seats[1]. The amphitheatre of seats was divided into thirteen blocks by the passages which ran upwards from the orchestra. It is a very plausible conjecture that in the arrangement of the audience each tribe had a special block assigned to it. Not that there was any correspondence between the number of the blocks and the number of the tribes. The blocks of seats were thirteen from the first: the tribes were originally ten, and were only raised in later times to twelve and thirteen. If therefore particular blocks were really appropriated to particular tribes, there must have been from one to three blocks unappropriated during a considerable period of Athenian history. But the recent excavations in the theatre afford grounds for inferring that there was a connexion between certain blocks and certain tribes, and the thing is not improbable in itself[2]. The tribal divisions played a large part in the various details of Attic administration, and an arrangement by tribes would have greatly facilitated the process of distributing the enormous mass of spectators among their proper seats.

Before leaving this part of the subject it may be useful to give a complete list of the priests and officials for whom the front row was reserved in later times. It is still possible, as

[1] Aristoph. Pax 962-966 καὶ τοῖς θεαταῖς ῥίπτε τῶν κριθῶν. ΟΙ. ἰδοῦ. | ΤΡ. ἔδωκας ἤδη; ΟΙ. νὴ τὸν Ἑρμῆν, ὥστε γε | ... οὐκ ἔστιν οὐδεὶς ὅστις οὐ κριθὴν ἔχει. | ΤΡ. οὐχ αἱ γυναῖκές γ' ἔλαβον. Alexis, Γυναικοκρατία, fr. 1 (Meineke, Frag. Com. Gr. iii. p. 402) ἐνταῦθα περὶ τὴν ἐσχάτην δεῖ κερκίδα | ὑμᾶς καθιζούσας θεωρεῖν ὡς ξένας.

[2] In the central block, on the third step, was a statue of Hadrian, of which the basis is still preserved, erected in 112 A.D. by the Areopagus, the Council of Six Hundred, and the people of Athens (C. I. A. ii. 464). Besides this, the bases of three other statues of Hadrian, erected by different tribes, are still in existence. They are all on the second step. The first, erected by the tribe Erectheis, is in the first block from the eastern end; the second, erected by the tribe Acamanthis, is in the sixth block from the eastern end; the third, erected by the tribe Oeneis, is in the sixth block from the western end (C. I. A. iii. 466-468). Thus the place of each statue in the series of blocks corresponded exactly with the place of the tribe in the official list of tribes. It is therefore a highly plausible conjecture that, in addition to the statue of Hadrian in the central block, there were twelve other statues erected by the twelve tribes in the remaining blocks; and that each tribe had a special block appropriated to itself. See Benndorf, Beiträge zur Kentniss des att. Theaters p. 4 ff.

already stated, to determine the occupants of fifty-four out of the sixty-seven seats; and the arrangement, with a few exceptions, is that of Hadrian's time[1]. The list of names is not

without interest, as it enables us, better than any description, to form a general conception of the sort of arrangement which

[1] Corp. Inscr. Att. iii. 240–298. There is a very full account of the inscriptions on the thrones in Wheeler's article on the Theatre of Dionysus, in Papers of the American School of Classical Studies at Athens vol. i. p. 152 ff.

was probably adopted at an earlier period. It also affords a curious glimpse into the religious side of the old Athenian life, and helps us to realise the variety and multiplicity of priests, deities, and ceremonials. In the very centre of the front row, in the best place in the whole theatre, sat the priest of Dionysus Eleuthereus, on a throne of elaborate workmanship. A representation of the throne is here inserted [1]. As the theatre was regarded as a temple of Dionysus, and the drama was a celebration in his honour, it was only fitting that his priest should occupy the most conspicuous and distinguished position. There is a reference to the arrangement in the Frogs of Aristophanes, in the scene where Dionysus is terrified by the goblins in Hades, and desperately appeals to his own priest for protection [2]. Of the thirty-three seats to the left of the priest of Dionysus the occupants of twenty are still known, and were as follows:—

Priest of Zeus the Protector of the City.
The Sacrificer.
The Hieromnemon [3].
Priest and Chief Priest of Augustus Caesar.
Priest of Hadrian Eleuthereus.
Chief Archon.
King Archon.
Polemarch.
The Six Thesmothetae.
The Iacchus-carrier [4].
The Sacred Herald.
Priest of Asclepius the Healer.
Fire-bringer from the Acropolis [5].
Priest of the People, the Graces, and Rome.
Holy Herald and Priest.

[1] The illustration is taken from Zeitschrift für bildende Kunst vol. xiii. p. 196. On the back of the chair are depicted two Satyrs, holding a bunch of grapes. In the front, underneath the seat, are two Oriental figures, engaged in a fight with winged lions. On the arms of the throne are figures of Cupids, setting cocks to fight. The appropriateness of the Satyrs, as a decoration in the theatre of Dionysus, is obvious. The cocks, no doubt, refer to the annual cock-fight held in the theatre (see above, chap. iii. p. 162). The significance of the Oriental figures has not yet been explained.

[2] Aristoph. Ran. 297.

[3] I. e. the representative of Athens at the Amphictyonic Council.

[4] I. e. the priest who carried the Iacchus, or sacred statue of Dionysus, at the Eleusinian procession.

[5] I. e. the priest who looked after the sacrificial fire in the temple of Athênê on the Acropolis.

All the thrones to the right hand of the priest of Dionysus have been preserved, and were occupied by the following persons:—

> Interpreter appointed by the Pythian Oracle[1].
> Priest of Olympian Zeus.
> Hierophant.
> Priest of Delian Apollo.
> Priest of Poseidon the Nourisher.
> Fire-bringer of the Graces, and of Artemis of the Tower.
> Interpreter chosen from the Eupatridae by the people for life.
> Priest of Poseidon the Earth-holder and Poseidon Erectheus.
> Priest of Artemis Colaenis.
> Priest of Dionysus the Singer, chosen from the Euneidae.
> Bullock-keeper of Palladian Zeus.
> Priest of Zeus of the Council and Athênê of the Council[2].
> Priest of Zeus the Deliverer and Athênê the Deliverer.
> Priest of Antinous the Dancer, chosen from the Company of Actors[3].
> Priest of Apollo Patrôus.
> Priest of Dionysus the Singer, chosen from the Company of Actors.
> Priest of Glory and Order.
> Priest of Asclepius.
> Priest of the Muses.
> Priest of Zeus the god of Friendship.
> Priest of the Twelve Gods.
> Statue-cleanser of Zeus at Pisa.
> Priest of the Lycean Apollo.
> Statue-cleanser of Olympian Zeus in the City.
> Priest of the Dioscuri and the Hero Epitegius[4].
> Priest of Heavenly Nemesis.
> Priest of Hephaestus.
> Priest of Apollo the Laurel-wearer.
> Priest of Dionysus of Aulon.
> The Stone-carrier[5].
> Priest of Theseus.
> Bullock-keeper of Zeus the Accomplisher.
> Priest of Demeter and Persephone.

The priests enumerated here were the principal dignitaries in the Athenian hierarchy. Behind them sat a large gathering

---

[1] He was one of the three Exegetae, or Interpreters of sacred law, and was appointed by the Pythian oracle. A second was chosen by the people from the Eupatridae, and also had a seat in the front row.

[2] They were the guardians of the βουλή, and their altars were in the βουλευτήριον.

[3] This Antinous was a favourite of Hadrian's, and was drowned in the Nile, and afterwards deified.

[4] Unknown.

[5] Probably an official who carried a sacred stone in some procession; but nothing is known about him.

of inferior priests and priestesses. Their presence in such numbers at performances like the Old and Middle Comedy affords a curious illustration of the religious sentiment of the Athenians, and indicates clearly that the coarseness of the early comedy, and its burlesque representations of the gods and their adventures, did not constitute any offence against religion, but formed an appropriate element in the worship of Dionysus.

§ 4. *Various arrangements in connexion with the Audience.*

The performance of plays began soon after sunrise, and continued all day long without intermission. There was no such thing as an interval for refreshments; one play followed another in rapid succession [1]. Apart from direct evidence upon the subject, it is manifest that, considering the large number of plays which had to be gone through in the time, any delay would have been out of the question. Consequently the spectators were careful to have a good meal before starting for the theatre [2]. There was also a plentiful consumption of wine and various light refreshments in the course of the actual performances. The time for such an indulgence was during the tedious portions of a play, but when one of the great actors came upon the stage, the provisions were laid aside, and the audience became all attention [3].

The theatre must have presented a bright and festive appearance. Crowns were worn in honour of Dionysus by the express command of the oracle [4]. The gaily-coloured dresses of the spectators would add greatly to the brilliancy of the scene. At the same time the comfort of the audience was not very much

---

[1] Aeschin. Ctesiph. § 76 ἅμα τῇ ἡμέρᾳ ἡγεῖτο τοῖς πρέσβεσιν εἰς τὸ θέατρον. Dem. Meid. § 74 ἐγὼ δ' ὑπ' ἐχθροῦ νήφοντος, ἕωθεν, κ.τ.λ. Aristoph. Av. 786-789 αὐτίχ' ὑμῶν τῶν θεατῶν εἴ τις ἦν ὑπόπτερος, | εἶτα πεινῶν τοῖς χοροῖσι τῶν τραγῳδῶν ἤχθετο, | ἐκπτόμενος ἂν οὗτος ἠρίστησεν ἐλθὼν οἴκαδε, | κᾆτ' ἂν ἐμπλησθεὶς ἐφ' ἡμᾶς αὖθις αὖ κατέπτατο.

[2] Philochorus ap. Athen. p. 464 E Ἀθηναῖοι τοῖς Διονυσιακοῖς ἀγῶσι τὸ μὲν πρῶτον ἠριστηκότες καὶ πεπωκότες ἐβάδιζον ἐπὶ τὴν θέαν.

[3] Philochor. ap. Athen. l.c. παρὰ δὲ τὸν ἀγῶνα πάντα οἶνος αὐτοῖς ᾠνοχοεῖτο καὶ τραγήματα παρεφέρετο. Aristot. Eth. Nic. x. 5 καὶ ἐν τοῖς θεάτροις οἱ τραγηματίζοντες, ὅταν φαῦλοι οἱ ἀγωνιζόμενοι ὦσι, τότε μάλιστ' αὐτὸ δρῶσιν.

[4] Philochor. ap. Athen. l.c. καὶ ἐστεφανωμένοι ἐθεώρουν. Dem. Meid. § 52.

consulted. The seats were of stone, and without backs; and the people had to sit there all day long, packed together as closely as was possible. Rich men brought cushions and carpets with them. Aeschines draws a contemptuous picture of Demosthenes escorting Philip's ambassadors to the theatre in person, and arranging their cushions and spreading their carpets with his own hands. The toady in Theophrastus, when he accompanies a wealthy man to the theatre, is careful to take the cushion out of the slave's hands, and to insist upon placing it ready for his patron[1]. But luxuries of this kind were confined to the richer classes, and the common people were probably contented with the stone seats.

There was no shelter from the sun. The theatre faced towards the south, and was entirely uncovered. But as the dramatic performances took place at the end of the winter, or early in the spring, the heat would not usually be excessive. Probably the sun was in most cases very welcome. If however any shelter was required, hats appear to have been worn, though the Athenians generally went bare-headed except upon a journey[2]. It has been suggested that small awnings were sometimes erected upon rods by individual spectators for their own convenience, and that the 'purple cloths' which Demosthenes spread out for Philip's ambassadors were awnings of this description[3]. But it is most improbable that anything of the kind was permitted, at any rate during the period of the democracy. Such awnings would have seriously interfered with the view of the persons immediately behind.

To keep order among a gathering of about thirty thousand persons, crowded together in a comparatively small space, must have been a matter of some difficulty. Certain officers called

---

[1] Aeschin. Ctesiph. § 76, Fals. Leg. § 111; Theophrast. Char. 2.

[2] Suidas v. Δράκων· ὑπὸ τῶν Αἰγινητῶν ἐν τῷ θεάτρῳ, ἐπιρριψάντων αὐτῷ ἐπὶ τὴν κεφαλὴν πετάσους πλείονας καὶ χιτῶνας καὶ ἱμάτια, ἀπεπνίγη.

[3] In one or two places in the theatre of Dionysus holes appear to have been cut in the stone for the reception of rods, to support small awnings; but they date from Roman times, and their purpose is not quite certain. The φοινικίδες mentioned by Aeschines (Ctesiph. § 76) were probably coverlets or carpets.

'staff-bearers' were stationed in the theatre for the purpose [1]. Disturbances were not infrequent, and arose from various causes. Sometimes the rivalry between two choregi resulted in actual violence. For example, on one occasion, when Taureas and Alcibiades were competitors in a dithyrambic contest, a fight broke out between them, in the course of which Alcibiades, being the stronger man of the two, drove Taureas out of the orchestra [2]. That the feeling between the choregi often ran very high has already been pointed out in a previous chapter. Disputes about seats were another fertile source of disturbance. With the exception of the front row, the individual places were not separated from one another, but the people sat together on the long stone benches. Such an arrangement was very likely to cause confusion. Demosthenes mentions the case of a highly distinguished citizen, who ran great risk of being put to death, owing to his having forcibly ejected a man from his seat. Personal violence in the theatre was regarded as a crime against religion, and was strictly prohibited. If any dispute arose, the proper course was to appeal to the officers; and the man who took the law into his own hands was guilty of a capital offence [3].

§ 5. *Character of Attic Audiences.*

The Athenians were a lively audience, and gave expression to their feelings in the most unmistakable manner. The noise and uproar produced by an excited crowd of thirty thousand persons must have been of a deafening character, and is described in the most uncomplimentary language by Plato [4]. It was exceedingly difficult for the judges to resist such demonstrations, and to vote in accordance with their own private judgment. The ordinary modes of signifying pleasure or disgust were much the same in ancient as in modern times, and consisted of hisses and groans on the one hand, and shouts and clapping of hands on the other [5]. The Athenians had also a peculiar way of marking their dis-

---

[1] Called ῥαβδοφόροι (Schol. Aristoph. Pax 734), and ῥαβδοῦχοι (Pax 734).
[2] Andocid. Alcibiad. § 20.
[3] Dem. Meid. §§ 178, 179.
[4] Plat. Legg. 700 C.
[5] Dem. Meid. §§ 14, 226; Alciphron, Epist. iii. 71.

approval of a performance by kicking with the heels of their sandals against the front of the stone benches on which they were sitting[1]. Stones were occasionally thrown by an irate audience. Aeschines was hissed off the stage, and 'almost stoned to death,' in the course of his theatrical career. There is an allusion to the practice in the story of the second-rate musician, who borrowed a supply of stone from a friend in order to build a house, and promised to repay him with the stones he collected from his next performance in public[2]. Country audiences in the Attic demes used figs and olives, and similar missiles, for pelting unpopular actors[3]. On the other hand, encores were not unknown, if particular passages took the fancy of the audience. Socrates is said to have encored the first three lines of the Orestes of Euripides[4].

If the Athenians were dissatisfied with an actor or a play, they had no hesitation about revealing the fact, but promptly put a stop to the performance by means of hisses and groans and stamping with the heels. They were able to do so with greater readiness, as several plays were always performed in succession, and they could call for the next play, without bringing the entertainment to a close. In this way they sometimes got through the programme very rapidly. There is an instance of such an occurrence in the story of the comic actor Hermon, whose play should naturally have come on late in the day; but as all the previous performers were promptly hissed off the stage one after another, he was called upon much sooner than he expected, and in consequence was not ready to appear[5]. If the tale about the comic poet Diphilus is true, it would seem that even the authors of very unsuccessful plays were sometimes forcibly ejected from the theatre[6].

A few scattered notices and descriptions, referring to the

[1] Poll. iv. 122 τὸ μέντοι τὰ ἰδώλια ταῖς πτέρναις κατακρούειν πτερνοκοπεῖν ἔλεγον· ἐποίουν δὲ τοῦτο ὁπότε τινὰ ἐκβάλοιεν.
[2] Dem. Fals. Leg. § 337; Athen. p. 245 E.
[3] Dem. de Cor. § 262.
[4] Cic. Tusc. iv. § 63. Αὖθις seems to have been the word used; cp. Xen. Symp. ix. 4 ἅμα δὲ ἐβόων αὖθις.
[5] Poll. iv. 88. he word for hissing an actor off the stage was ἐκβάλλειν; to be hissed off was ἐκπίπτειν. See Dem. de Cor. § 265, Poll. iv. 122.
[6] Athen. p. 583 F.

spectators in the Athenian theatre, show that human nature was very much the same in ancient times as at the present day. Certain types of character, which were generally to be met with among an Attic audience, will easily be recognised as familiar figures. There was the man of taste, who prided himself upon his superior discernment, and used to hiss when everyone else was applauding, and clap when every one else was silent[1]. There was the person who made himself objectionable to his neighbours by whistling an accompaniment to tunes which happened to please him[2]. There were the 'young men of the town,' who took a malign pleasure in hissing a play off the stage[3]. There were the people who brought out their provisions during the less exciting parts of the entertainment[4]. There was the somnolent individual who slept peacefully through tragedies and comedies, and was not even waked up by the noise of the audience going away[5]. Certain indications show that the employment of the claque was not unknown to Greek actors and poets. The parasite Philaporus, who had recently taken up the profession of an actor, and was anxious about the result of his first public appearance, writes to a friend to ask him to come with a large body of supporters, and drown with their applause the hisses of the critical part of the audience. Philemon, in spite of his inferior talents as a comic writer, is said to have frequently won victories from Menander by practices of this kind[6].

The character of the Athenian audience as a whole is well exemplified by the stories of their treatment of individual poets. Although they were willing to tolerate the utmost ribaldry upon the stage, and to allow the gods and sacred legends to be burlesqued in the most ridiculous fashion, they were at the same time extremely orthodox in regard to the national religion. Any atheistical sentiments, and any violations of their religious law, were liable to provoke an outburst of the greatest violence.

---

[1] Theophrast. Char. 11.
[2] Theophrast. Char. l.c.
[3] Alciphron, Epist. iii. 71 ἵνα, κἄν τι λάθωμεν ἀποσφαλέντες, μὴ λάβῃ χώραν τὰ ἀστικὰ μειράκια κλώζειν ἢ συρίττειν.
[4] Aristot. Eth. Nic. x. 5.
[5] Theophrast. Char. 14.
[6] Alciphron, Epist. iii. 71 ; Aul. Gell. N. A. xvii. 4.

Aeschylus on one occasion was nearly killed in the theatre itself, because he was supposed to have revealed part of the mysteries in the course of a tragedy. He was only saved by flying for refuge to the altar of Dionysus in the orchestra[1]. Euripides also caused a great uproar by beginning his Melanippe with the line, 'Zeus, whoever Zeus be, for I know not save by report,' &c. In a subsequent production of a revised version of the play he altered the line to 'Zeus, as is reported by truth,[2]' &c. In the same way sentiments which violated the moral feeling of the audience were received with intense indignation, and sometimes resulted in the stoppage of the play. The Danaë of Euripides is said to have been nearly hissed off the stage because of a passage in praise of money[3]. On the other hand, wise and noble sentiments excited great enthusiasm. Aristophanes was rewarded with a chaplet from the sacred olive because of the splendid passage in which he counsels mercy to the disfranchised citizens. Sophocles is said to have been appointed one of the generals in the Samian expedition on account of the excellent political wisdom shown in certain passages of the Antigone[4]. The partiality of the Athenians for idealism in art is shown by the reception which they gave to Phrynichus' tragedy of the Capture of Miletus, an historical drama in which the misfortunes of the Ionians were forcibly portrayed. So far from admiring the skill of the poet, they fined him a thousand drachmas for reminding them of the miseries of their kinsfolk, and passed a law forbidding the reproduction of this particular play[5].

The enthusiasm of the Athenians for the drama was unbounded. Nowhere was the theatre more crowded. In the words of one of the old historians they 'spent the public revenues on their festivals, were more familiar with the stage than with the camp, and paid more regard to verse-makers than

---

[1] Aristot. Eth. Nic. iii. 2, and Eustath. ad loc.
[2] Plut. Amator. 756 C; Nauck, Trag. Gr. Frag. p. 405.
[3] Senec. Epist. 115; Nauck, Trag. Gr. Frag. p. 363.
[4] Vit. Aristoph. (Dindf. Prolegom. de Com. p. 12); Arg. to Soph. Antig.
[5] Herod. vi. 21.

to generals[1].' The speeches of Demosthenes are full of complaints in the same strain. The eagerness with which dramatic victories were coveted, and the elaborate monuments erected to commemorate them, have already been referred to in a previous chapter. It was not however till the middle of the fourth century that the devotion to this and similar amusements grew to such a height as to become a positive vice, and to sap the military energies of the people. The Athenians of the fifth century showed that enthusiasm for art and music and the drama was not inconsistent with energy of character. As a matter of fact the very greatest period of the Attic drama is also the period of the political supremacy of Athens.

As far as intelligence and discrimination are concerned, the Athenian audiences were probably superior to any audience of the same size which has ever been brought together. Their keen and rapid intellect was a subject of frequent praise among the ancients, and was ascribed to the exhilarating influence of the Attic climate[2]. They were especially distinguished for the refinement of their taste in matters of art and literature, and for the soberness of judgment with which they rejected any sort of florid exuberance. That they were keenly alive to the attractions of beauty of form and chastened simplicity of style is proved by the fact that Sophocles was by far the most successful of their tragic poets. Though Euripides became more popular among the later Greeks, Sophocles in his own lifetime obtained far more victories than any other tragic writer[3]. At the same time it is easy to form an exaggerated idea of the refinement of an Attic audience. They were drawn from all classes of the people, and a large proportion were ignorant and uncultured. Plato speaks in the most disparaging terms of them, and charges them with having corrupted the dramatic poets, and brought them down to

---

[1] Justin. 17. 9. The passage was very likely from Theopompus.
[2] Dem. Olynth. iii. § 15 καὶ γνῶναι πάντων ὑμεῖς ὀξύτατοι τὰ ῥηθέντα. Cic. de Fato § 7 Athenis tenue caelum, ex quo acutiores etiam putantur Attici.
[3] Cic. Orat. § 25 (Athenienses) quorum semper fuit prudens sincerumque iudicium, nihil ut possent nisi incorruptum audire et elegans; § 27 ad Atticorum igitur aures teretes et religiosas qui se accommodant, ii sunt existimandi Attice dicere.

their own level[1]. His evidence is perhaps rather prejudiced. But Aristotle, who had much greater faith in popular judgment, is not very complimentary. He divides the theatrical audience into two classes, the refined and cultured class on the one hand, and the mass of rough and ignorant artisans on the other. One of his objections to the profession of an actor or musician is that he must accommodate himself to the level of the ignorant part of his audience[2]. He mentions examples in the Poetics of the low level of popular taste, from which it appears that the average spectator in ancient times was, like his modern counterpart, fond of 'happy terminations.' He cared little for the artistic requirements of the composition; his desire was to see virtue rewarded, and vice punished, at the end of a play. Then again, a large part of the audience, Aristotle remarks, were so ignorant as to be unacquainted with the ordinary facts of mythology, which formed the basis of most tragedies. In judging a play, they paid more regard to the actor's voice than to the poet's genius[3]. At the same time, in spite of depreciatory criticisms, it must be remembered that the true criterion of a people's taste is to be found in the character of the popular favourites. The victorious career of Sophocles, lasting over more than fifty years, is a convincing proof of the fact that, at any rate during the fifth century, the dramatic taste of the Athenians was altogether higher than that of an ordinary populai audience.

---

[1] Plat. Legg. 659 B, C.
[2] Aristot. Pol. viii. 7 ἐπεὶ δ' ὁ θεατὴς διττός, ὁ μὲν ἐλεύθερος καὶ πεπαιδευμένος, ὁ δὲ φορτικὸς ἐκ βαναύσων καὶ θητῶν καὶ ἄλλων τοιούτων συγκείμενος, ibid. 6 ὁ γὰρ θεατὴς φορτικὸς ὢν μεταβάλλειν εἴωθε τὴν μουσικήν, ὥστε καὶ τοὺς τεχνίτας τοὺς πρὸς αὐτὸν μελετῶντας αὐτούς τε ποιούς τινας ποιεῖ.
[3] Aristot. Poet. c. 13 δευτέρα δ' ἡ πρώτη λεγομένη ὑπὸ τινῶν ἐστι σύστασις ἡ διπλῆν τε τὴν σύστασιν ἔχουσα καθάπερ ἡ 'Οδύσσεια καὶ τελευτῶσα ἐξ ἐναντίας τοῖς βελτίοσι καὶ χείροσιν. δοκεῖ δὲ εἶναι πρώτη διὰ τὴν τῶν θεάτρων ἀσθένειαν, ἀκολουθοῦσι γὰρ οἱ ποιηταὶ κατ' εὐχὴν ποιοῦντες τοῖς θεαταῖς. Ibid. c. 9 (of the old legends) ἐπεὶ καὶ τὰ γνώριμα ὀλίγοις γνώριμά ἐστιν, ἀλλ' ὅμως εὐφραίνει πάντας. Id. Rhet. iii. 1 ἐκεῖ μεῖζον δύνανται νῦν τῶν ποιητῶν οἱ ὑποκριταί.

APPENDIX A.

The information concerning the dates at which the plays of the great Attic dramatists were produced, and the success which they met with in the competitions, is derived from various brief notices, which occur mostly in the Arguments prefixed to the different plays, and which were ultimately derived from Aristotle's Didascaliae, or from other collections of the same kind (see chap. i. p. 63). A complete list of these notices is here appended:—

472 B.C.

Arg. Aesch. Persae : 'Επὶ Μένωνος τραγῳδῶν Αἰσχύλος ἐνίκα Φινεῖ, Πέρσαις, Γλαύκῳ, Προμηθεῖ.

467 B.C.

Arg. Aesch. Septem : 'Εδιδάχθη ἐπὶ Θεαγενίδου ὀλυμπιάδι οη'. ἐνίκα Λαΐῳ, Οἰδίποδι, Ἑπτὰ ἐπὶ Θήβας, Σφιγγὶ σατυρικῇ. δεύτερος Ἀριστίας Περσεῖ, Ταντάλῳ, Παλαισταῖς σατυρικοῖς τοῖς Πρατίνου πατρός. τρίτος Πολυφράδμων Λυκουργείᾳ τετραλογίᾳ.

458 B.C.

Arg. Aesch. Agamemnon : 'Εδιδάχθη τὸ δρᾶμα ἐπὶ ἄρχοντος Φιλοκλέους, ὀλυμπιάδι ὀγδοηκοστῇ ἔτει δευτέρῳ. πρῶτος Αἰσχύλος Ἀγαμέμνονι, Χοηφόροις, Εὐμενίσι, Πρωτεῖ σατυρικῷ. ἐχορήγει Ξενοκλῆς Ἀφιδνεύς.

455 B.C.

Vit. Eurip. p. 4 Dindf. : "Ἤρξατο δὲ διδάσκειν (ὁ Εὐριπίδης) ἐπὶ Καλλίου ἄρχοντος κατ' ὀλυμπιάδα πα' ἔτει α', πρῶτον δ' ἐδίδαξε τὰς Πελιάδας, ὅτε καὶ τρίτος ἐγένετο.

438 B.C.

Arg. Eur. Alcestis : 'Εδιδάχθη ἐπὶ Γλαυκίνου ἄρχοντος ὀλυμπιάδι πε'. πρῶτος ἦν Σοφοκλῆς, δεύτερος Εὐριπίδης Κρήσσαις, Ἀλκμαίωνι τῷ διὰ Ψωφῖδος, Τηλέφῳ, Ἀλκήστιδι.

431 B.C.

Arg. Eur. Medea : 'Εδιδάχθη ἐπὶ Πυθοδώρου ἄρχοντος κατὰ τὴν ὀγδοηκοστὴν ἑβδόμην ὀλυμπιάδα. πρῶτος Εὐφορίων, δεύτερος Σοφοκλῆς, τρίτος Εὐριπίδης Μηδείᾳ, Φιλοκτήτῃ, Δίκτυϊ, Θερισταῖς σατύροις. οὐ σώζεται.

430 B.C. (?)

Aristid. vol. ii. p. 334 Dindf. : Σοφοκλῆς Φιλοκλέους ἡττᾶτο ἐν Ἀθηναίοις τὸν Οἰδίπουν, ὦ Ζεῦ καὶ θεοί.

428 B.C.

Arg. Eur. Hippolytus: Ἐδιδάχθη ἐπὶ Ἀμείνονος ἄρχοντος ὀλυμπιάδι ὀγδοηκοστῇ ἑβδόμῃ, ἔτει τετάρτῳ. πρῶτος Εὐριπίδης, δεύτερος Ἰοφῶν, τρίτος Ἴων.

425 B.C.

Arg. Arist. Acharnenses: Ἐδιδάχθη ἐπὶ Εὐθύνου ἄρχοντος ἐν Ληναίοις διὰ Καλλιστράτου· καὶ πρῶτος ἦν. δεύτερος Κρατῖνος Χειμαζομένοις· οὐ σώζονται. τρίτος Εὔπολις Νουμηνίαις.

424 B.C.

Arg. Arist. Equites: Ἐδιδάχθη τὸ δρᾶμα ἐπὶ Στρατοκλέους ἄρχοντος δημοσίᾳ εἰς Λήναια, δι' αὐτοῦ τοῦ Ἀριστοφάνους. πρῶτος ἐνίκα· δεύτερος Κρατῖνος Σατύροις· τρίτος Ἀριστομένης Ὑλοφόροις.

423 B.C.

Arg. Arist. Nubes: Αἱ πρῶται Νεφέλαι ἐν ἄστει ἐδιδάχθησαν ἐπὶ ἄρχοντος Ἰσάρχου, ὅτε Κρατῖνος μὲν ἐνίκα Πυτίνῃ, Ἀμειψίας δὲ Κόννῳ.

422 B.C.

Arg. Arist. Nubes: Αἱ δὲ δεύτεραι Νεφέλαι ἐπὶ Ἀμεινίου ἄρχοντος. Arg. Arist. Vespae: Ἐδιδάχθη ἐπὶ ἄρχοντος Ἀμεινίου διὰ Φιλωνίδου εἰς Λήναια· καὶ ἐνίκα πρῶτος. δεύτερος ἦν Φιλωνίδης Προάγωνι, Λεύκων Πρέσβεσι τρίτος.

421 B.C.

Arg. Arist. Pax: Ἐνίκησε δὲ τῷ δράματι ὁ ποιητὴς ἐπὶ ἄρχοντος Ἀλκαίου, ἐν ἄστει. πρῶτος Εὔπολις Κόλαξι, δεύτερος Ἀριστοφάνης Εἰρήνῃ, τρίτος Λεύκων Φράτορσι.

415 B.C.

Ael. Var. Hist. ii. 8: Κατὰ τὴν πρώτην καὶ ἐνενηκοστὴν ὀλυμπιάδα .... ἀντηγωνίσαντο ἀλλήλοις Ξενοκλῆς καὶ Εὐριπίδης· καὶ πρῶτός γε ἦν Ξενοκλῆς, ὅστις ποτὲ οὗτός ἐστιν, Οἰδίποδι καὶ Λυκάονι καὶ Βάκχαις καὶ Ἀθάμαντι σατυρικῷ. τούτου δεύτερος Εὐριπίδης ἦν Ἀλεξάνδρῳ καὶ Παλαμήδει καὶ Τρῴασι καὶ Σισύφῳ σατυρικῷ.

414 B.C.

Arg. Arist. Aves: Ἐδιδάχθη ἐπὶ Χαβρίου διὰ Καλλιστράτου ἐν ἄστει, ὃς ἦν δεύτερος τοῖς Ὄρνισι, πρῶτος Ἀμειψίας Κωμασταῖς, τρίτος Φρύνιχος Μονοτρόπῳ.

412 B.C.

Schol. Arist. Ran. 53: Ἡ δὲ Ἀνδρομέδα ὀγδόῳ ἔτει προεισῆλθεν. Schol. Arist. Thesm. 1012: συνδεδίδακται γὰρ τῇ Ἑλένῃ.

411 B.C. (?)

Arg. Eur. Phoenissae: Ἐδιδάχθη ἐπὶ Ναυσικράτους ἄρχοντος ὀλυμπιάδ .... πρῶτος ...... δεύτερος Εὐριπίδης, τρίτος .... ὁ Οἰνόμαος καὶ Χρύσιππος καὶ Φοίνισσαι καὶ ... σατυρ ...... οὐ σώζεται.

APPENDIX B. 321

409 B.C.

Arg. Soph. Philoctetes : 'Εδιδάχθη ἐπὶ Γλαυκίππου. πρῶτος ἦν Σοφοκλῆς.

408 B.C.

Schol. Eur. Orest. 371 : Πρὸ γὰρ Διοκλέους, ἐφ' οὗ τὸν 'Ορέστην ἐδίδαξε.

405 B.C.

Arg. Arist. Ranae : 'Εδιδάχθη ἐπὶ Καλλίου τοῦ μετὰ 'Αντιγένη διὰ Φιλωνίδου εἰς Λήναια. πρῶτος ἦν· Φρύνιχος δεύτερος Μούσαις· Πλάτων τρίτος Κλεοφῶντι.

— B.C.

Schol. Arist. Ran. 67 : Οὕτω γὰρ καὶ αἱ Διδασκαλίαι φέρουσι, τελευτήσαντος Εὐριπίδου τὸν υἱὸν αὐτοῦ δεδιδαχέναι ὁμώνυμον ἐν ἄστει 'Ιφιγένειαν τὴν ἐν Αὐλίδι, 'Αλκμαίωνα, Βάκχας.

401 B.C.

Arg. Soph. O.C. : Τὸν ἐπὶ Κολωνῷ Οἰδίποδα ἐπὶ τετελευτηκότι τῷ πάππῳ Σοφοκλῆς ὁ ὑϊδοῦς ἐδίδαξεν, υἱὸς ὢν 'Αρίστωνος, ἐπὶ ἄρχοντος Μίκωνος.

388 B.C.

Arg. Arist. Plutus : 'Εδιδάχθη ἐπὶ ἄρχοντος 'Αντιπάτρου, ἀνταγωνιζομένου αὐτῷ Νικοχάρους μὲν Λάκωσιν, 'Αριστομένους δὲ 'Αδμήτῳ, Νικοφῶντος δὲ 'Αδώνιδι, 'Αλκαίου δὲ Πασιφάῃ.

APPENDIX B.

OUR knowledge of the Athenian drama has been very much increased in recent years by the discovery at Athens of a large number of inscriptions relating to dramatic contests. A complete collection of all the inscriptions which bear upon this subject will be found, admirably edited by Köhler, in the Corpus Inscriptionum Atticarum, vol. ii. pt. 2. p. 394 foll. A selection of the most important of them is here appended. They are all copied from Köhler's collection, with the exception of the second on the list, which was only discovered in 1886, and is published in the 'Εφημερὶς 'Αρχαιολογική for that year (p. 269 foll.).

I. List of victors in the four contests at the City Dionysia.

I.

[Ξε]νοκλείδης ἐχορήγει,　　　　　　　　　　Before
[Μ]άγνης ἐδίδασκεν.　　　　　　　　　　　　458 B.C.
Τραγῳδῶν,

Περικλῆς Χολαρ(γεὺς) ἐχορή(γει),
Αἰσχύλος ἐ[δ]ίδασκε[ν].

2.

['Επὶ Φιλο]κλέους, 458 B.C.
[Οἰν]ηὶς παίδων,
Δημόδοκος ἐχορήγει.
'Ιπποθωντὶς ἀνδρῶν,
Εὐκτήμων 'Ελευ(σίνιος) ἐχορή(γει).
Κωμῳδῶν,
Εὐρυκλείδης ἐχορήγει,
Εὐφρόνιος ἐδίδασκε.
Τραγῳδῶν,
Ξενοκλῆς 'Αφιδνα(ῖος) ἐχορή(γει),
Αἰσχύλος ἐδίδασκεν.
'Επὶ ῎Αβρωνος, 457 B.C.
'Ερεχθηὶς παίδων,
Χαρίας 'Αγρυλῆ(θεν) ἐχορή(γει).
Λεωντὶς ἀνδρῶν,
Δεινόστρατος ἐχορή(γει).
Κωμῳδῶν,
. . . . [ἐχο]ρήγ[ει],

3.

[Κωμῳδῶν],
. . . . . Παια[νιεὺς ἐχορήγει],
. . . . . . ος ἐδ[ίδασκεν].
[Τραγῳ]ιδῶν,
[. . . . . . ω]ν Παιανιε[ὺς ἐχορήγει],
[Με]νεκράτης ἐδί[δασκεν],
[ὑπ]οκριτὴς Μυνν[ίσκος].
['Ε]πὶ 'Αλκαίου, 421 B.C.
'Ιπποθωντὶς παίδων,
'Αρίσταρχος Δεκε(λεεὺς) ἐχορή(γει).
Αἰαντὶς ἀνδρῶν,
Δημοσθένης ἐχορήγει.
[Κω]μῳδ[ῶν],
[. . . . . ἐχορ]ή[γει],

4.

Μένανδρο[s . . . .] ἐχορήγει,

Θεύφιλ[ο]s ἐδίδασκεν,
ὑπο[κριτ]ὴ[s] Κλέανδρο[s].
Ἐπὶ Θεοδότου,   386 B.C.
  Ἀντιοχὶς παίδων,
  Εὐηγέτης Παλλ[η]νεὺς [ἐχορήγει].
  Αἰγηὶς ἀνδρῶν,
  Ἰάσων Κολλυτεὺς ἐχορήγει.

5.

Κεκρο[πὶς παίδων],   Middle of
Διοφαν [. . . . ἐχορήγει].   fourth cen-
Κεκροπὶς [ἀνδρῶν],   tury B.C.
Ὀνήτωρ [Μελιτεὺς ἐχορήγει].
Κωμῳδ[ῶν],
Διοπεί[θης . . . . . . ἐχορήγει],
Προκλε[ίδης ἐδίδασκεν].
Τραγῳδ[ῶν],

6.

[Ἐ]πὶ Ἀριστ[ο]φάνους,   330 B.C.
  Οἰν[ηὶς] παίδω[ν],
  . . . . τος [Ἀχα]ρν[εὺς ἐχορή(γει)].
  [Ἱπ]ποθωντὶς ἀν[δ]ρ[ῶν],
  . . . . ος [Πειρ]αιε[ὺς ἐχορή(γει)].

II. Record of tragic contests at the City Dionysia.

[παλαιᾷ]· Νε[οπτόλεμος]
[Ἰφιγε]νείᾳ Εὐ[ριπί]δο[υ]·
[ποη(ταί)]· Ἀστυδάμας
[Ἀχι]λλεῖ, ὑπε(κρίνετο) Θετταλός·
Ἀθάμαντι, ὑπε(κρίνετο) Νεοπτόλ[εμος]·
[Ἀν]τιγόνῃ, ὑπε(κρίνετο) Ἀθηνόδω[ρος]·
[Εὐ]άρετος [δεύ(τερος)] Τεύκρῳ,
[ὑπ]ε(κρίνετο) Ἀθηνόδωρος·
[Ἀχι]λ[λ]εῖ, [ὑπε(κρίνετο)] Θετταλός·
[. . . . . ει], ὑ[πε(κρίνετο) Νε]οπτόλεμος·
[. . . . . . . τ]ρί(τος) [Π]ελιάσιν,
[ὑπε(κρίνετο) Νεοπτ]όλεμος·
Ὀρέστῃ[ι, ὑπε(κρίνετο) Ἀθη]ν[όδωρος]·
Αὔ[γῃ], ὑπε(κρίνετο) Θεττ[αλό]ς·
ὑπο(κριτὴς) Νεοπτόλεμος ἐνίκ[α].

324 APPENDIX B.

    'Επὶ Νικομάχου· σατυρι(κῷ)·   340 B. C.
        Τιμοκλῆς Λυκούργῳ·
        παλαιᾷ· Νεοπτόλεμ[ος]
        'Ορέστῃ Εὐριπίδου·
        [π]οη(ταί)· Ἀστυδάμας
        Παρθενοπαίῳ, ὑπε(κρίνετο) Θετ[ταλός]·
        [Λυκά]ονι, ὑπε(κρίνετο) Νεοπτόλε[μος]·
        ..... οκλῆς δεύ(τερος) Φρίξῳ,
        [ὑπε(κρίνετο)] Θετταλός·
        [Οἰδί]ποδι, ὑπε(κρίνετο) Νεοπτόλ[εμος]·
        [Εὐδρ]ετος τρί(τος)
        [Ἀλκμ]έ[ον]ι, ὑπε(κρίνετο) Θεττα[λός]·
        ...... ῃ, ὑπε(κρίνετο) Νεοπτό[λεμος]·
        [ὑπο(κριτὴς) Θε]ρταλὸς ἐνίκα.
    ['Επὶ Θεο]φράστου· σατυ[ρι(κῷ)]·   339 B. C.
        ...... Φορκίσ[ι]·
        [παλαιᾷ ... ὁ]στρ[ατος]
        [........ Εὐ]ριπί[δου]·

III. Record of tragic contests at the Lenaea.

        [Π]ειρ[ιθόῳ, ...],
        ὑπε(κρίνετο) ....·
        ὑπο(κριτὴς) [....... ἐνίκα].
    'Επὶ [Ἀστυφίλου· ....]   419 B. C.
        Ἀγα[μέμνονι, ...,.........],
        ὑπ[ε(κρίνετο) ....]·
        Ἡρα[κ ......],
        Θησεῖ, ...,
        ὑπ[ε(κρίνετο) ....]·
        ὑπο(κριτὴς) [....... ἐνίκα].
    'Επὶ Ἀρχ[ίου ....]   418 B. C.
        Τυροῖ, Τ............,.........,
        ὑπε(κρίνετο) Λυσικράτ[ης]·
        Καλλίστρατος ....,
        Ἀμφιλόχῳ, Ἰξίο[νι],
        ὑπε(κρίνετο) Καλλιππί[δης]·
        [ὑπ]ο(κριτὴς) Καλλιππί[δης ἐνίκα].
    ['Επ' Ἀ]ντ[ι]φ[ῶ]ντος Σ .....   417 B. C.
        ...... π .....

APPENDIX B.

IV. Records of Comic Contests.

1.

[. . . . . τέ(ταρτος) . . . α]στίδι,
[ὑπε(κρίνετο) 'Αριστόμ]αχος·
['Αντιφάνη]ς πέμ(πτος) 'Ανασῳζο(μένοις),
[ὑπε(κρίνετο) 'Αντ]ιφάνης·
[ὑπο(κριτὴς) . . . .]ώνυμος ἐνίκα.
['Επὶ Δι]οτίμου· Σιμύλος   353 B.C.
. . . . . σίᾳ, ὑπε(κρίνετο) 'Αριστόμαχος·
Διόδωρος δεύ(τερος) Νεκρῷ,
ὑπε(κρίνετο) 'Αριστόμαχος·
Διόδωρος τρί(τος) Μαινομένω[ι],
ὑπε(κρίνετο) Κηφίσιος·
[Φοι]νικ[ίδ]ης τέ(ταρτος) Ποητεῖ,
[ὑπε(κρίνετο) . . . . .]ης·

2.

[Τιμ]όσ[τρατος Λυτ[ρουμένῳ],   About
ὑπε(κρίνετο) Διογείτων·   190 B.C.
ὑπο(κριτὴς) Κράτης ἐνίκα.
'Επὶ Συμμάχου οὐκ ἐγ[ένετο].
'Επὶ Θεοξένου οὐκ [ἐγένετο].
'Επὶ Ζωπύρου· [παλαιᾷ]·
  'Εράτων Με . . . . ·
  ποη(ταί)· Λαιν . . . . .

3.

['Επὶ . . . . παλαιᾷ]·   About
. . . . M . . . . ·   180 B.C.
[ποη(ταί)]· Κρίτων 'Εφεσίοις,
[ὑ]πε(κρίνετο) Σώφιλος·
Παράμονος Ναναγῷ,
ὑπε(κρίνετο) 'Ονήσιμος·
Τιμόστρατος Φιλοικείῳ,
ὑπε(κρίνετο) Καλλίστρατος·
Σωγένης Φιλοδεσπότῳ,
ὑπε(κρίνετο) 'Εκαταῖος·
Φιλήμων νεώ(τερος) Μιλησίᾳ,
ὑπε(κρίνετο) Κράτης·
ὑπο(κριτὴς) 'Ονήσιμος ἐνίκ[α].

326 APPENDIX B.

Επὶ Ἑρμογένου οὐκ [ἐγέ]νετο.
Ἐπὶ Τιμησιάν[ακτος· π]αλαιᾷ·
   Φιλόστρατο[ς Ἀποκλε]ιομένει Ποσει[δίππου]·
   ποη(ταί)· . . . . κλήρῳ,
   ὑπε(κρίνετο) . . . .

4.

[Παρά]μονος Χορηγοῦντι,   About
[ὑπε(κρίνετο)]·Μόνιμος·   170 B.C.
[ὑπ]ο(κριτὴς) Κριτόδημος ἐνίκα.
[Ἐ]πὶ Εὐνίκου οὐκ ἐγένε[το].
Ἐπὶ Ξενοκλέους· παλαι[ᾷ]·
   Μόνιμος Φάσματι Μεν[άνδρου]·
   ποη(ταί)· Παράμονος τεθνηκὼς . . . . ις,
   ὑπε(κρίνετο) Δάμων·
   Κρίτων Αἰτωλῷ,
   ὑπε(κρίνετο) Μόνιμος·
   Βίοττος Ποητεῖ,
   ὑπε(κρίνετο) Δάμων·
   Λάμπυτος . . . . ,
   ὑπε(κρίνετο) Κα . . . .
   Ἐπικ[ράτης . . . . . .],
   ὑπε(κρίνετο) . . . . . .].

5.

[Ἐπὶ] Εὐερ[γ . . . . . οὐκ ἐγένετο].   About
[Ἐ]πὶ Ἐραστο[ῦ οὐκ ἐγένετο].   165 B.C.
Ἐπὶ Ποσει[δωνίου οὐκ ἐγένετο].
. . . .
Ἐπὶ Ἀρίσ[τολα· παλαιᾷ]·
   Ἡρακ . . . .

6.

[ὑπε(κρίνετο) Καβεί]ριχος·   About
[Ἐπ]ιγέ[ν]ης Λυτρουμένῳ,   160 B.C.
ὑπε(κρίνετο) Καβείριχος·
ὑπυ(κριτὴς) Νικόλαος ἐνίκα.
Ἐπὶ Ἀνθεστηρίου οὐκ ἐγένε[το].
Ἐπὶ Καλλιστράτου οὐκ ἐγένε[το].
Ἐπὶ Μνησιθέου· παλαιᾷ·

APPENDIX B.

Δάμων Φιλαθηναίῳ Φιλιππ[ίδου]·
πο(ηταί)· Φιλοκλῆς Τραυματίᾳ,
ὑπε(κρίνετο) Καλλικράτης·
Χαιρίων Αὑτοῦ καταψευδομέ[νῳ],
ὑπε(κρίνετο) Δάμων·
Τιμόξενος Συνκρύπτον[τι],
ὑπε(κρίνετο) Καλλικράτης·
Ἀγαθοκλῆς Ὁμονοία[ι],
[ὑπε(κρίνετο) Νικόλ]αος·
. . . .

V. Lists of tragic and comic poets, and tragic and comic actors, with the number of their victories at the Lenaea and the City Dionysia.

1. Tragic poets, with their victories at the City Dionysia.

1.

[Αἰ]σχύ[λος . . . .]
[. . .]έτης |
[Πολ]υφράσμ[ων . . .]
[. . . .]ιππος |
[Σοφο]κλῆς ΔΓ|||
. . . . . τος | . .
[Ἀριστί]ας . . .

2.

[Καρκί]νος Δ|
Ἀστ]υδάμας Γ[||]|
[Θεο]δέκτας Γ||
[Ἀφα]ρεύς ||
[. . . . . ων] |

2. Comic poets, with their victories at the City Dionysia.

1.

[Ξε]νόφιλος |
[Τ]ηλεκλείδης Γ
Ἀριστομένης ||
Κρατῖνος |||
Φερεκράτης ||
Ἕρμιππος ||||
Φρύνιχος ||

Μυρτίλος |
[Εὔ]πολις |||

2.

Τιμο[κ]λῆς |
Προκλείδης |
Μ[έν]ανδρος | . . .
Φ[ιλ]ήμων |||
['Απ]ολλόδωρο[ς . . .]
Δίφιλος |||
Φιλιππίδης || . . .
Νικόστρατος . . .
Καλλιάδης |
'Αμειν[ία]ς |

3. Tragic actors, with victories at the Lenaea.

Θεόδωρος ||||
Ἵππαρχος Γ|
['Α]μεινίας |
['Αν]δροσθένης |
[Νεο]πτόλεμος |
[Θεττα]λός ||

4. Comic actors.

['Αρίστ]ων ||||
Πα[ρ]μένων |
Λύκων ||
Ν[α]υσικ[ράτης . . .]
['Αμ]φιχ[άρης . . .].

GREEK INDEX.

Α.

ἀγορά, 106, 126.
ἀγῶνες Χύτρινοι, 43.
ἆθλον, 86.
αἰγείρου θέα, 106.
αἰῶραι, 189.
ἀναβαθμοί, 194.
ἀναβαίνειν, 103, 144.
ἀναδιδάσκειν, 92.
ἀνάπαιστα, 245.
ἀνάπαιστοι, 266.
ἀναπίεσμα, 194.
ἀνδρῶν χορός, 14, 18.
ἀντεπίρρημα, 244.
ἀντιχόρια, 281.
ἀπαγγέλλειν, 88.
ἀπ' αἰγείρου θέα, 106.
ἀπὸ μηχανῆς, 191, 193.
ἀποκρίνεσθαι, 203.
ἀπολαχεῖν, 45, 47.
ἀριστεροστάτης, 270, 271.
ἀρχιτέκτων, 304.
ἄρχων, 86.
αὖθις, 314.
αὐλαία, 195.
αὐληταὶ ἄνδρες, 14.
αὐλητής, 272.
αὐλός, 244, 292.
ἁψίς, 135, 176.

Β.

βάθρον, 108.
βαρύστονος, 249.
βῆμα, 132, 141.
βομβῶν, 249.
βουλευτικόν, 301, 306.
βροντεῖον, 194.
βωμός, 132, 133, 154, 183.

Γ.

γέρανος, 193.
γραμμαί, 135.
γραμματεῖον, 45, 47.
γραμματεύς, 97.
γραφαί, 170, 183.

Δ.

δεικηλίκτας, 256.
δείξεις, 286.
δεξιοστάτης, 270, 271.
δευτεραγωνιστής, 77.
δευτεροστάτης, 271.
δήμαρχος, 305.
διαζώματα, 120.
διασκευή, 93.
διαύλιον, 293.
διδασκαλεῖον, 79.
διδασκαλία, 21, 80, 205.
διδασκαλία ἀστική, 10, 21.
διδασκαλία Ληναϊκή, 21, 36.
διδασκαλία τραγική, 21, 80.
Διδασκαλίαι, 26, 63, 75.
διδασκολίαν καθιέναι, 45.
διδάσκαλος, 74, 75, 80, 81.
διδάσκειν τραγῳδίαν, 39, 80.
διθύραμβος, 14, 198.
Διονύσια τὰ ἀστικά, 10.
Διονύσια τὰ ἐν ἄστει, 10, 30.
Διονύσια τὰ ἐπὶ Ληναίῳ,
Διονύσια τὰ κατ' ἀγρούς, 43.
Διονύσια τὰ μεγάλα, 10, 30.
διπλῆ, 290.
διστεγία, 170.
διχορία, 281.

Ε.

ἐγκύκληθρον, 185.

ἐγκύκλημα, 185, 193.
εἰς ἄστυ καθιέναι, 10.
εἰς ἄστυ καταλέγεσθαι, 43.
εἰσκυκλεῖν, 188.
εἰσκύκλημα, 185.
εἴσοδος, 135.
ἐκβάλλειν, 314.
ἐκκλησία ἐν Διονύσου, 11.
ἐκκυκλεῖν, 185, 188.
ἐκκύκλημα, 182, 185.
ἐκπίπτειν, 314.
ἔκσκευα πρόσωπα, 221.
ἐλεός, 103, 145, 198.
ἐμβάς, 240.
ἐμβάτης, 224.
ἐν ἄστει διδάσκειν, 10.
ἐν τοῖν δυοῖν ὀβολοῖν, 302.
ἔξοδος, 245, 272.
ἐξώστρα, 189.
ἐπὶ Ληναίῳ ἀγών, 10, 36, 105.
ἐπιπάροδος, 276.
ἐπίρρημα, 244.
εὐημερεῖν, 50, 59, 205.
εὐφωνία, 247.
ἐφαπτίς, 228.
ἐφηβικόν, 306.
ἐώρημα, 189.

Z.

ζυγόν, 269.
ζῶναι, 120.

H.

ἡγεμών, 271.
ἡμικύκλιον, 126, 194.
ἡμιστρόφιον, 194.
ἡμιχόριον, 275, 281.

Θ.

θέα, 297.
θέα παρ' αἰγείρῳ, 106.
θεᾶσθαι, 88.
θεατής, 126.
θέατρον, 109, 113, 318.
θεατροπώλης, 304.
θεατρώνης, 304.
θεολογεῖον, 193.
θεὸς ἀπὸ μηχανῆς, 191, 193.
θερμαυστρίς, 290.
θεωρικόν, 303.
θυμέλη, 133, 141, 154, 155.

I.

ἰαμβεῖον, 242.
'Ιάονιοι νόμοι, 292.
ἴδια ᾄσματα, 278.
ἴκρια, 104, 105, 107, 124, 301.
ἱματιομίσθαι, 83.
ἱματιομισθωταί, 83.
ἱμάτιον, 266.

K.

καθάρσιον, 89.
καθέζεσθαι, 45.
καθίζειν, 45.
καινοὶ τραγῳδοί, 30, 40.
καινὸς ἀγών, 30.
καλαθίσκος, 290.
καταβαίνειν, 144.
καταβλήματα, 170.
καταλέγειν, 244.
καταλογή, 244.
κατατομή, 114.
κέραμος, 172.
κεραυνοσκοπεῖον, 194.
κερκίς, 120, 305.
κίνησις, 251.
κλεψίαμβος, 244.
κλίμακες, 147, 194.
κλιμακτῆρες, 147.
κόθορνος, 224.
κόμμος, 243, 278.
κονίστρα, 126, 154.
κόρδαξ, 290.
κορυφαῖος, 271.
κράδη, 193.
κρασπεδίτης, 271.
κριτής, 44, 45, 46.
κροῦσις, 243.
κυβίστησις, 290.
κύκλιος χορός, 14.
κῶμος, 14.
κωμῳδοί, 14, 18, 37, 42, 43, 133, 249.

Λ.

λαρυγγίζων, 249.
λαυροστάτης, 270.
ληκυθίζων, 249.
Λήναια, 9, 52.
Λήναιον, 105.
λογεῖον, 133, 141, 146.

GREEK INDEX.

M.

μεγαλοφωνία, 247.
μέλος, 242.
μετάστασις, 276.
μέτρον, 242.
μηχανή, 181, 182, 183, 189.
μηχανοποιός, 189, 192.
μῖμοι, 132, 154, 155.
μισθός, 53.
μονῳδία, 243.
μουσική, 294.
μυρμηκία, 294.
μύρμηκος ἀτραπός, 294.

N.

νεμήσεις θέας, 6, 305.
νεμήσεις ὑποκριτῶν, 77, 83.
νικᾶν, 55, 66.
νικᾶν ἐπὶ Ληναίῳ, 36.
νίκη ἀστική, 10.
νίκη Ληναϊκή, 36.

Ξ.

ξένος, 297.
ξιφίζειν, 290.
ξιφισμός, 290.
ξύλου παράληψις, 290.

O.

ὀκρίβας, 88, 141, 224.
ὄρχησις, 251, 284.
ὀρχηστής, 285.
ὀρχηστοδιδάσκαλος, 284.
ὀρχήστρα, 106, 126, 132, 133, 135, 141, 147, 151, 154, 155.

Π.

παίδων χορός, 14, 18.
παρ' αἰγείρου θέα, 104, 106.
παραβαίνειν, 126, 275.
παράβασις, 92, 244, 261, 275.
παραβῆναι τέτταρα, 290.
παρακαταλογή, 243, 245.
παραπέτασμα, 139, 170, 175, 195.
παρασκήνια, 132, 149, 154, 175.
παρασκήνιον, 213.
παραστάτης, 271.
παραχορήγημα, 212.
πάροδος, 135, 176, 189, 273, 278.
πεπλασμένως, 248.

περίακτοι, 170, 175, 181, 182.
περιβομβῶν, 249.
περίζωμα, 265.
πίναξ, 53, 64, 170.
ποικίλον, 226.
πομπή, 14, 37, 42.
προάγων, 88.
προεδρία, 304, 305.
πρόλογος, 200.
πρὸς χορὸν λέγειν, 244, 289.
προσκήνιον, 141, 147, 170, 195, 271.
προσωπεῖον, 237, 266.
πρυτάνεις, 45.
πρωταγωνιστής, 170, 175.
πρῶτον ξύλον, 107, 304.
πρωτοστάτης, 271.
πτερνοκοπεῖν, 314.
πυρριχισταί, 15.

P.

ῥαβδοῦχοι, 313.
ῥαβδοφόροι, 313.
ῥῆσις, 200, 244, 289.

Σ.

σατυρικόν, 20.
σάτυροι, 265.
σίγμα, 114, 126.
σιμὴ χείρ, 29.
σκηνή, 139, 147, 151, 154, 170, 189, 195.
σκηνογραφία, 170.
σκώπευμα, 291.
στάσιμον, 278, 279, 288.
στεφανοῦν, 52.
στοῖχος, 126, 141, 269.
στροφεῖον, 194.
σχήματα, 284, 286, 290.

T.

τὰ ἀπὸ τῆς σκηνῆς, 243, 278.
τὰ ἐκ τῶν ἁμαξῶν σκώμματα, 9.
ταινία, 53.
ταμίας, 45.
τάφοι, 183.
τετραλογία, 20, 21, 26.
τετράμετρον, 242, 244.
τεχνίτης, 204, 252, 289.
τραγῳδοί, 14, 18, 30, 37, 42, 133, 249.
τραγῳδῶν χοροί, 35.
τράπεζα, 103, 133.
τριλογία, 26.

τρίπους, 14, 15, 114.
τρίτος ἀριστεροῦ, 271.
τριτοστάτης, 271.
τρυγῳδοί, 288.

Υ.

ὑδρία, 45.
ὑποδιδάσκαλος, 81.
ὑποκρίνεσθαι, 203.
ὑπόκρισις, 205.
ὑποκριτής, 77, 139, 151, 170, 199, 203, 206.
ὑπορχηματικός, 278.
ὑπόρχησις, 289.
ὑποσκήνιον, 146.
ὑφάσματα, 170.

Φ.

φαλλικά, 198.
φαρυγγίζων, 249.
φαρυγγίνδην, 80.
φοινικίδες, 313.
φοραί, 286.

Χ.

Χαρώνιοι κλίμακες, 194.
χεὶρ καταπρηνής, 240.
χειρίδες, 226.

χιτών, 226.
χιτὼν ἀμφίμαλλος, 233.
χιτὼν μαλλωτός, 233.
χιτὼν χορταῖος, 233.
Χόες, 9.
χοραγός, 271.
χορευτής, 80, 103, 269.
χορηγεῖν, 82.
χορηγεῖν ἀνδράσι, 14, 115.
χορηγεῖν κωμῳδοῖς, 53.
χορηγεῖν παισί, 114.
χορηγεῖν τῇ φυλῇ, 15.
χορηγεῖν τραγῳδοῖς, 15.
χορηγεῖον, 79.
χορηγία, 50.
χορηγός, 45, 75, 82, 86, 261, 271.
χορολέκτης, 79.
χορὸν αἰτεῖν, 70.
χορὸν διδόναι, 66.
χορὸν εἰσάγειν, 90.
χοροῦ τυγχάνειν, 66.
Χύτροι, 43.

Ψ.

ψαλίς, 135.
ψιλεύς, 271.

Ω.

ᾠδεῖον, 87, 88, 109.

GENERAL INDEX.

A.

Acoustics, attention paid to, 159.
Acrae, theatre at, 117.
Acting, importance of voice in, 245. Musical training necessary for, 248. Mode of enunciation used in, 249. Gestures used in, 250.
Actors, contests between, 55, 57. Importance of protagonist, 56. Reproduction of old plays by, 58. Originally chosen by the poets, afterwards by the state, 76. Paid by the state, 83. Tamper with the text of old plays, 97. Meaning of the term 'actor,' 197. Gradual introduction of, 198 ff. Number of actors in tragedy, comedy, and satyric drama, 200. Effect of small number of, 201. Rise of the actor's profession, 204. Increase in importance of, 205. Distribution of parts among, 207. Changes of costume by, 209. Costume of tragic actors, 216 ff.; of comic actors, 235 ff.; of satyric actors, 231 ff. Importance of the voice in, 245. Musical training of, 248. Style of Greek acting, 249. The Actors' Guild, 251. Privileges of, 252. Social position of, 254. General character of, 255. Celebrated actors, 255 ff.
Aegis, worn by Athênê, 227.
Aeschines, called the 'rustic Oenomaus,' 42. Hired by Socrates and Simylus, 43. As tritagonist, 210. His accident at Collytus, 255. Taunted by Demosthenes, 254.
Aeschylus, his first appearance as a dramatist, 16, 107, 123. His Oedipodeia, 16, 24. His Oresteia, 17. His Lycurgeia, and Promethean trilogy, 17, 24. Trilogies and tetralogies of, 22 ff. Number of his victories, 47. Records concerning his Oresteia, 60, 64. Exhibits at an early age, 67. Actors of, 76. Trains his choruses, 81. Reproduction of his plays, 94. Text of his plays, 95, 97. Not popular in later times, 98. His statue in the theatre, 160. Scenery in his plays, 166. Invents scene-painting, 170. Invents stage decorations, 183. Introduces the second actor, 199. Ceases to act in person, 204. His Persae, 216. Invents the tragic mask and costume, 219, 223. Introduces the cothurnus, 224. His choruses, 259, 262. Designs the dress for the Erinyes, 264. Improves the tragic dance, 286. His Eumenides, 299. Nearly killed for impiety, 316.
Agathon, his first victory, 91. At the Proagon, 145. His choruses, 261. Adopts the new style of music, 294.
Agyrrhius, commissioner of the treasury, 54.
Aixonê, comedies at, 42.
Alcibiades, corrupts the judges, 49. Assaults Taureas, 86, 313. Admired for his beauty, 13, 299.
Alexander, the Great, wishes to build a stage of bronze, 159.
Alexandria, literary supremacy of, 29.
Altar, in the orchestra, 132. On the stage, 184.
Ambassadors, provided with front seats, 296, 306.
Anapaests, given in recitative, 244. Often delivered by the coryphaeus, 279.
Anapiesma, the, 194.
Anaxandrides, never revises his comedies, 93.
Andronicus, victorious in the Epigoni, 58.
Anthesteria, the, 42.

A

Antichoregi, 86.
Antisthenes, his success as choregus, 50, 82.
Aphareus, engages in eight contests, 29. Exhibits at the Lenaea, 39. A rhetorician as well as poet, 81.
Apollonius, disregards tetralogies, 27.
Applause, mode of expressing, 313.
Araros, son of Aristophanes, 69.
Archilochus, invents recitative, 243.
Archinus, commissioner of the treasury, 54.
Archons, the, granted the proedria, 305. The archon basileus, 65. The archon eponymus, 65.
Aristarchus, disregards tetralogies, 27.
Aristerostatae, the, 270, 271.
Aristias, competes with Aeschylus, 16, 25.
Aristodemus, the actor, 252, 255, 257.
Aristophanes (the grammarian), 26. His Arguments, 64.
Aristophanes (the poet), competes at the City Dionysia, 30; and at the Lenaea, 36, 40. Story about his Clouds, 51. Third in a certain contest, 54. Exhibits at an early age, 67. Entrusts his plays to others, 68. His Ecclesiazusae, 90. Proud of his originality, 92. His Frogs much admired, 92. Scenery in his plays, 169. Discards the phallus, 235; and the kordax, 290. Honoured with a chaplet from the sacred olive, 316.
Aristotle, makes no mention of tetralogies, 26. His Didascaliae, 63. Censures extravagance in choregi, 83. His opinion concerning the deus ex machina, 191. His definition of acting, 247. His opinion about actors, 255. His definition of dancing, 285. His remarks about the admission of boys to comedies, 301. His description of Attic audiences, 318.
Arsis, 283.
Artists of Dionysus, 204.
Aspendos, theatre at, 150.
Assembly, in the theatre, 91 ff., 162, 163.
Astydamas, his conceit, 161.
Athenodorus, the actor, 207, 255, 257.
Audience, the, representative character of, 3. Enthusiasm for the drama, 3, 316. Overrules the judges, 51. At the Lenaea, 296. At the City Dionysia, 296. Includes women, boys, and slaves, 297 ff. Distribution of seats among, 304 ff. Price of admission, 302. The proedria, 304. Occupants of the front row, 307. Comfort of, 311. Regulations for keeping order among, 313. Their mode of expressing pleasure and disapproval, 314. Characteristics of, 315. Their orthodoxy, 316. Their intelligence and taste, 317.
Auditorium, shape of, 113. Interior of, 117. Passages in, 119. Size of, 122. In the theatre at Athens, 113 ff.
Awnings, not used in early Greek theatres, 160, 312.

B.

Back-wall, the, 149.
Basis (metrical term), 283.
Birds, chorus of, 267. Their mode of entrance, 271.
Boys, admitted to the theatre, 297 ff.
Bronteion, the, 194.

C.

Callimachus, the grammarian, 64.
Callippides, the actor, 251. Stories about him, 256.
Callistratus, exhibits plays of Aristophanes, 69. Not an actor, 78.
Carpets, in the theatre, 312.
Changes, of scenery, 178 ff. Of costume, 209 ff.
Chariots, on the stage, 184.
Charon's Steps, 193.
Chionides, 8.
Chlamys, the, 226.
Choerilus, 7. Number of his plays, 8. Competes with Aeschylus, 16, 107, 123. His improvements in masks, 217.
Choregi, how appointed, 71. Their age, 72. Scarcity of, 73. Assignation of poets to, 73. Duties of, 79. Rivalry between, 86.
Choregia, abolished, 73. Expenses of, 82 ff.

GENERAL INDEX. 335

Choreutae, their appetite, 80. Delivery of words by single choreutae, 280. Decline in the excellence of, 287.

Chorus, granted by the archon, 66. Training of, 79. Paid by the choregus, 82. Its dresses supplied by the choregus, 83. Cost of different kinds of choruses, 84. Appearance on the stage, 152. Supposed platform for, 154 ff. Gradual decline of, 259. Its size in tragedy, comedy, and the satyric drama, 262. Its costume in tragedy, 264; in the Old Comedy, 266. Rectangular arrangement of, 268. Its mode of entrance, 269. Irregular entrances of, 272. The parodos, 273. Its formation when in the orchestra, 274. Manœuvres of, 275. Delivery of words by the whole chorus, 277; by the coryphaeus, 279; by single choreutae, 280; by half-choruses, 281. Decline of choral dancing, 286. Accompanies actors' speeches with mimetic dances, 289. Sings in unison, 292.

Chorus trainer, paid by the choregus, 82.

Chytri, the, 43.

City Dionysia, meaning of the name, 10. Date of, 11. Character of the proceedings at, 11. The procession at, 13. Contests at, 14. Tragedy at, 16 ff. Comedy at, 30 ff. Order of contests at, 33 ff. Compared with the Lenaea, 41. Proclamation of crowns at, 89. Tribute displayed at, 89. Orphans paraded at, 89.

Clâque, the, 315.

Cleander, actor of Aeschylus, 76.

Cleon, terror inspired by, 235.

Cock-fight, in the theatre, 162, 309.

Collytus, dramatic performances at, 42.

Comedy, first institution of contests in, 8, 30. At the City Dionysia, 30 ff. Number of poets and plays in the comic contests, 31. At the Lenaea, 40. Actors in, 200. Costume of actors in, 235 ff. Size of chorus in, 263. Costume of chorus in, 266. Dances used in, 290. Its connexion with religion, 300.

Conjurors, in the theatre, 163.

Contests, the dramatic, confined to the Dionysia, 1, 9. Managed by the state, 2. Universal prevalence of, 4. First institution of, 6 ff. Tragic contests at the City Dionysia, 15 ff. Comic contests at the City Dionysia, 30 ff. Tragic contests at the Lenaea, 37 ff. Comic contests at the Lenaea, 40. The judges in, 44 ff. Prizes for, 52 ff. Contests between actors, 55 ff. Records of, 59. Commence at daybreak, 89, 311. Preceded by a sacrifice, 89. Order determined by lot, 89. Announced by a trumpet, 90.

Coryphaeus, the, 271.

Costume, of the actors, 216 ff. Of the chorus, 263 ff. Tragic masks, 217 ff. Tragic dress invented by Aeschylus, 223. The cothurnus, 224. The tragic tunic, 225. The tragic mantle, 226. Head-coverings, 227. Special costumes in tragedy, 227. General character of the tragic costume, 228 ff. Costume of satyric actors, 231. Costume of actors in the Old Comedy, 235. Costume of actors in the New Comedy, 236 ff. Costume of the tragic chorus, 263; of the satyric chorus, 265; of the comic chorus, 266.

Cothurnus, the, 224. Not worn in satyric dramas, 232.

Council, special seats for the, 306.

Courtesans, special seats for, 306.

Crane, the, 192.

Crates, actor to Cratinus, 78.

Cratinus, number of his victories, 62. Refused a chorus by the archon, 67. Employs Crates as his actor, 78. Called a 'dancer,' 80, 205, 286.

Crowns, proclaimed at the City Dionysia, 89, 162. Bestowed on victors at the contests, 90. Worn by kings, 228; by messengers, 228; at banquets, 311. Worn by the spectators, 311.

Cushions, in the theatre, 312.

D.

Dancing, importance of in the Greek drama, 283. Its mimetic character, 284. History of, 286. How far employed in the drama, 287. Used as an accompaniment to speeches from

the stage, 289. The tragic dance, 289. The comic dance, 290. The satyric dance, 291.
Delivery, different modes of, 241 ff. Louder in tragedy than in comedy, 249. More rhythmical than in modern times, 249. Delivery of the choral part, 276 ff.
Demosthenes, his dream, 50. Supplies his chorus with golden crowns, 83. Complains of the amount spent on choruses, 85. His remark about actors, 247. Assaulted by Meidias, 6, 297.
Deus ex machina, 190.
Deuteragonist, 207, 208, 211.
Deuterostatae, 271.
Dexiostatae, 270.
Diaulia, 293.
Dicaeogenes, his meanness, 50.
Didascalia, meaning of the word, 63. The comic didascaliae, 37.
Didaskalos, 80.
Diodorus, exhibits two comedies at one contest, 32.
Dionysius, exhibits at the Lenaea, 39.
Dionysus, his statue in the theatre, 87. His temples, 110, 160. His priest, 309.
Diphilus, ejected from the theatre, 312.
Distegia, the, 172.
Distribution, of the parts among the actors, 210 ff.
Dithyrambic contests, 14, 37 note.
Doors, leading to the stage, 173 ff. ; to the orchestra, 140, 146.
Dorian Mode, the, 293.
Drop-scene, the, 194 ff.

E.

Eisodoi, the, 135.
Ekkyklêma, the, 185 ff.
Eleusis, dramatic performances at, 42.
Emmeleia, the, 289.
Encores, 314.
Entrances, to the orchestra, 135. To the stage, 173 ff. Regulations concerning the entrances, 176.
Ephebi, place the statue of Dionysus in the theatre, 87. Their seats, 306. Receive their shields and spears in the theatre, 163.

Epidaurus, the theatre at, 102. Shape of the auditorium in, 115, 116, 117, 121. Size of, 122. Date of, 124, 141. Seats at, 125. The stage in, 127, 141, 142. Plan of, 130. The orchestra in, 140. View of the proscenium in, 147.
Erinyes, the chorus of, 264, 272.
Eubulus, entrusts his plays to Philip, 70.
Eumenes, Portico of, 160.
Euphorion, produces plays of Aeschylus, 96.
Eupolis, exhibits at an early age, 68. Entrusts one of his plays to Demostratus, 70.
Euripides, his Alcestis, 17, 20. His Medea, 17. His Hippolytus, 18. Defeated by Xenocles, 18 ; by Nicomachus, 48. His Iphigeneia in Aulis and Bacchae, 18, 21, 96. Reproduction of his tragedies in later times, 28, 99. His first play, 39. Exhibits a new tragedy at the Peiraeeus, 42. Number of his victories, 48. Exhibits at an early age, 67. His actor Cephisophon, 76. Trains his own choruses, 81. Text of his plays, 95, 97. His popularity, 99. His statue in the theatre, 160. Scenery in his plays, 168. His use of the deus ex machina, 191. Often introduces children on the stage, 214. Character of his tragedies, 229. His choruses, 260. Adopts the new style of music, 294. Predicts the speedy popularity of Timotheus, 294. Charged with writing immoral plays, 299. His Melanippe, 316. His Danaë, 316.
Exodoi, not usually accompanied by dancing, 288.
Exostra, the, 189.
Extra performers, 212 ff.

F.

Fig-Branch, the, 192.
Files, in choruses, 268.
Flute, the, regularly used in the drama, 245.
Flute-players, how assigned in the dithyrambic contests, 74. Paid by the choregus, 83.

GENERAL INDEX.   337

Foreigners, confined to the back seats, 307.

G.

Gates, leading to the orchestra, 134.
Generals, the ten, their seats in the theatre, 305.
Gestures, most important in the Greek drama, 250. Restrained in character, 251.
Gladiatorial combats, in the theatre, 163.
Guild, the Actors', 251 ff.

H.

Hadrian, his statues in the theatre, 161.
Harmonies, the, 292.
Harp, the, occasionally employed in the drama, 245.
Hats, worn by the spectators, 312.
Head-coverings, for the actors, 227.
Hemichoria, 280.
Hemikyklion, 194.
Hemistrophion, 194.
Hermon, the actor, 258, 314.
Himation, the, 226.
Horses, on the stage, 184.
Hypodidaskalos, 81.
Hypokritês, use of the word, 196. Its derivation, 203.
Hypophrygian Mode, the, 293.
Hyporchêmata, 278, 288, 290.
Hyposkênion, the, 146.

I.

Iambic tetrameters, given in recitative, 244.
Iambic trimeters, spoken without musical accompaniment, 241.
Ikria, the, 104, 107.
Ion, of Chios, his remark about virtue, 20. His present to the Athenians, 91.
Ionic Mode, the, 293.
Iophon, exhibits plays of his father Sophocles, 69.

J.

Judges, in the dramatic contests, their number, 44. Mode of selection, 45. The process of voting, 47. Value of their verdicts, 48 ff. Sometimes corrupted and intimidated, 48. Afraid of the audience, 51. Their seats, 306.

K.

Katalogê, 245.
Katatomê, the, 114.
Keraunoskopeion, the, 194.
Kerkides, the, 120. Assigned to particular tribes, 307.
Klepsiambos, the, 245.
Kolpôma, the, 228.
Kommos, the, 243. Accompanied by dancing, 288. The kommos in the Persae, 290.
Konistra, the, 126.
Kordax, the, 290.
Kraspeditae, 271.
Krêpis, the, 225.

L.

Laurostatae, 270.
Lenaea, the, meaning of the name, 10, 36. General character of, 36. Tragic contests at, 37. Comic contests at, 40. Less important than the City Dionysia, 41.
Lenaeum, the, performance of dramas at, 105. Chosen as the site for the theatre, 110.
Lessee, the, 304.
Leucon, 32.
Licymnius, victorious in the Propompi, 58, 247.
Logeion, the, 141.
Lucian, ridicules the tragic actors, 229, 247.
Lycurgus, the orator, his law concerning the Anthesteria, 43. Institutes dithyrambic contests at the Peiraeeus, 54. His law for preserving the text of the great tragic poets, 97. Completes the theatre, 108, 125, 137.

M.

Magnes, 8.
Mantineia, the theatre at, 115.
Market-place, dramatic performances in the, 104.
Masks, invention of, 217. Results of

z

GENERAL INDEX.

the use of, 217. The tragic mask, 219. Different kinds of tragic masks, 220 ff. The mask of Silenus, 232. The masks in the Old Comedy, 235. The masks in the New Comedy, 237 ff. Worn by the choruses, 264.
Mêchanê, the, 189 ff.
Megalopolis, the theatre at, 115. Its size, 122.
Meidias, corrupts the judges, 49. His assault on Demosthenes, 86, 297. Interferes with Demosthenes' chorus, 252.
Meletus, his Oedipodeia, 26.
Menander, reproduction of comedies of, 33. Defeated by Philemon, 49, 315. His statue in the theatre, 161. His desire for distinction as a dramatist, 299.
Miltiades, his statue in the theatre, 161.
Mitra, the, 227.
Mixolydian Mode, the, 293.
Modes, the, 292.
Monodies, 243.
Mummius, 159.
Music, in the Greek drama, 291 ff. Simple in character, 291. Subordinated to the poetry, 292. The Modes, or Harmonies, 293. Deterioration in Greek Music during the fifth century, 294.
Mute characters, 83, 213, 214.
Mynniscus, actor to Aeschylus, 76. Calls Callipides an ape, 251.

N.

Neoptolemus, the actor, 247, 252, 255, 257.
Nero, competes in tragic contests, 247.
Nicias, as choregus, 50, 86.
Nicostratus, the actor, 244.

O.

Obelisks, on the stage, 184.
Odeum, the, used for the Proagon, 87. Formerly used for performances by rhapsodists and harp-players, 162. The Odeum of Pericles, 160.
Okribas, 141.
Orange, the theatre at, 140, 150.
Orchêsis, 284.

Orchestra, the, importance of in Greek theatres, 104, 151. The orchestra in the market-place, 106. Its name, 125. Comparative size in Greek and Roman theatres, 126. The orchestra in the theatre of Dionysus, 128 ff.; in the theatre at Epidaurus, 180 ff. Character of in early times, 131. Pavement of, 132. Position of altar in, 132. The gutter, 135. Marked with lines, 135. Strewed with chaff, 135. Hermann's view concerning, 154.
Orphans, paraded in the theatre, 89, 162. Have the proedria, 306.
Ovid, his advice to lovers, 285.

P.

Parabasis, delivered partly in recitative, 244. Position of chorus during, 275.
Parachorêgêmata, 212 ff.
Parakatalogê, 243.
Paraskênia, 149, 213.
Parastatae, 271.
Parmenon, the actor, 258.
Parodoi, or entrances to orchestra and stage, 135.
Parodos, or entrance song, 273. Given by the whole chorus, 277. Generally accompanied with dancing, 287.
Passages, in the auditorium, 119 ff. Into the orchestra, 133 ff.
Peiraeeus, the, dramatic performances at, 42. Theatre at, 115, 117. Date of theatre at, 124. Stage in theatre at, 127, 142. Orchestra in theatre at, 132.
Periaktoi, 181 ff.
Phaedrus, stage of, 109, 128, 138.
Phallus, worn by comic actors, 235 ; by satyrs, 265.
Pherecrates, censures the music of Timotheus, 294.
Philemon, reproduction of his plays, 33. Defeats Menander, 49, 315.
Philip, son of Aristophanes, 70.
Philippides, reproduction of his plays, 33.
Philocles, writes a Pandionis, 25.
Philonides, exhibits various plays of Aristophanes, 31, 69. Not an actor, 78.

GENERAL INDEX. 339

Phlya, dramatic performances at, 42.
Phlyakes, Comedy of the, 234.
Phrygian Mode, the, 293.
Phrynichus, his first victory, 7. Called a 'dancer,' 80, 286. His capture of Miletus, 93, 316. Introduces female masks, 217. Skilful in inventing new dances, 286.
Plato (the philosopher), writes a tetralogy, 26. His opinion of Attic audiences, 52, 313, 317. Excludes tragic poets from his republic, 105; also actors, 247. Praises the tragic dance, 289. Disapproves of the kordax, 290. His remarks about the drama in connexion with boys and women, 298.
Plato (the poet), sells his comedies, 69. His remarks on the decline of choral dancing, 287.
Plutarch, his description of Greek dancing, 285. His remark about music, 291.
nyx, the, stone seats at, 107. Disused as a meeting-place for popular assemblies, 162, 163.
Poets, number of at the different dramatic contests, 19, 28, 30, 31, 38, 40. Age of, 67. Produce plays in other persons' names, 68 ff. Originally also stage-managers, 69, 80. Assigned to the choregi, 73 ff. Act in their own plays, 204.
Polus, his salary, 255. Stories concerning, 256.
Polycleitus, architect of the theatre at Epidaurus, 116.
Polyphradmon, his Lycurgean tetralogy, 16.
Portico, in the auditorium, 121. Of Eumenes, 160.
Posidippus, reproduction of his plays, 33.
Praecinctiones, 121.
Pratinas, number of his plays, 8. Competes with Aeschylus, 16, 107, 123. Called a 'dancer,' 80, 286. Complains of the flute-players, 292.
Price, of admission, two obols, 302. Granted by the state to needy citizens, 303.
Priestesses, their seats, 305, 311.
Priests, their seats, 305, 309 ff.
Privileges, enjoyed by actors, 252.

Prizes, for choregi, 53, 90. For poets, 54, 90. For actors, 55.
Proagon, the, 87.
Probolê, the, 91.
Production, of a play, 66 ff. Concealment of the poet's name, 68 ff. Formerly managed by the poet himself, 69 ff. Posthumous production of plays, 96.
Proedria, the, 304. Conferred on priests, 305; on archons and generals, 305; on various other persons, 306.
Prologue, the, 273.
Proskênion, the, 141, 170.
Protagonist, his importance, 56, 208. Parts taken by him, 210, 211.
Ptolemy, the Third, a collector of manuscripts, 97.
Puppet-shows, in the theatre, 163.
Pythian games, dramatic performances introduced into the, 9.

Q.

Quintilian, his statement about Aeschylus, 95. His comparison of the orator and the dancer, 285.

R.

Ranks, in choruses, 268.
Recitative, how far employed in the Greek drama, 243 ff., 276.
Records, of dramatic contests, 59 ff. Erected in or near to the theatre, 161.
Refrains, 293.
Refreshments, in the theatre, 311.
Religion, its connexion with the drama, 5 ff., 300.
Reproduction of old tragedies, 28, 96; of old comedies, 32, 98; of plays of Aeschylus, 94. By the actors, 58, 92 ff. Almost unknown during the fifth century, 92. Favourite tragedies in later times, 98 ff.
Revision of plays, 93.
Rural Dionysia, the, 42.

S.

Salamis, dramatic performances at, 42.
Salaries, of the actors, 255.
Sannio, the chorus-trainer, 81, 252.
Satyric drama, at the City Dionysia, 19.

340 GENERAL INDEX.

Its relation to tragedy, 24. Decline in the importance of, 28. Number of actors in, 201. Size of chorus in, 263. Costume of satyric actors, 231 ff.; of satyric choruses, 265. The satyric dance, 291.
Satyrs, costume of, 265.
Satyrus, the actor, 99.
Scene-painting, 170.
Scenery, occasionally supplied by the choregus, 84. Simple in character, 164. Gradual introduction of, 165 ff. Number of scenes not large, 168 ff. Scene-painting, 170. Mechanical arrangements for scenery, 171 ff. Entrances to the stage, 174. Regulations concerning the entrances, 176. Changes of scene, 178 ff. The periaktoi, 181 ff. Stage-properties, 183. The ekkyklêma, 185 ff. The exostra, 189. The mêchanê, 189 ff. Various contrivances, 192 ff.
Seats, originally of wood, 104. In the theatre of Dionysus, 117 ff. Price of seats, 302.
Shepherds, on the stage, their costume, 227.
Side-wings, 148. Called paraskênia, 149.
Sigma, a name for the orchestra, 125.
Sikinnis, the, 291.
Simylus, the actor, 43, 249.
Skênê, origin of the term, 104. Various meanings of, 139, 170.
Slaves, admitted to the theatre, 297 ff., 302.
Soccus, the, 240.
Socrates (the actor), 43, 249.
Socrates (the philosopher), an admirer of Euripides, 42. His behaviour during the performance of the Clouds, 235.
Solon, witnesses a performance by Thespis, 7.
Solos, by actors, 243.
Song, used in lyrical passages, 243, 276.
Soothsayers, their costume on the stage, 227.
Sophocles, competes with Euripides, 17. Number of his victories, 20, 47, 62. Abandons the practice of writing tetralogies, 25. Defeated by Philocles, 48. Never third in a contest, 54. Refused a chorus by the archon, 67. Exhibits at an early age, 67.

Entrusts plays to his son Iophon, 69. His actor Tlepolemus, 76. Writes for the actors, 76, 207. Appears occasionally on the stage, 81, 205. His conduct after the death of Euripides, 87. The text of his plays, 95, 97. Popular tragedies of his, 99. His statue in the theatre, 160. Scenery in his plays, 168. Said to have invented scene-painting, 170. Introduces a third actor, 200. Prevented from acting by the weakness of his voice, 204. Invents the krêpis, 225; and the curved staff, 228. Increases the size of the chorus, 262. Appointed general, 316. His popularity, 317, 318.
Sparta, the theatre at, 122.
Speech, used in the delivery of iambic trimeters, 241, 276.
Sphyromachus, his regulation about the seats, 299.
Staff-bearers, 313.
Stage, height of, 141, 154 ff. Comparative size in Greek and Roman theatres, 142. Dörpfeld's theory concerning, 142 ff. Steps leading up to, 147. Supported by the hyposkênion, 146. The back-wall, 149. Intended for the actors, 150. Used occasionally by the chorus, 152. Its height during the fifth century, 158.
Stage-buildings, in the theatre of Dionysus, 136 ff. Long and narrow in shape, 139. The façade, 140. The side-wings, 148.
Stage-properties, 183 ff.
Stasima, movements of chorus during, 275. Delivered by the whole chorus, 277. Accompanied with dances, 287.
Statues, in the theatre, 160, 161. On the stage, 183.
Steps, between orchestra and stage, 147.
Stropheion, the, 194.
Sword-swallowers, in the theatre, 163.
Syrtos, the, 226.

T.

Taureas, assaulted by Alcibiades, 86, 313.
Tauromenion, the theatre at, 149.
Telestes, dancer employed by Aeschylus,

284. Dances the Seven against Thebes, 289.
Temples, of Dionysus, 110, 160.
Termessus, the theatre at, 117.
Tetralogies, 21 ff. Invention of, 21. Character of, 23. Disuse of, 25. Meaning of the term, 26.
Text, of old plays, officially preserved, 97.
Theatre, the Greek, general character of, 102. Originally of wood, 103. Site of the old wooden theatres at Athens, 104. Shape of the auditorium, 115 ff. Passages in the auditorium, 121. Size of different Greek theatres, 122. The orchestra, 125, 135. The eisodoi, 133. The stage-buildings, 139 ff. The stage, 141. The hyposkênion, 146. Steps to stage, 147. Side-wings, 148. Back-wall, 149. Acoustic properties of, 159.
Theatre, of Dionysus at Athens, history of the, 107 ff. Its site, 110. Plan of, 112. The auditorium, 113 ff. Date of the auditorium, 123 ff. The orchestra, 128 ff. The stage-buildings, 136 ff. The stage, 146, 158. Statues and monuments in, 160 ff. Buildings near, 160. Its various uses, 162 ff.
Themistocles, victorious in a dramatic contest, 53, 60. His statue in the theatre, 161.
Theodectes, engages in thirteen contests, 28. Victorious at the Lenaea, 39. A rhetorician as well as poet, 81.
Theodorus, excellence of his voice, 248. Stories about him, 257.
Theognis, the tragic poet, 95.
Theologeion, the, 193.
Theoric money, the, 303.
Thesis (metrical term), 283.
Thespis, the inventor of tragedy, 7. Called a 'dancer,' 80, 286. Acted his own plays, 204. Said to have used masks, 217.
Thessalus, the actor, 255, 257.
Thoricus, the theatre at, 42.
Thrasyllus, his dream, 58.
Thrones, in the theatre of Dionysus, date of, 125. Throne of the priest of Dionysus, 308.

Thymele, name for the altar in the orchestra, 132; for the orchestra itself, 133; for the stage, 155. Wieseler's view concerning it, 155.
Timotheus, the author of the new style of music, 294.
Tombs, on the stage, 184.
Tragedy, date of first institution of contests in, 6. At the City Dionysia, 16 ff., 27 ff. At the Lenaea, 37. Number of actors in, 200. Costume of actors in, 216 ff. Size of chorus in, 262. Costume of chorus in, 262. The tragic dance, 289.
Training, of the chorus, 80 ff.
Tribes, the Attic, dithyrambic contests between, 14, 15. Have no connexion with the dramatic contests, 14. Certain blocks in the theatre appropriated to them, 307.
Tribute, displayed at the City Dionysia, 89, 162.
Trilogies, 21 ff.
Tripods, the prizes in the dithyrambic contests, 53.
Tritagonist, the, 207, 208, 211.
Tritostatae, the, 271.
Trochaic tetrameters, given in recitative, 244.
Tunic, of tragic actors, 225. Of satyric actors, 232.
Turban, worn by Darius, 228.

V.

Voice, importance of in the Greek drama, 245. Its strength more regarded than its quality, 246. Training of the voice, 248.

W.

Windows, in the back-scene, 173.
Women, admitted to the theatre, 227 ff. Their seats, 307.

X.

Xenocles, defeats Euripides, 18.

Z.

Zeno, his remark about actors, 247.

THE END.

GREEK AND LATIN STANDARD AND EDUCATIONAL WORKS.

Virgil. Aeneid IX. Edited, with Introduction and Notes, by A. E. HAIGH, M.A. Extra fcap. 8vo., limp covers, 1s. 6d.

Aeschylus. In Single Plays. Extra fcap. 8vo.
    I. Agamemnon. With Introduction and Notes. By ARTHUR SIDGWICK, M.A. *Third Edition.* 3s.
    II. Choephoroi. By the same Editor. 3s.
    III. Eumenides. By the same Editor. 3s.
    IV. Prometheus Bound. With Introduction and Notes. By A. O. PRICKARD, M.A. *Second Edition.* 2s.

Aeschyli quae supersunt in Codice Laurentiano quoad effici potuit et ad cognitionem necesse est visum typis descripta edidit R. MERKEL. Small folio, 1l. 1s.

Aristophanes. In Single Plays. Edited, with English Notes, Introductions, &c., by W. W. MERRY, D.D. Extra fcap. 8vo.
    I. The Acharnians. *Third Edition.* 3s.
    II. The Clouds. *Third Edition.* 3s.
    III. The Frogs. *Second Edition.* 3s.
    IV. The Knights. *Second Edition.* 3s.
    V. The Birds. *In the Press.*

Aristophanes. A Complete Concordance to the Comedies and Fragments. By HENRY DUNBAR, M.D. 4to. 1l. 1s.

Euripides. In Single Plays. Extra fcap. 8vo.
    I. Alcestis. Edited by C. S. JERRAM, M.A. 2s. 6d.
    II. Hecuba. Edited by C. H. RUSSELL, M.A. 2s. 6d.
    III. Helena. Edited, with Introduction, Notes, etc., for Upper and Middle Forms. By C. S. JERRAM, M.A. 3s.
    IV. Heracleidae. By the same Editor. 3s.
    V. Iphigenia in Tauris. By the same Editor. 3s.
    VI. Medea. By C. B. HEBERDEN, M.A. 2s.

GREEK AND LATIN STANDARD AND EDUCATIONAL WORKS.

Sophocles. For the use of Schools. Edited with Introductions and English Notes. By LEWIS CAMPBELL, M.A., and EVELYN ABBOTT, M.A. *New and Revised Edition.* 2 vols. Extra fcap. 8vo. 10s. 6d.
 Sold separately: Vol. I, Text, 4s. 6d.; Vol. II, Explanatory Notes, 6s.

Or in single Plays:—
Oedipus Coloneus, Antigone, 1s. 9d. each; Oedipus Tyrannus, Ajax, Electra, Trachiniae, Philoctetes, 2s. each.

Sophocles. The Plays and Fragments. With English Notes and Introductions. By LEWIS CAMPBELL, M.A. 2 vols.
 Vol. I. Oedipus Tyrannus. Oedipus Coloneus. Antigone. 8vo. 16s.
 Vol. II. Ajax. Electra. Trachiniae. Philoctetes. Fragments. 8vo. 16s.

Chandler. A Practical Introduction to Greek Accentuation. By H. W. CHANDLER, M.A. *Second Edition.* 10s. 6d.

Head. Historia Numorum: A Manual of Greek Numismatics. By BARCLAY V. HEAD. Royal 8vo., half-bound, 2l. 2s.

Hicks. A Manual of Greek Historical Inscriptions. By E. L. HICKS, M.A. 8vo. 10s. 6d.

King and Cookson. The Principles of Sound and Inflexion, as illustrated in the Greek and Latin Languages. By J. E. KING, M.A., and CHRISTOPHER COOKSON, M.A. 8vo. 18s.

Liddell and Scott. A Greek-English Lexicon. By H. G. LIDDELL, D.D, and ROBERT SCOTT, D.D. *Seventh Edition, Revised and Augmented throughout.* 4to. 1l. 16s.

An Intermediate Greek-English Lexicon, abridged from LIDDELL and SCOTT's Seventh Edition. Small 4to. 12s. 6d.

Veitch. Greek Verbs, Irregular and Defective. By W. VEITCH, LL.D. *Fourth Edition.* Crown 8vo. 10s. 6d.

Oxford
AT THE CLARENDON PRESS
LONDON: HENRY FROWDE
OXFORD UNIVERSITY PRESS WAREHOUSE, AMEN CORNER, E.C.

Clarendon Press, Oxford.

SELECT LIST OF STANDARD WORKS.

DICTIONARIES . . . . page 1
LAW . . . . „ 2
HISTORY, BIOGRAPHY, ETC. . . . „ 3
PHILOSOPHY, LOGIC, ETC. . . . . „ 6
PHYSICAL SCIENCE . . . . . . „ 7

1. DICTIONARIES.

A New English Dictionary on Historical Principles, founded mainly on the materials collected by the Philological Society. Edited by James A. H. Murray, LL.D., and H. Bradley, M.A. Imperial 4to.

   Vol. I, A and B, and Vol. II, C, half-morocco, 2*l*. 12s. 6*d*. each.
   Vol. III, D and E.
      D. Edited by Dr. Murray. [*In the Press.*]
      E. Edited by Henry Bradley, M.A.
         E—EVERY, 12s. 6*d*. [*Published.*]
         EVERYBODY—EZOD, 5s. [*Published.*]

An Etymological Dictionary of the English Language, arranged on an Historical Basis. By W. W. Skeat, Litt.D. *Second Edition.* 4to. 2*l*. 4s.

A Middle-English Dictionary. By F. H. Stratmann. A new edition, by H. Bradley, M.A. 4to, half-bound, 1*l*. 11s. 6*d*.

An Anglo-Saxon Dictionary, based on the MS. collections of the late Joseph Bosworth, D.D. Edited and enlarged by Prof. T. N. Toller, M.A. Parts I–III. A–SÁR. 4to, stiff covers, 15s. each. Part IV, § 1, SÁR–SWÍÐRIAN. Stiff covers, 8s. 6*d*.

An Icelandic-English Dictionary, based on the MS. collections of the late Richard Cleasby. Enlarged and completed by G. Vigfússon, M.A. 4to. 3*l*. 7s.

A Greek-English Lexicon, by H. G. Liddell, D.D., and Robert Scott, D.D. *Seventh Edition, Revised and Augmented.* 4to. 1*l*. 16s.

A Latin Dictionary. By Charlton T. Lewis, Ph.D., and Charles Short, LL.D. 4to. 1*l*. 5s.

Oxford: Clarendon Press. London: HENRY FROWDE, Amen Corner, E.C.

A Sanskrit-English Dictionary. Etymologically and Philologically arranged. By Sir M. Monier-Williams, D.C.L. 4to. 4*l*. 14s. 6d.

A Hebrew and English Lexicon of the Old Testament, with an Appendix containing the Biblical Aramaic, based on the Thesaurus and Lexicon of Gesenius, by Francis Brown, D.D., S. R. Driver, D.D., and C. A. Briggs, D.D. Parts I–III. Small 4to, 2s. 6d. each.

Thesaurus Syriacus: collegerunt Quatremère, Bernstein, Lorsbach, Arnoldi, Agrell, Field, Roediger: edidit R. Payne Smith, S.T.P. Vol. I, containing Fasc. I–V, sm. fol. 5*l*. 5s.
Fasc. VI. 1*l*. 1s.; VII. 1*l*. 11s. 6d.; VIII. 1*l*. 16s.; IX. 1*l*. 5s.

2. LAW.

Anson. *Principles of the English Law of Contract, and of Agency in its Relation to Contract.* By Sir W. R. Anson, D.C.L. *Seventh Edition.* 8vo. 10s. 6d.

—— *Law and Custom of the Constitution.* 2 vols. 8vo.
Part I. Parliament. *Second Edition.* 12s. 6d.
Part II. The Crown. 14s.

Baden-Powell. *Land-Systems of British India;* being a Manual of the Land-Tenures, and of the Systems of Land-Revenue Administration prevalent in the several Provinces. By B. H. Baden-Powell, C.I.E. 3 vols. 8vo. 3*l*. 3s.

—— *Land-Revenue and Tenure in British India.* By the same Author. With Map. Crown 8vo, 5s.

Digby. *An Introduction to the History of the Law of Real Property.* By Kenelm E. Digby, M.A. *Fourth Edition.* 8vo. 12s. 6d.

Greenidge. *Infamia; its place in Roman Public and Private Law.* By A. H. J. Greenidge, M.A. 8vo. 10s. 6d.

Grueber. *Lex Aquilia.* The Roman Law of Damage to Property: being a Commentary on the Title of the Digest 'Ad Legem Aquiliam' (ix. 2). By Erwin Grueber, Dr. Jur., M.A. 8vo. 10s. 6d.

Hall. *International Law.* By W. E. Hall, M.A. *Third Edition.* 8vo. 22s. 6d.

—— *A Treatise on the Foreign Powers and Jurisdiction of the British Crown.* By W. E. Hall, M.A. 8vo. 10s. 6d.

Holland and Shadwell. *Select Titles from the Digest of Justinian.* By T. E. Holland, D.C.L., and C. L. Shadwell, B.C.L. 8vo. 14s.

Also sold in Parts, in paper covers:—
Part I. Introductory Titles. 2s. 6d.
Part II. Family Law. 1s.
Part III. Property Law. 2s. 6d.
Part IV. Law of Obligations (No. 1). 3s. 6d. (No. 2). 4s. 6d.

Holland. *Elements of Jurisprudence.* By T. E. Holland, D.C.L. *Sixth Edition.* 8vo. 10s. 6d.

Oxford: Clarendon Press.

Holland. *The European Concert in the Eastern Question;* a Collection of Treaties and other Public Acts. Edited, with Introductions and Notes, by T. E. Holland, D.C.L. 8vo. 12s. 6d.

—— *Gentilis, Alberici, De Iure Belli Libri Tres.* Edidit T. E. Holland, I.C.D. Small 4to, half-morocco, 21s.

—— *The Institutes of Justinian,* edited as a recension of the Institutes of Gaius, by T. E. Holland, D.C.L. Second Edition. Extra fcap. 8vo. 5s.

Markby. *Elements of Law considered with reference to Principles of General Jurisprudence.* By Sir William Markby, D.C.L. Fourth Edition. 8vo. 12s. 6d.

Moyle. *Imperatoris Iustiniani Institutionum Libri Quattuor;* with Introductions, Commentary, Excursus and Translation. By J. B. Moyle, D.C.L. Second Edition. 2 vols. 8vo. Vol. I. 16s. Vol. II. 6s.

—— *Contract of Sale in the Civil Law.* By J. B. Moyle, D.C.L. 8vo. 10s. 6d.

Pollock and **Wright.** *An Essay on Possession in the Common Law.* By F. Pollock, M.A., and R. S. Wright, B.C.L. 8vo. 8s. 6d.

Poste. *Gaii Institutionum Juris Civilis Commentarii Quattuor;* or, Elements of Roman Law by Gaius. With a Translation and Commentary by Edward Poste, M.A. Third Edition. 8vo. 18s.

Raleigh. *An Outline of the Law of Property.* By Thos. Raleigh, M.A. 8vo. 7s. 6d.

Sohm. *Institutes of Roman Law.* By Rudolph Sohm, Professor in the University of Leipzig. Translated by J. C. Ledlie, B.C.L. With an Introductory Essay by Erwin Grueber, Dr. Jur., M.A. 8vo. 18s.

Stokes. *The Anglo-Indian Codes.* By Whitley Stokes, LL.D. Vol. I. Substantive Law. 8vo. 30s. Vol. II. Adjective Law. 8vo. 35s. First and Second Supplements to the above, 1887–1891. 8vo. 6s. 6d. Separately, No. 1, 2s. 6d.; No. 2, 4s. 6d.

3. HISTORY, BIOGRAPHY, ETC.

Arbuthnot. *The Life and Works of John Arbuthnot, M.D.* By George A. Aitken. 8vo, cloth, with portrait, 16s.

Bentham. *A Fragment on Government.* By Jeremy Bentham. Edited with an Introduction by F. C. Montague, M.A. 8vo. 7s. 6d.

Boswell's *Life of Samuel Johnson, LL.D.* Edited by G. Birkbeck Hill, D.C.L. In six volumes, medium 8vo. With Portraits and Facsimiles. Half-bound, 3l. 3s.

Carte's *Life of James Duke of Ormond.* 6 vols. 8vo. 1l. 5s.

HISTORY, BIOGRAPHY, ETC.

Casaubon (Isaac). 1559–1614. By Mark Pattison. 8vo. 16s.

Clarendon's *History of the Rebellion and Civil Wars in England.* Re-edited from a fresh collation of the original MS. in the Bodleian Library, with marginal dates and occasional notes, by W. Dunn Macray, M.A., F.S.A. 6 vols. Crown 8vo. 2l. 5s.

Earle. *Handbook to the Land-Charters, and other Saxonic Documents.* By John Earle, M.A. Crown 8vo. 16s.

Finlay. *A History of Greece from its Conquest by the Romans to the present time,* B.C. 146 to A.D. 1864. By George Finlay, LL.D. A new Edition, edited by H. F. Tozer, M.A. 7 vols. 8vo. 3l. 10s.

Fortescue. *The Governance of England.* By Sir John Fortescue, Kt. A Revised Text. Edited, with Introduction, Notes, &c., by Charles Plummer, M.A. 8vo, half-bound, 12s. 6d.

Freeman. *The History of Sicily from the Earliest Times.*
  Vols. I. and II. 8vo, cloth, 2l. 2s.
  Vol. III. The Athenian and Carthaginian Invasions. 8vo, cloth, 24s.
  Vol. IV. From the Tyranny of Dionysios to the Death of Agathoklês. Edited by Arthur J. Evans, M.A. 21s.

—— *History of the Norman Conquest of England; its Causes and Results.* By E. A. Freeman, D.C.L. In Six Volumes. 8vo. 5l. 9s. 6d.

—— *The Reign of William Rufus and the Accession of Henry the First.* 2 vols. 8vo. 1l. 16s.

French Revolutionary Speeches. (See Stephens, H. Morse.)

Gardiner. *The Constitutional Documents of the Puritan Revolution,* 1628–1660. Selected and Edited by Samuel Rawson Gardiner, M.A. Crown 8vo. 9s.

Greswell. *History of the Dominion of Canada.* By W. Parr Greswell, M.A. Crown 8vo. With Eleven Maps. 7s. 6d.

—— *Geography of the Dominion of Canada and Newfoundland.* Crown 8vo. With Ten Maps. 6s.

—— *Geography of Africa South of the Zambesi.* With Maps. Crown 8vo. 7s. 6d.

Gross. *The Gild Merchant;* a Contribution to British Municipal History. By Charles Gross, Ph.D. 2 vols. 8vo. 24s.

Hastings. *Hastings and the Rohilla War.* By Sir John Strachey, G.C.S.I. 8vo, cloth, 10s. 6d.

Hodgkin. *Italy and her Invaders.* With Plates and Maps. By T. Hodgkin, D.C.L. Vols. I–IV, A.D. 376–553. 8vo.
  Vols. I. and II. *Second Edition.* 2l. 2s.
  Vols. III. and IV. 1l. 16s.
  Vols. V. and VI. *In the Press.*

—— *The Dynasty of Theodosius;* or, Seventy Years' Struggle with the Barbarians. By the same Author. Crown 8vo. 6s.

Hume. *Letters of David Hume to William Strahan.* Edited with Notes, Index, &c., by G. Birkbeck Hill, D.C.L. 8vo. 12s. 6d.

Oxford: Clarendon Press.

HISTORY, BIOGRAPHY, ETC.

Johnson. *Letters of Samuel Johnson, LL.D.* Collected and edited by G. Birkbeck Hill, D.C.L., Editor of Boswell's 'Life of Johnson' (see Boswell). 2 vols. half-roan, 28s.

Kitchin. *A History of France.* With Numerous Maps, Plans, and Tables. By G. W. Kitchin, D.D. In three Volumes. *Second Edition.* Crown 8vo, each 10s. 6d.
Vol. I. to 1453. Vol. II. 1453–1624. Vol. III. 1624–1793.

Ludlow. *The Memoirs of Edmund Ludlow, Lieutenant-General of the Horse in the Army of the Commonwealth of England,* 1625–1672. Edited, with Appendices and Illustrative Documents, by C. H. FIRTH, M.A. 2 vols. 8vo. 1l. 16s.

Luttrell's *(Narcissus) Diary.* A Brief Historical Relation of State Affairs, 1678–1714. 6 vols. 1l. 4s.

Lucas. *Introduction to a Historical Geography of the British Colonies.* By C. P. Lucas, B.A. With Eight Maps. Crown 8vo. 4s. 6d.

—— *Historical Geography of the British Colonies:*
Vol. I. The Mediterranean and Eastern Colonies (exclusive of India). With Eleven Maps. Crown 8vo. 5s.
Vol. II. The West Indian Colonies. With Twelve Maps. Crown 8vo. 7s. 6d.
Vol. III. West Africa. With Five Maps. Crown 8vo. 7s. 6d.

Machiavelli. *Il Principe.* Edited by L. Arthur Burd, M.A. With an Introduction by Lord Acton. 8vo. Cloth, 14s.

Prothero. *Select Statutes and other Constitutional Documents, illustrative of the Reigns of Elizabeth and James I.* Edited by G. W. Prothero, Fellow of King's College, Cambridge. Crown 8vo. 10s. 6d.

Ralegh. *Sir Walter Ralegh.* A Biography. By W. Stebbing, M.A. 8vo. 10s. 6d.

Ramsay (Sir J. H.). *Lancaster and York.* A Century of English History (A.D. 1399–1485). By Sir J. H. Ramsay of Bamff, Bart., M.A. With Maps, Pedigrees, and Illustrations. 2 vols. 8vo. 36s.

Ranke. *A History of England, principally in the Seventeenth Century.* By L. von Ranke. Translated under the superintendence of G. W. Kitchin, D.D., and C. W. Boase, M.A. 6 vols. 8vo. 3l. 3s.

Rawlinson. *A Manual of Ancient History.* By George Rawlinson, M.A. *Second Edition.* 8vo. 14s.

Rhŷs. *Studies in the Arthurian Legend.* By John Rhŷs, M.A. 8vo. 12s. 6d.

Ricardo. *Letters of David Ricardo to T. R. Malthus* (1810–1823). Edited by James Bonar, M.A. 8vo. 10s. 6d.

Rogers. *History of Agriculture and Prices in England,* A.D. 1259–1702. By James E. Thorold Rogers, M.A. 6 vols., 8vo. 7l. 2s.

—— *First Nine Years of the Bank of England.* 8vo. 8s. 6d.

—— *Protests of the Lords,* including those which have been expunged, from 1624 to 1874; with Historical Introductions. In three volumes. 8vo. 2l. 2s.

Smith's *Wealth of Nations.* With Notes, by J. E. Thorold Rogers, M.A. 2 vols. 8vo. 21s.

London: HENRY FROWDE, Amen Corner, E.C.

Stephens. *The Principal Speeches of the Statesmen and Orators of the French Revolution,* 1789-1795. With Historical Introductions, Notes, and Index. By H. Morse Stephens. 2 vols. Crown 8vo. 21s.

Stubbs. *Select Charters and other Illustrations of English Constitutional History, from the Earliest Times to the Reign of Edward I.* Arranged and edited by W. Stubbs, D.D., Lord Bishop of Oxford. *Seventh Edition.* Crown 8vo. 8s. 6d.

—— *The Constitutional History of England, in its Origin and Development. Library Edition.* 3 vols. Demy 8vo. 2l. 8s.

Also in 3 vols. crown 8vo. price 12s. each.

Stubbs. *Seventeen Lectures on the Study of Medieval and Modern History.* Crown 8vo. 8s. 6d.

—— *Registrum Sacrum Anglicanum.* An attempt to exhibit the course of Episcopal Succession in England. By W. Stubbs, D.D. Small 4to. 8s. 6d.

Swift (F. D.). *The Life and Times of James the First of Aragon.* By F. D. Swift, B.A. 8vo. 12s. 6d.

Vinogradoff. *Villainage in England.* Essays in English Mediaeval History. By Paul Vinogradoff, Professor in the University of Moscow. 8vo, half-bound. 16s.

4. PHILOSOPHY, LOGIC, ETC.

Bacon. *The Essays.* With Introduction and Illustrative Notes. By S. H. Reynolds, M.A. 8vo, half-bound. 12s. 6d.

—— *Novum Organum.* Edited, with Introduction, Notes, &c., by T. Fowler, D.D. *Second Edition.* 8vo. 15s.

—— *Novum Organum.* Edited, with English Notes, by G. W. Kitchin, D.D. 8vo. 9s. 6d.

Berkeley. *The Works of George Berkeley, D.D., formerly Bishop of Cloyne; including many of his writings hitherto unpublished.* With Prefaces, Annotations, and an Account of his Life and Philosophy. By A. Campbell Fraser, Hon. D.C.L., LL.D. 4 vols. 8vo. 2l. 18s.

The Life, Letters, &c., separately, 16s.

Bosanquet. *Logic; or, the Morphology of Knowledge.* By B. Bosanquet, M.A. 8vo. 21s.

Butler's *Works, with Index to the Analogy.* 2 vols. 8vo. 11s.

Fowler. *The Elements of Deductive Logic, designed mainly for the use of Junior Students in the Universities.* By T. Fowler, D.D. *Ninth Edition,* with a Collection of Examples. Extra fcap. 8vo. 3s. 6d.

—— *The Elements of Inductive Logic, designed mainly for the use of Students in the Universities.* By the same Author. *Sixth Edition.* Extra fcap. 8vo. 6s.

Fowler and **Wilson.** *The Principles of Morals.* By T. Fowler, D.D., and J. M. Wilson, B.D. 8vo, cloth, 14s.

Green. *Prolegomena to Ethics.* By T. H. Green, M.A. Edited by A. C. Bradley, M.A. 8vo. 12s. 6d.

Hegel. *The Logic of Hegel.* Translated from the Encyclopaedia of the Philosophical Sciences. With Prolegomena to the Study of Hegel's Logic and Philosophy. By W. Wallace, M.A. *Second Edition, Revised and Augmented.* 2 vols. Crown 8vo. 10s. 6d. each.

Hegel's *Philosophy of Mind.* Translated from the Encyclopaedia of the Philosophical Sciences. With Five Introductory Essays. By William Wallace, M.A., LL.D. Crown 8vo. 10s. 6d.

Hume's *Treatise of Human Nature.* Edited, with Analytical Index, by L. A. Selby-Bigge, M.A. Crown 8vo. 9s.

Hume's *Enquiry concerning the Human Understanding, and an Enquiry concerning the Principles of Morals.* Edited by L. A. Selby-Bigge, M.A. Crown 8vo. 7s. 6d.

Locke. *An Essay Concerning Human Understanding.* By John Locke. Collated and Annotated, with Prolegomena, Biographical, Critical, and Historic, by A. Campbell Fraser, Hon. D.C.L., LL.D. 2 vols. 8vo. 1l. 12s.

Lotze's *Logic,* in Three Books; of Thought, of Investigation, and of Knowledge. English Translation; Edited by B. Bosanquet, M.A. *Second Edition.* 2 vols. Cr. 8vo. 12s.

—— *Metaphysic,* in Three Books; Ontology, Cosmology, and Psychology. English Translation; Edited by B. Bosanquet, M.A. *Second Edition.* 2 vols. Cr. 8vo. 12s.

Martineau. *Types of Ethical Theory.* By James Martineau, D.D. *Third Edition.* 2 vols. Cr. 8vo. 15s.

—— *A Study of Religion:* its Sources and Contents. Second Edition. 2 vols. Cr. 8vo. 15s.

5. PHYSICAL SCIENCE.

Chambers. *A Handbook of Descriptive and Practical Astronomy.* By G. F. Chambers, F.R.A.S. *Fourth Edition,* in 3 vols. Demy 8vo.
Vol. I. The Sun, Planets, and Comets. 21s.
Vol. II. Instruments and Practical Astronomy. 21s.
Vol. III. The Starry Heavens. 14s.

De Bary. *Comparative Anatomy of the Vegetative Organs of the Phanerogams and Ferns.* By Dr. A. de Bary. Translated by F. O. Bower, M.A., and D. H. Scott, M.A. Royal 8vo. 1l. 2s. 6d.

—— *Comparative Morphology and Biology of Fungi, Mycetozoa* and Bacteria. By Dr. A. de Bary. Translated by H. E. F. Garnsey, M.A. Revised by Isaac Bayley Balfour, M.A., M.D., F.R.S. Royal 8vo, half-morocco, 1l. 2s. 6d.

De Bary. *Lectures on Bacteria.* By Dr. A. de Bary. *Second Improved Edition.* Translated by H. E. F. Garnsey, M.A. Revised by Isaac Bayley Balfour, M.A., M.D., F.R.S. Crown 8vo. 6s.

Goebel. *Outlines of Classification and Special Morphology of Plants.* By Dr. K. Goebel. Translated by H. E. F. Garnsey, M.A. Revised by Isaac Bayley Balfour, M.A., M.D., F.R.S. Royal 8vo, half-morocco, 1l. 1s.

Sachs. *Lectures on the Physiology of Plants.* By Julius von Sachs. Translated by H. Marshall Ward, M.A., F.L.S. Royal 8vo, half-morocco, 1*l.* 11*s.* 6*d.*

—— *A History of Botany.* Translated by H. E. F. Garnsey, M.A. Revised by I. Bayley Balfour, M.A., M.D., F.R.S. Crown 8vo. 10*s.*

Fossil Botany. *Being an Introduction to Palaeophytology from the Standpoint of the Botanist.* By H. Graf zu Solms-Laubach. Translated by H. E. F. Garnsey, M.A. Revised by I. Bayley Balfour, M.A., M.D., F.R.S. Royal 8vo, half-morocco, 18*s.*

Annals of Botany. Edited by Isaac Bayley Balfour, M.A., M.D., F.R.S., Sydney H. Vines, D.Sc., F.R.S., D. H. Scott, M.A., Ph.D., F.L.S., and W. G. Farlow, M.D.; assisted by other Botanists. Royal 8vo, half-morocco, gilt top.

Vol. I. Parts I–IV. 1*l.* 16*s.*
Vol. II. Parts V–VIII. 2*l.* 2*s.*
Vol. III. Parts IX–XII. 2*l.* 12*s.* 6*d.*
Vol. IV. Parts XIII–XVI. 2*l.* 5*s.*
Vol. V. Parts XVII–XX. 2*l.* 10*s.*
Vol. VI. Parts XXI–XXIV. 2*l.* 4*s.*
Vol. VII. Parts XXV–XXVIII. 2*l.* 10*s.*
Vol. VIII. Parts XXIX, XXX. 12*s.* each.

Biological Series.

I. *The Physiology of Nerve, of Muscle, and of the Electrical Organ.* Edited by J. Burdon Sanderson, M.D., F.R.SS. L.&E. Medium 8vo. 1*l.* 1*s.*

II. *The Anatomy of the Frog.* By Dr. Alexander Ecker, Professor in the University of Freiburg. Translated, with numerous Annotations and Additions, by G. Haslam, M.D. Med. 8vo. 21*s.*

IV. *Essays upon Heredity and Kindred Biological Problems.* By Dr. A. Weismann. Vol. I. Translated and Edited by E. B. Poulton, M.A., S. Schönland, Ph.D., and A. E. Shipley, M.A. *Second Edition.* Crown 8vo. 7*s.* 6*d.*

—— Vol. II. Edited by E. B. Poulton, and A. E. Shipley. Crown 8vo. 5*s.*

Prestwich. *Geology, Chemical, Physical, and Stratigraphical.* By Joseph Prestwich, M.A., F.R.S. In two Volumes.

Vol. I. Chemical and Physical. Royal 8vo. 1*l.* 5*s.*
Vol. II. Stratigraphical and Physical. With a new Geological Map of Europe. Royal 8vo. 1*l.* 16*s.*

Price. *A Treatise on the Measurement of Electrical Resistance.* By W. A. Price, M.A., A.M.I.C.E. 8vo. 14*s.*

Smith. *Collected Mathematical Papers of the late Henry J. S. Smith, M.A., F.R.S.* Edited by J. W. L. Glaisher, Sc.D., F.R.S. 2 vols. 4to 3*l.* 3*s.*

Oxford
AT THE CLARENDON PRESS
LONDON: HENRY FROWDE
OXFORD UNIVERSITY PRESS WAREHOUSE, AMEN CORNER, E.C.

www.ingramcontent.com/pod-product-compliance
Lightning Source LLC
Chambersburg PA
CBHW031423230426
43668CB00007B/410